Symbolism and Power in Central Asia

With the collapse of communism, post-communist societies scrambled to find meaning to their new independence. Central Asia was no exception. Events, relationships, gestures, spatial units and objects produced, conveyed and interpreted meaning. The new power container of the five independent states of Kazakhstan, Kyrgyzstan, Tajikistan, Turkmenistan and Uzbekistan would significantly influence this process of signification. Post-Soviet Central Asia is an intriguing field to examine this transformation: a region which did not see an organised independence movement develop prior to Soviet implosion at the centre, it provokes questions about how symbolisation of a new political container begins in the absence of a national will to do so.

The transformation overnight of Soviet republic into sovereign state provokes questions about how the process of communism-turned-nationalism could become symbolised, and what specific role symbols came to play in these early years of independence. Characterized by authoritarianism since 1991, the region's ruling elites have enjoyed disproportionate access to knowledge and to deciding what, how and when that knowledge should be applied. The first of its kind on Central Asia, the study not only widens our understandings of developments in this geopolitically important region but also contributes to broader studies of representation, ritual, power and identity.

This book was previously published as a special issue of *Europe-Asia Studies*.

Sally N. Cummings teaches at the University of St. Andrews. Her current research focuses on the politics of culture and identity, primarily in Central Asia. Her publications include: *Domestic and International Perspectives on Kyrgyzstan's 'Tulip Revolution'* (ed. Routledge, 2009), *Kazakhstan: Power and the Elite* (IB Tauris, 2005), *Oil, Transition and Security in Central Asia* (ed., Routledge, 2003) and *Kazakhstan: Centre-Periphery Relations* (Royal Institute of International Affairs and Washington, DC: Brookings Institution, 2000).

Routledge Europe-Asia Studies Series

A series edited by Terry Cox
University of Glasgow

The **Routledge Europe-Asia Studies Series** focuses on the history and current political, social and economic affairs of the countries of the former 'communist bloc' of the Soviet Union, Eastern Europe and Asia. As well as providing contemporary analyses it explores the economic, political and social transformation of these countries and the changing character of their relationships with the rest of Europe and Asia.

Challenging Communism in Eastern Europe
1956 and its Legacy
Edited by Terry Cox

Globalisation, Freedom and the Media after Communism
The Past as Future
Edited by Birgit Beumers, Stephen Hutchings and Natalia Rulyova

Power and Policy in Putin's Russia
Edited by Richard Sakwa

1948 and 1968 – Dramatic Milestones in Czech and Slovak History
Edited by Laura Cashman

Perceptions of the European Union in New Member States
A Comparative Perspective
Edited by Gabriella Ilonszki

Symbolism and Power in Central Asia
Politics of the Spectacular
Edited by Sally N. Cummings

Symbolism and Power in Central Asia

Politics of the Spectacular

Edited by
Sally N. Cummings

Routledge
Taylor & Francis Group
LONDON AND NEW YORK

University
of Glasgow

First published 2010
by Routledge
2 Park Square, Milton Park, Abingdon, Oxon, OX14 4RN

Simultaneously published in the USA and Canada
by Routledge
711 Third Avenue, New York, NY 10017

Routledge is an imprint of the Taylor & Francis Group, an informa business

This book is a reproduction of *Europe-Asia Studies*, vol.61, issue 7. The Publisher
requests to those authors who may be citing this book to state, also, the bibliographical
details of the special issue on which the book was based.

Typeset in Times by Value Chain, India

British Library Cataloguing in Publication Data
A catalogue record for this book is available from the British Library

ISBN13: 978-0-415-57567-6 (hbk)
ISBN13: 978-0-415-81597-0 (pbk)

Contents

List of Contributors

LAURA L. ADAMS is conducting research which explores the interactions between globalisation and the nation state in the context of the performing arts, specifically in Soviet and post-Soviet Central Asia. Currently she is teaching in the Sociology Department and the Expository Writing Program of Harvard University, and is Co-director of Harvard's Program on Central Asia and the Caucasus. Laura received her BA in sociology and Russian area studies from Macalester College (USA) and her PhD in sociology from the University of California, Berkeley. Her book manuscript, *The Spectacular State: Culture and National Identity in Uzbekistan* will be published in 2010 by Duke University Press. *Address*: Davis Center for Russian and Eurasian Studies, Harvard University, 1730 Cambridge St., Cambridge, MA 02138, USA.

SARAH S. AMSLER is Lecturer in Sociology at Aston University in the UK. Her main research interests are in the sociology and politics of culture, and the sociology and philosophy of knowledge, education and science. Her first book, *The Politics of Knowledge in Central Asia: Science from Marx to the Market* was published by Routledge in 2007, and she has written several articles on the colonial politics of higher education reform in the Central Asian region. She is currently working on a project on the 'sociology of hope' as it relates to problems of human agency and social change, and a project on the practices of critique and judgment in critical social theory. *Address*: Aston University, School of Languages and Social Sciences, Aston Triangle, Birmingham B4 7ET, UK.

SALLY N. CUMMINGS is Senior Lecturer in International Relations at the School of International Relations, University of St Andrews, in the UK. She is particularly interested in the post-Soviet politics of culture, especially in the region of Central Asia. Her publications include *Kazakhstan: Power and the Elite* (London: IB Tauris, 2005), *Oil, Transition and Security in Central Asia* (ed.) (London and New York: Routledge, 2003), *Power and Change in Central Asia* (ed.) (London and New York: Routledge, 2002) and *Kazakhstan: Centre–Periphery Relations* (London and Washington DC: Royal Institute of International Affairs/ Brookings Institution, 2000). *Address*: School of International Relations, Arts Faculty Building, Library Park, The Scores, St Andrews, Fife KY16 9AX, UK.

MICHAEL DENISON is Special Adviser to the UK Foreign Secretary and Lecturer in International Security at the University of Leeds (currently on leave). His recent publications include: 'Führerkult in Turkmenistan. Überwachen und überzeugen', *OstEuropa*, 08–09/2007 and 'Turkmenistan in Transition—A Window for EU Engagement' in Neil J. Melvin (ed.) *Engaging Central Asia: The European Union's New Strategy in the Heart of Eurasia* (Brussels and Washington DC: CEPS/Brookings Institution, 2008). *Address*: School of Politics and International Studies, University of Leeds, Leeds LS2 9JT, UK.

WILLIAM FIERMAN received his BA in Slavic Languages & Literatures and East Asian Languages and Literatures from Indiana University, and his MA and PhD in Political Science from Harvard University. He began conducting research on Central Asia before he went to Uzbekistan as a Fulbright-Hays Scholar in 1976–1977 to conduct research on Soviet language policy in that republic. Fierman has published many articles on the politics of Central Asia, especially on language, literary, religious, and other cultural policy. He is professor of Central Asian Studies and adjunct professor of Political Science at Indiana University. *Address*: Indiana University Bloomington, Department of Central Eurasian Studies, Goodbody Hall 157, 1011 E. 3rd St., Bloomington, IN 47405-7005, USA.

JOHN HEATHERSHAW is Lecturer in International Relations at the University of Exeter. He completed his PhD at the London School of Economics and Political Science in 2007. Dr Heathershaw has previously held teaching and research posts at the University of Notre Dame, the American University in Central Asia, and King's College London. He has also held research and consultancy positions at the UK Ministry of Defence and Department for International Development and with various non-governmental organisations in the UK, Central Asia and West Africa. His research interests include the politics of humanitarian aid, development, peacekeeping, peacebuilding and security assistance in Central Asia, particularly in Tajikistan. Dr Heathershaw has published widely on these issues. He has co-edited special issues of *Central Asian Survey* (2005) and the *Journal of Intervention and Statebuilding* (2008). *Address*: University of Exeter, Department of Politics, The Queen's Drive, Exeter, Devon EX4 4QJ, UK.

STUART HORSMAN is a policy support officer on Central Asia at the OSCE Secretariat. Between 2000 and 2008, he was the research analyst on Central Asia and then Iran at the British Foreign and Commonwealth Office. He has also taught at the Department of Politics, University of Sheffield, and Department of Peace Studies, University of Bradford. He has published extensively on Central Asian politics, environmental issues, political Islam and Soviet mountaineering. His publications include 'Environmental Security: Regional Cooperation or Conflict?' in Allison, R. & Jonson, L. (eds) *Central Asian Security: The New International Context* (London and Washington DC: The Royal Institute of International Affairs and Brookings Institution Press, 2001) and 'Themes in Official Discourses on Terrorism in Central Asia' in *Third World Quarterly*, 26, 1, 2005. His PhD examined political security in Kazakhstan and Uzbekistan. *Address*: Organization for Security and Cooperation in Europe, Wallnerstraße 6, Vienna, 1010, Austria.

ERICA MARAT is a Research Fellow with the Central Asia–Caucasus Institute & Silk Road Studies Program Joint Center. The Joint Center is affiliated with Johns Hopkins University-SAIS and the Stockholm-based Institute for Security and Development Policy. Dr Marat specialises in military institutions, state-building processes and organised crime in Central Asia and beyond. She is the author of over 200 publications at various policy and academic journals, and a collection of her articles on Kyrgyzstan were published as a book named *Tulip Revolution: Kyrgyzstan a Year Later* (Washington DC: The Jamestown Foundation, 2006). Dr Marat is also a co-editor of the *Journal of Power Institutions in Post-Soviet Societies* and guest editor of the *China and Eurasia Forum Quarterly*. Previously she taught at the University of Bremen in Germany, Uppsala University in Sweden, and the Tajik–Slavic University in Tajikistan. *Address*: 1701 16th Street, Apt 632, Washington, DC, USA.

ANNA MATVEEVA is a Visiting Senior Fellow at the Crisis States Research Centre at the London School of Economics. She has previously worked as a Research Fellow at the Royal Institute of International Affairs and as the UNDP Regional Adviser on Peace and Development. She has published extensively as an academic and a journalist, including a Chaillot Paper for the EU Institute for Security Studies on 'EU Stakes in Central Asia', a Chatham House Paper on 'The North Caucasus: Russia's Fragile Borderland', articles in the *Problems of Post-Communism* on 'Exporting Civil Society' and 'Chechnya: Dynamics of War and Peace', 'Return to Heartland: Russia's Policy in Central Asia', in *The International Spectator* and a recent book chapter on 'Conflicts in the Wider Black Sea Area'. She is a regular contributor to

The Guardian's Comment is Free. *Address*: Crisis States Research Centre, London School of Economics, Houghton Street, London WC2A 2AE, UK.

ERIC M. MCGLINCHEY is Assistant Professor of Government and Politics at George Mason University. He received his PhD from Princeton University in 2003. Prior to joining George Mason University as an Assistant Professor of Politics and Government in August 2005, Dr McGlinchey held positions as an Assistant Professor of Politics at Iowa State University (2003–2005) and as a Postdoctoral Fellow in Central Asian Studies at Stanford University (2002–2003). McGlinchey's areas of research include comparative politics, Central Asian regime change, political Islam, and the effects of Information Communication Technology (ICT) on state and society. *Address*: Department of Public and International Affairs, George Mason University, Robinson A201–MSN 3F4, 4400 University Drive, Fairfax, VA 22030, USA.

ASEL MURZAKULOVA is a Senior Lecturer at the Oriental Studies and International Relations Department of Bishkek Humanities University. She is pursuing a PhD in Political Science at the Kyrgyz–Slavonic University in Bishkek. She is a recipient of the CARTI Fellowship of the Open Society Institute's Higher Education Support Program and has been a Visiting Scholar at the Davis Center for Russian and Eurasian Studies at Harvard University. Her research focus has been on the Shanghai Cooperation Organization and on state-building in post-independence Kyrgyzstan. *Address*: Kyrgyz–Russian Slavic University, ul. Kievskaya, 44, 720 000 Bishkek, Kyrgyzstan.

MADELEINE REEVES is a UK Research Councils Academic Fellow in Social Anthropology at the University of Manchester. She has conducted research in Kyrgyzstan and Uzbekistan since 1999, exploring issues such as language policy in Kyrgyzstan and Kazakhstan; rural–urban and international migration in Kyrgyzstan; and the dynamics of post-Soviet 'border work' in the Ferghana valley, which was the subject of her 2007 doctoral dissertation. She has taught at Batken State University, the American University–Central Asia and the University of Cambridge and has published on the politics and practice of social science reform in Kyrgyzstan. She is the co-author, with Alan De Young and Galina Valyaeva, of *Surviving the Transition? Case Studies of Schools and Schooling in the Kyrgyz Republic since Independence*, and between 2006 and 2009 co-directed, with Nina Bagdasarova, the HESP Regional Seminar on Nationhood and Narrative in Central Asia: History, Context, Critique. *Address*: Centre for Research on Socio-Cultural Change, 178 Waterloo Place, University of Manchester, Oxford Road, Manchester M13 9PL, UK.

ASSEL RUSTEMOVA is a PhD candidate in Global Affairs at Rutgers University in New Jersey. Before coming into the programme she previously worked at the Political Science Department, Kazakhstan Institute of Management, Economics and Strategic Research in Almaty, Kazakhstan. She has been a recipient of the E. Muskie Graduate Fellowship from the US State Department. She obtained her MA in International Affairs from the American University in Washington, DC. Her dissertation research focuses on exploring the styles of governmentality in Central Asia through the comparative studies of Kazakhstan and Uzbekistan. *Address*: Division of Global Affairs, Rutgers University, 123 Washington Street, 5th Floor, Newark, NJ 07102, USA.

JOHN SCHOEBERLEIN is Director of the Program on Central Asia and the Caucasus at Harvard University, where he teaches on the society, politics and culture of Central Asia. He is a social anthropologist and has conducted over five years of research in the field in Central Asia since 1986. His research focuses on issues of identity, including the development of national identity under post-Soviet state-building, the changing role of Islam in former-Soviet countries, and the interaction between national ideologies and other kinds of identity. *Address*: Program on Central Asia and the Caucasus, 1730 Cambridge Street, Room S-320, Harvard University, Cambridge, MA 02138, USA.

Inscapes, Landscapes and Greyscapes: The Politics of Signification in Central Asia

SALLY N. CUMMINGS

IN THE POST-COMMUNIST WORLD, KATHERINE VERDERY (1999, p. 25) argues that the fate of famous political corpses helps

> us to see political transformation as something more than a technical process—of introducing democratic procedures and methods of electioneering, of forming political parties and nongovernmental organisations, and so on. The 'something more' includes meanings, feelings, the sacred, ideas of morality, the nonrational ….

Almost 30 years earlier Harold D. Laswell (1971, p. 545) had encouraged 'political science to examine in detail the process of … symbolization'. This work echoes these concerns; while it does not reject the importance of more traditional political studies, it encourages a broadening of its field to incorporate a study of symbolism in political life.

Symbolism is largely about producing, conveying and interpreting meaning. Language, discourse and image all produce such meaning. Specifically, this collection asks how, why and with what effects politics interacts with aural, visual and linguistic symbols in Central Asia. It reflects how political science can usefully collaborate with other disciplines, particularly cultural, psychological, anthropological and geographical studies, to incorporate the symbolic in its political analysis (Halas 2002). Victor Turner (1966, p. 19) points out how the *Concise Oxford Dictionary* refers to a 'symbol' as a thing 'regarded by general consent as naturally typifying or representing or recalling something by possession of analogous qualities or by association in fact or thought'. The symbolic observed by various contributors here ranges hugely from objects, activities, relationships, events, to gestures and spatial units.

Post-Soviet Central Asia is an intriguing field to examine this process of signification. A region which did not see an organised independence movement develop prior to Soviet implosion at the centre, it provokes questions about how symbolisation begins in the absence of a national will to do so. An externally imposed collapse of certainty led to a scramble for internally invented signs of certainty. The power container overnight had become a national one. This provokes questions about

My sincere thanks to Terry Cox for accepting this idea as a project for *Europe-Asia Studies*. My indebtedness also to Terry and to Sarah Lennon for their support in the final stages of completion; and my gratitude to an army of referees for their insights and promptness.

how the process of communism-turned-nationalism could become symbolised, and what specific role symbols came to play in these early years of independence. Second, this period has witnessed, on the one hand, a growing authoritarianism in the region as a whole, and on the other, very different types of authoritarianism between Kazakhstan, Kyrgyzstan, Tajikistan, Turkmenistan and Uzbekistan. Questions about links between regime type and symbolisation emerge, such as whether the production of meaning is helped or hindered by stronger authoritarianism; and whether the absence of formal electoral procedures places emphasis on non-electoral forms of buttressing power. Furthermore in an authoritarian system certain elites have disproportionate access to knowledge and to deciding what, how and when that knowledge should be applied.

Theories of (non-)representation

No consensus exists on the relationship between politics and symbols, however. Writers are broadly divided between those who view symbols as representational and those who do not. On the representational side, the study of representation in politics is split into three broad approaches: the reflective, intentional and constructivist approaches (Hall 2007). In simplified terms, reflective approaches mirror or imitate 'really existing' truth (mimesis). Signs bear a relationship to the shape and texture of the objects they represent. Intentional approaches, by contrast, are a function of what the agent wants something to mean; here meaning derives from the goals set by actors. Constructivists also do not deny the existence of the material world but their representation

> involves making meaning by forging links between three different orders of things: what we might broadly call the world of things, people, events and experiences; the conceptual world—the mental concepts we carry around in our heads; and the signs, arranged into languages, which 'stand for' or communicate these concepts. (Hall 2007, p. 61)

Ferdinand de Saussure (1959) argued that these links can be made linguistically meaningful by exposing the link between, on the one hand, language codes (*la langue*) and, on the other, different forms of speech used by language (*la parole*). *La parole* refers in the broadest sense to, for example, speech, writing, drawing or other types of representation. These forms of speech he labelled the signifiers and the mental concepts associated with them, the signifieds. As he explains in his *Course in General Linguistics* Part One:

> One characteristic of the symbol is that it is never wholly arbitrary; it is not empty, for there is the rudiment of a natural bond between the signifier and the signified. The symbol of justice, a pair of scales, could not be replaced by just any other symbol, such as a chariot. (de Saussure 1959, p. 68)

In Saussurian terms, therefore, the signifier (image) plus the signified (concept) equal the sign (meaning). We shall return to the arbitrariness of the symbol in conclusion.

In his study of semiotics, Roland Barthes (1972) built on the work of Saussure by incorporating the role of culture in the encoding, coding and decoding of signs. He referred to the sign as denotation and to connotation when these signs were linked to broader cultural themes. In his essay 'Myth today', Barthes (1972, p. 19) calls connotation a myth. In this reading, he adds,

> French imperiality is the very drive behind the myth. The concept reconstitutes a chain of causes and effects, motives and intentions...Through the concept...a whole new history...is implanted in the myth...the concept of French impartiality...is again tied to the totality of the world: to the general history of France, to its colonial adventures, to its present difficulties.

Barthes (1972, p. 114) proceeded to argue that myth was a 'second-order semiological system'. While in a first-order system the Saussurian logic of 'signifier + signified = sign' prevails, in the second-order system, the sign is a mere signifier.

Discourse replaced semiotics with the work of Michel Foucault. Foucault argued that it is impossible to understand symbolism without understanding the particular historic juncture at which the subjects found themselves. The uncovering of 'relations of power' trumped those of 'relations of meaning' (Foucault 1980, p. 115), and these power relations would be reflected in discursive formations (Foucault 1975). Discourse showed what was possible and not possible in language and practice by revealing where meaning originated. Mutually constituent, power and knowledge dictated how ideas came into practice and in turn regulated practice. A Foucauldian analysis of the post-Soviet space is therefore interesting precisely because it would be expected that with Soviet collapse forms of knowledge, objects, subjects and practices of knowledge would be radically altered.

On the non-representational side, debates on symbolism are similarly structured around the relationship between the material and the discursive. They focus on how these two realities interact, if at all. Kertzer and Wedeen both show how practice and meaning are mutually constituent. As David Kertzer (1998, p. 2) writes, 'Politics is expressed through symbolism. Rather little that is political involves the use of direct force, and, though material resources are crucial to the political process, even their distribution and use are largely shaped through symbolic means'. Lisa Wedeen (1999, p. 6) makes the distinction between obedience and compliance: between genuine reverence and citizens acting as though they revere their leader. For Wedeen, symbols assume a political life of their own, becoming mechanisms of domination and enforcement, and this process can be 'paradoxically both self-defeating and self-serving, both inviting transgression and delimiting its content' (Wedeen 1999, p. 31).

For some these symbols are not simply an act: they constitute that very reality. Guy Debord's broad understanding of the term 'spectacle' was informed by such an all-dominant view, and 'cannot be understood as a mere visual deception produced by mass-media technologies. It is a world-view that has actually been materialised, a view of a world that has become objective' (Debord 2006, p. 7). In the terms of Lyotard and Thebaud (1985, p. 41): 'Who are the tribes of interpreters, who are the narrators in this decoding of symbolic landscapes? The narrators are being narrated too, remember'.

Jean Baudrillard (1983, p. 5) unmistakably merges the worlds of the material and discursive, arguing that signifiers become objects in themselves: 'Someone who feigns an illness can simply go to bed and make believe he is ill. Someone who simulates an illness produces in himself some of the symptoms'. It is about self-referential production: 'Whereas representation tries to absorb simulation by interpreting it as false representation, simulation envelops the whole edifice of representation as itself a simulacrum' (1983, p. 11). Ultimately, 'the transition from signs which dissimulate something to signs which dissimulate that there is nothing, marks the decisive turning point' (1983, p. 12). Baudrillard's later work, *The Gulf War Did Not Take Place* (1995), epitomises this threshold.

As James Der Derian (1995, p. 38) writes, Baudrillard's conclusion that the real disappears into its representational form has

> a long lineage. It can be traced from Siegfried Kracauer's chronicling of the emergence of a 'cult of distraction' in the Weimar Republic, to Walter Benjamin's incisive warning of the loss of authenticity, aura, and uniqueness in the technical reproduction of reality, to Guy Debord's claim that, in modern conditions, spectacles accumulate and representations proliferate, and, finally to Jean Baudrillard's own notification that the simulated now precedes and engenders a hyperreality where origins are forgotten and historical references lost.

In the field: evidence and theory, the material and the discursive

Encounters between the material and the discursive have varied substantially in post-Soviet Central Asia. A single theory alone often inadequately captures the complexity of the signification process. Viewing power legitimation still largely through a Weberian lens, and suggesting primary emphasis on the representational theory of intentionality, Anna Matveeva's contribution to this collection suggests that elites are conscious beings that are able autonomously to produce the mechanisms that keep them in power, and these mechanisms of legitimation are partly symbolic. Murray Edelman (1985 (first published 1964)) draws attention to the symbolic nature of participation in politics. His argument concentrates on the mechanisms through which politics influences what people want, what they fear, what they regard as possible and even who they are. In these participatory fields, Matveeva argues, Central Asian regimes manoeuvre, often obliged to compete against domestic and external alternative sources of legitimacy.

Externally, communicative strategies by elites target international audiences of various kinds: investors, donors, tourists and sometimes external providers of national security. Erica Marat illustrates how Kazakhstan and Kyrgyzstan have produced largely new brands to sell themselves to the outside world, in contrast with Uzbekistan's relying on the symbolic resources it inherited from the Soviet Union, namely, its famous cities and cultural artefacts which also predate the Soviet Union. Framing suggests the deliberate selection of certain narratives over others and in turn their careful shaping to appeal to domestic and international audiences. Like Matveeva, Marat views images as produced by the ruling elite, and like Matveeva, therefore, sees that elite as a conscious actor whose own images shape the images of the state as a whole.

Although not strictly Weberian in approach, Eric McGlinchey also looks at the primacy of intentional symbolism and at the motivations behind Islam Karimov's attempts to co-opt and mobilise, particularly the *Kamalot* youth group. But unlike Matveeva and Marat, McGlinchey views this group's attendant symbolism as indicative of regime weakness rather than strength. Precisely because symbolism was underestimated, he argues, many Sovietologists failed to appreciate the fundamental weakness of the previous system. In the post-Soviet context, even if it fails to mobilise as in the case of the Uzbek youth, symbolism should be taken seriously, because its hollowness reflects growing authoritarianism as a response to a declining real hold on power. Symbols are not, therefore, reflective of a virtual reality but in fact are a mimesis of actually existing relations. McGlinchey would appear to combine intentional and reflective approaches of symbolism.

As Jacques Derrida (1981) quipped, writing always leads to more writing. The French philosopher argued that difference cannot be accurately expressed within any binary system. The possibility for multiple interpretations is captured by Stuart Horsman and Michael Denison. Symbols must hold meaning to the population to be useful, when they do not, they flounder. Taking an example from the Soviet period, Horsman's analysis of Michael Romm's *The Ascent of Mount Stalin* provides a firsthand account of the planning and progress of the expedition, the climbing of Mount Stalin and the physical and human landscape in which it took place. The 'virtual tourism' (Hirsch 2003) offered by the ascent of the mountain did not sustain the imagination of those reading it, did not enthuse them to 'imagine themselves into the emerging developmentalist narrative of Soviet-sponsored evolution and achieve-ment' (2003, p. 696). This might be compared to those 'Walt Disney characters who rush madly over the edge of a cliff without seeing it: the power of their imagination keeps them suspended in mid-air, but as soon as they look down and see where they are, they fall' (Vaneigem 2006, p. 21).

In Denison's contribution, different interpretations, this time of the past rather than the future, are seen as having shaped Turkmenistan's symbolic landscape under the late President Saparmurat Niyazov. The very possibility of differing interpretations seems foreclosed in the context of that regime's close intertwining of a strong cult of personality (borrowing heavily from Stalin and Ataturk, as well as Turkmen traditions of tribal governance), semi-sultanistic rule (Cummings & Ochs 2001) and elaborate, all-embracing ideologised symbolisation. Even within this tightly controlled narrative, however, the ruling elite seems unable, in Denison's view, to have monopolised meanings, which he interprets as the limiting nature of this early post-Soviet nationalising project. In both Denison's commemoration and Horsman's devel-opmentalist projects, it is suggested, in Saussurian terms, that the signifiers did not signify the same for the elite and the population. In Denison's account the Great Patriotic War has not reached the elite's unquestioned associations that French imperiality had in Roland Barthes' example. In the case of Mount Stalin, the incongruity was less a result of the signified being misinterpreted than the signifier, namely the image of the mountain, whose non-anthropomorphic nature did not conjure up the associations the Soviet regime had hoped it would.

'The Kyrgyzstani university landscape is also a striking example of competing (often borrowed) images, corporate cultures and ideologies influenced by distinctly foreign dominants (Turkish, American, Russian–Slavonic and Uzbek)'.[1] Sarah Amsler (in this collection) argues that education is a key site for the articulation of social imaginaries and for defining the cultural and political practices through which they may legitimately be realised. She explores how the idea of education in Kyrgyzstan has been articulated within and against wider cultural discourses of Marxism–Leninism and neoliberal capitalism, and discusses how these processes of articulation have shaped the present-day imagination of the futures education might promise, rather in the way Pierre Bourdieu (2001) discussed how the idea of education may become an *idée-force* (an idea which has social force).

Language politics in the four Turkic-speaking republics, as discussed by William Fierman, is another national resource of collective identity. As in the educational sphere, decisions are made with an acute sense of their symbolic significance but within the constraints of what is practically possible and instrumentally desirable. Language policies suggest that symbolism and material concerns operate alongside each other, often in quite different worlds. Although since 1991 the status of Russian in Central Asia (possibly excepting Turkmenistan) has significantly declined, Russian has continued to secure a symbolic niche, largely through its continued widespread practical use. By contrast, when indigenous languages have been used symbolically their implementation has often been sustained because they as yet had not acquired practical relevance. Russian-language tracks in higher education were given up as a real criterion for entry but were kept as a principle, symbolically.

A Foucauldian approach has as its assumption multiple sources of meaning, underscoring how the very subject is produced in discourse. Certain actors at certain periods of history are better placed than others to put ideas into practice; at the same time, however, these ideas then regulate the conduct of these very agents as well as others. In the post-Soviet era language policy elites have often lost their former abilities to be the sole producers, conveyors and, in some cases, consumers of this symbolism. In contributions to this collection, Asel Murzakulova and John Schoeberlein on national ideology, Laura Adams and Assel Rustemova on mass spectacle, and Madeleine Reeves on creeping migration, show how state discourse and practice are mutually constituent.

Murzakulova and Schoeberlein demonstrate how the formation of national ideology in Kyrgyzstan has not been simply about serving the interests of elite ideology producers. Rather, the ideological system is produced by a wide variety of social actors, and, crucially, their interaction has differed under Kyrgyzstan's first two presidents, Askar Akaev and Kurmanbek Bakiev respectively. The mass spectacle, the subject of Adams and Rustemova's analysis, is a different instance of where ideas from below are channelled into popular representations from above and then again interpreted by both above and below. The comparison of mass spectacle in Kazakhstan and Uzbekistan also underscores very different approaches to govern-mentality and, if we add the example of Kyrgyzstan, how symbolism can show us that states in Central Asia differ not just in degree but in type of regime.

The Wittgensteinian blurring of the material and the symbolic assumes analytical purchase in Madeleine Reeves' analysis of 'creeping migration'. Referring to the illegal

---

[1] I am grateful to an anonymous reviewer for this depiction.

purchase or lease of land and property in Kyrgyzstani border villages by citizens of neighbouring border villages in Tajikistan, Reeves argues that this practice is, on the one hand, both the result of state (and international) discourse on the need for post-Soviet demarcation and state fixing, and the 'creep' of the state border itself, on the other. This reaction is both discursive and material: that is, there has emerged a particular account of threat posed by 'creeping migration' which has tangible material effects. In Hanna Fenichel Pitkin's words, such a blurring of meaning (semantics) and use (pragmatics) ensures that: 'Semantic meaning is compounded out of cases of a word's use, including all the many and varied language games that are played with it; so meaning is very much the product of pragmatics' (Pitkin 1972, p. 54).

Finally, John Heathershaw combines a virtual with a Baudrillardian analysis of symbolism in post-conflict Tajikistan. He argues that international peacebuilding initiatives have created a virtual multi-party system 'constituted of ambiguous authoritarian-democratic signs'. This virtual reality is unrepresentative of existing relations. But the central argument is that the type of symbols chosen has had a real effect on helping to keep peace—even if these symbols do not reflect reality. The suggestion is that this disjuncture works, at least in the short term. In Baudrillard's (1983, pp. 12–13) terms:

> When the real is no longer what it used to be, nostalgia assumes its full meaning. There is a proliferation of myths of origin and signs of reality; of second-hand truth, objectivity and authenticity. There is an escalation of the true, of the lived experience; a resurrection of figurative where the object and substance have disappeared. And there is a panic-stricken production of the real and the referential, above and parallel to the panic of material production: this is how simulation appears in the phase that concerns us—a strategy of the real, neo-real and hyperreal whose universal double is a strategy of deterrence.

Questions ahead

The foregoing analysis of theories of (non-)representation and their application to post-Soviet Central Asia suggests further research avenues: first, the selection, content and function of symbols in cultural strategising; second, different symbolic functions; and, third the links between symbolism and regime type.

Symbols as cultural strategising: from the arbitrary to the unifying

The signification process is intimately linked to cultural stratification. Symbols reflect and infuse the varied strategies of cultural collective identities and discourse that lay claim to operating in the name of 'the nation'. In the absence of a 'wish of nations' (Renan 1990) for independence, symbolism took on specific significance: devoid of visible structural and elite change, symbols assumed added importance. Often signification has preceded narration: symbols in Central Asia have provided an immediate means to narrate the new sovereign nation. The discourse of sovereignty and nationhood had already become part of the *episteme* for these states in the Gorbachev era; that discourse seems to have aided the production of symbols in the newly independent era, itself generating new discourse. The symbols that were chosen in the early 1990s in Central Asia with few exceptions tended to emphasise the unchanging or the traditional. But at the same time the traditional is often challenged by the desire for the nation to become part of a sovereign globalised world, where images or discourse are not necessarily nationally produced, conveyed or interpreted, as Marat's national branding strategies or Amsler's ideological debates over education portray.

It is, however, misleading to claim that the content of the chosen symbols expresses cultural authenticity or essence. Identity as a process of becoming (Eley & Suny 1996) captures better the nature of a journey that can often be quite arbitrary in the form it ends up adopting. Symbols are often in the grey zone, rather than expressive of a central inner sphere or a specific outer landscape. Narrating is not a historicist, essentialist exercise. It is a practice that is contested at the margins (Bhabha 1990). The post-Soviet experience is most telling at these margins. In other words further explorations are encouraged as much to look at the liminal, the temporal and the counter-narratives as they are at the essentialist, traditional or official narratives.

A note of caution is in order however. Even if symbols can be contingent, arbitrary and everyday, their overall purpose is a unifying one:

> Nationalism is not what it seems, and above all not what it seems to itself...The cultural shreds and patches used by nationalism are often arbitrary historical inventions. Any old shred would have served as well. But in no way does it follow that the principle of nationalism...is itself in the least contingent and accidental. (Gellner 1983, p. 56)

Debord (2006, p. 7, italics and capitals in original) similarly refers to a unification process:

> *Fragmented* views of reality regroup themselves into a new unity as a separate pseudo-world that can only be looked at...THE SPECTACLE presents itself simultaneously as society itself, as a part of society, and as a means of *unification*.

Even if the Niyazov regime has employed isolated historical moments and symbols, rather than a coherent narrative, to represent Turkmen nationhood, few would contest that its aim was to unify rather than fragment. But these attempts to fixate and reify, however, often do not hold resonance for the population at large. It is, in any case, often as much intended for the elites in their process of self-legitimation (Cummings 2006). For Debord (2006, p. 13, capitals in original) again: 'THE SPECTACLE is the ruling order's non-stop discourse about itself, its never-ending monologue of self-praise, its self-portrait at the stage of totalitarian domination of all aspects of life'.

Symbols and their multiple functions

The varied functions of symbolism explain why they may end up meaningless for the population. Referential, condensation and dominant symbols dot the post-Soviet Central Asian 'scapes'. Referential symbols are 'economical devices for purposes of reference' (Turner 1966, p. 29). These predominantly cognitive symbols were encountered primarily by Matveeva, Marat and McGlinchey, where symbols or branding have been crafted with very specific audiences in mind. The second class, which includes most ritual symbols, consist of 'condensation' symbols, which Sapir (1964, p. 54) defines as 'highly condensed forms of substitutive behavior for direct expression, allowing for the ready release of emotional tension in conscious or unconscious form'. Some symbols of course can simultaneously perform both functions, such as ritual symbols. As Turner (1966, p. 30) explains,

> Durkheim was fascinated by the problem of why many social norms and imperatives were felt to be at the same time 'obligatory' and 'desirable'. Ritual, scholars are coming to see, is precisely a mechanism that periodically converts the obligatory into the desirable.

These emotionally charged symbols are often found in everyday objects (Reeves) or practices in our landscape:

> We are like Gulliver, lying stranded on the Lilliputian shore, with every part of his body tied down; determined to free himself, he looks keenly around him: the smallest detail of the landscape, the smallest contour of the ground, the slightest movement, everything becomes a sign on which his escape may depend. The surest chances of liberation lie in what is most familiar. (Vaneigem 2006, p. 23)

In the mass spectacle, and in discussions of education and language, governments are targeting quite different types of emotions, be they based on pride in past grandeur (in Uzbekistan) or confidence in a grand future (in Kazakhstan) or hope for better times (as described by Amsler on Kyrgyzstan). McGlinchey, Horsman and Denison show how emotional symbols can fail to mobilise. Fierman demonstrates how language can be at once a cognitive and emotional symbol, but when it is released only as an emotional one it can remain solely at the symbolic level.

Turner's 'ideological . . . pole of meaning' (1966, p. 29) is often neglected in discussions of symbolism which tend to emphasise the referential or sensory. It is, however, captured in some of this work's accounts. An ideological pole of meaning refers to the 'norms and values inherent in structural relationships' (Turner 1966, p. 28). Murzakulova and Schoeberlein's opening description of an interview they conducted with one of the ideological entrepreneurs of Kyrgyzstan captures well how a particular symbol held meaning for him but, to his surprise, was also understood by a younger researcher and also a foreign researcher. This was less because the symbol was condensational or sensory or emotional than because it contained meaning inherent in structural relationships that are historical and that were understood by both interviewers.

The World War II commemoration project (described by Denison) seemed similarly to be responding to what the elite conceived as certain norms and values inherent in structural relationships, real or desired; the failure of these symbols to mobilise suggested, however, that the norms and values associated with those signifiers had been misunderstood by the elite. The mass spectacle also tries to structure behaviour along norms and values inherent in society; in Uzbekistan's those are more past-related, in Kazakhstan's more future-related. The mass spectacle seems to be working in what Emile Durkheim described as a process making the obligational desirable. As Turner (1966, p. 30) explains:

> Within its framework of meanings, the dominant symbol brings the ethical and jural norms of society into close contact with strong emotional stimuli. In the action situation of ritual, with its social excitement and directly physiological stimuli, such as music, singing, dancing, alcohol, incense, and bizarre modes of dress, the ritual symbol, we may perhaps say, effects an interchange of qualities between its poles of meaning. Norms and values, on the one hand, become saturated with emotion, while the gross and basic emotions become ennobled through contact with social values.

It would be interesting to pursue further why some states seem to have, for example, a surfeit of the referential or a deficit of the ideological.

Symbols as a window on the nature of authoritarianisms

Finally, the politics of signification is just that—it both is and reflects a struggle for power and knowledge. The process of signification is not an easy one in any of these states, even in the most strictly controlled such as Uzbekistan or Turkmenistan. This supports the argument that authoritarianism is not a static reality handed to the leaders, but a dynamic that has to be worked at. To remain authoritarian, and without the constant use of repression or military force, the regimes have to work at staying authoritarian. To keep themselves in power, authoritarian rulers require considerable strategies of co-optation, de-politicisation and de-ethnicising of the political space (Cummings 2005) and symbols can reflect or be used in that struggle.

While it is often argued that authoritarian systems are more predictable than democratic ones, the study of symbolism has shown that a strong element of unpredictability remains. This unpredictability arises from another feature of the politics of signification in Central Asia after Soviet implosion: the process is multidirectional. This is despite the fact that many of the post-Soviet nation builders have used Soviet nation-building and state top-down building strategies. But, to follow the Foucauldian line, post-Soviet societies are at a different historical moment. The *episteme* is different. What is thinkable now is different to what was conceivable then. Different symbolic spheres have underscored how knowledge about the topic has acquired authority, a sense of its embodying the truth, and how the subjects involved in this discourse themselves have changed. So if it is not surprising that the Kyrgyz polity has a harder time achieving consensus on what a national ideology is than a Turkmen one, it may be surprising that its Turkmen counterpart still has to count on a degree of unpredictability in the reception of that ideology.

Differences in the strategies and fates of signification confirm that the blanket label of authoritarianism, if correctly applied to the regimes in Central Asia, covers very different state–society relations and styles of government. Depending on which function type we focus on, symbols can predict regime development—and even, in some authors' views, collapse. With the exception of branding (more referential and often devoid of meaningful content), symbols often convey meaning about domestic self-images and politics that cut-and-thrust political bargaining may not. In each of the five Central Asian politics, they give a sense of the bigger picture, of what the stakes are about, about what aspects of collective identity matter or have ceased to matter. Different regimes of power have produced different regimes (structures and practices) of meaning.

University of St Andrews

References

Barthes, R. (1972) 'Myth Today', in Barthes, R. (1972) *Mythologies* (London, Cape).
Baudrillard, J. (1983) *Simulations* (New York, Semiotextte).
Baudrillard, J. (1995) *The Gulf War Did Not Take Place* (Bloomington, Indiana University Press).
Bhabha, H.K. (1986) 'The Other Question: Difference, Discrimination and the Discourse of Colonialism', in Barker, P., Hulme, M.I. & Loxley, D. (eds) (1986) *Literature, Politics and Theory: Papers from the Essex Conference 1976–84* (London & New York, Methuen).
Bhabha, H.K. (ed.) (1990) *Nation and Narration* (London & New York, Routledge).
Bourdieu, P. (2001) *Acts of Resistance* (Cambridge, Polity Press).
Cummings, S.N. (2005) *Kazakhstan: Power and the Elite* (London, Routledge).
Cummings, S.N. (2006) 'Legitimation and Identification in Kazakhstan', *Nationalism and Ethnic Politics*, 12, 2.
Cummings S.N. & Ochs, M. (2001) 'Turkmenistan—Saparmurat Niyazov's Inglorious Isolation', in Cummings, S.N. (ed.) (2001) *Power and Change in Central Asia* (London, Routledge).
De Saussure, F. (1959) *Course in General Linguistics* [translated by Wade Baskin, edited by C. Bally & A. Sechehaye, in collaboration with A. Reidlinger] (London, Peter Own) (reference is to the 1964 second edition).
Debord, G. (2006) *Society of the Spectacle* [translated by Ken Knabb] (London, Rebel Press).
Der Derian, J. (1995) 'The Value of Security: Hobbes, Marx, Nietzsche, and Baudrillard', in Lipschutz, R.D. (ed.) (1995) *On Security* (New York, Columbia University Press).
Derrida, J. (1981) *Dissemination* [translated by Barbara Johnson] (Chicago, Chicago University Press).
Edelman, M. (1985) *The Symbolic Uses of Politics*, 2nd edn (Champaigne, University of Illinois Press).
Eley, G. & Suny, R.G. (1996) *Becoming National: A Reader* (Oxford, Oxford University Press).
Foucault, M. (1975) *Discipline and Punish: the Birth of the Prison* (New York, Random House).
Foucault, M. (1980) *Power/Knowledge* (Brighton, Havester).
Gellner, E. (1983) *Nations and Nationalism* (Oxford, Basil Blackwell).
Halas, E. (ed.) (2002) *Symbols, Power and Politics, Studies in Sociology: Symbols, Theory and Society* (Bern, Peter Lang Publishing).
Hall, S. (ed.) (2007) *Representation: Cultural Representations and Signifying Practices* (London, Sage).
Hirsch, F. (2003) 'Getting to Know "The Peoples of the USSR": Ethnographic Exhibits as Soviet Virtual Tourism, 1923–1934, *Slavonic Review*, 62, 4.
Kertzer, D.I. (1998) *Politics and Symbols: The Italian Communist Party and the Fall of Communism* (London, Yale University Press).
Laswell, H.D. (1971) 'The Politics of Prevention', in Greenstein, F.I. & Lerner, M. (eds) (1971) *A Source Book for the Study of Personality and Politics* (Chicago, Chicago University Press).
Lyotard, J.-F. & Thebaud, J.-L. (1985) *Just Gaming* [translated by Wlad Godzich] (Manchester, Manchester University Press).
Pitkin, H.F. (1972) *The Concept of Representation* (Berkeley, University of California Press).
Renan, E. (1990) 'What is a Nation?', in Bhabha, H.K. (ed.) (1990) ['Qu'est-ce qu'une nation', trans. I.M. Synder] (Paris, Calmann-Levy, 1882).
Sapir, E. (1964) 'Symbols', in *Encyclopedia of the Social Sciences*, XIV (New York, Macmillan).
Turner, V. (1966) *The Forest of Symbols: Aspects of Ndembu Ritual* (Ithaca & London, Cornell University Press).
Vaneigem, R. (2006) *The Revolution of Everyday Life* [translated by Donald Nicholson-Smith] (London, Rebel Press).
Verdery, K. (1999) *The Political Lives of Dead Bodies: Reburial and Postsocialist Change* (New York, Columbia University Press).
Wedeen, L. (1999) *Ambiguities of Domination: Politics, Rhetoric, and Symbols in Contemporary Syria* (Chicago, University of Chicago Press).

Legitimising Central Asian Authoritarianism: Political Manipulation and Symbolic Power

ANNA MATVEEVA

THIS ESSAY ENGAGES WITH THE DILEMMA OF LEGITIMISATION OF authoritarian states that move away from democracy by examining the cases of the Central Asian countries. These states have consolidated their independence since 1991, despite continuous internal tensions, and have withstood the impact of their turbulent neighbourhood. Achieving a degree of 'legitimacy' which fosters compliance with the existing domestic order, has made the rule of the current leaderships easier and has reduced the pressure on them to simply rely on coercion. Nevertheless, underlying challenges remain and will only grow in significance as these states struggle to balance the construction of state identities, elite cohesion and international recognition with the maintenance of some degree of internal legitimacy.

Assessing legitimacy in authoritarian conditions

The subject of legitimacy in authoritarian states needs to be addressed by scholars and policy makers because empirical evidence suggests that the authoritarian tide is growing stronger and demonstrates a degree of resilience to internal pressures and adverse regional circumstances. Political thought in the twentieth century was dominated by the view that democracy is the best and most advanced form of government, culminating in the idea that democratisation is in fact inevitable (Fukuyama 1992). The fall of the Berlin Wall and the post-communist states' transition towards both market economy and the ensuing liberal democracy seemingly confirmed this idea.

However, in the last decade political analysis has highlighted the phenomenon of 'hybrid' regimes which combine authoritarian features with a democratic façade, noting that several of the former 'transition' states have entered a political 'grey zone' (Carothers 2002). Some turned towards outright authoritarianism. Central Asia followed a different—in fact, an opposite—model of political development from that which it was expected to do by policy and academic communities. Despite earlier expectations that the Central Asian regimes were fragile, unsustainable and a temporary aberration from transition, these states have proved their viability and do not appear to be on the brink of a collapse. Their durability can be explained, on the one hand, by repression and the coercive power that the rulers have over the ruled, and on the other hand, by the degree of legitimacy these regimes have managed to achieve.

Of course, the very concept of legitimacy is open to question in an authoritarian context. Theory suggests that 'legitimacy, in and of itself, may be associated with many forms of political organisation, including oppressive ones' (Lipset 1981, p. 28) and that 'one can call a state legitimate without thinking it perfect or even inspiring. It's legitimate if it's good enough, if it passes a threshold' (Herzog 1989, p. 206). However, in authoritarian states it is difficult both for outsiders and insiders to interpret the extent to which citizens identify with the political order. How do we know that the state is 'good enough' and, importantly, that it remains above the threshold? How can legitimacy be measured and identified in societies where public expression of political preferences is so restricted, hidden, manipulated or disguised? We have recognised that our conception of the notion of legitimacy in such states has to include that it is not a normative idea as such, and that it includes a very complex view of consent. The political leadership structures itself is not certain of this consent and is more prone either to overestimate or to underestimate consensus over the existing rule. An authoritarian leader has less ability to see an approaching crisis and is likely to misinterpret symptoms by treating them too leniently or vastly exaggerating the threats. This study analyses the ways in which the rulers create and maintain their legitimacy, and the process by which the goal of legitimisation is being pursued. It discusses the issue of legitimisation in its two facets: performative and symbolic, and in the interplay between the two, as seen in the way the publics are misled about performance, and about threats to order and stability. It will analyse the pillars upon which legitimacy rests and what the symbolic means employed to maintain it are.

The literature tells us that 'legitimacy is that aspect of authority which refers to entitlement' (Schaar 1984, p. 108). The three grounds for legitimacy described by Weber—tradition, legal statute and charisma—are insufficient to understand the political development of Central Asia, although charisma is used by the leaders in a form of personality cult (Weber 1993, pp. 78–80). In Weberian terms, legitimacy secures obedience as determined by fear and hope. However, in Central Asia, 'hope' is seldom present, and is replaced by a lack of choice. Theoretically, the source of power ought to matter, since 'power is embedded in a realm of things beyond the wills of the holders of power: the legitimacy of power stems from its *origin*' (Schaar 1984, p. 111, emphasis in original). However, law or right deriving from a greater source than the ruler himself does not appear to constitute a cornerstone of legitimacy in the given context: there is little sense of illegitimacy in the way Uzbekistan's Islam Karimov or Kazakhstan's Nursultan Nazarbaev gained office.

Thus, although Weber's approach may be used as a starting point, because it provides for an intellectual framework marking the ingredients missing in polities such as the Central Asian ones, it should be kept in mind that it is only partly explanatory and other factors have more interpretive value. This study uses a performative approach, focusing on the idea that citizens think that the ruling group delivers on the basic security and developmental agenda, and a symbolic approach, based on the assumption that the leaders try to solicit consent to their rule by framing it in a way that renders the rule acceptable, or inevitable. This exploration will help to cast light on how decisive symbols prove to be in achieving the goal of legitimisation.

It will argue that efforts to employ symbolism for legitimisation of state power produce only partial results, because the Soviet and Islamic symbols are fairly likely to draw Central Asian populations away from their leaders and towards alternatives. To support their claims to power, leaders, while relying heavily upon symbols related to the establishment of the state and all its trappings, as well as on the personality cults, are left with a combination of their performance and popular apathy.

Legitimacy is also understood in the literature as a belief or opinion that existing institutions are morally proper. Lipset (1981, p. 83) writes that 'legitimacy involves the capacity of the system to engender and maintain the belief that the existing political institutions are the most appropriate ones for the society'. In authoritarian states, it is difficult to know whether the belief in the appropriateness of existing institutions is real or whether people merely demonstrate compliant behaviour and act as if they believe in the appropriateness of institutions. Moreover, they seldom have a coherent notion of the alternative institutions which could be better than the existing ones. It is ultimately not possible to be certain: compliant behaviour can mask tensions and resentment, but it can also reflect a genuine preference for the prevailing order. Thus, Lipset's criteria may not be easily applicable to the states of Central Asia. Additionally, Herzog (1989, p. 207) notes that 'any plausible account of legitimacy and obligation must centre on whether the state is for the most part responsive to the people'. An authoritarian ruler may act in good faith thinking that he is responsive to the people, but since popular opinion is not allowed to be expressed, belief that their rule is 'morally proper' cannot be confirmed.

Treading in these uncertain waters, the rulers pursue the process of legitimisation by trying to make a plausible case that the institutions are 'most appropriate', and hope that this works. Heathershaw observes that 'political scientists have reduced the concept to the top-down attempts by governments to convince their populations that their domination is justified—a campaign of legitimation, or what might today be considered part of a campaign of statebuilding' (Heathershaw 2007, p. 109). Beetham (1985, p. 33) describes the crucial benefits of legitimacy that are in the mutual interests of the rulers and the subordinates as 'enhanced order, stability, effectiveness—these are the typical advantages that accrue to a legitimate system of power as a result of the obligations upon the subordinate that derive from its legitimacy'. The leaders have to demonstrate that their rule is not merely a crude grip on power that relies on coercion, but reflects the principle of common interest, 'to serve not merely the interests of the powerful, but those of the subordinate also, or else to make possible the realisation of larger social purposes of which they have concern' (Beetham 1991, p. 59). Thus, the leaders employ symbolic means to link their own interest in maintaining power with convincing the citizens that this power is in their best interests and that it serves the realisation of a larger social purpose. They functionally use the benefits of legitimacy—enhanced order, stability, effectiveness, as described by Beetham—to serve as building blocks of a particular representation of the regime in the eyes of the citizens and base their rule on their demonstrable ability to deliver these benefits.

Lipset draws attention to the significance of 'effectiveness' or the 'actual performance, the extent to which the system satisfies the basic functions of government as most of the population and powerful groups within it' see it (Lipset 1981, p. 83).

These are the grounds for legitimacy which Central Asian presidents certainly employ, because painting an image of a regime as effective both in security provision (that crises will be managed even before they arise) and in economic growth (that every year is better than the past) has been a successful way of legitimising their rule, especially since the regimes can refer to some real achievements. Representing that rule as effective is also consistent with the modernisation message the leaders seek to project.

Thus, we may take from this theory the idea that state building, order, stability, effectiveness and a degree of common interest between the rulers and the ruled are the ingredients for legitimisation applicable in this context. In addition, as Schatz (2006) notes, we may also include the notion that there are international grounds for legitimacy. Next, we need to understand what the leaders do with these ingredients to create a degree of consent to their rule in order to avoid relying solely on coercion.

The literature on symbolism helps us to understand how legitimisation can be performed in the states when the citizens are restricted in their ability to choose their rulers, join meaningful parties or publicly express political preferences, and when elections do not play the role of a genuine competition between political forces. Edelman (1964) draws attention to the symbolic nature of participation in politics. His argument concentrates on the mechanisms through which politics influences what people want, what they fear, what they regard as possible and even who they are. These are the areas in which the Central Asian regimes try to act, but have to fight against the competing alternatives.

This exploration of symbolism will build upon Lisa Wedeen's (1999) work on authoritarianism in Syria in an attempt to unlock the dynamics of regimes where the confirmation of an established order's legitimacy cannot be tested through a ballot box. The relevant issues for our discussion are outlined below.

What are the symbols of legitimacy in an authoritarian state? How do the regimes attempt to control and manipulate the symbolic world, just as they attempt to control material resources and construct institutions of enforcement and punishment (Wedeen 1999)? Do they follow the same pattern derived from the common Soviet root, and what are the post-Soviet creations?

Which functions do the symbols perform and why do the regimes spend time and money on inventing and spreading symbolic goods? One possible explanation is that they aim to fight alternative, competing ideologies, such as Sovietism and Islam, by seeking to occupy most of the available public space. 'National symbols are political strategies that clutter public space, producing acts of narration that are depoliticising. They are politically fundamental even in the absence of belief or loyalty' (Wedeen 1999, p. 157). Another explanation lies in the function of national symbols, that they are charged with the difficult task of creating a nation out of the state rather than of creating a state out of a nation (Geisler 2005). Symbolism functions as a power display: 'in exercising its capacity to appropriate meanings and to insist on the momentary stability of signs, the regime advertises its power. By representing this power the regime creates it anew, continually upholding the circumstances that produce citizens' compliance' (Wedeen 1999, p. 157).

What is the content of symbolism? Does it appeal to citizens' reason or does it expect that apathy and cynicism would prevail, and that implausible claims would not be taken at face value? As in Asad's cult, where sometimes the rhetoric is patently absurd or blends consensual understanding with obviously false statements, the regimes produce a mixture of plausible and implausible claims. The former Soviet citizens of Central Asia who are accustomed to absurd statements, such as 'Lenin lived, Lenin lives, Lenin will [always] live' are not expected to take them literally. However, is there a degree of shared beliefs and expectations, 'whether it be tradition, divine command, scientific doctrine, popular will, or whatever' (Beetham 1985, p. 70) to make a claim to power appear plausible? Does official propaganda reflect any shared beliefs or notions upon which there is a broad consensus in society, and if so, what are they?

What are the effects of the symbols? Are symbols successful as an instrument of state building, performing a function of helping the regimes to legitimise their rule? According to Wedeen (1999, p.157),

> in the postcolonial context where regimes are forced to build an effective state and enforce their dominance while cultivating a sense of national identification, political cults may serve to redefine the terms of national membership by both occasioning the enforcement of compliance and also generating the shared experience of that compliance.

Do symbols define the terms, or are the rival symbols more significant?

This study inquires into how the legitimisation of authoritarian states is constructed and maintained through a complex process of symbolisation. Legitimacy rests on several pillars which form the cornerstones of state ideologies, but the significance of these ingredients and their application varies across the region. Projection of each requires employment of some symbolic means.

Appreciation of state-building success

Migdal (2001) notes that the state remains the paramount political idea of our age and it continues to be invoked in law, public performance and informal behaviour. The key symbols of state building are elections with predictable results, televised parliamentary sessions, historical writings and addresses to the nation. In state building, the new states do not break institutional continuity with their Soviet roots, but they are in competition with the Soviet past and Sovietism as a culture. Lipset (1984, p. 91) notes that 'a major test of legitimacy is the extent to which given nations have developed a common "secular political culture", mainly national rituals and holidays'. However, this aspect is a weak point for Central Asian rulers as they have not succeeded (yet) in bringing about the internalisation by citizens of the national rituals and holidays and of making them 'their own'.

Projection of fear

Internal and external threats loom large in the public displays and mindsets of the elites and the population. Provision of security is a critical asset of the regimes, upon which much of their legitimacy rests. 'A continuing tension between threat and reassurance is a central theme explaining the reactions of general publics to political symbols' (Edelman 1964, p. 188). This agenda reflects some shared beliefs and expectations between the rulers and the ruled which largely centre around notions and attributes of stability and social harmony. Stability and security are the crucial points that are emphasised in the projection of legitimisation and are expressed in symbols such as military displays or the televised trials of Islamists.

Representation of effectiveness

The representation of effectiveness includes the infrastructural power of the state and its ability to govern the whole of its territory and provide essential public services. This justifies a continuous need for a state in the eyes of the citizens. Referential symbols are utilised, such as indicators of economic achievements, growth references or comparisons with the chaos of the 1990s. The visibility of the state in remote corners of its territory is maintained.

High-profile leadership

The leaders personify the new states. Public cultivation of the leaderships forms an important part of legitimisation, where personality politics performs an important state-building function. Presidents loom large with their flattering portraits, televised appearances, public speeches, inscriptions of their words of wisdom and presidential palaces. Traffic is normally paralysed when a leader travels.

Dichotomy between international and internal legitimacy

Rejection of Western political imports and adverse examples from the wider region, to where democratisation brought chaos and instability, tend to resonate in societies. The conclusion fed to the public is that the status quo may be preferable, as the alternatives appear worse. Comparison between a domestic situation and adverse developments in regional neighbours is a useful way to demonstrate that the situation is better within the country. When the official information emanating from the state shows that the neighbours or regional states (which provide an easy reference for the citizens) suffer misfortunes because of the lack of a state which exercises strong control, this demonstrates in a clear, recognisable way that people in these other states suffer; that people in 'our' state do not and have a better, more secure life; and that the citizens should appreciate the role of the regime in achieving this.

Thus, the ruling groups spend time, energy and funding on the pretence that order, stability and effectiveness are indeed provided by the state, while the actual political legitimacy of Central Asian regimes remains weak and struggling. The situation may be that in highly authoritarian states elite legitimacy is really key, while popular consent can be manipulated by a combination of coercion and symbolic goods to ensure compliance. In the end, all these efforts only produce weak legitimacy because the states are not very effective and the popular attachment to symbols of Sovietism undermines the leaders who cannot claim it as their own, while Islamic symbolism is deeply contested despite the rulers' attempts to wrap themselves in it. Weak legitimacy requires maintenance of crucial patronage networks and elite coalitions, along with delegitimisation of opponents, while symbols and discourses are dispersed for public consumption. The art of political manipulation is matched by the popular apathy that underpins the atmosphere of consent and works towards 'legitimacy by default', corresponding to Schaar's (1984, p. 110) description of the social milieu for contemporary legitimacy as 'about confusion and indifference, stability and efficiency'.

Legitimisation framework

The five states of Central Asia range from various degrees of soft authoritarianism (Kazakhstan and Kyrgyzstan) to hard authoritarianism (Uzbekistan, Tajikistan and Turkmenistan). Broadly speaking, the states share a similar regime type which combines bureaucracy, tradition and personalised rule. Initially, the state in Central Asia was a Soviet creation, a commodity imported—or imposed—by the Soviet system. Eventually, the Soviet-type security–developmental state which, on the one hand emphasises external and internal security and, on the other hand, guarantees extensive provision of social welfare, became successfully indigenised. Nowadays, the states rely upon an extensive bureaucratic apparatus, inherited from the past, which also personifies the state and holds the countries together. The essential features of this model include power centralisation and concentration, a large state presence in economic regulation and management, and extensive commitment to the provision of welfare. The resilience of the Soviet bureaucratic culture and its management institutions, and the fact that they have adapted to the new circumstances and even grown in legitimacy has proved quite remarkable, given that the state which developed them no longer exists.

A legitimisation framework is provided by the justification of the presence of the central state, which citizens are reminded of through regularly held elections and the rulers' commitment to stability and social harmony. It is framed in vague references to nation, history and culture. National symbols are orchestrated by the regime, such as landslide electoral victories, Independence Day parades with displays of military might, historical writings, leaders' addresses to the nation, national holidays, flags and anthems, the currency, the capital and major national monuments. President Nazarbaev of Kazakhstan went so far as to create a new capital for the new state.

Formally, the state presents itself as 'democratic, constitutional and secular'.[1] In reality, the last has been the most plausible. However, the Central Asian regimes' central claim for legitimacy is not based on democracy or inviolability of a constitutional order, but upon their ability to provide security, growth and welfare. Compliance is reinforced by the state's resort to varying degrees of coercion. The late Soviet experience provides a useful reference point, seen as successful on a performance level and in which compliance required little overt repression. Coercion takes place, but symbolic legitimisation also works to ensure compliance. Wedeen (1999, p. 152) points out that 'symbolic power is inherently fragile and less

---

[1] President of Tajikistan Imomali Rahmon's 'Address to the Nation', 25 April 2008, delivered to bi-cameral parliament session. Text available on official presidential website, at: http://www.prezident.tj/rus/novostee_250408.html, last assessed 31 March 2009. Other leaders make similar claims.

determinate, but also more economical and more encompassing than forms of power involving overt violence and coercion'. The Central Asian leaders would like to rely upon symbolic power more than enforcement, given the cost of maintaining a large security apparatus, but the record to date is far from inspiring.

Competing alternatives

The way that cultural coherence is achieved and communication between the rulers and the ruled is maintained makes an important contribution to framing and legitimising the rule. In a post-colonial context development of alternative symbolism is a means of disentanglement from competing ideologies undermining the new states from within. The struggle for legitimacy in Central Asia involves a palpable tension between symbols of secular and religious modernity, on the one hand, and a competition with Sovietism on the other. The states find it difficult to define themselves against the competing ideologies of Islam and Sovietism.

In countries with predominantly Muslim populations, albeit with different degrees of religious adherence, the major question was how to treat Islam in the legitimisation framework. Talal observes that

> from the point of view of secularism, religion has the option either of confining itself to private belief and worship or of engaging in public talk that makes no demands on life. In either case such religion is seen by secularism to take the form it should properly have. Each is equally the condition of its legitimacy. (Talal 2003, p. 199)

There is a tension between secularism which comes from the state and pressures from society, especially from the younger generation which tends to be more religious than their more secularised fathers. Political regimes in Uzbekistan and Tajikistan preside over religiously active and young populations, where Islamic symbolism has a powerful cultural resonance. The governments of the other states cannot ignore the issue of Islam without being susceptible to potential condemnations by devout Muslims that the state is, like the Soviet Union of the 1920s and 1930s, 'anti-God'. In all cases the current secular order is fighting the alternative symbolism of Islam embodied in a domestic and foreign clerical elite.

Alternative Islamic symbolism has been claimed by political movements, such as *Nashriya-i Hizb-i Nahzati Islomii Tojikiston* (Islamic Renaissance Party, IRP), or *Hizb ut-Tahrir*, and by mainstream conservative Islamic clergy more concerned with the observance of religious norms and practices in public, and Islamic education. Religious associations such as *Hizb ut-Tahrir* claim that they can be better in providing security, growth and welfare at the local level where the secular state is failing, as they have a fear of God and are not corruptible. However, there are no demonstrable examples of that effect in Central Asia, as the states do not give religious associations a chance.[2] Even in Kyrgyzstan, the most liberal of the five, the 2008 Nookat events

---

[2]The only real case of religious associations and field commanders being in charge of security and welfare provision took place in Gharm in Tajikistan during the civil war and their rule presented an adverse demonstration example.

showed that the authorities would not tolerate *Hizb ut-Tahrir*'s attempts to substitute the state and claim alternative legitimacy.[3]

The state also makes offensives on a symbolic front. The Law on Religious Freedom and Religious Organisations (1998) in Uzbekistan imposes strict controls on religious observance, including on the wearing of Muslim dress in public by non-clergy. Local customs and traditions are counterpoised to the alien message of foreign clergy. Imams have to pass a political awareness test, know the national anthem, be familiar with Karimov's writings and express support for the state, president and constitutional order. The president has reinforced this policy by using the media to explain to the mosques what their function should be (Khalid 2007, p. 185). Kazakhstan and Tajikistan follow the same pattern of fighting radicals, and imposing controls over mosques and religious education as that employed in Uzbekistan, although with less brutality and heavy-handedness.[4]

Since the states are profoundly secular, the rulers' claim to power cannot be justified by references to Islam. The state is a product of the Soviet lineage in which it firmly controls religion. Control is seen to be especially important nowadays, as religion is viewed as a security problem by the ruling establishment. Moreover, the religious credentials of the ex-Soviet bureaucrats are dubious and the pretence of their being pious Muslim rulers cannot be stretched too far without making them look ridiculous. Khalid's (2007, p. 190) perspective is that

> the Soviet legacy makes Central Asia a world apart. In no other part of the Muslim world is the distance between the state and Islam so great as it is in Central Asia. After a brief period of flirtation with Islamic symbols at the beginning of independence, today's Central Asian regimes allow not the slightest hint of Islamic ritual to intrude on their functions.

In this author's view, this statement omits nuances. The choice the rulers made was to assume the formal attributes of Islam, such as rituals and festivities, as well as historical claims to Muslim heritage, but to preserve the inner substance of the regime as deeply secular. Islamic doctrine is in no way a guide to action, but actions can be justified through references to Islam. Thus, religion gained respect and state patronage, but within the parameters firmly established by the state, framing the discourse without influencing it.

Khalid's other relevant point is that due to the de-Islamisation of the Soviet period the assumptions carried over from the Middle East are not always applicable to

---

[3]*Hizb ut-Tahrir* operated freely in the Nookat district of Osh province, despite being officially banned. Clashes with the authorities took place on 1 October 2008 when the administrators attempted to ban *Hizb ut-Tahrir*-organised celebrations to mark the end of Ramadan. A total of 32 people were arrested and sentenced to 15–20 years in prison. See http://www.ferghana.ru/news.php?id=11170&mode=snews, last accessed on 31 March 2009.

[4]The regimes in Kazakhstan and Tajikistan employ policies which broadly follow the same line as that by the leadership of Uzbekistan: they also suppress radical groups and movements, exercise control over mosques and religious education, but do so with less vigour, they sometimes exercise discretion and on occasion demonstrate lenient attitudes when the implementation of policies may have gone too far. These are the same type of policies, but their application differs from that in Uzbekistan.

Central Asia where the authority of Islam and those who carry its message, as well as its public presence, is much weaker. Common references are the former Soviet countries, while emotional links with the rest of the Muslim world are weak (2007, p. 201). The new states are in acute competition with the Soviet past and with Sovietism as a culture. Two contradictory factors have marred developments since independence: a split from the Soviet roots that gave way to the construction of new state identities; and the fear contained in this departure. The leaders of Uzbekistan and Tajikistan, as well as the late leader of Turkmenistan, developed a particular aversion to Sovietism, unlike their Kyrgyz and Kazakh counterparts, where monuments to Lenin have survived amidst indifference. However, popular identification with Sovietism has not gone away: common people in Tajikistan continue to call the *somoni* (the national currency) the *ruble*, and use Soviet-era place names instead of the official ones. The same is observed in Turkmenistan despite the experience of Turkmenbashism.[5]

In 2007 Imomali Rahmon dropped the Russified ending 'ov' from his last name to distance himself from the Soviet Russian heritage and sound more Tajik. Several officials, such as Foreign Minister Zafiri, followed suit, but quite a few kept their surnames as they were. The timing of the move away from the shared past ran contrary to the feeling among ordinary people. Whereas in the late 1980s and early 1990s distancing oneself from the Soviet Russian culture and a return to ethnic roots was a popular aspiration, in the 2000s the main preoccupation of citizens became migration to Russia to find work. The practicalities of living in a Russian speaking milieu dictate the need to make names sound more user-friendly: so for example Alisher becomes Sasha.

The battle against Soviet Russian cultural influence had been the most advanced in Turkmenistan under its first president, Saparmurad Niyazov. In April 2001, less than 10 years after his country became independent, the former Soviet official declared that opera and ballet were 'alien' art forms that came from outside and had no meaning for Turkmens. Opera and ballet performances, along with the circus and cinemas, were closed down and replaced with works based on Turkmen folklore and television programmes glorifying Niyazov's life (Pannier 2008). The next president, Gurbanguly Berdymuhammedov, quickly recognised that this nonsense could not continue if he was to base his rule on anything but the projection of fear. A year after Turkmenbashi's death, arts were restored, much to popular satisfaction. In fact, one of the first moves of the new president was to restore Soviet festivities, such as International Women's Day.

In Uzbekistan Soviet and, by default, Russian symbolic power remains strong below the surface, although it is resented by the Uzbek leadership which is forced to compete against it, even if only in the minds of its own citizens. President Karimov has shown some sensitivity to the parallels with the Soviet past. Joseph Kobzon, a Soviet pop icon, was denied permission to perform in Tashkent during his grand tour of Central

---

[5]In 1993, a year after his election as President of Turkmenistan, Saparmurat Niyazov took on the title 'Turkmenbashi' or 'leader of all Turkmen'. A pseudo-ideology of Turkmenbashism was constructed around him. It involved the writing of the *Ruhnama* or 'soul book' which was supposed to act as spiritual guidance for the nation and was part of a larger nation-building campaign.

Asia. Years later Karimov explained to Kobzon why he was banned from singing in Uzbekistan: 'Because, Joseph, in half-an-hour your songs turn me into a Soviet man, and I don't want that...' (Dubnov 2007a). Meanwhile, the population is quite comfortable with the Soviet heritage. Attempts by the Uzbek leadership to eradicate Soviet symbolism, such as celebrations of Victory Day, were unpopular. The holiday was eventually restored when relations with Moscow improved.

Russian political and cultural symbolism resonates for Central Asians as a modern evolution of Sovietism. The contagious effects of the Russian model developed under Vladimir Putin were strongly felt. This model of a functioning alternative to democracy rests upon a systemic political monopoly by the ruling group, restricted expression of dissent and freedom of the press, and manipulated elections. Its appeal lies in its response to the weakness of the state, perceived to have been brought about by attempts at democratisation prompted by home-grown or 'external forces'. The other side of this model, however, is that the population is rather passive and the majority is prepared to accommodate to the regime. In the eyes of the Russian and the Central Asian publics, the state improved on a performative level, and this is what matters most. Where protests have occurred, the state has proved resilient to challenges.

National ideological constructs

There are noteworthy differences in the content of the new national ideologies. In contrast to its counterparts to the south, the Kazakhstani leadership did not try to battle Sovietism, but absorbed it. It did not base its legitimacy on the rejection of the Soviet past and on the victimhood of Kazakh people in the hands of the Russians, as in the Baltic states. Schatz notes that Kazakhstan's claims to legitimacy based on a common cultural and historical identity of ethnic Kazakhs were made problematic by the country's ethnic diversity (Schatz 2006, p. 270). In fact, after several botched attempts to construct nationhood upon an ancient Kazakh mythology, the leadership used exactly this diversity as a basis for state identity. In this new myth, the regime acts as a guarantor of the preservation of multi-ethnic diversity, and actively promotes the idea of 'Kazakhstan—our common home' in the public sphere.

The Kazakhstani state identity is based on positive aspirations, such as its stated desire to become one of the 50 most prosperous world nations and to chair the Organization of Security and Cooperation in Europe (OSCE). Nazarbaev did not frame the debate in terms of whether the Soviet past was good or bad, but rather endorsed it in its entirety as a shared historical experience which made the country what it is. He projected a forward looking new state identity that would not undermine the past foundations which many among his fellow countrymen hold dear.

However, although all rulers feel that the erection of symbols of power is important, maintenance of the new symbolism is dependent on the resources that the regimes possess. Energy windfalls in Kazakhstan and Turkmenistan made state financing available for monuments and palaces and provided for the creation of a new capital (Astana) or for a revamp of the old one (Ashgabat). In the meantime, Kyrgyzstan and

Tajikistan have to play the weak cards they have at their disposal. Still, President Rahmon persevered with the building of a new presidential palace while the international community was sending food aid to his country.

Much effort was dedicated to the production of pseudo-scholarly writings to create some academic foundation for the new state ideologies. Legitimisation is 'done by the book', as it was in the Soviet era when Stalin and Brezhnev authored masterpieces of dubious intellectual value. Books by Central Asian presidents become set texts for their countrymen. Nursultan Nazarbaev has authored two books—*The Strategy of Independence* (2003) and *In the Heart of Eurasia* (2005)— along with dozens of academic papers.[6] The late President Niyazov's infamous *Ruhnama*, which offered guidance on every aspect of life, history and morality, was in evidence everywhere in the country; it inspired a monument to itself and was compulsory reading in order to pass a driving test. In Tajikistan Rahmon's historical works are used as textbooks in schools. President Karimov has published around 30 books, and the latest, *Morality is Invincible Power* (2008), was presented in official propaganda as 'the best book on philosophy and morality since the times of Socrates' (Najibullah 2008b).

Ideologies based on the primacy of titular nations have been proclaimed in Turkmenistan, Uzbekistan and Tajikistan. In his book *Tajikistan in the Mirror of History*, published in 2006, Rahmon presented a romanticised notion of history portraying Tajiks as the heirs to 'Aryan civilisation'. The year 2006 was a year of Aryan civilisation, and 2008 was designated as the year of the Tajik language. In his address to the nation the president stated that 'State independence, Language, Mother, Motherland, culture and ancient civilization are connected chains that guide us to national accord, unity and solidarity'.[7] Official ideology insists that the Samanide dynasty of the eighth century advanced the idea of Tajik statehood. A monument to King Somon was built at one of the Dushanbe squares, which ironically was a central location in the run up to the civil war. Although it is hard to draw firm conclusions on whether the ideology is taking root, the proliferation of jokes in Dushanbe about the monument serves as an indication.[8]

Having made determined efforts to move away from the Soviet past, Islam Karimov failed to come up with a coherent alternative for Uzbek nationhood. The replacement ideological construct has been full of contradictions, with little real conviction on the part of the elites. The regime made violent shifts between the rediscovery of its Islamic roots, pro-Western orientation and the recreation of the cult of Amir Timur as a

[6]The books and academic papers are available to download at the president's official site, available at: http://www.akorda.kz/www/www_akorda_kz.nsf/sections?OpenForm&id_doc=7917981ACDDB34D146 2572340019E70E&lang=ru&L1=L7&L2=L7-49, accessed 28 April 2008.

[7]President of Tajikistan Imomali Rahmon's 'Address to the Nation', 25 April 2008, delivered to bi-cameral parliament session. Text available on official presidential website, at: http://www.prezident.tj/rus/novostee_250408.html, assessed 31 March 2009.

[8]My personal favourite is about a soldier who hears the voice of King Somon every midnight as he guards his monument. King Somon says: 'Soldier, bring me a horse' The terrified solider tells President Rahmon that King Somon is talking at midnight. The president gets curious and decides to stay with the soldier. As Rahmon and the soldier stand by the monument at midnight, the voice of King Somon comes. It says: 'Man, I asked for a horse. Why did you bring me an ass?'.

glorious forebear.[9] According to Tursynov (2002), Karimov pronounced at the opening of the Timur monument that the

> image of our great ancestor recreated today is deeply symbolic: he holds the reigns of a hot-blooded fighting horse with one hand, and with the other free hand that stretches forward, he wishes peace and prosperity to the peoples, proclaiming the principle 'Power is in justice!'.

The net result of this new ethno-history has been popular disbelief and confusion, rather than cultural resonance in a nation where religious symbols are far more important than Timur's reinvented cult.

In Tajikistan some symbols, such as the distinctiveness of a Persian-speaking nation in the Turkic world emphasised by the government, found a cultural resonance among Tajik cultural elites and the rural intelligentsia. This concept was downplayed in the Soviet era and became more powerful thereafter, but it cannot be stretched too far without inviting an unflattering reference to Afghanistan. The idea of an 'Aryan civilisation' and 'us' (Tajiks) having been here before 'them' (Uzbeks) is popular among the ethnic Tajik titular group. However, the major gap in Rahmon's ideology is that it does not provide an official, plausible interpretation of the history of the 1992–1997 war.

Most of the ideological constructivism leaves the recipient societies largely unaffected. What works better for the public is a comparative perspective. The populations of the Central Asian states tend to compare their wellbeing to the recent Soviet past (a Golden Age for many), and the early days of independence (an unqualified disaster). They also draw contrasts—often reinforced by the official propaganda—between their experiences and the misfortunes of their neighbours. There is a certain hierarchy of regional disasters, making people think that 'here it is still not as bad as elsewhere'. Thus, citizens of Kazakhstan feel that, despite tight controls upon the political space, their situation is infinitely better than in Uzbekistan, where people can be arrested and executed with little regard for human life or due process. In Uzbekistan it is believed that the country could have gone down the path of Tajikistan, which, the public thinks, is still suffering from the effects of the civil war. In Tajikistan a glance across the border into Afghanistan makes the faults of the current establishment pale in comparison. All of the regional neighbours look down on Kyrgyzstan as unstable, crime-ridden and possibly falling apart after the 2005 'Tulip Revolution'. Akaev's failed democratic experiment has served as an important claim for the Kazakhstani leadership that democracy is futile without a strong economy to back it up.

These comparisons reflect some commonly shared beliefs in the region, such as the vital importance of stability compared to democracy; that the state is vital as a pillar of social order; and that religion should be respected, but kept within its own space. These shared values are at the same time the outcome of a period of a relative stability, and also generate stability. Thus, although the national ideologies are not very

---

[9]Timur died in 1405, and the unity of the vast empire he founded did not survive him. Among other battles, he was known to fight against people called 'the Ozbeks of Shibani'.

coherent or particularly culturally resonant, they perform a function of depoliticising potential sources of instability.

Security, growth and welfare

Legitimacy based on the promise of security

The claim to power stems from the process of state building. The state is of central importance in the provision of stability and security. Citizens of Central Asian states tend to cherish stability and security, since they have gone through a fear of disorder that followed the early years of independence when they had to pull themselves from an abyss of economic collapse and social turmoil (Matveeva 1999). Having lived through a period when the state nearly vanished from their lives, they can appreciate the role it plays.

The public stance of legitimisation consists of pledges to maintain stability and praise for the nation. In the words of President Nazarbaev,

> in over 16 years of independence we implemented our own model for securing public stability and inter-ethnic accord, moulding the Kazakhstani identity and shared Kazakhstani patriotism. This is our Kazakhstani know-how of which we are justly proud and which we must carefully guard. (Nazarbaev 2008)

The idea of stability and social harmony is no less relevant for Tajikistan, given the context of the recent civil war. Heathershaw (2007, p. 307) describes what happened in Tajikistan as

> 'complex legitimacy': the gradual move from a military conflict to political order, a process that represents the legitimization of power and the recreation of authority, livelihoods, and sovereignty. The principal triumph of 'peacebuilding' for the Tajik elite has been its ability to recentralise the legitimate terrain of political authority—to become the state.

Threats to security and the public perception that the ruling regime is the main protector from external or internal foes is a powerful driver for legitimisation. For that to be credible, the population has to experience a sufficient degree of 'healthy fear' and believe in the reality of the threats. The Soviet example is illustrative. After a massive land invasion during the Second World War, many Soviet people believed that they were surrounded by enemies and that the repetition of a large-scale war on Soviet territory was possible. The Soviet regime was a protector, and sacrifices for the sake of defence were justified. Such beliefs waned in the 1960s and almost evaporated in the 1970s, giving way to jokes about 'bloody imperialists' and paving the way for a crisis of legitimacy of the Soviet state.

The leaderships of Tajikistan and Uzbekistan rely in large measure on security threats to legitimise the regime. In the case of Tajikistan, Heathershaw (2007, p. 311) characterises legitimacy as 'inter-subjective'. Legitimacy constitutes the quantitative reduction of physical violence, and the qualitative transformation of cultural and physical violence. Legitimacy potentially provides a richer, 'positive' description of a 'peace' such as Tajikistan's than that provided by 'negative peace' or 'war weariness'. Unlike the idea of 'negative peace', legitimacy sets limits on power which extend beyond the simple absence of widespread political violence. On the other hand, legitimacy does not cause peace or order. Rather, it constitutes the degree and form of peace in a given context. This is how peace holds.

However, legitimacy based on peacemaking has its limits as the war experience becomes more remote and the population becomes less concerned about a resumption of violence. Indeed, if 'war echo' security incidents in Tajikistan occur, they have less resonance in the society. In the latest clash that took place in Gharm in February 2008, the population did not back those who were in conflict with the state, as people are more concerned about economic problems than political ones (Olimova 2008).

Islam Karimov continues to present himself as a last bastion against Islamists, drug traffickers and other criminals. Although not of the same magnitude as in Tajikistan, the security threats in Uzbekistan are not without foundations, as episodes of violence have plagued the nation's short history and that of its neighbours. The approach to deal with these threats is reflected in a saying attributed to Islam Karimov that 'it is better to have hundreds of arrested than thousands killed'. This stance seems to be shared by the ruling elite, while a sufficient constituency of ordinary people experience a fear of radical Islamists who seek to violate the established order and impose a Taliban-style rule. From this perspective, overwhelming repression against real or bogus terrorists is not entirely unjustified. Such fears are often underestimated by outside analysts.

Economy and welfare first

Security threats alone are not sufficient for legitimisation and vary in credibility across the region. In Uzbekistan and Tajikistan security is a major pillar for legitimacy, but still the state has to show that it is effective in its delivery of growth and welfare. Performance on the development agenda underscores the validity of the existing institutions. Kazakhstan is a good example of giving priority to economy over democracy. Economic prosperity has been the key to Nazarbaev's search for legitimacy. Growth references have been accompanied by forward-looking slogans such as 'Kazakhstan—2030', which the regime employs in a subtle legitimisation of the current restrictions it lays upon political freedoms in return for economic growth and prosperity in the future. The primacy of economy rather than security has distinguished Nazarbaev from his Uzbek and Tajik counterparts. In his annual State of the Nation Address in 2008, Nursultan Nazarbaev proudly named the achievements of Kazakhstan, including rapid economic growth, a modernised political structure, enhanced social welfare and the reversal of negative demographic trends.

A commitment to the provision of social welfare inherited from the Soviet past is also a part of gaining consent to rule. Here highly authoritarian states meet with some success. Comparative research in Kyrgyzstan and Uzbekistan concludes that, 'the Uzbek state not only possesses more despotic power than the Kyrgyz state, it also exercises more infrastructural power and shapes perceptions that the state is useful' (Radnitz *et al.* 2009, p. 16). However, the government in Uzbekistan faces a problem when it has to convince the proactive part of the population of its *bona fide* credentials.

The state struggles to make the citizens cooperate in a proactive, positive way when it needs them to trust it. The state is capable of ensuring compliant behaviour and soliciting passive cooperation when citizens act as recipients of public goods and services. However, it is difficult for the state to make the citizenry act as its ally since it lacks their trust. For instance, a tax amnesty reform in Kazakhstan aimed at allowing 'grey' capital to enter the formal economy was fairly successful as the people in Kazakhstan trust their state more. A similar undertaking in Uzbekistan failed due to distrust by businessmen and labour migrants, despite active government propaganda that the source of money which enters the banking system would not be investigated.[10]

By contrast, a 'reformist' agenda can prove a liability. Kyrgyzstan's President Akaev initially had been genuinely committed to market and democratic reforms, but failed to build strong institutions and prevent corruption. His initial legitimacy claims had been linked to Western-oriented reforms, but backfired since the reforms failed to bring efficiency and prosperity. The reforms came to be seen as imposed from outside, and Akaev as naïve to have blindly followed foreign recipes:

> The brief and hesitating liberalization in Kyrgyzstan presented problems for an eventual authoritarian turn. Liberalisation was the centrepiece of Akaev's legitimacy claims, and when economic change bore little fruit and political change went rapidly into reverse, he encountered a legitimacy crisis. (Schatz 2009)

Since the governments partly base their legitimacy on their ability to look after the people, they are especially vulnerable to a crisis over welfare. The present circumstances are testing this ability: the global financial crisis, rises in food price, high inflation and crumbling infrastructure present challenges that the governments may not be able to cope with. Multiple crises hit Tajikistan in 2008[11] and the situation deteriorated in Uzbekistan as well. Popular protests focusing on the social and economic agenda erupted in February 2008 in Uzbekistan, in Jizzak and Karakalpakstan (Khamidov 2008). Tajikistan experienced several protests in the capital, Dushanbe, as well as in the cities of Kulob, Panjekent and Khorog. Both countries had previously experienced very low levels of protest due to a fear of repression. The authorities did not crush the protests by force in a sign that they recognised their failure to fulfil their social promise and indirectly admitted responsibility for reaching the point where basic needs were unmet. Karimov seems invincible as the welfare crisis in Uzbekistan is of manageable proportions, but in Tajikistan the shifting perception of the government's ability to provide for the population leaves Rahmon in a more vulnerable position.

---

[10]'Uzbekistan: Capital Amnesty Initiative Stalls in the Face of Public Skepticism', *Eurasianet*, 18 July 2008.

[11]These ranged from a demand by the International Monetary Fund to repay the $17 million debt obtained by fraud by the government, a 40% increase in drug trafficking, and flour and energy shortages to an invasion of locusts. See 'Tajikistan: Government Shakes Down Population Amid Deepening Economic Dysfunction', *Eurasianet Business & Economics*, *Eurasianet*, 7 May 2008.

The art of political manipulation

The Central Asian regimes continue to make the claim that their states are 'democratic'. They hold regular, if symbolic, elections, the outcomes of which are determined in advance. Even in 'soft authoritarian' Kazakhstan the president has ruled virtually unopposed since the Soviet era, and his party *Nur Otan* took all the seats in the lower house of parliament in the August 2007 elections.

The function and place of elections in authoritarian states is an interesting subject. The leaders feel that the elections are needed for more than just a hypothetical international audience. On the fifteenth anniversary of the adoption of Uzbekistan's Constitution, President Karimov addressed his fellow citizens on 'the noteworthy features of the presidential elections' of December 2007, where Karimov ran practically unopposed. The president noted that their 'thoroughly thought-out model is based on international standards, advanced experience of democratic states and entirely reflects the values and mentality of our people'. It was essential, in Karimov's view, to 'maintain the rule of law and freedom of expression, and completely reject approaches and stereotypes remaining from the Soviet period' (Dubnov 2007b).

The absence of formal electoral competition places a greater emphasis on their informal meaning. Rather than being a means of political choice, elections are expressions of loyalty and perform the function of regularly held rituals where citizens are reminded of the existence of the central state and of mutual obligations between the state and the citizens. To ensure this, 'the administrative system has to be sufficiently independent of the shaping of legitimising will. This occurs in a legitimisation process that elicits mass loyalty but avoids participation' (Habermas 1984, p. 138). In some respect the citizens go along with this largely consensually.

Still, this begs two questions. First, why create a pretence of democracy and mimic its attributes? On a performative level, formal democracy could just as easily be replaced by a conservative, authoritarian welfare state that reduces the political participation of the citizens to a harmless level (Habermas 1984, p. 148). Hypothetically, the rulers may think that in future, full democracy could be allowed when the citizens can be trusted not to use it to harm themselves and the state, thus making it worth creating the vehicles for it, even if they are presently devoid of meaning. Second, why falsify and manipulate elections if the regimes are confident of victory anyhow? In Kazakhstan, Schatz points out, 'the regime required little election-day fraud to ensure a favourable outcome, given social circumstances' (Schatz 2009, p. 212). In others the presidents are most likely to secure electoral victories, even for the simple reason of the lack of decent competition. This, however, was almost never allowed. The practice of holding elections in which presidents stand virtually unopposed implies that the regimes doubt their own popularity.

The leaderships' claim of legitimacy is helped by a lack of viable alternatives in the eyes of the population, and, in the case of Kazakhstan and Tajikistan at least, in the eyes of the international community. Heathershaw argues that 'while a certain legitimacy is present in Tajikistan, it is contingent. Tajiks resign to authoritarian government not because they appreciate it, but because they see no meaningful alternative' (Heathershaw 2007, p. 307).

There are two main techniques employed by the government to delegitimise their political opponents. One is to evoke fear that if they come to power, their rule would threaten the security and viability of the state. For example, in Tajikistan it is implied that if the IRP (*Nashriya-i Hizb-i Nahzati Islomii Tojikiston*) comes to power, it would attempt to impose an Islamic state and open a floodgate through which Islamist movements would pour in. The second technique, which is gaining in prominence, is to present opponents as corrupt, ineffective and incapable of governance. Thus, the alternatives presented to the public entail that there is no meaningful choice: it is between those who never had the experience of managing state affairs and would be unable to govern, and those who served in the government, but proved so corrupt that the incumbents appear more honest by comparison, such as Ahedjan Kajegeldin in Kazakhstan. Typically, evidence of corruption is in abundance and does not need to be fabricated. In Tajikistan the former opposition 'heavyweights'—Mahmadruzi Iskandarov, Mirzo Ziyoev and Ali Akbar Turajonzoda—are in the list of the top 100 richest people, thanks to the fortunes they amassed during the 'national reconciliation' process (Najibullah 2008c).

Delegitimisation of political opponents achieved by skilful manipulation ensures that no alternative grouping or prominent personalities have a chance to evolve into credible forces. The way this is done differs depending upon the nature of the regime: what separates the soft authoritarian ruler from his harder counterpart is the degree to which he relies on persuasive techniques (Schatz 2009; Cummings 2005). Typically, three strategies have been employed. The first is suppression (direct physical violence, such as imprisonment, torture, abduction of relatives, along with cultural and political pressure, such as restrictions on party activities, freedom of assembly, electoral fraud, and black PR). Secondly there is co-option into the ruling establishment (often by confronting opposition figures with evidence of corruption). By doing this the ruler 'pre-empts challengers by offering access to the crucial spoils that power brings' (Schatz 2009, p. 206). For instance, the Bakiev regime after the December 2007 parliamentary elections nominated several of his former opponents for government jobs. These opponents accepted the appointments and subsequently changed their opposition stance. The third strategy is to force opponents into exile. This tactic invariably works. So far, there is no figure among Central Asian expatriates who fits into the Boris Berezovskii mould of a high-profile émigré who can act against the current regime from abroad. Despite the well meaning hopes of the international community that political exiles would play a prominent role in their societies if domestic conditions changed (International Crisis Group 2004), Turkmenistan's case suggests that there is little evidence to support such a claim.[12]

The damage inflicted by the regimes to delegitimise their rivals should not be underestimated. Despite conditions that are ripe for discontent, there are no viable competitors to claim alternative legitimacy, and nobody among the opposition forces has a chance to evolve into a credible figure. Because the state leaders have

---

[12]On the inability of the Turkmen opposition in exile in Russia to play any role in their country after the power change, see interview with Khudaiberdy Orazov, 'Turkmenistan: Diktatura po vtoromu krugu', 26 May 2008, available at: http://www.ferghana.ru/article.php?id—5716, accessed 29 April 2009.

delegitimised their competitors, there is little sense of how change may come about. Thus, legitimacy is in large measure based on fear and the inability to change, and on the lack of options. Habituation to obedience—the combination of a cynical lack of belief and compliant behaviour—may be characteristic of authoritarian regimes (Wedeen 1999, p. 154).

Leadership matters

Since rule is highly personalised, we need to recognise that leadership matters: 'The personal traits and political inclinations of particular rulers should not be dismissed, least of all in authoritarian contexts' (Schatz 2009, p. 218). Personality continues to play a role, but it can be a liability as well as an asset.

The political systems in Central Asia are often called 'superpresidential', in which the leaders personify their states. At the same time the presidents are hardly impressive as popular figures and do not demonstrate sufficient leadership qualities to generate a following. Perhaps only Nazarbaev can boast that he connects with the citizens in some emotional ways, but this still pales in comparison with such leaders as Vladimir Putin in Russia. In Syria, as Wedeen (1999, p. 157) observes, the regime may not be able to create an extraordinary leader, but it does make President Asad extraordinary in the sense that people are publicly obedient to him. If charisma does not explain the phenomenon, are we then dealing with personality cults? This also seems not quite to be the case. With the exception of the late Niyazov, none of the presidents has a developed cult in the same fashion as Stalin, Saddam Hussein or Asad, although Uzbekistan, Tajikistan and present-day Turkmenistan have some makings of it. However, ordinary citizens can easily bypass these 'cults' in everyday interactions, which was not the case with Stalin. And there is little evidence of a coherent cult in Kyrgyzstan, where the president clings to power almost apologetically.

Still, what the countries have in common is that all the presidents loom large in public life, with portraits, slogans, TV appearances and celebrations cluttering the space. The leaders of Kazakhstan, Tajikistan and Uzbekistan depict themselves as the best guarantors of security and stability. In the turbulent time of the Soviet empire's collapse they went through a 'baptism of fire' as the new states were born. They can present themselves on a par with historical rulers who did great things in the past: they can claim they established the new states and rescued them from a real or potential failure. For example, Imomali Rahmon was elected the Chairman of the Supreme Soviet (head of state) at the height of the civil war in November 1992 after a number of more prominent Tajik politicians rejected the job as too dangerous.

By contrast, maintenance of 'greatness' presents a challenge for 'second tier' leaders such as Gurbanguly Berdymuhammedov, who came to rule Turkmenistan through bureaucratic succession, and certainly for Kurmanbek Bakiev of Kyrgyzstan who came to power almost by accident when Askar Akaev was ousted. Interestingly, Bakiev's leadership hesitated for three years on how to present the 'Tulip Revolution' events until, in 2008, the decision was made to mark 24 March as a public holiday in an attempt to legitimate the current government. However, the government felt vulnerable to the opposition parties' claims that it was illegitimate, and its staging of celebrations was brief and nervous (Cummings 2008).

A leader can also change the basis for his public persona and modify his image according to the message the regime seeks to project in the given times. In the period of 'lasting peace' (2003 onwards) Imomali Rahmon started to play down his war hero image by negating the civil war through a 'forget-and-forgive' policy and sought to invent a new style based on the notion of 'stability and prosperity'. Construction of the city gates marking the entrance to the capital and the new presidential palace has begun. The eightieth anniversary of the founding of Dushanbe in 2004 celebrated how far the city has developed from a market town in the pre-Soviet era, but mentioned nothing of the vicious civil war battles and considerable reconstruction the city has undergone recently. In his annual Address to the Nation in 2008 Rahmon did not make any overt references to the war. Instead, he outlined an agenda of development and survival, stressing three 'national strategic interests—to guarantee energy independence of the country, to get the country out of communication isolation and ensure food security'.[13] This was a risky move because he has been unable to deliver on any of them, and has made himself vulnerable to be blamed for their absence.

As presidents are symbols of their nations, they are required to look personally impeccable, but are vulnerable to the 'human factor'. An ability to make strategic decisions at a moment of choice is a crucial quality to hold the reigns of authoritarian power. A 'weak Tsar' is ill-suited to resist political storms, as his legitimacy can quickly decline if a strong presence is not maintained. Hesitancy in public is not to be forgiven. The 'Tulip Revolution' in Kyrgyzstan provides a stark example of that. Initially, Akaev enjoyed sufficient popular respect as the first president of the independent state and as a unifier of regional and ethnic groups in a common project. However, in the electoral year of 2005, he was unable to choose a strategy of succession management, and his entourage pursued several mutually exclusive strategies simultaneously. Moreover, Akaev lost his former ability to directly connect with his people. Nazarbaev, by contrast, had a clear idea of where he wanted to go with the parliamentary and presidential elections, and had enough spirit to engage proactively and personally with the challenges from various opposition forces.

The other dimension of vulnerability is family politics where scandals are an important symptom of delegitimisation. In many countries the public is interested in the affairs of the great and the good, and the 'first family' acquires an exaggerated significance. Still, family matters in Central Asia are different. Presidents tend to bring the immediate relatives into politics, and political problems can result from an outgrowth of family battles. In Kazakhstan, influence groups are formed along the principle of personal loyalty and affiliation with the president (Kimmage 2006). Family members can be expelled for 'bad behaviour', such as Rahat Aliev, former head of the National Security Committee and a presidential son-in-law married to Nazarbaev's elder daughter Dariga. Although Dariga Nazarbaeva divorced Aliev shortly after the Aliev scandal erupted, her party *Asar* was virtually dissolved and her influence in politics has receded (Najibullah 2008a).

---

[13]President of Tajikistan Imomali Rahmon's 'Address to the Nation', 25 April 2008. Available on the President of Tajikistan official website, at: http://www.prezident.tj/eng/news_150409.html, accessed on 29 April 2009.

In Uzbekistan Gulnara Karimova, the president's daughter, is the deputy Foreign Minister and an influential business figure in her own right.[14] She appears to have high aspirations, plays a prominent role in politics and the social life of the society, and she presides over charitable foundations and media outlets. These ambitions unleashed speculation as to whether the public could accept a female head of state were she to succeed her father, and a debate about how a woman should conduct herself in public politics in a country with a Muslim population. Although views upon these matters seldom find their way into officially sanctioned media, the divergence of opinions can be passionate and expose deeply held values. Gulnara responded by cultivating an image as an 'Uzbek Princess' in fashionable glossy magazines in Moscow, such as Russian *Hello!* She presented herself first and foremost a as woman—beautiful, feminine, and a good mother. This strategy was chosen in appreciation of the commonly held cultural beliefs among elites in Uzbekistan which imply that it is possible for a woman to engage in different pursuits provided that she does not neglect her womanhood, since young women may want to follow her as a role model.

Political leaders walk a very fine line between tolerating family scandal and undermining their symbolic power. President Akaev paid dearly for the ambitions of his wife and children. Developments in Tajikistan and Kyrgyzstan in 2008 are quite illuminating suggesting that President Bakiev may be heading along the same unfortunate path of his predecessor. His son Maxim, dubbed 'The Prince', is believed to control important businesses, including some that had belonged to Aidar Akaev, the son of the deposed president. One of the president's brothers, Janysh, heads the State Protection Service, and is Maxim's arch-rival for control over lucrative assets. Several episodes of scandal and violence between Maxim and Janysh Bakiev have been alleged.

The government in Tajikistan is largely based around President Imomali Rahmon's family, incorporating relatives and personal associates of the president whose loyalty he can trust and whose corrupt appetites he can control. In May 2008 his brother-in-law Hassan Sadulloyev, head of *Orienbank* and the man in charge of other lucrative companies, disappeared, and was believed to have been killed by one of the sons of President Rahmon in a dispute over assets. Sadulloyev appeared after a few months, but has been compromised by rumours that it is in fact his twin brother posing for him. Regardless of what exactly took place, the rumours by themselves have inflicted a blow on Rahmon's leadership. An important element in any authoritarian regime is the aura of invincibility. Within the post-Soviet context, a leader that cannot control his own relatives, or has shown any sign of weakness in family politics, has faced serious challenges to his authority (Najibullah 2008a).

The international arena

While in authoritarian regimes, such as in Central Asia, it may be impossible to distinguish between domestic legitimacy and enforced compliance, this does not apply to the international dimension, where compliance cannot be substituted for legitimacy.

---

[14]Gulnara Karimova was appointed as a deputy minister in February 2008. See: http://www.oreanda.ru/ru/news/20080204/common/events/article276710/, accessed 28 April 2009.

Domestic and international legitimacy are two different notions, differently constructed and not necessarily bearing upon each other, given the countries' isolation and restrictions on information flow. The international and internal audiences are different, and they care about different aspects of domestic political development. Moreover, the Central Asian elite is insufficiently internationalised and only a small segment has a horizon beyond the CIS. For example, the domestic audience in Uzbekistan believes in a threat from radical Islamists and therefore tends to view the regime as a protector, which ascribes legitimacy to it. The international audience does not share this perception to the same degree, but suspects that the Islamist threat is employed as manipulation of the regime in order to stay in power.[15]

While international legitimacy is somehow more objective, domestic legitimacy can be forced and the former can also be manipulated to a certain degree. Symbols of democracy adopted by Akaev worked well for international legitimacy, serving as a kind of super-trademark, stabilising the image and identity of the nation (Geisler 2005, p. xvii). In the 1990s Askar Akaev was the first in Central Asia to introduce national brands for international consumption. Two distinctive brands for Kyrgyzstan were coined: 'The Island of Democracy' and 'The Switzerland of Central Asia' (Marat 2007). This brought kudos to Kyrgyzstan well beyond the scope of the actual political reforms.

There is an argument that international development assistance can work towards legitimisation of policies and practices which may not be in the best interests of the countries of Central Asia. Heathershaw asserts that international efforts in peace-building shaped and aggravated Tajikistan's problems with regards to authority, livelihoods and sovereignty to some extent. 'Simulated "elections" and an "opposition", "border management" and "community self government" feign the existence of a sovereign and legitimate state to the international community, however "weak"' (Heathershaw 2007, pp. 309–10). Likewise, the international community, with the OSCE as a vehicle, legitimised the questionable presidential elections of 2005 in Kyrgyzstan. The elections were 'won' by Kurmanbek Bakiev, but in fact had a pre-determined outcome as a result of a bargain between Bakiev (a southerner) and Felix Kulov (a northerner), who became the prime minister in a so-called 'tandem' alliance deal.

Using international development clichés can be precarious for a regime, as they may acquire meaning and become a self-fulfilling prophecy, an unintended outcome of sloganeering performed for the international community's benefit. In Kyrgyzstan, 2004 was declared a 'year of social mobilisation' in an attempt to please the World Bank and United Nations Development Programme (UNDP), both of which promoted social mobilisation as a way of community development in the countryside. Slogans translated from English to this effect were placed on the roadsides, initially producing more bewilderment than appeal. However, social mobilisation indeed happened throughout the year and culminated in the 2005 'revolution'.

Schatz (2006, p. 274) distinguishes between hard (Uzbekistani) and soft (Kazakhstani) authoritarianism and attributes the variation to the role of interna-tional actors. In discussing Kazakhstan, Schatz seems to equate international and

---

[15] The following from Khalid (2007, p. 169) is a fairly typical stance: 'Islamic militancy does exist in Uzbekistan, but if it didn't, the regime would have invented it'. A number of influential scholars, such as Shirin Akiner (2005), have been more sympathetic to the position of the Uzbek President.

domestic legitimacy, pointing out that engagement with international actors became the established *sine qua non* of Kazakhstan's conception of statehood. The argument is that the Kazakhstani elite made a choice to frame state legitimacy as being moored to engagement with the international community. In this paradigm, one is substituted for the other: 'international engagement was a way to frame legitimacy for a domestic audience'. However, international claims would have been an empty promise, were they not supplemented by tangible social and economic improvements at home.

International legitimacy can vary more wildly than internal legitimacy. People inside the country may not deny legitimacy to a regime to the same extent as external commentators do. Uzbekistan is considered by international media and NGOs to be an outright dictatorship. After Andijan, its leader is seen as one of the world's worst villains. Kazakhstan is in a different category. Its successful attempts to gain international legitimacy started with Nazarbaev's nuclear disarmament policy, which demonstrated that he was a responsible international player. Favourable treatment of Western investors also helped to promote the country's credentials. Kazakhstani companies are listed on the London Stock Exchange. Corruption charges against Nazarbaev and his associates in the USA have also been dropped. Kazakhstan is to chair the OSCE in 2010, a high mark of recognition of international legitimacy. Meanwhile, the differences in domestic arrangements are not necessarily so stark. Nevertheless, Kazakhstan was awarded the OSCE presidency without any real conditions, and so it is no wonder that there is 'no concern' for political reform in the statements made by the authorities (Dosybiev 2008).

While societies may be disinterested, their leaderships care about international legitimacy and, increasingly, about the image they have abroad. The reaction of the reasonably confident Kazakhstani leadership to the *Borat* misfortune, from which it suffered accidentally, is quite telling. Even leaders who defy most of the world became more sensitive about their reputation. Uzbekistan had a project pursued by the Ministry of Foreign Affairs in partnership with UNDP on the improvement of its image abroad. Even the Tajik leadership became alarmed about its negative profile in the international arena, being typically called 'the main corridor for transit of Afghan drugs into Europe', 'supplier of cheap labour for Russia' and 'the poorest country in Central Asia'. A decision was made by the Security Council to set up a Committee on Information Resistance (*protivostoyanie*) under the president in July 2008.[16] However, the leadership of Tajikistan acquired international notoriety when it became publicly known that it has paid over $126 million in legal fees over the past three years to a British law firm in connection with a TadAZ (Tajik Aluminium Plant) embezzlement case. This incident is likely to adversely affect the reputation of the country until the regime changes.[17]

---

[16]See http://www.centrasia.ru/newsA.php?st=1216234980, accessed 28 April 2009.

[17]According to papers filed with a London court, the British firm Herbert Smith has continued to bill the Tajik government $11 million every month. Legal costs were going to set the UK and possibly the world record in legal fees. The Tajik Aluminium Plant's (TadAZ, renamed TALCO) litigation is set to rank as the third most-expensive lawsuit contested in the English courts to date. For further details see Murphy (2008) and 'Tajikistan: Government Shakes Down Population Amid Deepening Economic Dysfunction', *Business & Economics, Eurasianet*, 7 May 2008.

Delegitimisation of democracy through the presentation of 'failed' attempts at democratisation in Kyrgyzstan and Tajikistan is a crucial part of delegitimisation of the negative international perspective on Central Asian politics. This strategy forms an aspect of the legitimisation campaign based on sovereignty, non-interference and anti-Western sentiment aimed to foster regional solidarity to resist international political pressure. Resentment of Western lecturing on how these countries should be ruled and what the right values are expresses some commonly held standards. Delegitimisation of international criticism of internal politics forms a discourse along the lines of, 'who are you to criticise us if you don't understand the conditions in which we live'. In this, international (seen as 'Western') verdicts regarding flawed elections are presented in a dubious light. Counter-legitimisation is performed via representatives of the CIS or Shanghai Cooperation Organization (SCO) electoral observers. For example, views of external observers on the quality of the parliamentary elections in 2007 in Kyrgyzstan differed: the SCO issued a favourable verdict, while in the OSCE's view the elections represented a decline in the democratic process and an increase in the government's interference.

Conclusions

All five Central Asian states have made efforts to construct new national symbols. How many resources they invest in their production depends on their available income, with energy-rich countries ahead of others, but all aspire to a standard of high visibility. The content is not very sophisticated, mixing plausible and implausible claims, but the Soviet experience taught citizens to treat propaganda with a pinch of cynicism in any case. The pillars of legitimisation consist of representation of achievements in state-building, stability and security guarantees, projection of effectiveness and successful delegitimisation of international criticism and political opponents.

Authoritarian states which undergo the transition away from democracy can be more or less convincing in legitimising their rule even without making many concessions to democracy. The regimes achieved a degree of consent to their rule by a combination of coercion, manipulation of the political landscape to portray an absence of meaningful alternatives and performative accomplishments. The continuation of their legitimisation will depend upon their ability to deliver what their people expect of them: security, growth and welfare. Since legitimacy in large measure is based on threats to the stability of social order, citizens have to continue to believe that insecurity is real. Regional comparisons help to reinforce this message.

Symbolism is important in the legitimisation of state-building where presidential personalities clutter the political space and the sheer volume of state propaganda produces depoliticising effects. Presidents loom large in public life as symbols of power concentration and state strength. Elections, parliaments, armies and addresses to the nation may not play the same role as in democracies, but they fulfil a significant function as national symbols to frame and legitimise the rule. Most importantly, national symbols project an image of a strong rule, thus legitimising power as an empirical, visible fact.

Still, the ideological foundations remain shaky. In Kazakhstan's case popular consent has not merely been forced or bought; it is more nuanced, but in general the new state identity has not contributed greatly to legitimacy due to citizens' weak association with the new states. This, for example, is reflected in the attitudes towards the establishment of interstate borders, resentment of which creates a powerful emotional resonance among populations who had been happy living in a common state of the USSR without internal borders. Making nations out of states through the construction of national symbols has not been very effective.

However, delegitimisation strategies have been fairly effective whether in portraying the opposition as incapable, dangerous or corrupt, leaving the public with no meaningful choice, or in delegitimisation of international criticism as a rejection of Western recipes. Delegitimisation of Western criticism has found a cultural resonance because it reflects shared beliefs of sovereignty and fatigue with being lectured by outsiders. Western liberalism, by contrast, is presented as culturally too distant, with its appeal undermined by messy policies abroad and financial crisis at home (Lewis 2008). If, at the onset of independence, the image of the West was definitely positive, the applicability and popular resonance of Western notions in Central Asia has become far less certain. Still, successful acquisition of international legitimacy can be a symbolic tool at home, as Nazarbaev showed with his personal crusade to obtain OSCE chairmanship for his country.

Nowadays, Central Asia's leaders are hostages to their own positions, having outwitted or suppressed their opponents. They preside solely upon the political Olympus, bearing the sole responsibility for future crises. They depend upon being effective at what they set out to do, as they have made themselves vulnerable if things go wrong, while their personal and familial behaviour can turn into a weapon against them. The absence of a free press does not mean that compromising information is not spread around, as the public relies upon oral circulation through social networks, which these societies have a high density of. Their symbolic legitimisation remains uncertain and in competition with the stronger opposing forces of Sovietism and Islam. Since both Islamic and Soviet or Putinist alternatives are culturally resonant, albeit for different groups of society, the Central Asian rulers are vulnerable and challenged, because these alternatives emanate from sources beyond their control. So far, there is no sign that the intensity of these challenges is diminishing.

Attempts by the Central Asian leaders to wrap themselves up in the symbols of Islam are not very convincing, as they cannot claim these symbols as their own and because Islamic symbolism can easily be used against them. Its appeal is likely to increase in the future and be important in shaping the perceptions of a model ruler, who is against corruption and is renowned for austere personal behaviour with no scandals and no relatives in politics. Khalid predicts that the Muslims of Central Asia will invoke Islam in their struggles over the destinies of their societies (Khalid 2007, p. 203). To legitimise themselves, the next generation of leaders will have to pay more than lip service to religious symbolism.

The political outcomes of acquiring a degree of legitimacy have been partially achieved through a combination of coercive, performative and symbolic means. However, legitimacy remains weak. It presents a balancing act which requires constant maintenance, and competes against powerful and culturally resonant symbols. The present stability could quickly unravel if a regime's grip on power were to be visibly loosened. Stability also rests upon general popular passivity which feeds the atmosphere of consent, but it cannot be taken for granted in the long term.

London School of Economics

References

Akiner, S. (2005) *Violence in Andijan, 13 May 2005: An Independent Assessment*, Silk Road Paper, Central Asia–Caucasus Institute, Silk Road Studies Program (Washington, DC, John Hopkins University).

Beetham, D. (1985) *Max Weber and the Theory of Modern Politics* (Cambridge, Polity).

Beetham, D. (1991) *The Legitimation of Power* (London, MacMillan).

Carothers, T. (2002) 'The End of the Transition Paradigm', *Journal of Democracy*, 13, 1.

Connolly, W. (ed.) (1984) *Legitimacy and the State* (New York, New York University Press).

Cummings, S.N. (2005) *Kazakhstan: Power and the Elite* (London, Routledge).

Cummings, S.N. (2008) 'The Tulip Revolution: Mixed Messages of Official Memory', *CACI Analyst, Silk Road Programme*, 4 April, available at: http://www.cacianalyst.org/?q=node/4828, accessed 28 April 2009.

Dosybiev, D. (2008) 'OSCE Pressure Unlikely to Prompt Kazak Reforms', *Reporting Central Asia*, 534, Institute of War and Peace Reporting, 28 February, available at: http://www.iwpr.net/?p=rca&s=f&o=342990&apc_state=henirca2008, accessed 19 May 2009.

Dubnov, A. (2007a) 'Karimov gotovitsya stat' Presidentom Uzbekistana i ne khochet byt' sovetskim chelovekom', *Vremya Novostei*, 22 November.

Dubnov, A. (2007b) 'Karimov obeshchaet zapadu ottepel', *Vremya Novostei*, December.

Edelman, M. (1964) *The Symbolic Uses of Politics* (Urbana, University of Illinois Press).

Fukuyama, F. (1992) *The End of History and the Last Man* (London, Hamish Hamilton).

Geisler, M.E. (2005) 'Introduction: What are National Symbols—and What Do They Do to Us?', in Geisler, M.E. (ed.) (2005) *National Symbols, Fractured Identities: Contesting the National Narrative*, Middlebury Bicentennial Series in International Studies (Middlebury, Middlebury College Press and Lebanon, NH, University Press of New England).

Habermas, J. (1984) 'What Does a Legitimization Crisis Mean Today?', in Connolly, W. (ed.) (1984).

Heathershaw, J. (2007) *Peace as Complex Legitimacy: Politics, Space and Discourse in Tajikistan's Peacebuilding Process, 2000–2005*, unpublished PhD thesis, Department of International Relations, London School of Economics.

Herzog, D. (1989) *Happy Slaves: A Critique of Consent Theory* (Chicago, University of Chicago Press).

International Crisis Group (2004) *Repression and Regression in Turkmenistan—A New International Strategy*, Asia Report, No. 85, 4 November (Brussels, International Crisis Group).

Khalid, A. (2007) *Islam after Communism: Religion and Politics in Central Asia* (Berkeley, University of California Press).

Khamidov, A. (2008) 'Uzbekistan: Having Weathered Winter, Authorities Brace for Spring', *Eurasianet*, 28 February.

Kimmage, D. (2006) 'Kazakhstan: a Shaken System', *Eurasia Insight*, 5 March, available at: http://www.eurasianet.org/departments/insight/articles/pp030506.shtml, last accessed 31 March 2009.

Kislov, D. (2008) 'Doch' prezidenta Uzbekistana dala interv'yu moskovskomu glamurnomu zhurnalu', available at: http://www.ferghana.ru/article.php?id=5754, last accessed 29 April 2009.

Lewis, D. (2008) *The Temptations of Tyranny in Central Asia* (London, Hurst & Company).

Lipset, M.S. (1981) *Political Man: The Social Bases of Politics*, 2nd edn (Baltimore, John Hopkins University Press).

Lipset, M.S. (1984) 'Social Conflict, Legitimacy, and Democracy', in Connolly, W. (ed.) (1984).

Marat, E. (2007) 'Branding the New Nations of Central Asia and South Caucasus', *CACI Analyst, Silk Road Programme*, 14 November.

Matveeva, A. (1999) 'Legitimacy, Democracy and Political Change in Central Asia', *International Affairs*, 75, 1, January.

Migdal, J.S. (2001) *State in Society: Studying How States and Societies Transform and Constitute One Another* (Cambridge, Cambridge University Press).

Murphy, M. (2008) 'Tajikistan Case Set to Test Fee Records', *Financial Times*, 30 April.

Najibullah, F. (2008a) 'Central Asia: Ambition Often the Downfall of Powerful Presidential Relatives', *Eurasia Insight*, 31 May, available at: http://www.eurasianet.org/departments/insight/articles/eav053108.shtml, accessed 28 April 2009.

Najibullah, F. (2008b) 'Uzbekistan: Authoritarian President Publishes Tome on "Morality"', *Radio Free Europe/Radio Liberty*, 19 May, available at: http://www.rferl.org/content/article/1117512.html, last assessed 31 March 2009.

Najibullah, F. (2008c) 'Tajikistan: Politicians and their Friends Make Up Much of "100 Richest" List', *Radio Free Europe/Radio Liberty Central Asia Report*, 8, 10, 10 April, available at: http://www.rferl.org/content/article/1109550.html, accessed 19 May 2009.

Nazarbaev, N. (2008) 'Growth of Welfare of Kazakhstan's Citizens is the Primary Goal of Our Policy', Annual State of the Nation Address, *KazInform*, 6 February.

Olimova, L. (2008) 'Cops and Robbers in Tajikistan', *Reporting Central Asia*, 546, Institute of War and Peace Reporting, 6 June, available at: http://www.iwpr.net/?p=rca&s=f&o=345055&apc_state=henprca, last accessed 31 March 2009.

Pannier, B. (2008) 'Turkmenistan: Lions and Tigers and Mozart to Return to Cultural Life', *Eurasia Insight*, 30 January, available at: http://www.eurasianet.org/departments/insight/articles/pp013008.shtml, accessed 31 March 2009.

Radnitz, S., Wheatley, J. & Zürcher, C. (2009) 'The Origins of Social Capital: Evidence from a Survey of Post-Soviet Central Asia', *Comparative Political Studies*, 42.

Schaar, J. (1984) 'Legitimacy in the Modern State', in Connolly, W. (ed.) (1984).

Schatz, E. (2006) 'Access by Accident: Legitimacy Claims and Democracy Promotion in Authoritarian Central Asia', *International Political Science Review*, 27, 3.

Schatz, E. (2009) 'The Soft Authoritarian "Tool Kit": Agenda-Setting Power in Kazakhstan and Kyrgyzstan', *Comparative Politics*, 41, 2, January.

Talal, A. (2003) *Formations of the Secular: Christianity, Islam, Modernity* (Stanford, CA, Stanford University Press).

Tursynov, A. (2002) 'Sil'nyi chelovek v "zalozhnikakh"', *Kontinent*, 20.

Weber, M. (1993) *Essays in Sociology* (London, Routledge).

Wedeen, L. (1999) *Ambiguities of Domination: Politics, Rhetoric, and Symbols in Contemporary Syria* (Chicago, University of Chicago Press).

Nation Branding in Central Asia: A New Campaign to Present Ideas about the State and the Nation

ERICA MARAT

RELAXING IN A LUXURY HOTEL ROOM IN PARIS, WORLD TRAVELLERS are exposed to TV commercials for Kazakhstan, a 'land of democracy' located in the 'Heart of Eurasia'. Similar advertisements have been featured since the 1990s on CNN, the BBC, and ABC, in the pages of *The New York Times*, *The Wall Street Journal*, *The Economist* and other Western mass media outlets. During their public speeches Kazakhstan's diplomats distribute hundreds of leaflets about the latest economic developments and political achievements in their country. Such public relations campaigns aimed at building an international identity pose a new public policy challenge in post-Soviet states. This goal has not yet been met, but the governments of Kazakhstan, Uzbekistan and Kyrgyzstan are seeking to make the world more aware of their countries.

This essay examines the national images that Central Asian states are trying to present to international audiences. Since 1991 all Central Asian states have created national ideologies, but only three—Kazakhstan, Kyrgyzstan and Uzbekistan—have programmes in place to capture the attention of foreign businessmen, politicians and tourists. Following the pattern of crafting national ideologies for domestic audiences in all three states, the ruling elites have led the effort to create a unique national 'brand' identity for their country. The process has become a means of public diplomacy for embassy officials, as ruling elites seek to raise their country's prestige, primarily among international businesses and the global political community. Indeed, the creation and promotion of nation images serve as a new form of communication among countries, marketing to the needs of the globalised economy and international politics. It is a highly politicised activity involving stakeholders, usually national governments and local businesses interested in allocating funds to promote the brand (Akutsu 2008, pp. 209–11).

Using three case studies, this article discusses the international experience of the nascent process of nation branding, outlines emerging academic debates in the field, and analyses a few existing nation brands. The three Central Asian countries differ in the way they propagate their messages. While Kazakhstan disseminates similar narratives for both domestic and international audiences, the Uzbekistani regime filters messages presented abroad and at home. In both countries, images are developed and circulated by ruling elites and diplomats under the government's strict supervision, but both employ different persuasive techniques abroad. In Kyrgyzstan, by contrast, the process of communicating images about nation and state is less centralised, with the Ministry of Culture taking charge of most activities, while public diplomacy abroad is loosely coordinated by the regime. Importantly, however, the activities of the three countries increasingly resemble standard international practices for promoting nation brands. Indeed, representatives of these countries are gradually adopting the vocabulary and techniques used by the international nation-branding industry.

National brands, old and new

Most countries have an international image that is fairly stable and consistent over time and space. Some countries, such as Great Britain, Japan, Germany and Australia, have more enduring images, with stable sets of symbols associated with them, such as tourist attractions, signature export products and unique cultures. These international images developed quite passively, without any specific or consolidated effort by local actors. However, once they have solidified, such images have been largely reinforced by national businesses and governments, as well as individual citizens of these states who travel internationally. In the past decade states like India, Malaysia and Turkey have launched active campaigns to boost their international images and attract tourists and investments. None of these countries has an image as famous as Japan's or Germany's, but the slogans 'Incredible India' and 'Malaysia—truly Asia' have already taken root. These brands were developed by New Delhi and Kuala Lumpur with the help of the business community and they have been extensively transmitted through international mass media (Dinnie 2008, p. 35).

The concept of 'nation branding' emerged in the mid-1990s, describing the practice of constructing and communicating a unique image about a specific nation to the rest of the world through public diplomacy, trade, exports promotion and tourism (Anholt 2007, p. 3). A nation brand reflects the complex reality of a country by encapsulating its culture, history, peoples, government and business in a short motto or image (Anholt 2007, p. 405). According to marketing experts Thomas Cromwell and Savas Hadji Kyruacou, who take a more conservative approach toward the concept, numerous countries may currently seek to establish their brands, but none has yet developed a successful one. However, they believe Singapore and Spain have been able to promote comparatively more successful brands through subtle and coordinated communication of their positive traits, such as services, tourist attractions and products to the international audience.[1] Nation branding is, in turn, a process of creating an international reputation about a state and its people, but this reputation is also often contingent on various historic or cultural events that altered the external perception of the nation.

---

[1]Author's interview with Thomas Cromwell and Savas Hadji Kyruacou from East–West Communications, Washington, DC, 6 January 2009.

For instance, the Rose Revolution in 2003 helped Georgia to be seen as a developing democracy, while the government's violent suppression of riots in Andijan, in 2005, tarnished Uzbekistan's international reputation. Georgia and Armenia have also devised a somewhat coherent promotion strategy. Georgia, aside from its claim to be the 'cradle of wine', is spreading its red and white flag with five crosses in Western outlets, including *The Economist* magazine. Armenia, in turn, emphasises its Christian identity, proclaiming 'Noah's Route, Your Route'. Both countries hope to do well in the annual Eurovision song contest to confirm their rightful place in Europe. Azerbaijan, in turn, bought a number of commercials on CNN that feature colourful national dresses, food and dances.

Central Asian leaders are making their first attempts to promote their own nation internationally. Through authorised publications, films, speeches and cultural events both the embassies of Kazakhstan and Uzbekistan advertise their countries' potential, embellish its achievements and conceal negative developments. New narratives about the state and the nation are created in the process, with Kazakhstan typically presented as a geopolitical crossroads and Uzbekistan as a cultural gem. These narratives are often tailored specifically for the international—usually Western—public.

Unlike the domestic public, the international audience is difficult to define precisely, but it can be divided into three broad groups: businesses, politicians and tourists. In their efforts to create an international image, Kazakhstan, Uzbekistan and Kyrgyzstan have actively used public diplomacy to communicate with specific representatives of the business and political communities, as well as mass media to target a broader audience. Potential tourists, on the other hand, are harder to reach for most states. Partly because the wider international audience is so diverse, the messages produced by Central Asian states are quite haphazard, often lacking a single unifying idea. They rather serve as a means and medium for communication between diplomats and foreign actors. Therefore, such images of state and nation represent the ideas of the diplomats and the ruling elites, not the collective of people living in their respective countries. They also reflect the commercial or political interests these diplomats seek to attract.

Among the numerous messages promoted in the international media about economic growth, rich cultures and democratic development, 'Kazakhstan—the Heart of Eurasia' stands out. This message highlights the country's geostrategic advantages, revealing the Kazakh government's efforts to achieve international recognition of the county's vast territory (the ninth largest in the world), its natural resources and political weight. Uzbekistan, in turn, promotes its cultural treasures and tourist destinations, sometimes presenting itself as a 'Crossroads of Civilisations'. The Kyrgyz government has been less pretentious in choosing a slogan, navigating between 'Kyrgyzstan—a land of wonders' and the rather curious 'Kyrgyzstan—a land of Santa Claus', an offhand remark spontaneously picked up by the Kyrgyz Ministry of Culture. Unlike the Kazakhstani and Uzbekistani regimes, which have been actively targeting international audiences to build positive country images, Kyrgyzstan's information campaign is conducted mostly within the country to attract international media.

Images prepared for an international audience are not necessarily intended to maintain the national identity at home. The international images are not burdened

Source: http://baurzhan.kz/wp-content/uploads/smal.jpg, accessed 15 January 2009.

FIGURE 1. 'THE HEART OF EURASIA', A STATUE IN ZHASTAR SAYABAGY PARK, ASTANA, KAZAKHSTAN

with the task of creating a nation or reinforcing patriotism, because the attributes of a country's international image might or might not resonate with domestic ideas about the nation. The government of Uzbekistan, for example, has created an external image about its state and people that is different from the one promulgated at home. While Uzbekistan's external emphasis on its cultural richness resonates with the images promoted domestically, public diplomacy leaves out the Amir Timur heritage that is central to Uzbekistan's national identity. The Kazakhstani leadership, in contrast, promotes similar sets of ideas about its central location in Eurasia both internationally and domestically. Uzbekistan's focus on Amir Timur supports President Islam Karimov's authoritarian state power, while Kazakhstan's focus on Eurasia offers a more general idea about Kazakhstan as a member of the international community.

In both Kazakhstan and Uzbekistan, the ruling regimes have monopolised the process of creating and spreading images of the nation and the state both domestically and internationally. The countries face little challenge from domestic audiences when framing images for international consumption. Their regimes, therefore, tend to promote themselves more than represent the sentiments of the people. State leaders use activities associated with nation branding to justify political and economic decisions and explain political achievements. Kazakhstan's OSCE chairmanship is the most notable example of a national image that is closely linked with government achievement. Most justifications for seeking the chairmanship were explained through the prism of Kazakhstan's geopolitical location and Kazakhstani President Nursultan Nazarbaev's zeal to peacefully accommodate multiple ethnicities, given the country's geographic location between Europe and Asia. In other words, the OSCE chairmanship confirms that inter-ethnic peace has been realised thanks to the Nazarbaev regime.

These two cases show that although states have limited control over the information spread about them abroad, state leaders nevertheless actively seek to frame discourse in their favour. Images and symbols promulgated by these countries for foreign consumption shore up the identity of the rulers and grow out of existing narratives promoted for the domestic public. They downplay some parts of the story while inflating others. For instance, cultural events organised by Uzbekistan's embassies never bring up such negative issues as child labour or human rights abuse, which experts believe exist inside the country. While positioning Kazakhstan as a harmonious multicultural and multiethnic nation, its leaders gloss over its ongoing inter-ethnic confrontations at the village level and rampant nepotism in state structures. Kyrgyzstan, with its more liberal political culture, abandoned political image-making altogether, concentrating instead on reaching out to tourists.

On a national level, leaders can embrace political symbols that ignore daily reality and 'externalise' domestic problems, such as economic hardship (Edelman 1985, p. 8). The leaders' hegemonic narratives often act as a means of persuasion for the domestic public, complementing their coercive strategies.[2] In the Central Asian context, the governments' political symbols might not always be popular among the masses, but ruling regimes promote their own rigid ideas about the nation and the state despite ambivalent public perceptions. Furthermore, countries face greater competition in formulating an image on the international scene compared with the ideas and symbols circulated domestically. Whereas national ideologies are often imposed coercively through education and public events, governments and businesses cannot manipulate or coerce foreign audiences. International competition for tourists and investment takes place in an uncontrolled space, and therefore governments must use considerably greater resources and be more creative in promulgating their images, whereas at home governments are able to control mass media, holiday celebrations, and public institutions such as education, culture and the military. Ruling elites have limited leverage as to how they present their country for an international audience, as those narratives are much more transparent and will be scrutinised by sceptical tourists and investors.

The recipe for a successful international brand is not straightforward. Unlike national flags, emblems and anthems—the standard components of sovereign identity—a country's international image can be formed in a variety of ways. Scientific innovations, tourist destinations, historic and cultural attractions, famous persons, literary works, nature, movies and important political events are just a fraction of the possible ideas. Because of the wealth of possibilities from which to form an appealing image, the states must approach their international PR campaign strategically.

---

[2]For an insightful analysis of the power of persuasion in soft authoritarian regimes, see Schatz (2008).

But regime leaders are ready to face the challenge, as communicating images of the nation has a strong political value for them. By finding ways to embellish their countries, they seek to persuade international political leaders and businesses of their own achievements. Improving a country's reputation also has commercial value in terms of attracting more people and capital to the country. Like other states, the Central Asian countries are aware of the influential tags assigned by international organisations,[3] such as political and economic country ratings, or endorsements, such as Kazakhstan's long but successful quest to hold the OSCE chairmanship in 2010. These international factors inevitably influence the way countries are perceived by international businesses, governments and potential tourists. States can unexpectedly benefit from unplanned images created through films, appealing cultural artefacts and captivating historic writings. Alternatively, their images can suffer from negative cultural connotations or violent events taking place within their borders.

Accidental brands emerged for some former Soviet states. The democratic Orange Revolution in Ukraine and the Rose Revolution in Georgia quickly ascribed recognisable symbols to these countries. At least in the international policy world, the colour orange and the flower are now closely associated with these two states. Western debates about the genocide of Armenians have drawn international attention to the Armenian state and diaspora. The Andijan massacre in Uzbekistan attracted negative attention to President Islam Karimov, defining him as just another dictator. Finally, *Borat*, the comedy film featuring Sacha Baron Cohen, became an accidental international brand for Kazakhstan. The Kazakhstan portrayed in the comedy had little resemblance to the actual Kazakhstan and its native culture, but as one of the most successful films of 2006 it did bring name recognition. A successful national image, therefore, cannot be separated from the processes taking place inside the country.

Likewise, there are already a few passive brands for each Central Asian state. These have developed independently of the efforts of the political elites and business communities. For instance, Kyrgyzstan's celebrated writer Chingiz Aitmatov is a recognisable name in Europe and the former Soviet states, where his books were especially popular. The city of Samarkand is internationally associated with Uzbekistan. The eccentric regime of the late Turkmen leader Saparmurat Niyazov makes Turkmenistan an intriguing place to visit. The Tajik government's ideological project on Aryan identity has also attracted some international public attention. To date, Central Asian states are far from enjoying internationally known brands similar to those developed by, for instance, Germany, Japan and Sweden, but a combination of domestic factors such as the business interests of local companies and political processes that might affect the country's image, as well as the 'Borat effect', encourage the new independent states to consciously burnish their international reputations.

Kazakhstan and Uzbekistan

Both Kazakhstan and Uzbekistan promote themselves as crossroads of civilisations and cultures. While the governments of both states monopolised the construction and

---

[3]For instance, Transparency International, Freedom House and the World Bank.

dissemination of national images, the methods and media for communicating these messages have varied. Kazakhstan's efforts to place itself on the global map have involved the use of mass media, commemorative books, conferences and public events at its embassies abroad. Uzbekistan, on the other hand, has mostly relied on personal communication between diplomats and international political and business circles at its embassies' numerous public events.

Kazakhstan   *powerful geostrategic actor*

After gradually eliminating his political opponents, Nazarbaev increasingly relied on the power of persuasion to argue for the legitimacy of his regime at home (Schatz 2008). The president portrayed Kazakhstan as a rapidly emerging economic and political power with a peaceful and harmonious society. Kazakhstan's location between Russia and China served as the main justification to label the country a crossroads of civilisations in Eurasia. Kazakhstan's diplomats employ a similar technique utilising the same symbols. Since the 1990s, Kazakhstan has been investing large sums of money to ameliorate its international images, and Astana produced a tremendous amount of publications and organised numerous conferences and cultural exhibitions specifically to improve its image abroad.

The contest for the OSCE chair played an important role in transmitting Nazarbaev's vision for Kazakhstan to domestic and international audiences. During the campaign for the OSCE chairmanship, Astana emphasised the country's multicultural and multiethnic society. Kazakhstan's Ministry of Foreign Affairs commissioned an international advertising campaign to point out that 'Kazakhstan is located right at the crossroads of civilizations and for this reason it blends away, in a most harmonious way, all the contrasts between the East and the West'.[4] This line of branding is consistent with Nazarbaev's ambitious plan to construct a 'Palace of Nations' in Astana that would house a mosque, an Orthodox church and a Buddhist temple all under one roof.

In 2005 Nazarbaev published a monograph, *V serdtse Evrazii* [*In the Heart of Eurasia*], that outlined the rationale behind moving the national capital from Almaty to Astana (Nazarbaev 2005). The president explained that Astana can rightly be called the centre of Eurasia, since it is located between Europe and Asia and thus has soaked up the cultural heritage of both West and East for centuries. Since this book was published, Kazakhstani officials regularly use the 'Heart of Eurasia' slogan in their speeches. Nazarbaev personally took his slogan to major Western cities, mentioning it during his speeches and presentations of books about Kazakhstan.

At the 2005 Eurasian Media Forum in Almaty, Kazakhstani officials discussed following Croatia's very successful lead and creating a special Ministry for International Branding (Danayeva 2005). Instead, the government formed a special Department of International Information under the Ministry of Foreign Affairs in May 2007, with an official responsibility to create and promote Kazakhstan's image abroad. The Department of International Information worked closely with various PR companies to counteract the bad publicity brought by *Borat*, and helped create

[4]Country advertisement of Kazakhstan, *The Economist*, 13 December 2008.

numerous 'infomercials' in Western and Russian media to promote the 'Heart of Eurasia' message (Verhotunmov 2007).[5] Kazakhstan's diplomats took an active part in countering the racial and religious slurs made by the character in the movie. Kazakhstan's Ambassador to the United Kingdom, Erlan Idrissov, was especially eloquent, publishing an opinion piece in *The Times* requesting readers to 'please understand why our laughter [about the film] is selective. I suspect that when you know more about the real Kazakhstan, yours will be too' (Idrissov 2006).

Significant financial resources were spent on a public campaign promoting the slogan in *The New York Times,* the BBC and CNN in 2006–2007 in order to divert attention from Cohen's movie. In 30-second 'infomercials' on various foreign TV channels, Kazakhstan presented itself as a country 'committed to freedom and democracy' and as the 'Central Asian leader and a reliable strategic partner of the United States'. The advertisements also emphasised Nazarbaev's achievements in economics, international security and politics. Furthermore, at the May 2007 international PR Forum in Almaty, the Kazakhstani government announced plans to spend more than $10 million over the next few years towards creating a positive international image of Kazakhstan.[6]

For the years 2009–2011, along with the 'Heart of Eurasia' campaign, Kazakhstan has developed another programme with a catchy title that aims to firmly link the country with Western states, entitled 'Road to Europe'. The programme is designed to increase Kazakhstan's cooperation with European states in technology, energy and transport, improving national legislation to attract international investments, and preparing Kazakhstan for the OSCE chairmanship. The government tried to counter particular foreign perceptions about Kazakhstan, such as claims that the country is authoritarian and corrupt. Leaflets distributed by the government to foreign guests emphasise that Kazakhstan is a stable country with strong property rights granted to its citizens. Along these lines, Kazakhstan's evolving democracy is described in leaflets as having an 'extraordinary degree of political freedom … [achieved] without any violence at all'.[7] The multitude of slogans and media campaigns involved in Kazakhstan's promotions reflects the lack of a cohesive government strategy. Several ministries and agencies, including far-flung Kazakhstani embassies, simultaneously seek to improve the country's image, leading to overlapping and contradictory activities.

Kazakhstan's slogans are reinforced by numerous events organised by the government, both at home and abroad. For example, Kazakhstan's Ministry of Foreign Affairs sponsored the Congress of Leaders of World and Traditional Religions and a meeting of foreign ministers with the theme 'Common World: Progress through Diversity'. Kazakhstan, furthermore, entered the contest to host the

[5]Countries occasionally find themselves affected by accidentally negative images. For instance, the *Hostel* movie is comparable to *Borat* in its effect, as is *Transsiberian* in the case of Russia.

[6]'Boratu-brata? Pravitel'stvo Kazakhstana vydelyaet $10 mln na sozdanie imidzha strany za rubezhom' ['Brother for Borat? Government of Kazakhstan is Allocating $10 Million to Create the Country's Image Abroad'], available at: www.ktk-tv.kz, accessed 29 December 2008.

[7]'Common Misconceptions in the West about Kazakhstan', a handout distributed during the presentation by Kazakh Minister of Foreign Affairs Marat Tazhin, *Kazakhstan in a Globalizing World* at the Carnegie Endowment for International Peace, 1 October 2008.

2014 Winter Olympic Games in Almaty. Although Kazakhstan lost to Russia, no other Central Asia country dared to enter. Finally, Kazakhstan's government has commissioned Western analysts to write a series of favourable reports about the country's economic and political developments. These reports embellished some events in the country, while overlooking criticism of the regime. Several local, private PR companies also sought to contribute to Kazakhstan's positive image by announcing nationwide contests to create an attractive commercial about the country to be broadcast abroad.

Kazakhstan has been so aggressive in promoting its 'Crossroads of Civilisations' and 'Heart of Eurasia' brands that neighbouring Central Asian states would risk charges of plagiarism if they adopted a similar slogan. Kazakhstan's monopoly over the 'Heart of Eurasia' slogan is comparable to Uzbekistan's 'monopoly' over the Amir Timur heritage. Internationally, however, the 'civilisation' slogan may be trivial. Dozens of countries and regions have proclaimed themselves to be the crossroads or gateways to one region or another.[8]

With active campaigns to herald Kazakhstan's political achievements and economic freedoms, Astana is, in fact, promoting an image that is still forming. Nazarbaev's Kazakhstan-2030 Strategy, announced in 1997, promises to achieve security, economic prosperity and political stability by utilising Kazakhstan's geostrategic location, natural and human resources, and historic heritage (Nazarbaev 1997). But most Western research and policy papers tend to view Kazakhstan as a petro-state with an authoritarian political system, as Nazarbaev's presidency faces no term limits, while opposition forces are muted across the country.[9] The premature announcement of its political and economic 'democratisation' was probably a ruse to bolster the government's efforts to chair the OSCE.

Uzbekistan *accentuate ancient traditions & modern culture*

While Kazakhstan seeks to position itself as a powerful geostrategic actor, Uzbekistan seeks to accentuate its ancient traditions and modern culture by organising celebrations of its major public holidays and staging fashion shows of traditional clothing at embassies. Frequent cultural events at Uzbekistani embassies keep Uzbekistan's cultural brand on public display despite the regime's poor political image. The Uzbekistani government essentially promotes two differing national images, one for domestic consumption and another for the international community. Holiday celebrations, such as *Navruz* and Independence Day (1 September), are carried out differently inside Uzbekistan and at Uzbekistani embassies. When embassies organise dinners, fashion shows, exhibitions and concerts, reference to Amir Timur is minimised in favour of traditional artefacts and modern paintings depicting Uzbek culture. The events promote national ceramics and *suzani* (embroidery), accompanied by traditional cuisine. Images of the blue domes of Samarkand's historic sites regularly decorate official leaflets, books and websites about Uzbekistan. Although embassy officials are

[8]'How Countries Compete to Look Good', *The Economist*, 9 November 2006.
[9]According to Freedom House, the overall democracy score in Kazakhstan was 6.39 (with 7 being the worst) (Dave 2008).

loyal supporters of President Karimov, his name is rarely mentioned at foreign cultural events. By contrast, Karimov is the central figure in cultural celebrations inside Uzbekistan, and he personally visits many of the festivities.

Following the government's violent suppression of protests in Andijan in May 2005, Uzbekistan drew fierce criticism from the international public and the EU imposed travel sanctions on some Uzbek officials. However, according to the Uzbekistani embassy to the USA, the frequency of cultural events such as photo exhibitions and fashion shows organised by them has continued apace since then, and attendance rates in Washington, DC—usually 600–800 people—have remained level.[10] The embassies collaborate closely with the Ministry of Culture, but do not have a special budget for such events.[11] The Uzbekistani embassy in Washington, DC, for instance, organises cultural events on a monthly basis seeking funds from its own budget. Uzbekistani officials also cooperate with a number of influential Western academics who depicted the Andijan events in a favourable way.

Furthermore, Tashkent has focused on promoting tourist attractions such as Samarkand, Bukhara and Khiva, as well as other historic places, directly or indirectly through events in Uzbekistani embassies and various publications. According to their government data, tourism has increased by between 15% and 20% each year since the early 2000s.[12] As Uzbekistani officials maintain, Uzbekistan's cities attract tourists interested not as much in the political situation in the country, but curious about religious and civilisational history.[13] Fortunately for Uzbekistan, its major tourist sites have long been popular in the West, even during the Soviet period.

Kyrgyzstan

Unlike his Central Asian counterparts, Kyrgyz President Kurmanbek Bakiyev has not been interested in formulating a national ideology or an external image. The president has paid little attention to structuring public diplomacy abroad, preferring to concentrate on mostly coercive methods of limiting freedom of speech and curtailing domestic opposition. Kyrgyzstan's efforts to build a country image were not directed by the government or president, but initiated by separate individuals from government structures acting on their own enterprise, as well as by opposition forces and private companies. Actors, such as the Ministry of Culture or PR agencies, lack the funds needed to access international mass media or organise events abroad. Most events to attract international attention, therefore, are held inside Kyrgyzstan.

Under Bakiyev, the Ministry of Culture tried to develop the slogan 'Kyrgyzstan—a land of wonders', which captures the country's natural beauty and dynamic political situation, but few government bureaucrats were enthusiastic about the slogan. Beginning in late 2007, officials began to link Kyrgyzstan with Santa Claus. The idea originated in Sweden, when the SWECO logistics company casually noted that

---

[10]Author's interview with Abdusattor Mukhamedov, Uzbekistani Embassy in Washington, DC, December 2008.

[11]Author's interview with Uzbekistani official, Washington, DC, December 2008.

[12]Author's interview with Abdusattor Mukhamedov, Uzbekistani Embassy in Washington, DC, December 2008.

[13]Author's interview with Uzbekistani official, Washington, DC, December 2008.

Kyrgyzstan would be the most logical place for Santa Claus to operate, since the country is located in the centre of Eurasia and is mostly mountainous (MacWilliam 2007). The idea, however, was quickly picked up by the Kyrgyz Ministry of Cultural Affairs, which organised thematic events to attract more tourists, such as arranging for several mountaineers dressed in various costumes representing international equivalents of Santa Claus to climb mountains near the Issyk-Kul Lake.[14]

Source: http://morrire.livejournal.com/tag/santa, accessed 15 January 2009.

FIGURE 2. WORLD SANTAS UNITE AT LAKE ISSYK-KUL, FEBRUARY 2008

The image of Santa Claus is not used to reinforce Bakiyev's legitimacy either domestically or abroad. The project is the result of Kyrgyz government and business structures' realisation that the tourist industry's potential must be explored in the country. Furthermore, the idea of developing a national brand to develop the tourist industry has been actively discussed by local mass media outlets and PR agencies for the past few years. Kyrgyzstan did not have its own Borat to advertise the country to a wide range of international viewers but the image of Santa Claus might become a national emblem to reach out to international tourists.[15] The idea of accommodating Santa Claus, in turn, is humorous and unexpected, but such positive associations have the potential to attract curious tourists to ski resorts in Kyrgyzstan and resorts in Issyk-Kul.[16]

According to Ryskul Borombayev, director of the National Cultural Centre in Bishkek, Kyrgyz officials acted fast during January 2008, shortly after SWECO's

[14]The various images included Russian '*Ded Moroz*' (Ice man) and Kyrgyz '*Ayaz ata*' (adopted from Russian) dressed in a Kyrgyz ethnic outfit. In January 2009 a new website was launched to support the idea: see www.kyrgyzsanta.org/en, accessed 7 April 2009.

[15]Some Kyrgyz experts dealing with brands regretted that Sacha Baron Cohen did not choose Kyrgyzstan, but there were, of course signs of relief among Kyrgyz, Uzbek, Turkmen and Tajik citizens that the film was not about their country.

[16]'Propishitsya li Santa v Kyrgyzstane?' ['Will Santa be a Resident in Kyrgyzstan?'], *Moya Stolitsa—novosti*, 11 January 2008.

comment. Over 200 soldiers from the National Guard (a unit mainly used for military parades and celebrations) dressed in Santa Claus costumes to perform a theatrical play in the mountains.[17] They were joined by a multitude of 'Santas': the Russian *Ded Moroz,* Danish Santa Claus, Iranian *Haji Feruz,* Uzbek *Karbobo* and Kazakh *Ayaz Ata.* The event was hastily organised and *ad hoc,* lacking any follow-up or future planning but the campaign still proved to be fairly successful, since several Western mass media outlets, including the BBC and Fox News, as well as numerous European, Russian, US and Central Asian news agencies, picked up the story. And, the event piqued the curiosity of many in Kyrgyzstan.

Thanks to the relative freedom in organising celebrations such as the Santa festival, Kyrgyz officials responsible for cultural affairs invented their own explanations of how the character, despite his Christian heritage, fits into Kyrgyz culture. 'Santa Claus, *Ded Moroz* and *Ayaz Ata*—are all the same man' argued Brombayev.[18] Interestingly, however, '*Ayaz Ata*' is a direct translation of Russian *Ded Moroz,* and it was actually the Soviet regime that brought him to Central Asia. Overall, the image of Santa Claus, who became widely known in the region after the collapse of the Soviet Union due to the spread of Western culture, is meant to personify the idea of Kyrgyzstan as an international hub.

After the popular Santa Claus shows in early 2008, the Kyrgyz government allocated additional funds to organise similar celebrations in the winter of 2008–2009. One phase included building a central Santa's post-box, where people from across the world could send their Christmas wish lists. A similar winter festival was staged in February 2009 with even greater publicity and a greater number of Santa Clauses visiting Kyrgyzstan from around the world. During December 2008 and early January 2009 public transport workers in Bishkek dressed in Santa Claus costumes. A number of similar events involving Santa Claus were organised across Kyrgyzstan simultaneously. Both the government and tourist firms sponsored the events.

Unlike in Kazakhstan and Uzbekistan, Kyrgyz opposition leaders are able to challenge the government's narratives presented to the international public. Political opposition activists provided another venue for image making, as they sought international contacts to help their cause. For instance, opposition leader Alikbek Jekshenkulov promoted the slogan 'Kyrgyzstan is a country of edelweiss'. He collected and distributed an extensive photo album (over 1,000 pictures) of Kyrgyzstan's places, peoples and traditions and presented copies of his album at his various meeting with US and EU representatives. Importantly, Jekshenkulov's campaign focused on two audiences: foreign leaders and the Kyrgyz public, to approve his presentation of the image abroad as part of his party's political platform.

In sum, Bakiyev's lack of interest in controlling the domestic or international discourse through inventing official narratives has opened up space for more spontaneous interpretations of what Kyrgyzstan's international image should be. Competition among government representatives and opposition members on the appropriate content of Kyrgyzstan's international image continues. For the

[17]*Moya Stolitsa—novosti,* 11 January 2008.
[18]'Propishitsya li Santa v Kyrgyzstane?' ['Will Santa be a Resident in Kyrgyzstan?'], *Moya Stolitsa— novosti,* 11 January 2008.

government, the image is less important. The political opposition, however, attempts to present its own image of Kyrgyzstan to the international public.

A glimpse of the past, a look into the future

The Soviet past is still used to identify the modern Central Asian states. The 'post-Soviet' label is frequently applied to the states by international media and academics, as well as tourist agencies. For many international travellers, Central Asia is a quaint former Soviet outpost where daily life, urban architecture and people's behaviour are still heavily influenced by its communist heritage. Such an image may raise the curiosity of investors and tourists, but it also makes the region appear less culturally distinctive and attractive in its own right. One of the positive impacts of the *Borat* film was the realisation by Kazakhstan and its neighbours that a knowledge gap existed among the international public about the region and its countries. Today, the Central Asian states have a unique opportunity to promote themselves in a positive light by developing their individual brands, either political or cultural, as well as by devising a joint regional brand. In the mid-2000s the post-Soviet Baltic states launched such a double strategy, promoting each nation as well as the region as a whole. The Central Asian states will benefit from similar international exposure.

One of the challenges these states face is to convince the international public that communism no longer influences their homelands, which today are flourishing, independent countries. In particular, the Central Asian states will need to be creative in communicating their national images. The conventional technique of emphasising a country's pre-Soviet history may prove to be counter-productive, as it is likely to blur differences between the states. Contemporary borders are a Soviet construct and delving into lengthy explanations of pre-Soviet history might require more work than a tourist cares to pursue. To say the least, such complex arguments on the historical development of the states may be hard for the international public to grasp. Highlighting the contested borders between the states, in turn, could drive away tourists and businesses.

To a large extent, Central Asian governments have improvised national brands for international audiences. Kazakhstan reacted to *Borat*; Uzbekistan's cultural events are diffuse and contingent; while the Kyrgyz Ministry of Culture seized upon a throwaway comment by a business organisation. This *ad hoc* reaction to creating new state brands sharply contrasts with more systemic and coherent national ideologies developed by ruling elites. According to Cromwell and Kyruacou, the problem of emerging democracies is that they celebrate their progress in terms of their history, a gauge that may not interest outsiders.[19] Former Soviet states claim great success in democratic development but that, however, is of little relevance to investors or tourists from established democracies. Instead, Central Asian elites and businessmen would find more success in choosing their distinctive traits from post-independence times, be it in the form of products, people or places. The stakeholders must think beyond the national borders and choose qualities that are most appealing across countries and continents, such as technological developments, new services, ecological movements or

---

[19]Author's interview with Thomas Cromwell and Savas Hadji Kyruacou from East–West Communications, Washington, DC, 6 January 2009.

trends in education. Like Kazakhstan, Kyrgyzstan and Uzbekistan must think beyond their present historic memory.

Central Asian leaders made their first attempts at nation branding in the 2000s specifically to present themselves favourably to the international public, not just to improve the image of the country in general. There was an upsurge in the production of national ideology in the 1990s up until the mid-2000s, but the ideas and symbols used to identify Kazakhstan and Uzbekistan, in particular, are mostly efforts by political elites to attract more tourists, international donors and investors. Uzbekistan seeks to be seen as a culturally rich country, while Kazakhstan stresses its economic potential, important location and ethnic diversity. Another significant difference between Kazakhstan and Uzbekistan is that Astana relies more on catchy slogans, as opposed to the more holistic cultural approach pursued by Tashkent. Kazakhstan also follows a more coherent, integrated strategy, combining political and business resources into distributing the 'Heart of Eurasia' slogan. Kazakhstan relies on a slogan that is more likely to resemble international propaganda funded by abundant economic resources than an attempt to create a nation brand. Kazakhstan's brand clearly links the country with the ruling regime, the president and his decisions.

Finally, Kazakhstan and Kyrgyzstan have produced new symbols to brand their nations internationally. Uzbekistan, conversely, has relied on the symbolic resources it inherited from the Soviet Union, namely, its famous cities and cultural artefacts. This comes as a contrast to Uzbekistan's national ideology, which centres on the much older image of Amir Timur. Kazakhstan's one-party system, control of mass media and corruption rates inevitably undermine the government's attempts to build a positive image abroad. But by focusing on culture, the Uzbekistani government has attempted to divert international attention from autocracy, poor human rights and international isolation.

Central Asia-Caucasus Institute & Silk Road Studies Program Joint Center

References

Akutsu, S. (2008) 'Current Practice and Future Horizons for Nation Branding', in Dinnie, K. (ed.) (2008).
Anholt, S. (2007) *Competitive Identity: The New Brand Management for Nations, Cities and Regions* (New York, Palgrave Macmillan).
Danayeva, Z. (2005) 'Imidzh strany', *Expert Online*, 9 May.
Dave, B. (2008) *Kazakhstan, Nations in Transit 2008* (Washington, DC, Freedom House).
Dinnie, K. (ed.) (2008) *Nation Branding: Concepts, Issues, Practice* (Burlington, Butterworth-Heinemann).
Edelman, M. (1985) *The Symbolic Uses of Politics* (Urbana, University of Illinois Press).
Idrissov, E. (2006) 'We Survived Stalin and We Can Certainly Overcome Borat's Slurs', *The Times*, 4 November.
MacWilliam, I. (2007) 'Kyrgyz to Name Peak after Santa', *BBC News*, 19 December.
Nazarbaev, N. (1997) 'Kazakhstan-2030', speech delivered to Kazakh public in 1997, available at: http://www.kazakhemb.org.il/?CategoryID=187&ArticleID=169, accessed 3 April 2009.
Nazarbaev, N. (2005) *V serdtse Evrazii*, available at: http://www.akorda.kz/www/www_akorda_kz.nsf/7917981ACDDB34D1462572340019E70E/$FILE/text2.pdf, accessed 9 December 2008.
Schatz, E. (2008) 'Transnational Image Making and Soft Authoritarian Kazakhstan', *Slavic Review*, 67, 1, Spring.
Verhotunmov, D. (2007) 'Imidzh Kazakhstana i ego razvitie', Russian State Humanitarian University, 26 December, available at: http://www.postsoviet.ru/page.php?pid=740, last accessed 27 April 2009.

Searching for *Kamalot*: Political Patronage and Youth Politics in Uzbekistan

ERIC M. McGLINCHEY

THE ISLAM KARIMOV GOVERNMENT IN UZBEKISTAN is precariously brittle. Signs that the regime might collapse, though, would not be readily apparent if one's analytical framework derived solely from the political science transitions literature. Paradoxically, though political scientists are preoccupied with change, our leading theories emphasise continuity. We stress path dependency, institutional stickiness, and enduring ethnic, national and indeed civilisational identities. When change does arrive, we attribute it to sudden disruptions, to 'exogenous shocks', 'punctuated equilibriums', mobilisation 'cascades', and to the contingencies of 'elite miscalculation' (North 1990; Steinmo *et al.* 1992; Kuran 1991; Huntington 1993; Pierson 2000). So much for predictive social science theory.

What if, however, we jettisoned the *ex-post* causal parsimony of transitology and, instead, rolled up our analytical sleeves and actually 'mucked around' in the messiness of day-to-day autocratic politics? What indicators, short of the familiar dichotomy between stability and collapse, might we use to assess the pulse of authoritarianism? And might these indicators actually help us, *ex-ante*, predict political change? In this essay I illustrate that we can evaluate the health and, furthermore, the likely longevity of autocracy. More specifically, by taking seriously that which political scientists often do not—symbols, spectacle and discourse—we can identify the stress points where authoritarian governments are most likely to crack.

The spectacles I study involve the Karimov government's efforts to mobilise the soon-to-be majority of the Uzbek population through the youth group *Kamalot*. To a certain degree, this study parallels the familiar social science model of inquiry; *Kamalot* became suddenly prominent in the early 2000s and one of the essay's goals is to explain this variation. At the same time, though, this analysis of past variation is decidedly forward looking. I argue that by understanding the causal factors behind changes in symbolic politics, we can understand the processes and the likelihood of Uzbek regime change. That is, I argue, the same factor that is driving symbolic politics in the *Kamalot* case—the spreading failure of patronage-based politics in the regions— will lead Uzbek regime change in the near future.

That this is a case study need not lessen the implication of the essay's broader methodological findings. Political change and revolutions are seldom 'now out of never' (Kuran 1991, p. 7). Just the opposite, as I demonstrate here, political change is almost always foreshadowed by identifiable changes in discourse, symbols and spectacles. Lamentably, political analysts rarely acknowledge these changes in symbolic politics until it is too late, until well after dramatic institutional changes come to pass. Sovietologists, for example, not only failed to acknowledge the potential importance of the changed discourse embodied in the 1975 Helsinki Final Act, they smugly derided the human rights language of this diplomatic effort. Thus, Anthony Lewis wrote of the Final Act in August 1976: 'Only a fatuous optimist would have expected its [the Soviet government's] attitudes to be transformed by the Helsinki Declaration' (Lewis 1976, p. 1). Some 25 years later we find political scientist Daniel Thomas offers a differing assessment:

> That the unraveling of the Communist party-state enabled by Gorbachev's reforms proceeded in a democratic and largely peaceful direction across Eastern Europe is explained by the continued salience of those activists and independent organisations who had made 'Helsinki' a watchword for human rights nearly a decade earlier. (Thomas 2001, p. 23)

While Thomas's is a superb study, of Sovietology and transitology more broadly, one cannot help but conclude that while our punchlines are good, our delivery is frequently too late. Political scientists justify the discipline's collective tardiness by appealing to the need for methodological rigour. John Hall, in his essay, 'Ideas and the Social Sciences', writes for example: 'Given the sloppiness to which facile idealist analysis is prone, this sort of explanation should, in my opinion, be entertained only after more structural accounts have been exhausted' (Hall 1993, p. 52). Thus, we are instructed that ideas—the shorthand political scientists use for symbols, discourse, norms, for causal variables that neither rational choice nor institutionalist explanations adequately address—should be treated as the residual, something to be analysed only as a last resort when all other explanations fail. Judith Goldstein and Robert Keohane's study of *Ideas and Foreign Policy* instructs aspiring PhDs that, for their 'null hypothesis', they should assume political outcomes as the result of actors following 'egoistic interests in the context of power realities'. Only when this 'null hypothesis is carefully addressed and comparative evidence brought forth', Goldstein and Keohane instruct, will we be in a position to evaluate the role ideas play in political change (Goldstein & Keohane 1993, pp. 26–27).

There are dissenters, of course. 'Symbolic change', David Kertzer writes, produces 'important political and material consequences' (Kertzer 1996, p. x). And political actors recognise this, even if political scientists often do not. Thus, Alison Brysk demonstrates, actors, even those who pursue egoistic interests, seek 'to achieve social change through symbolic collective action' (Brysk 1995, p. 564). This, as I next demonstrate, is what President Islam Karimov is attempting through *Kamalot*. No longer able to count on patronage politics to ensure monopoly power, Karimov is seeking to rally youth to his side through symbolic collective action. His efforts may not, and it is likely, will not prove successful. That he is engaging youth politics in symbolic collective action, though, is a ready indicator of the political change that is likely to come.

In the first section below I discuss the emergence of and the extraordinary spectacles conducted by the state-led Uzbek youth group, *Kamalot*. In the second section I explore what *Kamalot*'s spectacles potentially tell us about the health of the Karimov regime and the potential for change in Uzbek politics. The image I present, that of an aging and ailing autocratic leader attempting to enlist youth support, is notably at odds with the portrayal of liberalising youth politics in other post-Soviet contexts, for example in Georgia, Serbia and Ukraine. Critically though, I argue that just as reformists see youth as vigorous and symbolically potent allies in the fight against moribund autocracy, so too do autocrats see youth as a way to revitalise stalled authoritarianism. The third section concludes by exploring the implications of youth mobilisation for the future of Uzbek governance. Here I demonstrate that Karimov's attempt at youth mobilisation is an indicator of failing patronage politics. If the septuagenarian president's gambit at winning youthful affection fails, if *Kamalot* is but a one-sided romance, then Karimov's political star will quickly fade.

The Kamalot *youth organisation*

For any student of Soviet politics, Uzbekistan's *Kamalot* youth organisation is immediately familiar. Modelled after the Soviet *Komsomol*, *Kamalot* is designed to capture the hearts and minds of Uzbekistan's burgeoning youth population. It may be trite to conclude a country's youth is its future. Nowhere in Central Asia, though, is this more the case than in Uzbekistan. In 2015, 47% of Uzbekistan's population will have been born after the Soviet collapse. This 14 million strong, youth cohort of people aged 24 and under, moreover, will be larger than the total country populations of Kyrgyzstan, Tajikistan and Turkmenistan in 2015, and just two million less than the total population of Kazakhstan.[1] However, numeric strength need not equal political power. As the following paragraphs illustrate though, the Karimov government is intent on enlisting the support of younger generations through *Kamalot*'s carefully crafted programmes and events.

My description of *Kamalot*'s activities is derived largely from secondary sources, primarily from Uzbek media accounts of the youth organisation. This reliance on secondary sources is the result of political necessity rather than any lack of desire to research the organisation firsthand. For one decade, between 1995 and 2005, I conducted several extended research trips to Uzbekistan, working with Uzbek colleagues in Bukhara, Andijan, Namangan, Karshi and Tashkent. My last research trip to Uzbekistan was in June 2005, one month after the Karimov government's repression of protesters in Andijan. In September 2005 a Human Rights Watch representative informed me that several Uzbek colleagues—all human rights activists—were either under threat of state repression, actively being repressed, or in exile and seeking refugee status. The Human Rights Watch representative further added that one of my Uzbek colleagues noted in his United Nations High Commissioner for Refugees (UNHCR) asylum application that his collaborative research with me was what had elicited Uzbek government threats of repression. I have neither directly collaborated with Uzbekistan-based colleagues nor returned to conduct field research in Uzbekistan since June 2005.

---

[1]Calculations based on the *United Nations World Population Prospects, The 2008 Revision*. The full population dataset is available online at: http://esa.un.org/unpp/, accessed 29 April 2009.

Despite or perhaps because of these challenges, my interest in the Uzbek polity has grown. More specifically, in the light of my colleagues' trials and given what I had witnessed of youth–state interactions during my own field research, I became increasingly puzzled as to why Uzbek youth broadly did not appear to share the dismal view of the Karimov government that my Uzbek friends and I did. Upon reflection, I realised my research interests[2] brought me into contact with youth who, understandably given the often fraught relations between state and Islam and the state and consumer goods traders, probably harboured more animosity toward the Karimov government than did the average Uzbek teenager or person in their twenties. If I could return now to study *Kamalot*, would the Uzbek youth I encountered be any different from the frustrated traders and young religious scholars I had encountered during previous visits? If the following media-derived accounts are even partially true, then the answer is almost certainly yes; that far from fearing the Karimov regime, many youth value the state-run *Kamalot* for the entertainment and education opportunities the organisation provides. And that it is uncertain whether this appreciation might translate into mobilised political support for the Karimov government.

In addition to studying markets, mosques and *madrassahs*, by June 2005 I had attended enough weddings, dance clubs and football matches, and frequented enough internet cafes, to know that Uzbek youth share the same aspirations and gravitate to the same forms of entertainment that youth the world over do. And it is here, in the arena of entertainment, that *Kamalot* particularly excels. In January 2006, for example, *Kamalot* and the government's Forum on Culture and Art televised the *Kelazhak Ovozi* [*Voices of the Future*] ceremony, a government-sponsored celebration in which medals are awarded to promising young leaders in the arts, businesses and sciences.[3] Headlining the event were singers Tohir Sodiqov and Gulnora Karimova. (Karimova, in addition to her musical career, is serving her father's government as Uzbekistan's Representative to the United Nations Office in Geneva.) Sodiqov, immensely popular in Uzbekistan, provided a fitting start to this equally popular annual celebration of youth achievement. *Kelazhak Ovozi* has grown from 3,000 competitors in 2005 to over 54,000 in 2008. So as to reach the broadest possible audience, *Kelazhak Ovozi* rotates the categories of competition every year—2009's fields include 'Architecture and Design, Information Communication Technology, Traditional Arts and Crafts, and Poetry and Prose' as well as a competition for 'the best collection of materials covering *Kelazhak Ovozi* contest'.[4] Participants compete at the local level before advancing to the final, national level selection. Those who win, in addition to being honoured on national television by household names like Sodiqov and Karimova, receive stipends to further their education.

[2]In the 1990s I studied the development of post-Soviet Uzbek bazaars and in the 2000s I have focused on the emergence of local Islamic associations and elites.

[3]'Uzbek President's Daughter Sings in Patriotic Chorus', *BBC Monitoring of International Reports*, 7 January 2006, available via: https://web.lexis-nexis.com/universe, accessed April 2009. For more on *Kelazhak Ovozi*, see the organisation's website, available at: http://www.kelajakovozi.uz, accessed 29 April 2009.

[4]'Journalism Contest Announced for News Agencies, Printed and Online Media', *UzReport.com*, 19 August 2008, available via: https://web.lexis-nexis.com/universe, accessed April 2009.

For the more athletically inclined, *Kamalot* sponsors a range of sporting institutions and events. The youth group runs summer camps for disadvantaged children. The goal of these camps 'is to bring children up in the spirit of love and loyalty towards their motherland, to prepare them for service in the Uzbek armed forces, to strengthen their health, to temper them physically and spiritually'.[5] *Kamalot* regularly sponsors sports festivals. In September 2003 it organised an 'Extreme Sports' festival in Tashkent where skaters competed while organisers worked the crowds to raise awareness about the dangers of drug abuse.[6] In December 2005 *Kamalot* coordinated a 'mass marathon' from Termez to Tashkent to commemorate the 13-year anniversary of the Uzbek constitution.[7] In Andijan in July 2006 *Kamalot* held an 'international youth martial arts tournament' under the slogan: 'we are against terrorism and drugs'.[8] And, together with the Presidential Fund for the Development of Children's Sports, *Kamalot* sponsors the annual 'Student Games' in which 2,400 of the best athletes from secondary schools and universities converge in Tashkent to compete in basketball, tennis, table tennis, football, track and field athletics, swimming, chess and wrestling.[9]

For Uzbek youth more interested in virtual games, *Kamalot* has opened computer cafes and provides free internet access points throughout the country (Novintskyi 2005). Should cerebral rather than virtual or athletic competitions be more attractive, *Kamalot* hosts 'Values, Customs, Traditions and Youth' contests in which university students are quizzed on the 'uniqueness of national customs, traditions and values of various regions, peoples and nationalities'.[10] For future lawyers and judges, *Kamalot* organises 'Do You Know the Law?' contests for high-school students.[11] There are also job fairs, and seed capital is offered to start small businesses for the entrepreneurially inclined.[12] For the more spiritually oriented, *Kamalot*'s Andijan branch has established a resource centre 'to prevent the spread of drug addiction and religious extremist ideas among minors'.[13] And for history enthusiasts, *Kamalot* organises tours of Tashkent's national monuments. The goal of these excursions, tour director Khilola Makhmudova explains, is 'to shape in forthcoming generation the sense of love to

[5]'Uzbekistan Founds Military Sports Camp for Difficult Children', *BBC Monitoring Central Asia Unit*, 24 July 2003, available via: https://web.lexis-nexis.com/universe, accessed April 2009.

[6]'Young Uzbeks Skate against Drugs', *BBC Monitoring Central Asia Unit*, 23 September 2003, available via: https://web.lexis-nexis.com/universe, accessed April 2009.

[7]'Marafontsy Napravalis' v Bukharu', *Narodnoe Slovo*, 1 December 2005, available at: http://old.narodnoeslovo.uz/?a=sport&c=show&id=65, accessed April 2009.

[8]'Young Andijan Athletes Compete to Condemn Terror', *BBC Monitoring International Reports*, 5 July 2006, available via: https://web.lexis-nexis.com/universe, accessed April 2009.

[9]'2008 the Year of Youth in Uzbekistan', *UzReport.com*, 31 January 2008, available via: https://web.lexis-nexis.com/universe, accessed April 2009.

[10]'Ferghana Implements "Values, Customs, Traditions and Youth" Project', *Times of Central Asia*, 28 March 2008, available via: https://web.lexis-nexis.com/universe, accessed April 2009.

[11]'"Do You Know the Law" Nationwide Contest Ends in Jizzakh Region', *UzReport.com*, 17 May 2007, available via: https://web.lexis-nexis.com/universe, accessed April 2009.

[12]'4th International Education and Career Exhibition Opens in Uzbek Capital', *UzReport.com*, 19 February 2009, available via: https://web.lexis-nexis.com/universe, accessed April 2009.

[13]'Uzbek Body Mulls Prevention of Religious Extremism among Minors', *BBC Monitoring Central Asia Unit*, 23 December 2006, available via: https://web.lexis-nexis.com/universe, accessed April 2009.

Homeland, respect to its invaluable culture and history, which serves an important factor in upbringing the youth [sic]'.[14] Should diplomacy capture an Uzbek teen's imagination, *Kamalot* organises biannual cross-cultural exchanges with youth groups in neighbouring countries. Occasionally, these exchanges result in diplomatic pronouncements. Thus, a 2005 visit to Azerbaijan concluded with Shohret Gasimov (*Kamalot*'s vice president) issuing the following statement on the Nargono–Karabakh conflict: 'We also understand the problems of the Azerbaijani youth and we believe that the territorial integrity of Azerbaijan should be restored'.[15]

Religious resource centres, internet cafes, sports tournaments, academic competitions, small business loans, cultural exchanges, arts and entertainment—these all sound like wonderful programmes, but how broad is *Kamalot*'s actual reach? *Kamalot*'s target age group is 15–30 (Karimov 2001). In 2005 there were approximately eight million Uzbeks between these ages,[16] and according to *Kamalot*'s leader, Botir Ubaydullayev, the organisation had 4.5 million members in February 2006.[17] This is an impressive figure and, if true, it begs the question why the Karimov regime has made this concerted effort to reach out to Uzbekistan's younger generation. No other post-Soviet state can claim half the 15–30-year old population as active members of a state-sponsored youth association. Indeed, one must look back to the Soviet period, to the *Komsomol*, to find a state-led effort to engage younger generations on such a massive scale.

The answer to the *Kamalot* puzzle, to these carefully designed sporting events, concerts, and nationalism and state-oriented competitions, I argue in the next section, lies in the growing crisis of Uzbek governance. The spectacle of youth politics is an indicator that President Karimov's traditional source of power, the patronage politics that had throughout much of the 1990s secured the deference of regional elites, is failing. Youth politics is Karimov's attempt to 'rebuild', to replace broken patronage networks among older, Soviet-era elites with a new younger polity that coheres not only as a result of state largesse, but also as a result of individuals' perceptions of a post-colonial, Uzbek-nationalist identity. Thus, *Kamalot*'s festivals, the organisation's executive secretary Said-Abdulaziz Yusupov unabashedly notes, are designed to promote youth 'loyalty to the mother land' (Sharai 2005, p. 1). Through symbolism and spectacle, through 'Patriots' Festivals', marathons celebrating the Uzbek constitution, and post-Andijan music concerts held under slogans such as 'Protect Your Motherland As You Would a Loved One', President Karimov is reaching out to a younger generation to replace an ossified political elite while, at the same time, redefining that which constitutes political legitimacy (Shukurov 2005).

---

[14]'The First Stage of Charity Campaign Held in Tashkent', *Times of Central Asia*, 24 July 2008, available via: https://web.lexis-nexis.com/universe, accessed April 2009.

[15]'Youth of Uzbekistan Interested in Cooperation with Azerbaijan Coevals', *Times of Central Asia*, 21 July 2005, available via: https://web.lexis-nexis.com/universe, accessed April 2009.

[16]Calculations based on the *United Nations World Population Prospects, The 2008 Revision*, available online at: http://esa.un.org/unpp/, accessed 29 April 2009.

[17]'Uzbek Youth Movement Leader Says its Ranks Increasing', *BBC Monitoring International Reports*, 2 February 2006, available via: https://web.lexis-nexis.com/universe, accessed April 2009.

Patronage politics: a failing policy of balance of power

Scholars, both Uzbek and foreign, have devoted considerable attention to the Karimov regime's strategy of balancing regional elites so as to maintain centralised power. Some analysts describe this balance as one among competing clans, among broad networks of familial (or perceived familial) relations with each network headed by a single charismatic leader (Collins 2004; Faizullaev 2005). Others argue that competing regional and state-institutional identities, rather than ones of blood and kin, are what drive Uzbek politics (Ilkhamov 2007; Jones Luong 2002). Regardless of the nature of the affiliation, the central government's strategy of divide and rule is the same—Karimov steadily rotates elites into positions of power so as to first promote loyalty by distributing the riches of the state, and second, to promote inter-regional or inter-clan competition so as to divert animosity away from his personalised authoritarianism. Thus, for example, the Samarkand regional elite compete with the Tashkent and Ferghana groupings or devotees of Rustam Inoyatov, head of Uzbekistan's National Security Service, unite against supporters of Zakir Almatov, Uzbekistan's former Interior Minister, so as to win the centre's attention and material largesse.

Problematically for the Karimov regime, resources for maintaining patronage politics are limited. In contrast to the oil-rich Nazarbaev regime in Kazakhstan, Karimov has struggled to replace Moscow's Soviet era largesse with easily exploitable industries or international supporters. To some extent, monopoly control over the domestic purchase and international resale of Uzbekistan's large cotton crop has yielded rents that Karimov can redistribute to the political elite.[18] The World Bank estimates that 25% of Uzbekistan's foreign reserves come from the international resale of cotton (Guadagni *et al.* 2005, p. 1). Declining cotton yields, however, and the Karimov government's attempt in recent years to offset this decline through some liberalisation of the industry, have eroded cotton's ability to deliver patronage funds. Net tax transfers from cotton production have declined from 10% to 3% of Uzbek GDP between 2000 and 2004 (Guadagni *et al.* 2005, p. 3).

Some, most notably the former British ambassador to Uzbekistan, Craig Murray, would argue that, beginning in late 2001, the Karimov government found in the US a ready substitute for declining cotton revenues. In October 2001, US troops began landing at Karshi-Khanabad, an Uzbek airbase 90 miles north of the Afghan border. A marked build-up in US troops at the base and a similarly marked increase in US assistance to Uzbekistan quickly followed. In 2002 the US extended $160 million in assistance to Uzbekistan, a figure equal to 77% of combined US assistance to Uzbekistan from 1993 to 2001 (United States General Accounting Office 2003, p. 20). Murray would later conclude of this build-up, and of US and UK military and intelligence cooperation with Uzbekistan more broadly, 'we are selling our souls for dross'.[19]

---

[18]Although the IMF has encouraged the Karimov government to liberalise the domestic pricing of cotton, Uzbekistan's cotton farmers receive only a fraction of the international market price for their crop. For more on how the Karimov government extracts rents from the cotton industry, see International Crisis Group (2005).

[19]*Financial Times*, 16 October 2004.

The US military presence, and with it, generous US assistance budgets, ended in November 2005, following five months of strained relations in the wake of the Karimov regime's bloody repression of the Andijan protestors. And while Uzbek experts like Murray may be correct to question the morality of Washington's and London's partnering with autocratic regimes, human rights have only worsened with the decrease in US assistance. The US government devoted more than half its 2002 US assistance to Uzbekistan to democracy, community development and humanitarian programmes (US Department of State Bureau of European and Eurasian Affairs 2002). These programmes proved critical in supporting, among others, Uzbekistan's human rights and democracy activists. In short, although US assistance from 2002 to 2005 may have, to a degree, offset declining cotton revenues thereby temporarily shoring up Karimov's weakening patronage system, US assistance equally aided Uzbekistan's democracy and human rights activists.

Although it is difficult to assess the net effect that US assistance between 2002 and 2005 had on Uzbek politics, what is clear is that revenues from international aid and from the cotton industry are now in decline. And while Uzbek regional elites continue to compete for an ever-shrinking economic pie, the long-run sustainability of Karimov's divide and rule strategy of patronage politics is ever less certain. Patronage politics demand that the state maintains a near monopoly on economic wealth.[20] As soon as alternative sources of wealth emerge, the effectiveness of centrally defined patronage networks weakens. Paradoxically, as the Karimov regime is now discovering, regional and familial identity networks—networks which the central leadership actively cultivated as part of its balancing strategy—rapidly turn against the executive once alternative, local sources of wealth become available.

Andijan—a window into weakening patronage politics

The May 2005 Andijan uprising illustrates both the dynamic of patronage politics and, at the same time, the potentially destabilising demonstration effects that mass mobilisation generally and youth mobilisation in particular may have on Karimov's weakening autocratic rule. Andijan, perhaps more clearly than any other event since the Soviet collapse, provides a window into why the Karimov government has initiated a new strategy of youth politics so as to pre-empt its declining power in the regions while, at the same time, to persuade younger generations of the ills of colour revolutions.

The Andijan protests, contrary to the Karimov leadership's claims of religious extremism, were a product of the leadership's failed attempts to reassert control over regional appointees and a regional population that had become more responsive to local rather than national-level sources of wealth. In May 2004 Karimov dismissed Qobijon Obidov, Andijan's governor, citing the negative effects of regionally based 'personal connections'.[21] Karimov's charge of corruption was an oblique reference to

---

[20]For a detailed discussion of inter-group competition and the politics of political survival, see Migdal (1988).

[21]'Uzbek President Slams Andijan Governor over Corruption', *BBC Monitoring International Reports*, 25 May 2004, available via: https://web.lexis-nexis.com/universe, accessed April 2009.

the growing influence a local cohort of wealthy Muslim businessman—a group the Uzbek regime labeled *Akramiya*—held both over Obidov's administration and among Andijan society more broadly. Karimov, however, was not content with simply sacking Obidov. Concerned that an administrative reshuffle alone was insufficient, Karimov proceeded to imprison and eventually to convict the Muslim businessmen on charges of religious extremism—an action which precipitated the May 2005 uprising (McGlinchey 2005).

Andijan is the most prominent but by no means the only case of failed patronage. Given the state's control over the Uzbek press, it is often difficult to uncover the full extent of patronage breakdown. That said, Karimov's own pronouncements suggest central authority breakdown at the local level is a common and geographically widespread phenomenon. In 2000 Karimov sacked Jora Noraliyev, the governor of Surkhandarya, citing that the governor had cultivated an environment of 'nepotism, cronyism and bribery'.[22] In October 2004 the Uzbek president removed Alisher Otaboyev, governor of Fergana, noting that his regional representative's 'instructions and orders are beginning to lose, or possibly have already lost, their power in the localities'.[23] And in December 2008 Karimov dismissed three district *hakims* as well as the governor of the Tashkent region, Ziyovuddin Niyozov, for embezzling state land and selling housing plots to political supporters.[24] Perhaps the most astonishing state acknowledgement of declining (and in this case, altogether absent) control over its regional appointees is the case of regional *hakim* Isoqov. Isoqov, Uzbek Prosecutor-General Rashid Qodirov explains:

> Wanted to get rich and paid no attention to solving social, economic, cultural and everyday problems. Feeling himself to be invulnerable and all-powerful, he stopped taking into consideration people's views and did not pay heed to their problems and needs. This former official gathered around him people loyal to him. He created an atmosphere of unlimited autocracy in the locality by exerting duress on his subordinates ... the arrogant governor was given a long prison term.[25]

Complementing these challenges at the elite level have been further mass mobilisation challenges at the local level. The Andijan protests, for example, were preceded by a string of 'market uprisings' in September 2004 in Fergana, Andijan, Quqon and Karshi, in which retailers marched on and, in several cases occupied, local administration buildings in protest against new central government laws regulating local commerce. These protests ended when regional administrators quietly ceased

---

[22]'President Karimov Sacks Regional Governor: "Nepotism, Cronyism, Bribes Rife"', *Uzbek Radio Second Programme*, 23 March 2000, available via: https://web.lexis-nexis.com/universe, accessed April 2009.

[23]'Uzbek Leader Warns of Perils of Mismanagement', *BBC Monitoring Central Asia Unit*, 16 October 2004, available via: https://web.lexis-nexis.com/universe, accessed April 2009.

[24]'Uzbek Leader Sacks Regional, District Governors', *BBC Monitoring Central Asia Unit*, 16 December 2008, available via: https://web.lexis-nexis.com/universe, accessed April 2009.

[25]'Uzbek Chief Prosecutor Points to Corruption Crack-Down', *BBC Monitoring of International Reports*, 23 April 2005, available via: https://web.lexis-nexis.com/universe, accessed April 2009.

implementing Tashkent's directive.[26] Uzbeks throughout the country as well as regional leaders learned from these demonstrations that protest was possible, and that Karimov's control was not absolute. Moreover, Uzbeks learned from their own success in these protests, as well as from the March 2005 Tulip Revolution in neighbouring Kyrgyzstan, and from the earlier Rose and Orange revolutions in Georgia and Ukraine, that uprisings could be successful, that citizens could constrain and, in some cases, turn out their autocratic rulers. Giving voice to this new optimism, Mukhammed Salikh, the leader of *Erk* opposition party, declared in the days following the Andijan events of 13 May 2005: 'We can transform this movement into a velvet revolution, just as in Georgia, Ukraine and Kyrgyzstan, without arms and bloodshed'.[27]

Given Uzbeks' growing inclination to protest and Tashkent's increasingly failed rule at the local level, it is understandable that the Uzbek President might pursue new strategies of control. Karimov's old regional elite are no longer responsive and reliable. In some cases, as in the September 2004 market protests, this elite simply lacked the power to be responsive. In other settings though, for example in the case of regional *hakims* Obidov, Isoqov, Noraliyev and Niyozov, these elite members chose not to be responsive. In all cases, though, Tashkent's authority is in retreat. And it is in this environment of central government retreat that the Karimov government initiated its new strategy of youth politics in an effort to restore executive rule in the regions.

The spectacle of youth politics—rejecting ex-post *causalities while anticipating the future*

Youth movements are often portrayed both in the popular media and in the social science literature as drivers of liberal political reform. Empirically and, no less important, symbolically, youth mobilisation causalities enjoy considerable support. Any reflection on the recent pro-democracy revolutions in Serbia, Ukraine and Georgia immediately evokes images of young protestors challenging—and winning over—equally young and armed government soldiers. Substantive explanations do exist for why younger generations appear so willing to challenge the authoritarian leanings of their elders. Importantly though, closer analysis suggests that the causality scholars attribute to youth protest may be mistaken. That is, although choreographed youth mobilisation is an indicator of impending political change, youth mobilisation need not be an indicator that liberalising political change is near.

This observation is soberingly at odds with the 'end of history' optimism that characterises much of the study of youth in post-Soviet transition. Valerie Bunce and Sharon Wolchik, for example, tell us that there are compelling reasons to believe younger generations are more inclined to liberal change than their elders. Writing of the Serbian, Slovakian and Georgian revolutions, Bunce and Wolchik find that youth, in addition to bringing 'fresh approaches [and] new techniques', are also 'untainted by

[26]Author interviews with Tulkun Karaev, Karshi, November 2004 and author interviews with a prominent, though not state 'accredited' local imam and a human rights/political activist in Quqon, November 2004.

[27]'Uzbekistan Possibly on Way to "Velvet Revolution"', *AFX News*, 17 May 2005, available via: https://web.lexis-nexis.com/universe, accessed April 2009.

the compromises many members of the opposition had made [with the old regime]'
(Bunce & Wolchik 2006, pp. 56–57). Importantly, however, though Bunce and
Wolchik's argument helps explain the demographics of revolutionary moments and
the enduring youthful face of post-revolutionary successor regimes, we should not be
deluded that this younger generation is any more committed to reform than their
elders. The '30 and 40-somethings' of the United National Movement who dominate
post-Shevardnadze Georgian politics, we now know, are no more democratic than the
pre-2003 Georgian political elite. President Saakashvili's cohort may be less tainted by
associations with the Soviet state, but these young, Western-educated leaders,
champions of NATO, the European Union, and a Euro-Atlantic future, are now
compromised in the eyes of Georgian voters by other associations—associations with
ballot rigging, corruption and 'Dr Dot'.[28]

In short, even if one accepts the hypothesis that younger generations are more open
to change, there is little evidence that youth are any more inclined toward liberal
rather than illiberal change. Perhaps because analyses of post-Soviet politics have
centred on liberal or partial reform rather than authoritarian retrenchment, the
question of illiberal youth politics has received comparatively little attention. New
research however, most prominently Lucan Way's analysis of Ukraine's Orange
Revolution, suggests that youth mobilisation may be an indicator of autocratic
weakness rather than a causal force behind liberal reform. More specifically, Way
questions Orange Revolution interpretations which attribute the winter 2004–2005
defeat of the Kuchma–Yanukovych alliance to mass youth protest. He instead argues
that it was internal discord within the Kuchma regime in the autumn of 2004, not 'the
idealistic youth who braved Kyiv's ice-cold streets' that precipitated the Orange
Revolution (Way 2005, p. 144). This does not mean youth politics is inconsequential.
Just the opposite, if as Joel Migdal suggests, we can assess a government's strength by
the degree to which it insures 'compliance, participation, and legitimation', then
sudden shifts in the nature of these processes may well indicate eroding, or a
government's perception of eroding state capacity (Migdal 1988, p. 32).

The Andijan events, as I illustrate above, suggest that the nature of compliance,
participation and legitimation is shifting in Uzbekistan. Given Tashkent's fading
economic influence relative to the growing resources of local business elites, Soviet-
style patronage politics no longer guarantees President Karimov the loyalty of
regional appointees. Rather, the Uzbek President must cultivate new sources of
legitimacy and, having lost the economic game, Karimov is turning to nationalism in
an effort to cultivate a new, less mercenary following among Uzbekistan's younger
generations. However, will Karimov, Central Asia's oldest remaining Soviet-era

---

[28]Both domestic observers and international organisations such as the OSCE Office for Democratic
Institutions and Human Rights (ODIHR) have forcefully criticised the United National Movement's
(the UNM is the ruling party) electoral manipulations. For a detailed report of electoral abuse, see
'OSCE/ODIHR Limited Election Observation Mission, Final Report, Georgia Municipal Elections, 5
October, 2006', available via: http://www.osce.org/documents/odihr/2006/12/22806_en.pdf, accessed
April 2009. Dr Dot is the working name of Dorothy Stein, a masseuse whose website list of satisfied
customers includes various show-business celebrities and the Georgian President, Mikhail Saakashvili.
Dr Dot's video narrative of her trip to Georgia can be found on her website: http://www.drdot.com/
index.php?movies=1.

autocrat, be able to reinvent himself and find legitimacy anew as the nationalist leader of a country where the majority of people were born after the Soviet collapse?

Given the forced nature of *Kamalot*'s many productions it is tempting to conclude that Karimov has not a hope at rallying Uzbekistan's youth. His efforts to cultivate nationalist mobilisation are awkward and contrived: a country-wide celebration of Uzbek culture that culminates with the televised performance of the president's aspiring pop star daughter; 'Do You Know the Law' contests for a country that has no rule of law; sporting events that honour the Uzbek constitution, this despite Karimov's running roughshod over his country's founding document. Yet it is the very inanity of these spectacles that may hold the key to their potential success. Here Lisa Weeden's analysis of the Syrian President Asad's similar use of spectacle is instructive:

> The images of citizens delivering panegyrics to Asad's rule, collectively holding aloft placards forming his face, signing oaths in blood, or simply displaying pictures of him in their shop windows communicated to Syrians throughout the country the impression of Asad's power independent of his readiness to use it. And the greater the absurdity of the required performance, the more clearly it demonstrated that the regime could make most people obey most of the time. (Wedeen 2002, p. 723)

Ultimately, Karimov's political future rests not in *Kamalot*'s ability to stage slick nationalist productions, but rather, in the organisation's ability to seemingly effortlessly rally youth *en masse* despite the artificiality of these clearly choreographed events. In order to achieve this appearance, Karimov must recognise that the power of spectacle exists only so far as his government is perceived as not expending considerable effort in the staging of *Kamalot*'s rallies. Asad's absurdity is compelling because the Syrian President appears aloof from spontaneous displays of public fealty. Indeed, in addition to learning from Asad, Karimov would do well to study the same youth he is attempting to mobilise; the perfected detachment of adolescent youth is exactly the image the Uzbek autocrat needs to convey to his target audience.

Conclusion

In Karshi, a city in southern Uzbekistan not far from the Afghan border, there was during my last visit in November 2004, a large billboard of President Karimov holding a young soldier aloft in a powerful bear hug (Figure 1). My colleague, Tulkin Karaev, and I would regularly joke about the obvious symbolism and the equally obvious insecurity this billboard conveyed. Karaev, father of two adolescent boys, was acutely aware of the billboard's true meaning. The Uzbek leader's embrace of youth politics was too tight. Karimov was suffocating the very population he hoped would breathe new life into his fading presidency.

If *Kamalot*'s recent activities are an accurate indication, then it is clear that neither Karimov's embrace nor his insecurity has lessened in the intervening years. What is less clear is whether Uzbek analysts broadly and political scientists in particular will take *Kamalot* and the spectacle of youth politics seriously. As I have argued in this essay, taking *Kamalot* seriously need not mean we ascribe symbolism and spectacle some invariably determinative causality. Karimov's effort to mobilise youth may, and

FIGURE 1. UZBEK PRESIDENT ISLAM KARIMOV EMBRACES A YOUNG SOLDIER. THAT UZBEK YOUTH WILL RETURN THIS EMBRACE IS UNCERTAIN. BILLBOARD, KARSHI, UZBEKISTAN, NOVEMBER 2004

indeed most likely, will fail. What taking *Kamalot* seriously does mean, though, is that we recognise Karimov's clumsy attempt at youth mobilisation as a sign of growing autocratic strain and, as such, a portent of change to come. Political scientists, Sovietologists and transitologists have thus far all proven slow to recognise and interpret such signs of existing regime weakness. From a discipline-specific point of view, this reticence to recognise and interpret symbols and spectacle is unfortunate in that it impedes a central goal of social science—the development of predictive causal theories. From a policy-specific point of view, this reticence is equally unfortunate in that it leads to ephemeral alliances with embattled autocrats. Such alliances, as the United States has discovered in Central and South Asia, may yield fleeting gains, but these gains come, more often than not, at the expense of long-run strategic and, no less important, humanitarian interests.

George Mason University

References

Brysk, A. (1995) 'Hearts and Minds: Bringing Symbolic Politics Back In', *Polity*, 27, 4, Summer.
Bunce, V. & Wolchik, S.L. (2006) 'Youth and Electoral Revolutions in Slovakia, Serbia, and Georgia', *SAIS Review*, 26, 2, Summer–Fall.
Collins, K. (2004) 'The Logic of Clan Politics: Evidence from the Central Asian Trajectories', *World Politics*, 56, 2, January.

Faizullaev, D. (2005) 'Uzbekistan–Kyrgyziya: Politiko-ekonomicheskie posledstviya territorial'nikh problem', *Aziya i Afrika segodnya*, 7.

Goldstein, J. & Keohane, R.O. (eds) (1993) *Ideas and Foreign Policy: Beliefs, Institutions, and Political Change* (Ithaca, Cornell University Press).

Guadagni, M., Raiser, M., Crole-Rees, A. & Khidorov, D. (2005) *Cotton Taxation in Uzbekistan: Opportunities for Reform* (Washington, DC, World Bank).

Hall, J.A. (1993) 'Ideas and the Social Sciences', in Goldstein, J. & Keohane, R.O. (eds) (1993).

Huntington, S.P. (1993) 'The Clash of Civilizations?', *Foreign Affairs*, 72, 3, Summer.

Ilkhamov, A. (2007) 'Neopatrimonialism, Interest Groups and Patronage Networks: The Impasses of the Governance System in Uzbekistan', *Central Asian Survey*, 26, 1, March.

International Crisis Group (2005) 'The Curse of Cotton: Central Asia's Destructive Monoculture', 28 February, available at: http://www.crisisgroup.org, accessed 29 April 2009.

Jones Luong, P. (2002) *Institutional Change and Political Continuity in Post-Soviet Central Asia: Power, Perceptions, and Pacts* (Cambridge, Cambridge University Press).

Karimov, A. (2001) 'Kamolot dolzhen stat' mostom mezhdu molodezh'yu i gosudarstvom', *Narodnoe slovo*, 16 March.

Kertzer, D.I. (1996) *Politics & Symbols: The Italian Communist Party and the Fall of Communism* (New Haven, Yale University Press).

Kuran, T. (1991) 'Now Out of Never: The Element of Surprise in the East European Revolution of 1989', *World Politics*, 44, 1, October.

Lewis, A. (1976) 'Echoes of Helsinki', *New York Times*, 2 August.

McGlinchey, E. (2005) 'Autocrats, Islamists, and the Rise of Radicalism in Central Asia', *Current History*, 104, 684, October.

Migdal, J.S. (1988) *Strong Societies and Weak States: State–Society Relations and State Capabilities in the Third World* (Princeton, Princeton University Press).

North, D.C. (1990) *Institutions, Institutional Change and Economic Performance* (Cambridge, Cambridge University Press).

Novintskyi, V. (2005) 'V Uzbekistane sozdaetsya obshchestvennaya obrazovatel'naya informatsionnaya set 'Ziyonet', *Narodnoe slovo*, 1 October.

Pierson, P. (2000) 'Increasing Returns, Path Dependence, and the Study of Politics', *The American Political Science Review*, 94, 2, June.

Sharai, Y. (2005) 'Vospityvaya patriotov, intellektualov, biznesmenov', *Narodnoe slovo*, 3 August.

Shukurov, S. (2005) 'Proyavlenie patriotizma i lubvyi k otchizne', *Narodnoe slovo*, 12 July.

Steinmo, S., Thelen, K. & Longstreth, F. (eds) (1992) *Structuring Politics: Historical Institutionalism in Comparative Analysis* (Cambridge, Cambridge University Press).

Thomas, D.C. (2001) *The Helsinki Effect: International Norms, Human Rights, and the Demise of Communism* (Princeton, Princeton University Press).

United States General Accounting Office (2003) *Central and Southwest Asian Countries: Trends in US Assistance and Key Economic, Governance, and Demographic Characteristics* (Washington, DC, United States General Accounting Office), available at: http://www.gao.gov/new.items/d03634r.pdf.

US Department of State Bureau of European and Eurasian Affairs (2002) *US Assistance to Uzbekistan—Fiscal Year 2002* (Washington, DC, US Department of State Bureau of European and Eurasian Affairs), available at: http://www.america.gov/st/washfile-english/2002/December 20021206090410lfenner@pd.state.gov0.8355219.html.

Way, L. (2005) 'Kuchma's Failed Authoritarianism', *Journal of Democracy*, 16, 2, April.

Wedeen, L. (2002) 'Conceptualizing Culture: Possibilities for Political Science', *The American Political Science Review*, 96, 4, December.

Michael Romm's *Ascent of Mount Stalin*: A Soviet Landscape?

STUART HORSMAN

IN 1933 THE USSR'S HIGHEST MOUNTAIN, PEAK STALIN ((7,495 m), subsequently renamed Peak Communism and ultimately Ismail Somoni) was climbed as part of a large expedition, the Tajikistan–Pamirs-expedition (TPE).[1] Several accounts of the expedition were published by Michael Romm (also known as Mikhail D. Romm). This article will focus on the 1936 English language edition of *The Ascent of Mount Stalin* (*Ascent* hereafter). *Ascent* provides a firsthand account of the planning and progress of the expedition, the climbing of Mount Stalin, and the physical and human landscape in which it took place. The expedition was a major scientific and mountaineering event, which involved leading Soviet scientific and political figures. Mount Stalin was the highest point in the USSR and the highest outside of the Himalayas to have been climbed at the time. This achievement was made and described by Romm in an overtly but changing ideological environment, during an increasingly dangerous political period within the USSR and in Europe more broadly, in which Nazi Germany and Fascist Italy also used exploration and mountaineering for national and ideological goals (Kenny 1991, p. 284).

Mountaineering and exploration, and their literary representations have to be seen in their political context (Ellis 2002, p. 7). Analysing such literature can illustrate the ideological norms and context of the times in which they were constructed (Ellis 2002, pp. 7, 48). Romm's *Ascent* was no exception. *Ascent*, in many ways a standard exploration narrative, was constructed in a highly ideological and politicised environment. Whilst *Ascent* did not become a seminal text, it was an original and singular one. It was an officially sanctioned, first-hand account; a novel case study to examine 1930s official Soviet discourses on and the symbolism of landscape, both physical and human, and of the USSR's cultural, political and physical periphery.

I would like to thank Dr Nick Megoran, Dr Denis Shaw, Professor Stephen Cunha, Dr Eva Maurer and the anonymous reviewers for their useful input and advice during the research and writing of this essay. The views, findings, interpretations and conclusions expressed in this article are those of the author alone and do not necessarily represent the official position of the OSCE and/or its participating States.

[1]The direct translation from the Russian 'pik' tends to use the word 'Peak' and would be better recognised in the climbing literature as such but throughout the book by Romm he uses the term 'Mount'. Following Romm's usage therefore, 'Mount' is used in the rest of this article.

Examination of *Ascent* 'allows us to explore the production, dissemination and reception of official narratives about a new type of multinational state', the USSR (Hirsch 2003, p. 684).

The 1933 Tajikistan–Pamirs-expedition

The TPE was one of a series of large scale, multi-disciplinary scientific expeditions in the Pamir mountains between 1928 and 1935. Similar expeditions with implicit ideological objectives, 'to build socialism', were carried out across the USSR (Hirsch 2003, p. 704). The Pamirs expeditions were significant events; 'a national matter to be financed by the state' (Rickmer Rickmers 1929, p. 219). Their collective abstracts and bibliography, published in 1936, comprised 249 pages alone (Middleton & Thomas 2008, p. 437).

The TPE's goal was to build on the 1932 Tajikistan–Complex-Expedition's (TKE) research on developing and modernising the Tajik Socialist Soviet Republic (TajSSR) and to exploit the republic's natural resources for Soviet industry's use. It differed from the TKE by focusing solely on the Pamir region and abandoning the TKE's agricultural and irrigation work (Romm 1936, p. 7). The TPE's 40 units surveyed the Pamirs for natural resources, mapped its landscape and recorded its weather, and one unit, the 29th, climbed Mount Stalin.[2]

The expedition had political resonance not just because of objectives in the Tajik SSR but also because of its participants. Among its cartographers, geologists, geographers, meteorologists and mountaineers were leading Soviet political and scientific figures. These included Nikolai Pertovich Gorbunov who had been Lenin's personal secretary and scientific advisor; Nikolai Vasil'evich Krylenko, the first Soviet Commander in Chief and, at the time of the TPE, Minister of Justice for the Russian Soviet Federal Socialist Republic and a Chief Prosecutor in the Shakhty case of 1928, a major political show trial which heralded the onset of the Great Purge; and Evgenii Abalakov, one of two famous mountaineering brothers. Gorbunov and Krylenko were in fact both influential veterans of the 1917 Revolution and experienced explorers (Horsman 2002).

The book

Ascent was the official record of the 1933 expedition. The 270-page text, accompanied by 30 black and white photographs and a single map of the Pamir range, was published in English in 1936. At least three Russian language versions were published: in 1934, 1936 and 1937. The 1934 edition was only 57 pages long, the 1936 edition was similar to the English version of the same year (268 pages) and the 1937 edition was only 200 pages long but with a preface by Gorbunov. Significantly, in the 1937 edition all the personal, subjective and potentially politically more dangerous material had been removed or reduced to the most banal and positive Soviet stereotypes.[3]

This shift in the content of the Russian editions demonstrates the political environment in which Romm was operating. The choice of Gorbunov for the preface

---

[2]For more on the actual climbing of Mount Stalin see Horsman (2002).
[3]Author's personal communication with E. Maurer (email), 11 December 2008.

of the 1937 edition also showed how quickly the political landscape could shift. By 1938, he and the TPE's other leading light, Krylenko, were victims of the system that had so recently treated them as heroes (Horsman 2002, p. 204). Romm was internally exiled at the end of the 1930s (Mininberg 1998). He survived however. Gorbunov died in prison and Krylenko was executed.

Romm, as a Moscow-based journalist, was aware of the wider domestic political context in which he was writing. He underplayed the broader political milieu throughout *Ascent*'s text however. This was probably a wise decision, though his subtle, considered and at times critical support for the Soviet system, seems with hindsight to have been political risky rather than balanced. In a rare moment of explicitly political commentary, Romm referred to the role of Krylenko (a leading member of the 1928, 1932 and 1933 expeditions) as prosecutor in the Shakhty trials stating that 'he [Krylenko] led the judicial struggle of the Soviet Government against counter-revolution' (Romm 1936, p. 115).

Structurally *Ascent* followed the standard linear, chronological, directional pattern of exploration literature (Ellis 2002, p. 71). Thus it began in Moscow, with the goals, plans and key participants of the expedition being introduced. It then chronicled the TPE's travel to its base camp in Osh and subsequently the 29th unit's movement as it travelled towards Mount Stalin. Romm was a member of the 29th unit, which was personally led by Gorbunov. The book then described the actual ascent of Mount Stalin before concluding with the unit's return to Osh.

Although the TPE was a major undertaking and the climbing of Mount Stalin a major mountaineering achievement, *Ascent* does not appear to have entered the canon of either the Soviet 'transition' or mountaineering literature. It does not appear to have had any impact, either immediate or residual, among either readerships. *Ascent*'s limited success may have been because there was actually little drama in the ascent and only a small proportion of the book was specifically devoted to climbing. The limited reference to the actual climb is not in itself unusual in such literature however (Ellis 2002, p. 71). *Ascent*'s style may have been a factor in its limited impact. As a highly critical British reviewer argued (K.M. 1937, p. 18), Romm had little knowledge of mountaineering himself and wrote in a journalistic style, although the latter was an odd criticism given that Romm was a self-acknowledged journalist.

The author, Michael Romm, was not very forthcoming about himself in *Ascent*. He was a football player, having played for the Russian national team before World War I.[4] By 1933 he was a newspaper journalist, probably a sports reporter for *Izvestia* (Keys 2003, p. 429; Romm 1936, pp. 143, 173). He claimed to have been a boxer of some note and probably saw military service during the Revolution or the Civil War (Romm 1936, pp. 25, 159). As to his book commission, he simply stated he was to write a book on the expedition and send telegrams to 'the chief newspaper' (Romm 1936, p. 143). This seems a rather self-deferential reference to his reporting on such a significant Soviet scientific expedition. It does not help to uncover the Soviet authorities' real interest or motives behind the production of a report on it. As noted earlier, 1936 saw numerous scientific publications on the expedition (Middleton & Thomas 2008, p. 437). It is conjecture but the Russian and English language edition of

---

[4]Author's personal communication with E. Maurer (email), 11 December 2008.

Ascent published in the same year may have been a general introduction to lay readers advertising this Soviet feat.

The choice of British publisher, Lawrence and Wishart, suggests *Ascent* had some political value at the time of its publication. Lawrence and Wishart was an avowedly left-wing publishing house formed in 1936, partly from the British Communist Party's press. *Ascent* was part of their cannon of socialist and communist works.[5] That said, however, it is now impossible to ascertain the publisher's and translator's interests or views of the book and its political significance. There is no record of the book in the archives of either Lawrence and Wishart or the translator, Alec Brown.[6] Some of the former's records were destroyed during World War II. However it is probably fair to assume that Lawrence and Wishart thought the book significant given it was one of, if not the, first one they published. In addition, in his generally scathing review, K.M. accepted that 'the ascent of the highest mountain in Russian territory ... certainly merit[ed] a translation into English' (1937, p. 18).

1930s Soviet views on landscape

Political regimes have frequently sought to represent, co-opt and manipulate landscapes to promote their own ideological and political objectives. These regime goals include legitimising their political and cultural hegemony and control of the physical and social space they inhabit (Azaryahu 1996, p. 311; Bassin 2000a, p. 250; Gill 2005, pp. 480–81). Whilst less overtly ideological regimes conceal or deny the extra-aesthetical symbolism of landscape, revolutionary and totalitarian regimes seek explicitly to emphasise it (Bassin 2000b, p. 314). They seek to present a single 'correct' interpretation of landscape, and prevent any alternative perspective. It is an instrument of their wider social and political transformative agenda (Azaryahu 1996, p. 320; Bassin 2000b, p. 314; Gill 2005, p. 480; Hirsch 2003, p. 691; Lefebvre 1991, p. 54). As Bassin (2000b, p. 315) has shown, however, providing a radical, singular and comprehensive, ideologically correct value to the exclusion of all other interpretations for a landscape can prove difficult even for totalitarian regimes. In addition, even in the most overtly ideological context, landscape is often portrayed as apolitical or even anti-political. Landscape is imbued with 'the impression of escaping from the realm of the social' (Bassin 2000a, p. 250).[7] Thus a singular coherent symbolism is difficult to achieve. Even in the most ideological attempts at landscape representation there was often an inconsistency with a highly political and instrumental interpretation grating against an apolitical, romanticised one.

As a 'propaganda state' the USSR sought a total shift in mass consciousness (Hirsch 2003, p. 687). As part of this process the USSR sought to interpret landscape in a novel and overtly ideological manner. Work by Bassin (2000a, 2000b) and Hirsch (2003) are key texts in understanding the evolution of Soviet thinking on its physical and cultural landscapes. Bassin focuses on the debates on landscape in early Soviet art

---

[5]Lawrence and Wishart website available at: http://www.lwbooks.co.uk/about.html, accessed 15 August 2008.

[6]Personal communications with the author, 30 September 2000 and 14 September 2001.

[7]For further discussion, see Ellis (2002, p. 63).

and art criticism, whilst Hirsch analyses the virtual travel through the USSR's territory, past and present, created by exhibitions housed in the Ethnographic Department of the Russian Museum in Leningrad. The work of both authors highlights the intricacies and inconsistencies in the ideological framing of landscape and place. As noted by Bassin (2000b, p. 313), landscape, or the representation of it to be more precise, was seen as a means of conveying important Soviet messages and values. The depiction of landscape was ideological and used to portray 'a highly articulated message about the meaning, direction and destiny of society itself' (Bassin 2000b, p. 318). However, Soviet landscape interpretation was not static; it shifted over time. Nor was landscape's ideological and symbolic value straightforward.

Between 1917 and the late 1920s official Soviet attitudes towards landscape were essentially orthodox Marxist, although also influenced by traditional Russian attitudes on the subject. During this period, the natural world was perceived as a hostile entity to be tamed, transformed and perfected by Soviet society. A modern, technologically advanced and implicitly Marxist society could and should manipulate and use nature for the society's own requirements (Bassin 2000b, pp. 315, 322). Contemporary artistic representations of landscape were influenced by this progressive, human-centric approach. Representations of landscapes without 'any human-social presence at all' were to be avoided as they undermined any transformative message (Bassin 2000b, p. 315).

By the mid-1930s, the period between the TPE and publication of *Ascent*, Soviet attitudes towards landscape were changing however. This was part of the broader 'Great Retreat', a shift from radical to conservative social and cultural policies (Keys 2003). In terms of landscape symbolism, there was a marked shift from the 'utilitarian and hard-headed sensibilities of the 1920s' (Bassin 2000b, p. 316). The transformation of nature and its material benefit to Soviet society were still important but not exclusive goals. The nature–human relationship could now be portrayed as one of 'organic harmony and ... eternal, unchanging rhythms' (Bassin 2000b, p. 316). Landscapes could now hold inherent qualities, autonomous from any social value. Nature could now be intrinsically beautiful. These 'autonomous' values attributed to landscape were in fact a return to far more universal, traditional ones, heavily influenced by nineteenth-century Russian nationalist and romantic ideas. The novelty was that they were being articulated as part of Stalinist cultural ideology (Bassin 2000b, p. 316). Landscape no longer had solely to symbolise the Soviet transformative agenda. However, the revival in the 'essential nature' did not result in a complete rejection of the ideological interpretation of landscape. It made the ideological narrative more complex and less stark. This shift took place against a backdrop of increased Communist Party control over the 'machinery of representation' (Hirsh 2003, p. 696). Portrayals of the USSR and its people were to be more closely managed. Thus whilst landscape representation may have appeared less rigid and less ideological in character, this 'naturalism' was directed from the centre with considerable authority.

The TPE and *Ascent* took place during this period, a cusp in the transformation in Soviet ideological thinking towards landscape and exploration and their representation as instruments of Soviet hegemony. Thus study of the expedition and Romm's book allows an insight into these objectives in this period of intellectual flux and political uncertainty. The study will focus on three key themes in *Ascent*—transition (tradition and modernity); integration (centre–periphery relations); and the representation of landscape *per se*. It will seek to place *Ascent* into the wider Soviet and non-Soviet literature on these debates, and examine to what extent the relevant academic literature can explain Romm's narrative.

Ascent offers a novel, alternative case study on these subjects. Most research has to date focused on high literature and artistic interpretations of landscape in the USSR or very specific issues such as toponyms (Azaryahu 1996; Bassin 2000a, 2000b; Bown 1991; Ely 2002; Horsman 2006). However *Ascent* is part of a different canon—exploration and mountaineering literature. It was a far less overtly aesthetic, intellectual or ideological text. However as Ely (2002, p. 21) states in his relevant research on landscape and national identity in Tsarist Russia, 'the commonplace, even hackneyed ... [and] mundane', as well as the high art representations of landscape are valuable source material, worthy of study.

The themes

Transition (tradition and modernity)

Romm's work can be assessed in relation to the 'classic Stalinist transformation narrative' of its period (Maurer 2009, p. 487; Hirsch 2003, pp. 683, 691.) Travel and ethnographic literature, which *Ascent* can be regarded as part of, shifted from an 'exoticising' to a 'modernising' discourse, after Stalin's 1929 declaration that the USSR was defeating 'backwardness' and moving rapidly towards socialism (Hirsch 2003, pp. 683, 696).

It is therefore unsurprising to see a strong transformative theme in *Ascent*. Romm established a dynamic between a traditional, conservative reactionary past with an improved present and an even better future. This offered a 'highly articulated message about the meaning, direction and destiny' of Soviet society in keeping with intellectual currents of the time (Bassin 2000b, pp. 317–18).[8]

The expedition was the crucible in which this transformation was taking place. Shared hardship and experiences, political debate, modern technology and communications were the instruments of this transformation. Road construction, for example, removed the ancient caravan route with 'the wide ribbon of a high road, ... the rhythmic throb of high compression motors' bringing 'new forms of civilisation' (Romm 1936, pp. 33, 36–37). Romm used an alleged dispute and the resultant debate between the European climbers and their Kyrgyz porters over the death of one of the latter from altitude sickness, as a catalyst for this intellectual transformation conversion (1936, pp. 131, 141–46). Romm claims he was instrumental in the process of removing the porters' initial wariness and scepticism towards the expedition and the Soviet project as a whole (1936, pp. 141–46).

He discussed the Soviet process of relocating the region from its past based in legend, mystery and tradition to a present and future founded on fact, rationalism and modernity. To paraphrase Romm, the Pamir's 'veil of legends [had only just been

---

[8]See also Hirsch (2003).

removed] and this tremendous mountains uplands complex ... [was] put on the map of planned socialist construction' (1936, pp. 4, 33). The Tajik Socialist Soviet Republic, only established in 1929, was the poorest and least developed of the Soviet republics (Breu *et al.* 2005, p. 139). It was being transformed by Soviet scientific endeavour including extensive exploration and research (Romm 1936, p. 5). This was the TPE's role; to establish 'a picture of the new technological and industrial possibilities and prospects of the country' (Romm 1936, p. 207).

The past was portrayed in a strongly negative light and pre-Soviet social and political structures were criticised. Thus the traditional local Muslim human landscape was described as 'rigid ... [and] stagnant', hampered by 'medieval feudal relation-ships ... patriarchal customs', 'slavery and exploitation' (Romm 1936, p. 3), inefficient agriculture, drug and women trafficking, syphilis, universal illiteracy and Islam (Romm 1936, pp. 35–36). Such criticisms of traditional structures were common in most Soviet literature of the time (Hirsch 2003, p. 694). These views were, for example, also echoed by the Soviet Tajik politician and leading historian, B. G. Gafurov (Sokol 1953, p. 174). Romm also criticised the previous Tsarist rule, albeit more mildly. He argued it had failed to modernise the region, address illiteracy, end oppressive and backward social and religious customs and deprived the local communities of their political rights (Romm 1936, pp. 14–15; Hirsch 2003, p. 694).

Romm reported with satisfaction that the past was in abeyance however. The present, in two senses—a historical one (the Soviet period) and an immediate one (the actual expedition)—was liberating the Central Asian peoples from their Muslim and Tsarist pasts (Romm 1936, p. 14). Rationalism and science were replacing religion and superstition (Romm 1936, pp. 27–28). However Romm presciently noted the persistence of the pre-Soviet clan networks, something that was still evident at the end of the Soviet era (Khazanov 1994, p. 146). As Romm stated, the 'ancient struggle around the pastures was still going on, only masked by soviet forms' (Romm 1936, pp. 35–36). Other Soviet commentators and practitioners were also engaged in attempts to remove superstition and traditional power relations. Leningrad's Ethnographic Department, for example, was equally aware of the survival of traditional society but unlike Romm, was criticised for failing effectively to counter them in its ethnological exhibitions (Hirsch 2003, pp. 691, 706).

Through the TPE's physical and intellectual work a brighter Soviet future was being created for the Tajik SSR (Romm 1936, p. 145). Romm's narrative strongly matched the contemporary views of the new society that was being constructed (Bassin 2000b, pp. 317–18). His imagined future for the Central Asian porters is one such example. Romm portrayed one of the porters as at a 'crossroads' between two alternative futures. One was the continuation of traditional life with its associations to Islam and patronage networks resulting in life as an émigré or *Basmachi*; the other was a 'long and difficult path, to study, to the KUTV or the Communist University of the Workers of the East, and to Moscow' (Romm 1936, p. 145). Soviet educational advances and opportunities for the Central Asians were a common feature of his narrative (Romm 1936, pp. 15, 145).

Romm suggested that the better future was rapidly approaching the region. The transformation of the Pamirs was emphasised in passages on the speed of construction of the Osh–Khorog road and the transformation of a Soviet military outpost from a foodless, deserted ruin to a base able to host a celebration of Felix Dzerzhinki's life in the space of one year (Romm 1936, pp. 63–65). Similar narratives of enlightenment from 'poverty, ignorance ... backwardness [and] ... Islam' were 'a stock Soviet story' in official literature on Central Asia (Kamp 2001, pp. 3–4; Hirsch 2003, pp. 689–90). Similarly, Central Asia's future was to be found in the urban development of Stalinabad and Tashkent. Stalinabad was emerging from the 'chaos' of the traditional settlement of Dushanbe, with metalled roads, petrol cars and aeroplanes replacing the ox-wagon and the 'biblical silhouettes of camels on mountain tracks' (Romm 1936, pp. 3–4). In Tashkent a planned and orderly settlement had been created, in which modern services, amenities and educational opportunities were available (Romm 1936, p. 15). The transition from past through the present to the future was rapid, from feudalism to socialism within a generation (Romm 1936, p. 16).

Modernity was not, however, an entirely positive development. Romm seemed to have held a romantic view of the periphery and its hardships. His narrative towards his return to Soviet normality and civilisation was not entirely positive. He made numerous references to political violence. Romm also makes reference to the lack of supplies available to a medical station he and the unit call on during their return. On a more personal level he claimed that when given the first chance in three months to sleep in a clean bed under a roof, he opted to sleep outdoors under the stars (Romm 1936, p. 264). Whether this is true or not it is illuminating. Modern society, for the returning wanderer, was not utopian. It was not functioning properly. His ambivalence towards civilised society was, as Ellis points out, a common attribute in mountaineering literature: 'The mountain [was] a place apart, a refuge ... from the complexities at home' (Ellis 2002, p. 63). Romm was not accused of presenting a lively and interesting past and 'pale and uninspiring present' however, something that Leningrad's Russian Museum was charged with over its exhibitions of Soviet nationalities' past and present socio-economic modes (Hirsch 2003, p. 702).

Integration (centre–periphery)

As with all the other Soviet republics, the Tajik SSR was undergoing 'nation-building from above' during the 1920s and 1930s (Carlisle 1994, p. 73; Akiner & Barnes 2001, p. 19). The TPE was part of this process, integrating this peripheral region into the Soviet mainstream. The expedition and its climbers were 'cultural ambassadors to the periphery' (Maurer 2009, p. 486; Hirsch 2003, p. 705). They were an elite vanguard of the Soviet mountaineering, scientific and in some instances, political communities. In the Pamirs, they carried out activist and unofficial diplomatic roles, promoting the benefits of their political system, offering aid and assistance and seeking to develop relationships with their Kyrgyz and Tajik hosts. Romm understandably, therefore, devoted considerable attention to issues concerning the periphery and its integration into the broader Soviet system.

The periphery was 'vanishing' as it became integrated into the Soviet mainstream, physically and intellectually (Romm 1936, p. 33). The expedition acted as a form of inspiration, conversion and education, promoting the concept of a *Homo Sovieticus*, as did other scientific expeditions across the USSR (Hirsch 2003, p. 705). The Kyrgyz and Tajik porters' 'narrow world, limited by their native village ... [was now] linked up by some kind of threads with distant Moscow' (Romm 1936, p. 144). 'Their antiquated nationalistic feelings and aloofness from other people [were being abandoned and they] ... began to feel themselves part of one great country' (Romm 1936, p. 34). Class-consciousness and common Soviet identity was replacing parochial, sub-national and religious identities (Romm 1936, pp. 34, 143–44).

Modern forms of communication, transportation and education were key tools in this integration process. For Romm (1936, p. 36), the road and Revolution were intertwined. Without the former the latter's authority in the region would have been weaker. Significantly, in terms of discourse on the periphery and its integration into the mainstream, the final act of the book was the arrival of a motor car to take Romm and other members of the unit out of the Pamirs (Romm 1936, pp. 267–68). Modern civilisation had arrived. A similar modernising and integration message had been used by Schneiderov, who talked of the 1928 expedition's short-wave broadcasts 'which maintained connection ... [from] the distant Pamir ... to Moscow' (1930, p. 270).

Cultural and physical differences and distance were central aspects of this integration narrative. Romm's perspectives on the periphery were not uniquely Soviet, however. Rather they corresponded with common traits that authors such as Daniels & Cosgrove (1993), Häyrynen (2004) and Ellis (2002) have highlighted. These writers have demonstrated how peripheries have been represented in literature as representing 'otherness' from the 'civilised core', and 'distance and movement' from the safe, familiar metropole to the uncertain, dangerous, difficult periphery (Häyrynen 2004, pp. 5, 24; Ellis 2002, p. 71). Romm's narrative closely corresponds with Ellis' assessment of MacKinder's near contemporaneous *The First Ascent of Mount Kenya*. Ellis (2002, p. 71) describes MacKinder's narrative as 'a move from the familiar, comprehensible, controllable environment [of the metropole] ... to one of difficulty, conflict, danger and often cultural incoherence [at the periphery]'. *Ascent* closely mirrored this progression with, in the opening passage of text, Romm meeting Gorbunov in a sedate office in Moscow, setting the tone for the rest of the book.

Soviet norms were evident in Romm's work, although not overplayed. Individual members of the TPE such as Gorbunov, Krylenko and Abalakov were experienced climbers and had visited the Pamirs before. In fact it is difficult to argue that Romm saw the Pamirs as a periphery in the sense of alien or hostile as MacKinder, Schneiderov or even the Ethnographic Department of the Russian Museum in Leningrad did (Ellis 2002; Schneiderov 1930; Hirsch 2003). Unlike Schneiderov, a Soviet filmmaker who accompanied the 1928 expedition, Romm did not suggest that the Pamir mountains were alien or unwelcoming. He actually made the Pamirs more immediate and accessible to his readers by using a more familiar periphery in Russian culture, Siberia, as a metaphor. When he discussed leaving Osh, he said he was 'going into distant exile' (Romm 1936, pp. 31–32).

It is fairer to say that Romm saw the region's landscape and society as a cultural and geopolitical border, exotic but comprehensible and ultimately familiar in character. The mountain range was a geo-political boundary, 'our most advanced outpost in Central Asia' (Romm 1936, p. 50). From 'over the frontier came religious fanatics' and support for the *Basmachi* rebels (Romm 1936, pp. 37, 51). On this point his opinions differed little from local Soviet or post-Soviet views (Horsman 2005, pp. 205–09; MacFarlane & Torjesen 2005, p. 14). He portrayed Central Asian characters in a paternal and possibly moderately patronising manner. Romm regularly mentioned their suspicious and superstitious nature. The local porters were, for example, 'afraid of the fearsome spirits of the mountains' who 'had thrown one of [the Europeans] down the side of the mountain' (Romm 1936, p. 141). However such traits Romm suggested were easily defeated with Soviet rationalism. As such the porters are shown as innocents, quickly won over to the TPE's mission and Soviet values by Romm's eloquence (Romm 1936, p. 144). However any Orientalism or cultural stereotypes evident in *Ascent* were mild and not extreme or uniquely Soviet. He was far more sympathetic towards the local communities than Schneiderov was for example. The latter described the lifestyle of the Kyrgyzs as 'semi-savage' though hospitable and easy-going (Schneiderov 1930, pp. 268–69). In doing so he fitted perfectly Rickmer Rickmers' (1929, p. 215) excellent anti-Orientalist critique: 'the popular mind places every explorer into a country peopled by savages'. Soviet attitudes had not dramatically improved two decades later when a Soviet commentator referred to the Sherpas as heroic but 'nameless coolies' of the 1953 'imperialist' ascent of Everest (Maurer 2009, p. 487). Romm (1936, pp. 146, 165) in fact emerges in a favourable light, talking of the Kyrgyz and Tajik porters as 'conscious and equal participant[s] in our difficult and dangerous task'. Even the far more culturally sensitive and articulate Rickmer Rickmers (1929, pp. 219, 222) talked about 'Europeans' and 'servants' and called the Tajiks 'an unenterprising race'.

References to distance and movement were common in *Ascent*. They were both narrative tools, a means of propelling the book, and also constant subjects of interest for Romm who used these two spatial devices to underpin *Ascent*. However as Ellis (2002, p. 71) and Häyrynen (2004, p. 24) have shown, distances travelled and time taken, as well as modes of transport, are also important symbols in discourses on peripheries. Modes of transport, rail, road, horse, camel, foot and even a proposed aircraft flight, were discussed at length by Romm. In an alleged exchange between Romm and two of the porters, both otherness and distance, characteristics of the periphery discourse, were combined. The porters asked Romm why he wrote so much about what appeared to them normal and mundane. Romm replied that what he was witnessing was alien, novel and different as his *kibitka* (tent or home), Moscow, was 'four days by train' from Tashkent and even more from the Pamir camp they were then in (1936, p. 91).

In the final section, distance and dislocation are again conjured up by the arrival of month old letters and newspapers that had travelled 'thousands of miles from Moscow, Leningrad, Siberia and Paris' to base camp. Reading out-of-date newspapers, Romm emphasised the significant socio-political events of Soviet life from which he had been long separated. These included the opening of the White Sea–Baltic Canal, a football match and, perhaps most significantly, 'the party purge proceeding in ... Moscow' (Romm 1936, pp. 229–30). As with other themes in the final third of the book, Romm appeared to be attempting to reintegrate himself, the expedition and the narrative into the wider Soviet reality. In his attempt to do so, he did not always refer favourably to the social and politicised world he was re-entering.

Conflict and danger were evident in *Ascent*'s periphery. They emerged from both natural and human sources. *Basmachi*, *kulaks* and other counter-revolutionaries were the principle sources of human danger but there were a variety of natural risks including avalanches, malaria and frostbite. They were also an impediment to the Soviet transformative agenda, although Romm did not labour this point (Hirsch 2003, p. 706). As Romm noted, the Pamirs were one of the last areas of the USSR to emerge from civil war (1936, pp. 3–21). At one point the natural and security dangers were combined with a tale of a group of *Basmachi* suffering from serious frostbite (Romm 1936, pp. 257–58).

However Romm, as always, did not fully adhere to a singular and correct ideological interpretation. His 'periphery as danger' narrative was fair and balanced. Significantly the social landscape of Central Asia's villages and roads was no more secure than the natural mountain environment. The presence of the *Basmachi*, evident throughout the book, became almost an omnipresent feature in the final chapters of the book when he returned to the settled valleys (Romm 1936, pp. 247, 253, 256–60).

He did not romanticise or glorify the periphery's danger for political or literary effect. Nor did he suggest that the physical and ideological ends, reaching Mount Stalin's summit, entirely justified the costs, the deaths of two individuals. The plaque erected to record the ascent was accompanied by one dedicated to the climber and porter who died during the expedition. He stated that '[m]ourning [and] inevitable sacrifices' tempered 'the magnificent victory of our Soviet climbers' (Romm 1936, p. 221). The impression given to the reader is that of an anti-climax and an achievement marred by the loss of life. After the death of the climber, Romm referred to a fellow climber as 'quite broken' and claimed that Gorbunov, the TPE's leader, was worried that the news could undermine the morale of the entire unit. Romm's response on hearing of the death implied a life had been unnecessarily cut short (1936, p. 102).

This apolitical, risk-averse narrative was markedly in contrast with contemporary Nazi and fascist discourses on mountaineering and its inherent dangers which would glorify the death of a mountaineer (Ellis 2002, p. 49). The most heroic language Romm could muster was Gorbunov declaring that the peak must be reached 'at all costs ... [as it is] a task set by the Government' (1936, p. 150). The lack of glorification of danger may be partly because of recent Russian and Soviet history. Some of the TPE, possibly including Romm, had fought in the Revolution and Civil War, some against the *Basmachi*. However, probably more importantly, unlike the rightwing totalitarian ideologies communism did not have an ideological fascination with conflict and death. This helps explain why the TPE, and mountains and mountaineering more generally, had limited symbolic value to the Soviet cultural agenda.

Representations of landscape

Romm's representations of the Pamiri landscape reflected the shift in Soviet attitudes towards landscape during the 1920 and 1930s. As Bassin's research suggests, it contained the complex, even contradictory, view of landscape prevalent at the time.

The TPE's *raison d'être* was to give the Pamirs a social value, placing humans and their needs at the centre of its landscape. Consequently these themes are prevalent in the book, particularly in its early chapters. Until the region had been mapped and surveyed it had no social value. It could not be possessed and utilised by the USSR. So there were regularly, for example, references to 'the mysterious western edge of the

Pamirs mountain plateau [which] till recently appeared on the map as a blank area', or 'the last secrets of the blank areas of the Pamirs', which the TPE was finally addressing (Romm 1936, pp. 2, 9). This strongly corresponded with Il'in's claim in 1931, as reported by Hirsch, that the first Five Year Plan (1928–1933) would turn 'empty spaces' into 'green pastures and cultivated lands' (Hirsch 2003, p. 384). To some extent Romm also portrayed some of the uninhabited landscape in a negative light. Thus the moraine landscape was 'chaotic, senseless ... confusion', 'oppressive ... and monotonous' (Romm 1936, pp. 106, 108). This valueless landscape contrasted with the more familiar, accommodating and human landscape of the Osh Valley with is vines and cultivated fields, favourably described by the author (Romm 1936, p. 206).

Ascent's photographs are perhaps the strongest evidence of the Soviet landscape aesthetics of the late 1920s, which emphasised human-centric landscapes, where nature was being transformed for the benefit of society. The images of motor vehicles on the Pamir highway and the newly constructed metrological observatory looking across snow-capped mountains were exemplary representations of 'industrial landscapes' (Romm 1936, pp. 33, 225). Such images of development and human domination of landscape testify to 'Soviet society's efforts to transform the environment' (Bassin 2000b, pp. 323–24). However in some of these photographs, the commitment to this agenda seemed cursory. It was only the accompanying text that provided the correct Soviet transformative interpretation in some cases. A similar piecemeal approach to making 'traditional' images ideologically correct took place at the Ethnological Department of Leningrad's Russian Museum. The curators simply relabelled old exhibits with 'scripts about the revolution's accomplishments' (Hirsch 2003, p. 693).

However Romm's view of the mountain landscape was more sensitive than that of the filmmaker Schneiderov. The two shared the clichéd language of mysterious and blank spaces but Schneiderov was far more dismissive and less enamoured of the landscape. He called the Pamirs 'wild', 'severe and inhospitable' and its fauna was of little merit. He claimed the term '[f]oothill of death' best described this region (Schneiderov 1930, pp. 266–69). Romm and Schneiderov's different attitudes may reflect the shift in official discourse towards landscape appreciation between the late 1920s and the mid-1930s. However it may have also been as much a result of differences in their own personal preferences. Romm appeared to be a far more empathetic writer than Schneiderov.

In addition, rather than presenting a single politicised interpretation of landscape, Romm appeared to modulate his analysis dependent upon the type of landscape he was viewing. Thus in the journey across the Central Asian Steppe and foothills to Osh, and the return from high altitude to the Tajik and Kyrgyz settlements he presented an ideological, socialised narrative. Away from society and human habitation, Romm's narrative became far less politicised, more escapist and more positive towards nature.

In fact his criticisms of the moraine landscape were the exception. And such landscapes are difficult and demoralising for any mountaineer. Romm's comments on the moraines were thus understandable and do not necessarily reflect his general view on uninhabited landscape. In fact most of his references to the non-human environment were positive, bordering on the romantic. Romm's approach was, whether intentionally or otherwise, within in the norms of mid-1930s Soviet thinking.

He valued the landscape for both its intrinsic as well as its instrumental value. His writing echoes the revival of traditional, romantic nineteenth-century attitudes towards landscape that Bassin (2000b, p. 316) notes was taking place in the 1930s. The mountain was not a place to be eschewed because of its peripheral, asocial character. Instead it was a place of unfettered beauty, vitality and value. It brought 'health and strength. Anyone who has spent time in the mountains will return there again and again, unless he is a hopeless town dweller or an international-express gentleman' (Romm 1936, p. 130). At the key moment of human triumph over nature, Abalakov's solo climbing of Mount Stalin, Romm placed the climber uncritically in a landscape devoid of human agency—'a grandiose design of glaciers and ranges ... the grandest mountain complex in the world' (Romm 1936, p. 214).

Elsewhere Romm referred to 'the poetry of the mountains' (1936, p. 131). Thus he was able to freely describe the Pamirs as 'incomparable' and 'beautiful' (Romm 1936, pp. 46, 232). He also gave nature an intrinsic worth above and beyond its value to society when he stated that the 1928 climbers 'were defeated by the charm of those spaces where the foot of man had never trodden' (Romm 1936, p. 115). Such terms were devoid of any transformative or Marxist ideological symbolism. They were views a Soviet author may have struggled to use five years previously as evident in Schneiderov's more critical landscape appreciation. As Bassin has noted, the new romanticised norm was evident in the view of Chegodaev, a contemporary Soviet art critic, who described nature as having 'elemental power' and 'cosmic scope' (Bassin 2000b, p. 316). This language was mirrored by Romm's description of 'landscape [that has] an evocative power that is universal and remarkable' (1936, p. 250). Romm's text may therefore be regarded as an early, possibly unwitting marker of this new, and more conservative and romantic appreciation of landscape.

Escapism was a strong element in Romm's landscape narrative. As Bassin notes, even in the most ideological environment there was a strong element of landscape narrative that emphasised 'the impression of escaping from the realm of the social into something more natural and therefore more genuine and appreciable' (Bassin 2000a, p. 250). Gautier, one of the climbers, Romm claimed, 'loved the expansive and carefree ways of ... climbing expeditions, so different from the routine existence of towns' and another loved 'being alone with the vast [mountain] world' (1936, pp. 26, 187–88). These romantic and individualistic views were out of place in contemporary Soviet landscape thinking. They were also, and remain, a universal theme, even a cliché, in most mountaineering literature. Similar views were expressed by a British climber in MacKinder's Kenya expedition who talked about 'being as free as Nature' (Ellis 2002, p. 63).

The multiple and at times confused attitude towards landscape was also evident in the book's accompanying photographs. As noted above, human-centred, transformative and industrial landscape images were prominent among them. However other photographs corresponded with the appreciation of landscape for its own sake, as in that titled *The Vast Massif of Mount Stalin ... Glittering With ... Frozen Snow* (Romm 1936, p. 144). Others were more voyeuristic and Orientalist in character, for example *Tadjikian Girls at Horog* (Romm 1936, pp. 48, 72). In neither of these cases did they advance a progressive ideological agenda or criticism of the images they portrayed.

Conclusion

Whilst *Ascent* was not a seminal text, it was not a commonplace, mundane journalistic piece as the hyper-critical *Geographical Journal* reviewer suggested. As Ely (2002, p. 21) notes, even if it were mundane and commonplace this should not preclude *Ascent* from being a valuable research opportunity. It remains a unique text worthy of serious study. Importantly, it was an officially sanctioned firsthand report on a major expedition involving senior Soviet scientific and political figures during which time the third highest ascent in the world was achieved. Most importantly it, and the other editions, were written in a highly ideological and politicised environment. Consequently it provides useful information about official discourses on the ideological utilisation of landscape by the USSR in the 1930s. It also provides a comparative case study to Bassin and Bown's analysis on landscape artists and critics.

The book did not come to symbolise the Soviet transition agenda because it proved difficult to utilise the image of the mountain for ideological goals and because the expedition's leading figures were to become enemies of the state, making the whole endeavour politically suspect. Similarly, public interest in exotic, border regions was not to be encouraged, for these areas symbolised danger, foreign contamination and subversion, as evident in accusations levelled against Soviet and post-Soviet 'traitors' (Horsman 2005, pp. 205–09). This was certainly the case by 1937 when the political context was shifting, as reflected in the shorter, more factual Russian language edition of *Ascent*.[9] Intriguingly, although considerable resources were invested in the preparation of the TPE and the resultant scientific outputs, there was little attempt to utilise the expedition or Romm's account for ideological purposes.

Analysis of *Ascent* supports and mirrors Hirsch's (2003) conclusions on 1930s virtual tourism. For Hirsch, virtual tourism 'was supposed to teach the population how to think about the past, the present and the future and to help the actual peoples of the USSR imagine themselves into the emerging developmentalist narrative of Soviet-sponsored evolution and achievement' (2003, p. 696). Soviet landscape representations, including *Ascent*, were supposed to promote the same agenda. However, neither the mountain nor *Ascent* provides an entirely satisfactory symbol or vehicle for communicating Soviet values or norms to a broader audience. The ideological problems of a non-anthropomorphic landscape, the transition within official Soviet landscape appreciation, and the political sensitivities around the expedition, especially its leading personnel, all conspired to prevent this.

Romm's attitudes toward the landscape he experienced in 1933 initially appear to be apolitical, unideological and confused. However, as others (Bassin 2000b; Hirsch 2003; Maurer 2009) demonstrate, the shifting and confused traits evident in *Ascent* can be explained by reference to the broader and difficult shift in cultural thinking in 1930s USSR. Romm was neither apolitical nor unique. Rather he was facing the same inherent contradictions as his peers, some possibly far more schooled in the nuances of Soviet ideology, landscape appreciation and art criticism (Bassin 2000b, p. 313). Study of Romm's *Ascent* supports the contention that at the very heart of 1930s Soviet attitudes towards landscape there was tension between anthropocentric transforma-

---

[9]Author's personal communication with E. Maurer (email), 11 December 2008.

tion and appreciation of nature for its own autonomous and inherent qualities (Bassin 2000b, p. 326). Whilst representations of landscape were politicised, 'the ambiguous and even contradictory nature of the messages' could not be removed. Political priorities could not entirely displace pastoral sensibilities (Bassin 2000b, pp. 313, 326). Romm should not be censured for an inability to address this ideological problematic. He was not alone in battling with this contradiction (Hirsch 2003, p. 686). Nor was his honesty about the problems of implementing the Soviet transformation agenda unique. Other authors faced and failed the same challenge (Hirsch 2003, p. 706). Romm's narrative illustrates the problems experienced by servants of a totalitarian and overtly ideological regime in its attempt to enforce and adhere to a single and 'correct' interpretation of landscape (Bassin 2000b, p. 314).

Organization for Security and Cooperation in Europe

References

Akiner, S. & Barnes, C. (2001) *The Tajik Civil War: Causes and Dynamics* (London, Conciliation Resources).

Azaryahu, M. (1996) 'The Power of Commemorative Street Names', *Environment and Planning D: Society and Space*, 14, 3.

Bassin, M. (2000a) 'Landscape and Identity in Russia and Soviet Art: An Introduction', *Ecumene*, 7, 3.

Bassin, M. (2000b) '"I Object to Rain That is Cheerless": Landscape Art and the Stalinist Aesthetic Imagination', *Ecumene*, 7, 3.

Bown, M. (1991) *Art under Stalin* (Oxford, Phaidon).

Breu, T., Maselli, D. & Hurni, H. (2005) 'Knowledge for Sustainable Development in the Tajik Pamir Mountains', *Mountain Research and Development*, 25, 2.

Carlisle, D. (1994) 'Soviet Uzbekistan: State and Nation in Historical Perspective', in Manz, B.F. (ed.) (1994).

Daniels, S. & Cosgrove, D. (1993) 'Spectacle and Text: Landscape Metaphors in Cultural Geography', in Duncan, J. & Ley, D. (eds) (1993).

Duncan, J. & Ley, D. (eds) (1993) *Place/Culture/Representation* (London & New York, Routledge).

Ellis, R. (2002) *Vertical Margins: Mountaineering and the Landscapes of Neoimperialism* (Madison, University of Wisconsin Press).

Ely, C. (2002) *This Meager Nature. Landscape and National Identity in Imperial Russia* (DeKalb, Northern Illinois University Press).

Gill, G. (2005) 'Changing Symbols: The Renovation of Moscow Place Names', *The Russian Review*, 64, 3.

Häyrynen, M. (2004) 'A Periphery Lost: The Representation of Karelia in Finnish National Landscape Imagery', *Fennia*, 182, 1.

Hirsch, F. (2003) 'Getting to Know "The Peoples of the USSR": Ethnographic Exhibits as Soviet Virtual Tourism, 1923–1934', *Slavic Review*, 62, 4.

Horsman, S. (2002) 'Peaks, Politics and Purges: The First Ascent of Pik Stalin', *Alpine Journal*, 107.

Horsman, S. (2005) 'An All-Encompassing Definition of Terrorism: Central Asian Governments' Portrayals of the IMU and Hizb ut-Tahrir', *The Third World Quarterly*, 26, 1.

Horsman, S. (2006) 'The Politics of Mountain Toponyms in the Pamirs', *Area*, 38, 3.

Kamp, M. (2001) 'Remembering the Hujum: Uzbek Women's Words', *Central Asian Monitor*, 1.

Kenny, A. (1991) *Mountains: An Anthology* (London, John Murray).

Keys, B. (2003) 'Soviet Sport and Transnational Mass Culture in the 1930s', *Journal of Contemporary History*, 38, 3.

Khazanov, A. (1994) 'Underdevelopment and Ethnic Relations in Central Asia', in Manz, B.F. (ed.) (1994).

K.M. (1937) 'Untitled Review of *The Ascent of Mount Stalin*', *The Geographical Journal*, 89, 3.

Lefebvre, H. (1991) *Production of Space* (London, Blackwell).

MacFarlane, S.N. & Torjesen, S. (2005) 'Distortions in the Discourse of Danger: The Case of Small Arms Proliferation in Kyrgyzstan', *Central Asian Survey*, 24, 1.

Manz, B.F. (ed.) (1994) *Central Asia in Historical Perspective* (Boulder, Westview Press).

Maurer, E. (2009) '"Cold War, Thaw and Everlasting Friendship": Soviet Mountaineers and Mount Everest, 1953–1960', *International Journal of the History of Sport*, 26, 4.

Middleton, R. & Thomas, H. (2008) *Tajikistan & the High Pamirs: A Companion and Guide* (Hong Kong, Odyssey).

Mininberg, L. (1998) *Evrei v rossiyaskom i sovetskom sporte (1891–1991)* (Moscow).

Rickmer Rickmers, W. (1929) 'The Alai-Pamirs in 1913 and 1928', *The Geographical Journal*, 74, 3.

Romm, M. (1936) *The Ascent of Mount Stalin* (London, Lawrence and Wishart).

Romm, M. (1937) 'Shturm Pika Stalina', *Molodaya Gvardiya*, available at: http://lib.dnipro.net/lat/ALPINISM/ROMM/pikkommunizma.txt, accessed 1 September 2008.

Schneiderov, V. (1930) 'Foothill of Death', *Pacific Affairs*, 3, 3.

Shaw, D.J.B. & Oldfield, J.D. (2008) 'Totalitarianism and Geography: L.S. Berg and the Defence of an Academic Discipline in the Age of Stalin', *Political Geography*, 60, 8.

Sokol, E.D. (1953) *The Revolt of 1916 in Russian Central Asia* (Baltimore, Johns Hopkins University Press).

Vaksberg, A. (1990) *The Prosecutor and the Prey: Vyshinsky and the 1930s Moscow Show Trials* (London, Weidenfeld and Nicolson).

The Art of the Impossible: Political Symbolism, and the Creation of National Identity and Collective Memory in Post-Soviet Turkmenistan

MICHAEL DENISON

OFFICIAL (DE)MONUMENTALISATION AND COMMEMORATION have emerged as important, and often bitterly contested, loci in the construction of post-socialist national identity.[1] New ethno-national foundation narratives, incorporating symbolic sites and practices, have been used across the post-Soviet space, and particularly in Central Asia, in order to bind together hitherto disparate and often inimic sub-national communities in support of new nation states that lack pre-Soviet historical precedent and, in certain cases, geographical logic. The contextualisation of the Soviet experience in the articulation of these narratives can be problematic. The Soviet period is often described as an aberration, and the narratives sometimes appear to be designed principally to provide cover for the compromised roles of the political elites in their past incarnations as Party bosses.

The creation of a national ethnos is supported by pseudo-historical appeals to a primordial attachment between land and indigenous people, allied to which are claims of defined and developed ancient national cultures. These provide justification for the territorial integrity of the new states, policies on language reform and nativisation, and even modes of (authoritarian) governance (Sabol 2003; March 2003; Karimov 1998; Turkmenbashi 2001; Alimov 1994, pp. 217–36). As Frederick C. Corney (2004, pp. 1–11) demonstrated in his account of memory production after the Bolshevik Revolution, when such myths are compellingly and insistently reproduced, they lend coherence, dynamism and drama to the authorised narrative. They also provide plausible explanations for post-Soviet dislocation, and a normative framework for the recovery of identity and belonging. Conversely, such accounts also require 'concerted

I am grateful for the constructive comments on an earlier draft provided by two anonymous reviewers.

[1] For example, a proposal made in 2007 by the Estonian Ministry of Defence to remove the Soviet Soldier Liberator monument from central Tallinn has elicited a hostile reaction from the country's normally quiescent ethnic Russian community and prompted Russia's Deputy Prime Minister Sergei Ivanov to urge Russians to boycott Estonian products (Osborn 2007).

forgettings' (Gillis 1994a, pp. 7–8)—a cult of new beginnings analogous to the cultural processes that followed the political upheavals in France and America in the eighteenth century (Hunt 1986)—in other words, the 'organised oblivion' (Koonz 1994, pp. 258–80) of the recent past where it might potentially interfere with the smooth linearity of the authorised meta-narrative. This repertoire contains an important spatial dimension. Official projects of memory and identity production are manifest not only in public sculpture, memorialisation, site sacralisation and urban design, but also in the conceptual mapping of the nation state, from both above and below, as self-consciously post-Soviet, European, Asian, Eurasian, or none of these.

While there is an emerging body of literature on identity production in contemporary Central Asia, this has focused exclusively on the dissemination of symbols, texts, rituals and practices that reproduce and impose these new, authorised national identities, rather than engaging with the legacies and cultural residue of the Soviet period (Adams 2004; Anacker 2003; Bell 1998; Megoran 2005; Schatz 2004; Forest & Johnson 2002). Even within this body of scholarship however, Turkmenistan is absent; problems of gaining entry to the country, together with official harassment, often prove to be a deterrent for many researchers working on the region.

Drawing on field research conducted between 2002 and 2008, including interviews with leading Turkmen 'court' artists and sculptors, personal observation of official events, and analysis of regime texts, this essay seeks to explore the intersections between official history, commemorative strategy, community memory, public sculpture and geopolitics in post-Soviet Turkmenistan. An illuminating example of this interplay is the commemoration and symbolisation of the Great Patriotic War, which has presented a complex challenge to authorised renditions of Turkmen identity, requiring the country's post-Soviet elites to devise new strategies, symbols and vocabularies to direct and accommodate, somewhat ineffectually, popular remembrance practices and the fleeting public visibility of the country's ethnic Russian minority. The essay argues that Great Patriotic War commemoration during the post-Soviet era is an example of a rare site of genuine community sentiment in a state where civil society has been extremely circumscribed. In doing so, Great Patriotic War commemoration practices expose the apparent limitations of the post-Soviet nationalising project in Turkmenistan.

The remainder of the essay is structured into four sections: the first part briefly reviews the place of official symbols, ritual and text, often manifested through the saturation of urban public space, in the construction of national identity in insecure and young states; the second section provides context for the peculiar Turkmen case, in which state identity after 1991 was largely subsumed into a pervasive cult of personality surrounding President Saparmurat Niyazov (1991–2006) and then has tentatively been reborn through an evolving but still undeveloped cult centred on his successor, President Gurbanguly Berdymuhamedov (2006–). The third part considers how the Niyazov regime formulated new formal remembrance patterns to circumvent the potential incongruities thrown up by Great Patriotic War commemoration, shaped by the peculiar nature of the Turkmen national project. A short concluding section assesses this case study and the way it illustrates how the unintended and 'uncontrollable' aspect of symbol production reveals the broader limitations of both official attempts to manipulate national memory and the wider nationalising projects under way in the post-Soviet Central Asian republics.

Commemorative strategy in public space

Knauer and Walkowitz (2004, p. 4) argue that nations are constructed and bound together by 'imaginative, narrative and symbolic means'. Where this process is successfully formulated and managed, nations 'loom out of an immemorial past and, still more important, glide into a limitless future' (Goonewardena 2004, p. 66). Multiple commemorative forms are deployed to give visual expression to the past, but the sacralisation of sites and the erection of national monuments is intended to be the most permanent mode of spatially and visually fixing the past: 'the visualisation of a relation between time and stone, the tracing in space of an image in time' (Verschaffel 1999, p. 333). Lewis Mumford (1938, p. 438) argued that national monuments were no longer relevant as long ago as 1938, while Gregory Pauleson's seminal article on monumentality, published in the aftermath of World War II, explicitly linked monuments to totalitarianism, declaring that 'monumentality is not desirable... intimacy, not monumentality should be the goal, even in cities, as far as is possible' (Pauleson 1948, p. 119). However, monuments and public sculpture remained a dominant form of official political expression in the 'People's Democracies' until the collapse of communism. Their function was not only to commemorate, but to radiate power, to legitimise the incumbent regime and, in the case of Socialist Realist commissions, 'to suggest the idea of material progress and the future in the present' (Fowkes 2004, p. 25). Thus, the permanence of the built form was intended to mirror the immortality of the regime responsible for its creation.

Paradoxically, monument commission, design and siting are invariably contingent and politicised, and the Soviet Union and its Eastern European satellites were no exception. The massive Soviet Army Memorial complex at Treptow Park in Berlin (1949) is clearly a monument to victory rather than liberation, while war monuments in other parts of the socialist bloc variously emphasised liberation (the Liberation Monument, Budapest, 1947) and fraternisation between Soviet (normally represented as Russian) troops and local communities (Soviet Army Memorial, Sofia, 1953) (Benton 2004a; Fowkes 2004). Abstract monuments, derided as inaccessible, self-referential and revisionist in the Stalinist period, became more common and their overt ideological content diminished following Khrushchev's major resolution 'On the removal of exaggerations in planning and building' in November 1955 (Åman 1992, pp. 2180–21). But within the former Soviet space, the dominant theme of many monuments remained the 'Eternal Friendship of the Peoples', most commonly expressed in the counterpoint of a transaction or relationship between a local and Russian figure. This is commonly expressed in monuments throughout Central Asia depicting a local elder waving off a departing Slavic soldier in uniform to war, either in Europe or Afghanistan, the implication being that the Central Asian supports and provides for the military on the home front and, in the case of Afghanistan, gives his blessing to fighting in a Muslim state populated by ethnic kin. Both abstraction and 'friendship' motifs feature strongly in the Soviet war memorial complex in Ashgabat

(1974).[2] Mitchell argues persuasively that, in the socialist bloc, public monuments represented the 'ultimate politicisation of art', where every detail of artistic design is carefully abstracted and generalised in order to better present socialist ideology (Mitchell 2003, p. 448).

Commemoration is also expressed through ritual. Lane explains how state rituals proved to be an important tool of cultural management and 'value integration' in the Soviet Union (Lane 1981, p. 22). Bolshevik leaders recognised the power of symbols from an early stage. Lenin initiated a monumental propaganda scheme as early as May 1918, and festivals, carnivals and re-enactments, often syncretising pre-revolutionary and communist imagery, were staged on a frequent basis to narrate the October Revolution and, later, the myths surrounding the cults of Lenin and Stalin (Corney 2004; Stites 1989, pp. 79–100; Tumarkin 1983). Ritual was viewed as an effective means of converting 'individual emotion into collectively oriented moral sentiment' (Lane 1981, p. 33), and breathing life into the relatively small menu of approved slogans and images available for use in the Soviet Union. As Michael Walzer (1967, p. 194) suggests: 'The state is invisible; it must be personified before it can be seen, symbolised before it can be loved, imagined before it can be perceived'. The complexity and uncertainty of meaning implicit within symbols conversely enables them to represent and unify a diversity of understandings. In a sense, their very multivocality not only connects past, present and future, but also enables individuals both to approach, and extract from, symbolic ritual different emotions within a common normative framework. So long as their messages avoid giving commands (for they bring to mind the possibility of disobedience), rituals can underwrite and harmonise the political status quo, and also engender solidarity with power, thereby forging unity between representer and represented, both of which outcomes are crucial for young and insecure political regimes (Kertzer 1988). Thus, for David Kertzer, the very ambiguity inherent in ritual construction smoothes out potential cognitive dissonance (1988, pp. 61–99). At the same time, however, the transmission of ideological power through ritual demands complete univocality on the part of ritual participants. The mass choreographed spectacles that characterised socialist regimes (and still do, to some extent, in Turkmenistan and a few other states such as the Democratic People's Republic of Korea) demand rigid conformity on the part of performers, each of whom occupies a separate analytical time and space in an invisible geometric grid, rendering their bodies 'legible' and docile to the point where the regime's desired 'soft power' objectives almost merge into physical coercion (Roubal 2003, pp. 1–25).

The use of texts, slogans and toponyms is also central to the occupation of public space deemed necessary for identity construction. Literature, memoirs, songs, radio and television programmes were all vital to configuring officially sanctioned meaning and engendering 'lofty collective feelings' about the Great Patriotic War during the

---

[2]Monumentalisation is not confined to public sculpture. It might be argued that, to name only a few examples, giant steel works and factories, avenues, the Palaces of Culture in many towns and cities, major canal projects, and model cities such as Nowa Huta, Stalinstadt (Eisenhüttenstadt) and Magnitogorsk, were all examples of socialist monumentalisation, but such projects do not fall within the scope of this essay.

Soviet period (Gudkov 2005). While spatial design of the official urban landscape, including the creation of 'legible' grid systems, as well as the siting of monumental complexes and government buildings (re)produces clear codes of cultural signification, there are non-territorial dimensions to planning control—economic, procedural and cultural—that embed disciplinary–symbolic power (Foucault 2002, pp. 349–64). Among the most important of these are the renaming of places and streets to represent both change and 'rediscovery' of earlier identities. Although lacking the visual impact of monuments and rituals, renaming places commemoration and official history into everyday settings, legitimising power relations and authorised histories in the literal mapping of the city (Azaryahu 1997). Official texts and slogans from the Soviet era, on billboards, public buildings and often the names of landmarks, farms, settlements and towns, are still common through the Soviet Union, or in many parts of Central Asia have simply been retouched with new injunctions, warnings and aspirations, many of which rather dubiously proclaim the uniqueness and historical importance of their particular location.

In all societies, public space is politicised, but in socialist and post-socialist states the claims made by the state on behalf of society intensified this experience. There was a conscious attempt to socialise people within public (and private) space (Harloe 1996). As Crowley and Reid (2002) suggest, places of work, leisure, public ceremony and family life were permeated by and charged with ideological meaning. Public space, and the wider configuration of cities, was invested with a social-transformative role. However, under mature socialism, as Yurchak (2006) has successfully illustrated, the spatial practices of individuals could only be partially and ambiguously contained. Private accounts of the everyday, the *byt*, reveal an unravelling of the claims and aspirations of socialist urban and cultural planning. Similarly, analysis of popular commemoration patterns in minimally reformed post-socialist societies also tests the parameters and penetration of official narratives. While authorised narratives remain important, they tell only a part of the story. The responses drawn from their intended audiences, though frequently overlooked in scholarship on public space, are critical to the contextualisation and anatomisation of the legitimacy, content and reach of the official repertoire.

Identity production in post-Soviet Turkmenistan

Although officially sanctioned and circumscribed expressions of Turkmen identity gained some currency among the small urban intelligentsia during the Soviet period, notably in the performing and visual arts, and perhaps architecture, the picture emerging from Soviet sources is of the relatively uneven, contingent and ambiguous overlapping development of Turkmen ethno-national consciousness, emerging Soviet and resilient tribal identities.[3] Soviet structures and nationalities policy played a

---

[3]In an artistic context, Khodjakuli Narliev's seminal 1972 film *Nevestka* [*Daughter-in-law*] movingly depicts the tensions between, on the one hand, material progress under the Soviet system and pride in the Soviet war effort and, on the other hand, the resilience of Turkmen and tribal values. On the fusion of Soviet and Turkmen architectural styles, see Kacnelson *et al.* (1987). Turkmen intellectuals defended the Turkmen language during the Khrushchev 'thaw' in the Turkmen language journal *Edibayat we Sungat*.

significant role in framing and articulating aspects of Turkmen ethno-national and territorial aspirations, particularly during the process of national delimitation in 1924 when local elites successfully framed their territorial demands within the discourse of Bolshevik nationalities policy. Side by side with the instrumental use of Soviet policy by early Turkmen nationalists, identification with local traditions and cultural practices, centred principally on (sub-) tribal identities, also proved resilient in everyday life (Barthold 1962; König 1962).[4]

Thus, the growth of Communist Party cells in the 1920s and 1930s appeared to be impressive but, on closer examination, often proved to be a simple continuation of the *maslakhat* (village council) structure (Edgar 2004, pp. 107–09). Soviet campaigns against polygyny, under-age marriage and *qalin* (bride-price) in Turkmenistan officially eradicated the problem, but these practices persisted covertly. Simultaneously, local officials appeared willing to cooperate with Moscow in some of the most egregious episodes of the Stalinist period such as the Great Purges of the late 1930s, again if only instrumentally, in order to settle old communal scores (Northrop 2004; Klevniuk 1998).

During the mid- to late-Soviet period, overlapping Soviet and Turkmen identities and practices were more successfully developed and embedded, among other ways, through formal institutionalisation, for example, service in the armed forces or membership of the Turkmen Academy of Sciences, the publication of 'approved' native authors such as Makhtumkuli, encouragement of local craft industries such as carpet weaving, and the rapid expansion of educational provision.[5]

Political expression of 'ethnic consciousness', even in the late Soviet period, appears to have surfaced only sporadically, and then only in response to particular local conflict situations or provocations. For example, irrigation disputes between Turkmen and Uzbek farmers near Charjou in April 1988, and ethnic riots in Nebit Dag and Ashgabat in May 1989 were blamed on Armenian traders increasing bread prices during shortages. Field interviews conducted by the author with former army officers in 2005 (of both Russian and non-Russian ethnicities) revealed that the principal concern of Soviet army officers serving in Turkmenistan was inimical relations between Turkmen tribal groups, rather with other nationalities.[6] As Communist Party First Secretary from December 1985, Niyazov himself recognised this problem, writing in February 1987 that 'family–clan hostility' and 'the creation of student groupings according to family and clan' would not be tolerated, and again on 5 May 1988, when he warned that 'feuds between tribes are a ruinous occurrence in our life that hampers the development of the republic and often leads to tragedy'.[7]

---

[4]On ethnic Turkmen communists learning to 'speak Bolshevik' in order to articulate their political and territorial objectives during the demarcation of Soviet national borders in 1924, see Arne Haugen's analysis of *Sovnarkom* archives (2003, pp. 176–77).

[5]For details see, Istoriya (1978a, pp. 32–35, 1978b, pp. 112–13, 186–87) and Kulturnoe (1958, pp. 42–43, 118–19).

[6]Author's interviews with Captain Dr M.T., former head of the Turkmen army's medical corps, Leeds, UK, 14 September 2005, O.M.; former Soviet army officer, Ashgabat, 3 August 2004; and L.K., former Soviet army conscript, Balkanabat, 10 May 2005.

[7]*Turkmenistan Iskra*, 15 February 1987; *Turkmenistan Iskra*, 5 May 1988.

Unlike almost all other Soviet republics at the end of the Soviet period—even those in Central Asia—the Turkmen SSR was characterised by the absence of manifestations of, or a significant push for, national cultural or political revival, either inside or outside Party structures. The Turkmen SSR's Declaration of State Sovereignty made on 21 August 1990 should be construed as a purely reactive measure to Boris Yel'tsin's earlier declaration in the Russian SFSR on 12 June 1990, rather than as preparation for independence. Indeed, Niyazov was one of those Republic leaders at the core of initiatives to save the Soviet Union. Gorbachev's proposals for a revised Union Treaty were almost unanimously approved (under official direction) in the March 1991 referendum, and Niyazov was still active in attempting to find a formula to save the Union as late as the end of November 1991.

While Turkmenistan was psychologically, institutionally and economically ill-equipped for independence in December 1991, this state of affairs paradoxically gave the political elite, now firmly dominated by Niyazov, fairly wide scope to shape the terms, if not the complete content, of national identity production in the early post-Soviet period. The content of the subsequent official nation-building project elaborated certain core themes to make sense of the present and the past: first, the projection of a monist political order legitimated by pre-Soviet practice and enacted in the person of Niyazov; second, an emphasis on the primordial bonds linking ethnic Turkmen, often through mythical rulers well known in the history and folklore of the Turkmen (notably Oghuz Khan), to the Turkmen lands—in other words the carving of a distinct Turkmen geocultural space; third, a highly selective and normatively laden ethno-national meta-narrative that only acknowledged historical context at very specific junctures, and in which the Soviet experience is barely registered.

These messages were transmitted through a variety of media. The first resolution passed by the Congress of People's Deputies (renamed the *Majlis*) in 1992 was for the unlimited production of state portraits of Niyazov. This set the tone not only for the institutionalisation of Niyazov's power (he was granted the presidency for life in December 1999), but for the saturation of public space with Niyazov's image—on banknotes, coins, brooches, carpets, posters outside and inside public buildings, statues, countless plaques and monuments, on commercial items such as watches, notebooks and bottles of vodka, as well as through blanket television coverage. Niyazov was also toponymically immortalised through the renaming of cities, airports, streets, natural landmarks and collective farms, often at the request of local officials, and his slogans can be found on public buildings, bridges and even chalked into hillsides.

In the latter period of Niyazov's rule (2001–2006), the principal mode of ideological transmission was through Niyazov's two-part treatise *Ruhnama* [*Book of the Soul*], a blend of pseudo-history, genealogy, homily, memoir and loosely articulated political analysis, which has become required reading in schools and universities and even in disassociated professional settings, such as hospitals where, according to a former paediatric neurologist from Dashoguz interviewed in November 2005, the readings interrupted time better spent on patient care.[8] The telling of history in *Ruhnama* fuses

---

[8]Author's interview with Dr N.A., a paediatric neurologist from Dashoguz who had gained political asylum in the UK, Barnsley, 4 November 2005.

the construction of the national meta-narrative with Niyazov's own persona. He emerges as 'the architect of national independence' who 'did not rest by day or night until your [the Turkmen people's] head could be held high' (Turkmenbashi 2001, p. 252). He is not merely part of Turkmenistan's history; he actively shapes its destiny. Turkmenistan is likened to a galley, with each citizen an oarsman: 'If all the oarsmen obey one captain, and row in accordance with the orders of the captain, the ship will be put out to sea' (2001, p. 68). Niyazov was seen to embody the state so completely that he was named (until March 2007) in the national oath: 'At the moment of my betrayal . . . to Saparmurat Turkmenbashi the Great let my breath stop'. According to local 'official' scholars, *Ruhnama*'s penetration into professional, military and educational life was necessary because it 'cultivates personality' and sets out 'the moral obligations of society' (Turkmen 2003, pp. 130–31). It acts as 'a bridge to the world of moral values and the rich cultural heritage of the Turkmen people' (Nepesova & Tugiev 2001, p. 128), a 'mirror of the national soul . . . making the heart wiser and kinder' (Odekov 2001, p. 131) and will be 'a source of power and striving to reach the [economic] targets of Turkmen's Golden Age' (Amansariev 2003, p. 116).

Where did all this come from? The Western media has had no doubts. Numerous newspaper articles portrayed Niyazov rather simplistically as a deluded dictator ruling by personal whim with no thought to the conventional rules of the political game (Jack 2002; Huggler 2004). However, the creation and operation of the monist system of power, accompanied by the cult of personality as its choice of ideological transmission, demands more careful and thorough interrogation.

At its core, the system appears to have fused selective aspects of pre-Soviet and Soviet conceptions of power and order. Although the absence of functioning institutions opened an important space for the gambits and political opportunism of President Niyazov in the immediate post-Soviet period, the almost complete absence of democratisation, in either form or content, after 1991 can, at least partially, be attributed to some congruencies between Turkmen tribal governance and Soviet practices.

Most sources agree that, until the immediate pre-Tsarist period, the Turkmen political order was acephalous—that is to say, it lacked a political leadership endowed with enduring authority and furnished with a permanent staff (O'Donovan 1882; Vambery 1865).[9] Leadership did exist but it was normally situational—equally conferred on, and withdrawn from, a *khan* or *serdar* (military leader) for an agreed purpose or duration. However, great care was taken in the village councils (*maslakhats*), which were comprised of elders and leading community figures, to ensure that decisions were reached consensually and in accordance with customary law (*adat*). Where unanimity could not be achieved, decisions were often postponed until an acceptable compromise could be attained. However, once a decision had been reached, any dissenting members were expected to fall completely into line, not least because joint liability existed for any trespasses that subsequently ensued. The emphasis on univocality in political decision making was therefore relatively compatible with the *pro forma* voting procedures of the Soviet period. This made the re-traditionalisation of post-independence Turkmen political institutions more

---

[9]For a summary of other accounts, see Geiss (2003).

acceptable, notably in the designation of Niyazov as *Serdar* and the creation of the *Khalk Maslahaty* (People's Council), a fusion of legislature, executive and judiciary that functions as the country's supreme representative body but, in practice, has proven to be politically compliant.

The visual forms of the Niyazov cult clearly draw from the imagery, texts and rituals of both Stalinist and Kemalist rule. Niyazov was raised for part of his childhood in a state orphanage in the period of High Stalinism following World War II, and the Soviet authorities clearly considered such institutions as important venues for ideological indoctrination. Certain Stalinist motifs have recurred under Niyazov's rule, clearly evident in official portraiture and ritual, and also in Niyazov's architectural ambitions for Ashgabat and the interest in bending nature for human purposes, notably in the earlier drive to complete the Karakum canal and the construction of a large desert reservoir.

Significantly, Niyazov visited Turkey for the first time in early December 1991, just as the Soviet Union moved towards final dissolution and Niyazov was facing up to the challenge of constructing a new political order. He soaked up Kemalist imagery at the vast mausoleum complex in Ankara and other sites, and subsequently singled out Atatürk as a leader of special significance in twentieth-century nation-state building projects in several speeches. The adoption by Niyazov of the appurtenance of Turkmenbashi in 1993 is an obvious referent to Atatürk. The principal difference between Niyazov and Atatürk lies not only in the obvious disparity in the quality of their political leadership, but that the image of Atatürk symbolises a certain abstract developmental path of secular modernisation and national unity—it embodies a set of values beyond the personage of Atatürk—whereas in Turkmenistan, the cult has been really rather indissoluble from Niyazov's own predilections and idiosyncrasies—and, as a consequence, really only came to stand for little more than Niyazov himself.

The second strand of official identity production in the Niyazov period was the construction of a new history of the Turkmen and their lands from earliest times, shorn of Soviet teleological determinism and engrained prejudice against nomadism. The main vehicles for transmission of this new account are in the only scholarly journal of note, *Miras* (which, translated into English and Russian, suggests a propagandising function), in passages of *Ruhnama*, which regrettably functioned until 2007 as the main history text used in schools and universities and, again, through the saturation of public space with television documentaries, statues, monuments and gold reliefs depicting mythical battles. This 'new' history telescopes in on only two periods of ethno-national history (one of which is entirely mythical in any event), and entails significant deviations from orthodox historical narratives of the period.

The forbears of the Turkmen, the nomadic Ashina clans who were nomads in western China and the Altai in the sixth century CE, only migrated west of the Aral Sea in the ninth and tenth centuries CE, and then settled in the isolated Aral Sea delta, Ust-Yurt plateau and Mangistau peninsula areas, none of which fall within the boundaries of contemporary Turkmenistan. The great migrations of the Turkmen tribes into Turkmenistan occurred between the seventeenth and nineteenth centuries in response to economic pressures and population displacements of Kazakhs and Kalmyks from the north. At that time, nearly all of what is now Turkmenistan was uninhabited. The regime has circumvented the lack of a primordial connection between 'blood' and 'soil' by reviving a traditional folkloric claim that the Turkmen descend from a mythical warrior named Oghuz Khan, himself a descendant of the Biblical prophet Noah. *Ruhnama* does not state with clarity when Oghuz Khan lived, but one can infer that his empire existed in approximately 3000 BCE. Niyazov states that the reign of Oghuz Khan was 'a golden age' which 'illuminated the path of the Oghuz people, our ancestors, for thousands of years' (Turkmenbashi 2001, pp. 79–100). Crucially, the land that Oghuz ruled is situated, according to Niyazov, almost co-terminously with the boundaries of the modern state of Turkmenistan, thereby materialising the organic, primordial, mystical connection between land and people.

Similarly, the Seljuk empire (985–1194) is depicted in the post-Soviet narrative as the apotheosis of Turkmen civilisation and influence, and is used ubiquitously to confer legitimacy on the Niyazov regime. Seljuk sultans figured prominently when the months of the year were renamed in 2002, their statues figure prominently next to Niyazov in central Ashgabat, elaborate gold reliefs recount battles (many of which were, inconveniently, fought against nomadic Turkmen tribes), and the eight-pointed Seljuk star design has been incorporated into the state emblem. Accounts of the Seljuk period are specifically portrayed within a normative framework: together, the Turkmen people will shape the world's destiny; divided, Turkmen identity disintegrates.

Of particular significance is the conscious geographical and historical 'de-anchoring' of Turkmenistan from surrounding peoples and events. In October 2000, Niyazov ordered a new high school history textbook to be pulped after it had traced the ethnogenesis of the Turkmen to the Mongolian Altai region. The impact of the Mongol conquest and the Timurid empire, which has been claimed by the Karimov regime in Tashkent as Uzbek, is completely ignored, although confusingly, *Ruhnama* claims that after the Mongol invasion, 'Turkmenistan was the most developed country in the world', devising the first carriages and perfecting the art of making tools with molten ores (Turkmenbashi 2001, p. 55). The Arabshahid rule in the sixteenth and seventeenth centuries is barely mentioned (probably because it is bound within the patterns of migration), and the khanates of Khiva and Bukhara, parts of the territories of which now lie in Turkmenistan, might never have existed. The terms of Russian expansion into the region, which embarrassingly elicited different responses of collaboration and opposition from the various Turkmen tribes (principally western Yomuts assisting and Ahal Tekes resisting), is not really elaborated upon, apart from in one-dimensional official commemoration of the defeat of the Ahal Teke tribe by Tsarist forces in the battles at Geok-Depe (1879 and 1881) that signalled the end of meaningful resistance to the Russian advance (Saray 1989).

Instead, Turkmen identity is presented on television, in public spaces and even in scholarly journals, almost purely in the form of depoliticised, dehistoricised symbols—the Ahal Teke horse, carpets, musical instruments, and particular spaces or buildings such as the Sultan Sanjar mausoleum at Merv—but without any context or referents (Gurbanov 2001; Yaziyev 2003; Turkmen 2003; Amansariev 2004). In the authorised narrative, the Turkmen people are almost entirely detached from surrounding civilisations. There is barely any mention of interaction with the Ghaznavids,

Khorasanians, Arabshahids or Sarts resident in the region's cities, or of Turkmen migrations within and beyond the territory of contemporary Turkmenistan. Spatial depictions of Turkmenistan dwell on how the country's timeless landscape surmounts tribal differences. To illustrate, in one passage of *Ruhnama*, Niyazov envisions Turkmenistan on maps as a strong bull goring the Caspian Sea. On his desk is a golden statue of a bull found at Altyn Depe. He notes that outside his presidential palace stands a huge bronze statue of a bull tossing the world, representing the Ashgabat earthquake of 1948, upon which a dying mother is depicted holding a golden child (Niyazov) aloft. In this short passage, Niyazov himself is therefore effortlessly interwoven with Turkmen land, history and people through text, symbol and monument (Turkmenbashi 2001, p. 241).

The Bolshevik Revolution and subsequent creation of the Soviet Union are also almost entirely absent from official renditions of Turkmen history. *Ruhnama* devotes one page to the Soviet era, describing the 'terrible conditions in our towns and villages' and lamenting: 'O Turkmen! You almost lost your native tongue in that period' (Turkmenbashi 2001, p. 296). Lenin, Stalin and successive Turkmen SSR Party First Secretaries might not have existed. Perhaps more surprisingly there is no place at all for Gaigasiz Atabayev, Nadirbai Aitakov and Halmirad Sahetmiradov, the three leading Bolshevik figures in the early Soviet period, who perished in Stalin's purges and thus could plausibly have been rehabilitated under Niyazov.

Not only is Turkmen identity temporally detached from any Soviet moorings, it has been almost entirely decontextualised on a spatial level. The other Central Asian Soviet Republics are barely mentioned in official narratives of the Soviet period, and neither are ethnic Turkmen (or Turcoman) communities resident in Afghanistan, Iran and Iraq. The decision made in the immediate post-Soviet period to pursue a policy of neutrality and diplomatic isolation from regional security affairs has also facilitated these silences. In other words, if Central Asia's existence need barely be acknowledged in the present, the requirement to explain its past concomitantly diminishes.

As Soviet values penetrated Turkmen society unevenly, officials involved in the formation and propagation of Soviet nationalities policy were also only partially successful in inculcating Turkmen national consciousness, safely nested within the larger Soviet family. Instead, unofficial identity remained stubbornly fixed at the tribal level, particularly in rural areas. Once Turkmenistan became independent, the country's cultural planners sought to locate repositories of 'Turkmenness' in order to bind the titular nation together beneath the entirely formal and perfunctory veneer of a civic, multi-ethnic national identity.

The ensuing project of ethno-national identity production entailed the elevation of Niyazov first to the level of founding president, then national father figure and, latterly, semi-divine prophet. But personalising national identity is, by itself, insufficient. By virtue of their remoteness, leaders cannot tell a people much about themselves. The crystallisation of Turkmen identity, according to the project, could only be achieved by isolating its constituent elements. The sweep of national history cannot be encapsulated neatly within the muddy ebbs and flows of empire, conquest and the pragmatic self-redefinition of ethnicity that characterise Central Asian history. Thus, the production of sites of official memory in Turkmenistan has been notable as much by absence as presence; temporal erasure from the Soviet past and spatial erasure from the Central Asian present combine with a small menu of sanctioned sites, symbols and icons to distil the essence of the Turkmen spirit and form a cultural template for downward transmission.

Great Patriotic War memory and autonomous remembrance

Popular memory and commemoration of the Great Patriotic War presents a problematic site for the Turkmen government, for it prevents 'concerted forgettings' and locks the new Turkmen nation back into the communist bloc and the Soviet past. Great Patriotic War memory requires official recognition of the Soviet Union's existence, and of Turkmenistan's role in a larger struggle, directed from Moscow by Stalin, and taking place a long way away. It forces confrontation with an alternative, unspoken and, for many younger children schooled principally on *Ruhnama*, an unknown history. It brings the regime face-to-face with an unsanctioned and unmediated community memory, with Soviet iconography and, given that the war reconnected Soviet state and society following the earlier excesses of Stalinism, with a palpable sense of Soviet nostalgia. Thus, popular war commemoration is a symbolic arena that does not narrate the nation according to the official story. The ensuing tensions created can be illustrated by looking at memorialisation, ritualisation and commemoration during the celebrations marking the 60th anniversary of VE day in 2005.

It seems that the remaking of the present often entails the remaking of history and, with it, the remaking of the city. Forest and Johnson suggest that, at critical junctures, memorials become a site of political contestation between elites (Forest & Johnson 2002, p. 531). They argue that, in post-Soviet Moscow, memorials fell into three categories: Tsarist, Orthodox and Great Patriotic War memorials which were co-opted by the new city authorities; statues depicting Lenin and other revolutionary figures which were contested by elites; and memorials linked to the Communist Party and Soviet economy which were unequivocally disavowed. In post-Soviet Turkmenistan, selected pre-revolutionary motifs (Oghuz and the Seljuks) were co-opted. Apart from one small statue of Lenin in Azadi Square (retained, it seems, for the ornate 'carpet' tiling on the plinth), cities have been fairly comprehensively 'de-Partified' and 'de-Leninised', although some revolutionary and anti-*Basmachi* monuments remain in remoter settlements, such as Yerbent in the Karakum desert, either through neglect or because they function as convenient village centre meeting places for local elders. Memorialisation of the Great Patriotic War in contemporary Turkmenistan has, however, undergone a fourth process, perhaps best described as authorised reconfiguration. Existing memorials have not been removed and replaced. Instead, new memorials have been erected that re-interpret the conflict. Almost all of these memorialise the war through the person of Niyazov's father, Atamurat, who purportedly died on active service in 1943, fighting with the Soviet Army in North Ossetia (although Niyazov's opponents maintain that Atamurat died after being thrown off a train during a drunken gambling dispute). The incremental augmentation of the cult surrounding Niyazov with lesser cults of Atamurat and Niyazov's mother Gurbansoltan Eje, who died when Niyazov was eight years old in the Ashgabat earthquake of 1948, was of central importance to the project of identity production in the period 1997–2007. At one level, the immortalisation of Niyazov's parents could be viewed as the public fetishisation of his grief for the parents he barely knew.

However, the cult surrounding Niyazov's parents also had important political functions. Sharing public space with long deceased family members alleviated the monotony of Niyazov's own cult without diluting or threatening his personal authority.[10] Moreover, in the absence of Niyazov's own family as a meaningful or— given his estranged wife's Jewish–Russian nationality—acceptable role model of kinship and social duty, Niyazov turned to the lives of his parents to embody traditional Turkmen values. Most importantly, however, is the way in which their deaths directly connect Niyazov to the two most traumatic events in Turkmenistan's recent history. The orphan Niyazov's tragedy personifies national grief (in the Soviet era), long struggle, and the eventual triumph of the national spirit in the form of independence. A substantial passage in *Ruhnama* embodies the idealisation of Atamurat. The young Niyazov is accosted in a Leningrad library by an old Russian man whom he does not know. The Russian tells Niyazov that he resembles closely 'a very great man . . . a real hero' who was captured by the Germans, and then killed for sharing a cigarette with a fellow prisoner, a Russian communist (Turkmenbashi 2001, pp. 31–45). In this implausible tale, Niyazov, through his father, is linked directly to an act of war heroism in which his father (embodying the Turkmen nation) makes the ultimate sacrifice to save Russia. The reader is left in no doubt who should be grateful to whom. The hagiography is further developed in other publications, notably Niyazov's book *My Relatives*. In one story, Atamurat bravely resists the excesses of Stalinist collectivisation in his village before going off to war, where he fights 'like a lion' until, 'betrayed by his countrymen he went to his death, like Christ sold to his enemies' (Amansariev 2004, p. 135). This betrayal signifies what awaits the Turkmen if they fail to unify against their enemies.

The symbolic representation of the war is consistent with the promotion of a nationalising dimension mediated mythically through Atamurat. Thus, the Soviet war memorial in the Caspian port city of Turkmenbashi (formerly Krasnovodsk), is now supplemented (or superseded) by a more prominent statue of Atamurat sited opposite the entrance to the railway station to greet visitors. In Ashgabat, two war memorial complexes occupy the end points of a mile long axis in the city, at the centre of which is the Arch of Neutrality. The spacious, abstract Soviet War memorial ensemble comprises four obelisks 'enclosing' the eternal flame. To its right, stands a statue of a grieving mother, between two soldiers—a Russian and a Turkmen—connected by an arch (Figure 1).

The new memorial depicts Atamurat, sculpted as an idealised Teutonic warrior with flowing cape, surrounded by a pool of water, shaped as an eight-pointed Seljuk star, cascading from a crescent fountain (Figure 2). Behind the crescent, a gold mural depicts five Turkmen women, representing the country's five tribes, working in unity behind the frontline. The memorial's subsidiary function is didactic and

---

[10]In other cases where living family members of leaders develop their own cults, they have become a threat to the leader's position. Rifat al-Asad, brother of former Syrian president Hafez al-Asad, is one such example.

FIGURE 1. SECTION OF SOVIET WAR MEMORIAL COMPLEX, ASHGABAT. COMPLETED 1974

FIGURE 2. SECTION OF NEW WAR MEMORIAL COMPLEX, ASHGABAT. COMPLETED 2003

contemporary, suggesting that the war acted as a tribal 'binding agent'. Unlike the Soviet memorial, Atamurat cannot be approached and there is no place where one would spontaneously deposit flowers.

The critical difference between the monuments, which were both the work of Saragt Babayev, lies in the contemporary messages they seek to convey. The Soviet memorial unites Turkmen and Russian communities in struggle and sombre reflection. The new memorial symbolises, through Atamurat (and by extension Niyazov), an explicitly and exclusively Turkmen contribution to the war, divorced from its Soviet–Russian context.

The de-Sovietisation of official war memory was also prevalent in the author's observations of the celebrations on 8–9 May 2005 to mark the 60th anniversary of VE Day. The formal ceremony was held at the Soviet memorial, where there is more space, on the morning of 8 May. Niyazov himself was not present, instead attending a remembrance service in Moscow at which a CIS heads of state summit had also been scheduled. The ceremony was well attended by a smartly dressed crowd comprised mainly of women and children. The most striking aspect of the occasion was its informality and fluidity, and the high visibility of an elderly ethnic Russian contingent. By 2005, the government had become so wary of unsanctioned gatherings that severe restrictions governed the holding of wedding parties, karaoke events and even satellite television screenings of international football matches. Music festivals and concerts held in Ashgabat were invariably state controlled, regimented and rehearsed, their content confined to traditional music, sometimes blended with anodyne Turkish pop music forms.

As a consequence, the crowd at the VE day ceremony seemed unfettered, genuine and even excitable. The official wreaths were laid first by the armed forces, security services, government ministries and foreign diplomats while the (entirely ethnic Turkmen) military band played. Then it was the turn of those gathered. Veterans laid their flowers at the memorial first. However, the large official wreaths interposed before the memorial were fashioned as Seljuk stars. People were therefore required to lay their flowers not before the memorial, but before the symbol of Turkmen nationality. They then proceeded to the arch where mothers and children posed for photographs with veterans of both Russian and Turkmen ethnicity alike. The stream of flower and wreath laying, intermingling between people of different ages and across ethnic communities for several hours, and unmediated by any official choreography or direction, starkly contrasted with the overtly nationalised official commemoration practices.

By contrast, there was no congregation of people during the day at the new war memorial and, until a series of official wreaths were neatly arranged in front of the memorial to Atamurat in the late afternoon (Figure 3), there was, in fact, no indication that the site had any relevance to the remembrance rituals.

Emerging from the observation of Great Patriotic War commemoration was a sense of resilience to official sites and modes of memory production, and a stubborn identification with the Soviet memorial. This, it seemed, was 'Russia's day' in the calendar, an event with which ethnic Turkmen of all ages could happily coalesce, and it therefore represented a site of memory production and nostalgia that could not quite be captured by the state. This became starkly apparent in the coverage of the ceremony on state television channel *Altyn Asyr* later in the day. The commemoration was shorn of grief or value. The camera focused only on ranks of seated Turkmen soldiers, with no shots of ethnic Russians or of members of the public paying their respects. There was no portrayal of the war or context to the celebrations, and the

FIGURE 3. SECTION OF NEW WAR MEMORIAL COMPLEX ASHGABAT ON 60TH ANNIVERSARY OF VE DAY,
8 MAY 2005

images cut repeatedly between the military and the new war memorial, with the formal speeches focusing on the role of Atamurat as the embodiment of Turkmen war heroism.

The following day (9 May 2005) was also a public holiday, and an open-air concert was held in the square between the Arch of Neutrality and the World Trade Complex. The concert consisted of Turkmen singers and musicians miming to nationalist songs, the majority of which extolled the greatness of Turkmenbashi. Veterans were absent and, while the event attracted a sizeable holiday crowd of young Turkmen, the event was far more regimented and closely choreographed, with children holding placards displaying the cover of *Ruhnama*. Television coverage of the concert broadcast later in the day again focused heavily on Atamurat, Niyazov and the new symbols of nationality, without any further contextualisation.

The public holiday to commemorate VE Day was clearly a complex site of symbolism and remembrance. My conspicuous position as an outsider and the heavy security presence precluded interviews, either directly or through a Turkmen language interpreter, with the participants—principally to avoid them being subject to subsequent questioning—but from observation alone, the ceremony at least appeared to reveal certain dissonances and brittleness in the Turkmen government's preferred rendition of the War. This rendition is predicated on detaching official memory from its 'Sovietness'—its multinational, Eurasian character—and instead creating a site where post-Soviet national identity can be affirmed. This task is performed principally by pressing into service Niyazov's deceased father as a vehicle for the narration of national wartime experience and, ultimately, sacrifice. The suddenness and poverty of this creation may go to explain the stubborn popular adherence to Soviet forms of commemoration. Were the same to be said for other commemorative sites and dates, the regime might intervene to alter forcibly patterns of public conduct, as it has done with other public holidays and private festivals. However, such is the symbolic weight and cultural residue of the Soviet cult of the Great Patriotic War that the Turkmen authorities leave unsanctioned commemoration practices alone. The regime does not sanction but also does not disrupt unofficial memory—in doing so, it becomes complicit, somewhat reluctantly, in practices that anchor the state back into its Soviet/Eurasian past.

Conclusion

Great Patriotic War commemoration in contemporary Central Asia provides an intriguing venue in which to test the sophistication, reach and content of post-Soviet nationalising projects. In Turkmenistan's case, even with the most circumscribed civic space of any country in the former communist bloc, and the most intense, uncontested and insistent messages from the regime, the poverty and limitations of post-Soviet identity production are laid bare.

As interviews conducted in 2004 with leading court sculptors Saragt Babayev and Babasary Annamuradov confirm, the cult of Niyazov stemmed more from mid-level officials than from the upper reaches of the regime itself.[11] The cult was viewed as a strategic resource by city, regional and local officials—a mechanism to demonstrate fealty to, and thereafter extract additional resources from, the centre. As a consequence, there has emerged only a very limited vocabulary, repertoire and portfolio of text, ritual and symbol. Berdymuhamedov has done the same, notably in relation to the large numbers of schoolchildren in traditional Turkmen costume arraigned to welcome him during official visits. However, Berdymuhamedov's injunction, at least in the earlier part of his presidency, appears to have been taken seriously, perhaps because it was expressed in terms of the harm done by removing children for many hours from school to take part in the ceremonies, rather than as a ritual expression of modesty. The inclusion of Niyazov's parents as supplementary subjects for cultic veneration broadened the vocabulary of the regime somewhat. In doing so, they removed any residual association Niyazov might carry from the Soviet period, instead building him into a deeper identification with Turkmen national life.

Official Great Patriotic War commemoration has also been co-opted, often rather crudely, into the nation-building project. The great Soviet struggle against fascism has, in common with other aspects of national history, been abruptly decontextualised and despatialised in order to be presented as a rather disembodied conflict in which only those events that pertain directly to the Turkmen people have any significance. The limits of this approach are laid bare when the practices of commemoration are analysed. In short, although one cannot preclude alternative explanations for preferring Soviet remembrances—simple habit, perhaps, or more general resistance to the regime's appropriation of significant anniversaries—at least to this outsider's perception, people appeared to be more content with Soviet renditions of the conflict.

[11]Author's interviews, Ashgabat, 9–10 April 2004.

Although many Turkmen lost their lives in World War II, conflict, mass killings, occupation and collaboration do not greatly 'muddy the waters' of either unofficial or official memory in the way that would be the case in the western former Soviet states. There, practices and popular attitudes may differ greatly. Nevertheless, the Turkmen case may shed some light on where people voluntarily situate their identity, half a generation after the collapse of the Soviet experiment.

The Soviet legacy seems to retain some cultural power and magnetism in Turkmenistan, in ways of doing and performing community memory, notwithstanding the almost total saturation of public space with messages to the contrary, and the concerted drive to remove reminders of Soviet authority. In the Turkmen case, it also exposes the limitations of cult production and propagation more generally. As noted above, lack of ambiguity in ritual construction facilitates rather than captures cognitive dissonance. Murray Edelman (1995, p. 64) argued that 'the more explicit the political message of art, the less influential it is likely to be, for explicit depictions are less able to incite and excite: they either evoke greater resistance or simply objectify conventional beliefs'. By devoting resources to representing and promoting, a very narrow conception of identity through public art and text, the Turkmen government might, in common with their Soviet forbears, inadvertently engender the construction of a very different reality.

Such an eventuality may, in time, lead to the modification of identity production strategies under Niyazov's successor, Gurbanguly Berdymuhamedov. However, the brief 'Ashgabat spring' of 2007 appeared, by mid-2009, to have given way to retrenchment and a reversion to tried and tested political and symbolic practices, albeit greatly toned down from the Niyazov era. Official portraits of Berdymuhamedov have proliferated, but are not as pervasive and have not yet been commodified in the way that Niyazov's cult was. *Ruhnama* has been downgraded in the school curriculum to a civic studies text rather than a history text. Portraits and statues of Niyazov have been removed, as has his portrait on banknotes. Niyazov's name has been removed from the national anthem and oath of allegiance. As discussed earlier, the lesser cults surrounding Niyazov's parents have been progressively and unobtrusively dismantled, although the major statuary, including the new war memorial, still remain intact. This incremental process of decultification has been undertaken with little official comment and, unlike its Stalinist forbear, with no discernible public backlash. The new cult surrounding Berdymuhamedov, official portraiture in public buildings and few hagiographical volumes notwithstanding, is far less brash and expensive. Thus, while Berdymuhamedov appears to be retreating into the governing style of his predecessor, continually purging or reshuffling senior officials and acting as the focal point (and bottleneck) for policy decisions, the regime has not attempted to replicate the Niyazov cult. The reasons are unclear, but the most likely explanation is that, being far less isolated and detached than Niyazov, Berdymuhamedov is aware of the external ridicule and internal indifference with which it was met.

Thus, far from fixing and engendering permanence to Turkmen identity, the political symbolism of Niyazov's cult, as illustrated in the case study, appears to have been shallow, contingent and transient. Its intended effect, to unify the Turkmen nation with Niyazov himself as its focal point, was manifestly unsuccessful, if it is evidenced by its relatively swift removal. Symbolism and spectacle in the Turkmen case is, like its socialist predecessors, a political 'soft power' tactic to legitimise both nation and regime with shaky foundations through visual force in both everyday life (through the urban redesign of Ashgabat) and on special occasions. As with many other insecure and young regimes, notably those created in the defeated Axis powers after World War II, legitimation of government is more likely to come from economic rather than ritual performance.

University of Leeds

References

Adams, L. (2004) 'Cultural Elites in Uzbekistan: Ideological Production and the State', in Luong, P.J. (ed.) (2004) *The Transformation of Central Asia: States and Societies from Soviet Rule to Independence* (Ithaca, NY, Cornell University Press).
Alimov, K.Z. (1994) 'The Rediscovery of Uzbek History and its Foreign Policy Implications', in Starr, S.F. (ed.) (1994) *The Legacy of History in Russia and the New States of Eurasia* (Armonk, NY, M. E. Sharpe).
Åman, A. (1992) *Architecture and Ideology in Eastern Europe during the Stalin Era: An Aspect of Cold War History* (Cambridge, MA, MIT Press).
Amansariev, B. (2003) 'Revived Spirituality', *Miras*, 1.
Amansariev, B. (2004) 'Unfading Symbol of Courage', *Miras*, 2.
Anacker, S. (2003) 'Geographies of Power in Nazarbayev's Astana', *Eurasian Geography and Economics*, 45, 7.
Azaryahu, M. (1997) 'German Reunification and the Politics of Street Names: The Case of East Berlin', *Political Geography*, 16, 3.
Barthold, V.V. (1962) *Four Studies on the History of Central Asia* (Leiden, Brill).
Bell, J. (1998) 'Redefining National Identity in Uzbekistan: Symbolic Tensions in Tashkent's Official Public Landscape', *Ecumene*, 9, 6.
Benton, C. (2004a) 'Introduction', in Benton, C. (ed.) (2004b).
Benton, C. (ed.) (2004b) *Figuration/Abstraction: Strategies for Public Sculpture in Europe, 1945–1968* (Aldershot, Ashgate).
Corney, F.C. (2004) *Telling October: Memory and the Making of the Bolshevik Revolution* (Ithaca, NY, Cornell University Press).
Crowley, D. & Reid, S.E. (2002) 'Socialist Spaces: Sites of Everyday Life in the Eastern Bloc', in Crowley, D. & Reid, S.E. (eds) (2002) *Socialist Spaces: Sites of Everyday Life in the Eastern Bloc* (Oxford, Berg).
Edelman, M. (1995) *From Art to Politics: How Artistic Creations Shape Political Conceptions* (Chicago, IL, Chicago University Press).
Edgar, A.L. (2004) *Tribal Nation: The Making of Soviet Turkmenistan* (Princeton, NJ, Princeton University Press).
Forest, B. & Johnson, J. (2002) 'Unravelling the Threads of History: Soviet-Era Monuments and Post-Soviet National Identity in Moscow', *Annals of the Association of American Geographers*, 92, 3.
Foucault, M. (2002) 'Space, Knowledge and Power', in Faubion, J.D. (ed.) (2002) *Power: The Essential Works of Foucault, 1954–1984*, Volume III (London, Penguin).
Fowkes, R. (2004) 'Soviet War Memorials in Eastern Europe, 1945–1974', in Benton, C. (ed.) (2004b).
Geiss, P.G. (2003) *Pre-Tsarist and Tsarist Central Asia: Communal Commitment and Political Order in Change* (London, RoutledgeCurzon).
Gillis, J.R. (1994a) 'Memory and Identity: The History of a Relationship', in Gillis, J.R. (ed.) (1994b).
Gillis, J.R. (ed.) (1994b) *Commemorations: The Politics of National Identity* (Princeton, NJ, Princeton University Press).
Goonewardena, K. (2004) 'Aborted Identity: The Commission and Omission of a Monument to the Nation, Sri Lanka circa 1989', in Walkowitz, D.J. & Knauer, L.M. (eds) (2004).
Grant, J. (2001) 'The Dark Side of the Grid: Power and Urban Design', *Planning Perspectives*, 16.
Gudkov, L. (2005) 'The Fetters of Victory: How the War Provides Russia with its Identity', *Eurozine*, 3 May.
Gurbanov, M.B. (2001) 'Ten Years of the Cultural Revival of Independent Turkmenistan', *Miras*, 3.

Harloe, M. (1996) 'Cities in the Transition', in Andrusz, G., Harloe, M. & Szelenyi, I. (eds) (1996) *Cities After Socialism: Urban and Regional Change and Conflict in Post-Socialist Societies* (Oxford, Blackwell).

Haugen, A. (2003) *The Establishment of National Republics in Soviet Central Asia* (Basingstoke, Palgrave Macmillan).

Huggler, J. (2004) 'Is This the World's Craziest Dictator?', *The Independent*, 14 April.

Hunt, L. (1986) *Politics, Culture and Class in the French Revolution* (London, Methuen).

Istoriya (1978a) *Istoriya Industrializatsii Turkmenskoi SSR, Tom 1* (Ilim, Ashgabat).

Istoriya (1978b) *Istoriya Industrializatsii Turkmenskoi SSR, Tom 2* (Ilim, Ashgabat).

Jack, M. (2002) 'His Own Little USSR', *Financial Times*, 7 December.

Kacnelson, J.I., Azizov, A.K. & Visocky, E.M. (1987) *Architektura Sovietskoi Turkmenii* (Moscow, Stroyisdat).

Karimov, I.A. (1998) *Uzbekistan on the Threshold of the Twenty-First Century: Challenges to Stability and Progress* (Basingstoke, Palgrave Macmillan).

Kertzer, D. (1988) *Ritual, Power and Politics* (New Haven, CT, Yale University Press).

Klevniuk, O. (1998) 'Les Mechanisms De La "Grand Terreur" des Annés 1937–1938 au Turkmenistan', *Cahiers du monde russe*, 39.

Knauer, L.M. & Walkowitz, D.J. (2004) 'Introduction', in Walkowitz, D.J. & Knauer, L.M. (eds) (2004).

König, W. (1962) *Die Achal-Teke: Zur Wirtschaft und Gesellschaft einer Turkmenen-Gruppe Im 19. Jahrhundert* (Leipzig, Veröffentlichungen des Museums für Völkerkunde zu Leipzig).

Koonz, C. (1994) 'Between Memory and Oblivion: Concentration Camps in German Memory', in Gillis, J.R. (ed.) (1994b).

Kulturnoe (1958) *Kulturnoe Stroitelstva, SSSR*, Central Statistical Board of the USSR, Council of Ministers (Moscow, Foreign Languages Publishing House).

Lane, C. (1981) *The Rites of Rulers: Ritual in an Industrial Society—The Soviet Case* (Cambridge, Cambridge University Press).

March, A. (2003) 'From Leninism to Karimovism: Hegemony, Ideology and Authoritarian Legitimation', *Post-Soviet Affairs*, 19, 4.

Megoran, N. (2005) 'The Critical Geopolitics of Danger in Uzbekistan and Kyrgyzstan', *Environment and Planning D: Society and Space*, 23, 4.

Mitchell, K. (2003) 'Monuments, Memorials and the Politics of Memory', *Urban Geography*, 24, 5.

Mumford, L. (1938) *The Culture of Cities* (New York, Harcourt).

Nepesova, R.G. & Tugiev, C.R. (2001) 'The Holy Ruhnama and the Students', *Miras*, 4.

Nissman, D. (1983) 'Iran and Soviet Islam: The Azerbaijan and Turkmen SSR', *Central Asian Survey*, 2, 4.

Northrop, D. (2004) *Veiled Empire: Gender and Power in Stalinist Central Asia* (Ithaca, NY, Cornell University Press).

Nurbadov, K. (2002) 'The Holy Rukhnama and the Alphabet of Turkmenbashi', *Miras*, 2.

Odekov, R.V. (2001) 'The Holy Rukhnama is Unbottomed Fount of Wisdom and Eternal Verities', *Miras*, 4.

O'Donovan, E. (1882) 'Merv and its Surroundings', in Anon. (ed.) (1977) *The Country of the Turkomans: An Anthology of Exploration from the Royal Geographical Society* (London, Oguz Press).

Osborn, A. (2007) 'Putin's "Successor" Picks Fight with Estonia', *The Independent*, 6 April.

Pauleson, G. (1948) 'In Search of a New Monumentality', *Architectural Review*, September.

Roubal, P. (2003) 'The Politics of Gymnastics: Mass Gymnastic Displays under Communism in Central and Eastern Europe', *Body and Society*, 9, 2.

Sabol, S. (2003) *Russian Colonization of Central Asia and the Genesis of Kazak National Consciousness* (Basingstoke, Palgrave Macmillan).

Saray, M. (1989) *The Turkmens in the Age of Imperialism* (Ankara, Turkish Historical Society).

Schatz, E. (2004) 'What Capital Cities say about State and Nation-Building', *Nationalism and Ethnic Politics*, 9, 4.

Stites, R. (1989) *Revolutionary Dreams: Utopian Vision and Experimental Life in the Russian Revolution* (Oxford, Oxford University Press).

Tumarkin, N. (1983) *Lenin Lives! The Lenin Cult in Soviet Russia* (Cambridge, MA, Harvard University Press).

Turkmen, F. (2003) 'Ruhnama in Soul and Spirit of Turkmen', *Miras*, 3.

Turkmenbashi, S. (2001) *Ruhnama: Reflections on the Spiritual Values of the Turkmen*, Vol. One (Ashgabat, Turkmen dowlet nesirat gullugy).

Turkmenbashi, S. (2004) *Strategic Partnership in the Ideals of Peace and Humanism* (Ashgabat, Turkmen dowlet nesirat gullugy).

Vambery, A. (1865) *Travels in Central Asia: Being the Account of a Journey from Teheran across the Turkoman Desert on the Eastern Shore of the Caspian to Khiva, Bokhara and Samarkand Performed in the Year 1863* (New York, Harper).

Verschaffel, B. (1999) 'The Monumental: On the Meaning of a Form', *Journal of Architecture*, 4, 4.

Walkowitz, D.J. & Knauer, L.M. (eds) (2004) *Memory and the Impact of Political Transformation in Public Space* (Durham, NC, Duke University Press).

Walzer, M. (1967) 'On the Role of Symbolism in Political Thought', *Political Science Quarterly*, 82.

Yaziyev, A. (2003) 'Cultural Doctrine of Saparmurat Turkmenbashi the Great', *Miras*, 4.

Yiftachel, O. (1998) 'Planning and Social Control: Exploring the Dark Side', *Journal of Planning Literature*, 12, 4.

Yurchak, A. (2006) *Everything was Forever, Until it was no More: The Last Soviet Generation* (Princeton, NJ, Princeton University Press).

Promising Futures? Education as a Symbolic Resource of Hope in Kyrgyzstan

SARAH S. AMSLER

PROGRAMMES OF EDUCATIONAL REFORM IN Central Asian societies—as in many other societies across the globe—are often presumed to be either reflections of dominant political and economic change or tools for achieving it. In this essay, which uses higher education reform in Kyrgyzstan as a case study for theoretical analysis, I argue for an alternative, more constructivist interpretation of the relationship between education and the political. This is that educational work is a key site for the articulation of social imaginaries and for defining the cultural and political practices through which they may legitimately be realised. My argument proceeds as follows. In the first part of the essay, I introduce some of the dominant claims made about the political meaning of higher education reform in contemporary Kyrgyzstan. I then offer a theoretical explanation of why education is an important space of cultural politics as well as an institution of socialisation, drawing on cultural theory, the sociology of knowledge and especially the work of Pierre Bourdieu to explicate how the idea of education may become an *idée-force*—'an idea which has social force'—in contexts of major social change (Bourdieu 2001, p. 34). Following this I explore how the idea of education in Kyrgyzstan has been articulated within and against wider cultural discourses of Marxism–Leninism and neoliberal capitalism, and discuss how these processes of articulation have shaped the present-day imagination of the futures education might promise. I illustrate this specifically by looking at how certain pedagogical styles have become articulated as signifiers of 'competing' political cultures within the society. Finally, I consider the implications of this signification for the development of alternative ideas about educational reform.

Understanding education as a resource of hope

As in many other post-Soviet societies, initial post-independence assessments of education in Kyrgyzstan were made against a background of 'total social collapse' and in the context of a predetermined 'transition' of the society from parochial communist authoritarianism to liberal democracy, free-market capitalism and global citizenship.[1]

---

[1] For an excellent critique of 'intellectual reductionism in the analysis of transition', see Thompson (2008, pp. 23–24). In my view, this is most accurately characterised as an embracing of neoliberalism, and for further reading on the economic, political and cultural dimensions of this regime I recommend exploring work by Antonio (2007), Bourdieu (2001) and Harvey (2005).

While the rhetoric of reform emphasised the importance of depoliticising education by disentangling it from the requirements of centralised state power, education continued to be conceptualised as both a tool for advancing new forms of cultural and economic change and a space in which such changes might be practised, observed and evaluated.

There were (and are) justifiable laments about the 'crisis of science and education', which was understood to be caused primarily by 'the economic collapse and the inevitable decline of state expenditures for the social sphere in these conditions' (Bokonbaev 1995, p. 50).[2] In the late 1990s, the situation in Kyrgyzstan was similar to that in Kazakhstan, as described by DeYoung and Valyayeva (1997, p. 34):

> The teachers we surveyed could in fact report that at one or another school, something positive might be happening. Nevertheless, they report, the national school system is in complete chaos. The overwhelming majority of those who answered our survey claim that schools are much worse than before and are steadily declining. They indeed do use the word chaos to describe this situation, as well as 'collapse', 'breakdown', 'ruin', and 'devastation'.

> Whatever their earlier hopes for freedom and autonomy and creativity had been, teachers today report their situation as disastrous: no respect, too little pay, and no coherent educational direction beyond what they may have in their own buildings.

However, these conditions have been an impetus for reform, and the criticisms have thus been matched by hopes that the crisis might open space for a new kind of education, either through relegislating its functions, funding and organisation (Kakeev 1995, p. 6), or by embarking upon its curricular 'humanisation' (Isaev 1993). Institutions and practices of education in Kyrgyzstan hence function as resources of private and social hope. At a societal level, this includes the hope that literacy of all kinds will enable autonomy and independence; that socialisation will enable civility; that knowledge will cement social stability and economic development or provoke innovative change; and that cognitive, affective and technical skills will ensure meaningful and competent labour.[3] For educators and students, education often privately promises the fulfilment of desires which are denied possibility through other means—the possibility of open futures and economic security; professional recognition and satisfaction of work; personal self-development; membership in a privileged elite; protection from marginalisation and exclusion; and legitimacy under a global gaze of third-world neglect and, in some cases, disrespect. There is little ambiguity here about the social and political import of education; indeed, the belief that education is the natural bridge between a damaged past and improved future makes these localised hopes intelligible parts of a more global faith in the social value of education itself (Grubb & Lazarsen 2006; Popkewitz 1991).

As a result of these subjective associations of education with social progress, discourses on educational reform are often framed in technical terms which focus on how knowledge production in general, and learning and teaching in particular, should

---

[2]See also Sabloff (1999).

[3]For more on education as a resource of hope in the contemporary global context, see Freyberg-Inan and Cristescu (2007), Giroux (2005), Lauder et al. (2006), Robertson et al. (2007) and Svi Shapiro (2009).

be conducted in order to accomplish these socially agreed-upon ends. There is, therefore, voluminous publication of reports about the contributions that formal education—primary and higher, cultural and political—might make to the society's economic, political and social 'development' (e.g. Anderson & Heyneman 2005; Berryman 2000; Briller & Iskakova 2004; Heyneman 1998). This is an internally contested body of knowledge which includes both academic research and organisational documentation, and a great deal of debate within Central Asian educational studies revolves around which types of education are most viable, progressive or desirable, and who (or what) should organise and finance them. On the other hand is a more minor collection of critical work which explores the ways that certain forms of education are implicated in creating or exacerbating social inequalities, studies the practical relationships between knowledge and power in classrooms and boardrooms, interrogates the politics of national and international educational policy, and highlights imbalances of cultural and economic power within programmes of 'development education'.[4]

However, despite voluminous output, there has been relatively little research into the idea of education in Kyrgyzstan: to what education means and how it is experienced by educators and learners; to why different notions of knowledge, learning and social change garner uneven cultural legitimacy within the society; or to how and why beliefs about education become forged in efforts to construct meaningful narratives of personal agency against the ideological backdrop of an autopoietic and dehumanised notion of social 'transition'.[5] These questions matter, because in practice the concept of education signifies complex fields of expectation and desire rather than describing or prescribing it (Giroux 2005; Popkewitz *et al.* 2001). Furthermore, because education is regarded as a set of institutions through which individuals and groups can self-consciously shape the future, struggles over the cultural meaning of the idea of education rise to the surface of political discourse particularly clearly in conditions of social crisis and transformation. In such moments, the symbolic meaning of education assumes particular import as 'both an ideal and a referent for change in the service of a new kind of society' (Giroux 1985, p. xiii). As educational theorist Henry Giroux suggests,

> education is that terrain where power and politics are given a fundamental expression, since it is where meaning, desires, language and values engage and respond to the deeper beliefs about the very nature of what it means to be human, to dream, and to name and struggle for a particular future and way of life. (1985, p. xiii)

Conceptualising education as a symbolic resource of hope in this way is thus important for understanding the complex politics of educational reform in

---

[4]I am thinking here of work by Madeleine Reeves (2004, 2005), Alan deYoung (2002, 2007), and Safarov Niyozov (2006), which engage more directly with the cultural politics of education and the ethnographic study of and with educators in Kyrgyzstan. Norma Jo Baker and Chad Thompson have, individually (Thompson 2008) and together (Baker & Thompson 2009), also made important interventions in critically reconceptualising 'liberal education' in Central Asia.

[5]For more on the project of the 'critical study of cultural practices' in the work of Pierre Bourdieu and other critical sociologists of culture, see Swartz (1997).

'transitional' societies; in this case, in post-Soviet Central Asian societies, and Kyrgyzstan in particular.[6] Here, questions about how to theorise human nature, which are implicit in all educational activities, have become sites of struggle between competing notions of the human subject. Here, the choice of educational 'models'—to follow an 'American' model in developing a system of standardised testing for university enrolment (Drummond & DeYoung 2004) for example, or to construct an institutional identity based on 'critical thinking' (Reeves 2005)—are choices about identity and geopolitical economy as much as they are problems of pedagogy and administration. They are intellectual and emotional investments not just in a particular way of doing things, but also in whole ways of being in the world. They are, in other words—and perhaps sometimes only in the deepest recesses of consciousness—investments of hope in alternative futures.

Shifting focus: from educational facts to the 'idea of education'

It is this deeper symbolic significance of education that interests me here, and that opens up possibilities for a critical analysis of educational reform from the perspectives of the sociology of knowledge and culture. Karl Mannheim once wrote that 'when any human activity continues over a long period without being subjected to control or criticism, it tends to get out of hand' (Mannheim 1991, p. 1). He also argued that by not subjecting our commonsense meanings to critical interrogation, we may find that 'those methods of thought by means of which we arrive at our most crucial decisions, and through which we seek to diagnose and guide our political and social destiny, have remained unrecognised and therefore inaccessible to intellectual control and self-criticism' (Mannheim 1991, p. 26). Much more recently, this insight has been developed by critical theorists such as Pierre Bourdieu, who 'stresses the active role played by the taken-for-granted assumptions and practices in the construction and resistance of power relations' (Swartz 1997, p. 89). Bourdieu argued that as a site of organised power over the determination and distribution of cultural, social and academic capital, education is one of the most politically significant institutions in any society. For Bourdieu, the uncritical understanding of education as simply or primarily a tool for technical progress prevents us from recognising that it is the 'preeminent institutional machinery for the certification of social hierarchies in advanced nation-states, and for this reason a central ground and stake in democratic struggles' (Wacquant 2005, p. 134).

The insights of Mannheim and Bourdieu may be usefully applied to unpack the idea of education in Kyrgyzstan today, for while 'education' is widely discussed in public space, its deeper political and affective meanings are seldom articulated in an explicit way. Talk about education in Kyrgyzstan is ubiquitous and appears on diverse registers. The state professes an ostensible commitment to supporting education, although in practice this has translated into very low levels of investment in schooling (Ministry of Education 2006; Shagdar 2006; Tiuliundieva 2006), and into what Muzaffar Toursunov has referred to as a 'gap between good intentions and tangible

---

[6]For further discussion, see Amsler (2007, pp. ix–xiv).

improvements' (2008).[7] Foreign governments have invested considerable sums of money in promoting and supporting particular forms of education, often as part of their more general 'development' and foreign policy programmes (de la Soblonnière *et al.* 2009; DeYoung 2002), and international organisations host a range of educational embassies and programmes, for example, the Asian Development Bank (Asanova 2006). Finally, individual philanthropists, namely George Soros and the Aga Khan, have built competing, multi-million dollar cultural empires around educational centres in the region (Silova & Steiner-Kamsi 2009).

Apart from basic facts of this sort, however, what might it mean to speak of the 'idea' of education? It is, of course, possible to identify formal institutions of education in Kyrgyzstan and to understand their declared functions within the society. It is also possible to distinguish a wide range of educational practices within the society, including teaching, learning, facilitating, training, managing knowledge, consulting and researching; and indeed, doing so is an important element of pedagogical science in the society. For example, both Russian and Kyrgyz languages retain clear semantic distinctions between *vospitanie* or *tarbiyaloo* (cultural socialisation and moral improvement) on the one hand, and *obrazovanie* or *bilem beruu* (the transmission or refinement of knowledge and skills), on the other.[8] Both languages have also incorporated the term *treining* (training), and each of these practices is further distinguished from the creative production of new knowledge through *issledovanie* (research). When prefixed by more narrowly focused adjectives—*narodnoe obrazovanie* (people's education) or *dukhovnoe vospitanie* (spiritual or moral guiding), for example, or *sovremennoe* as opposed to *traditsionnoe obrazovanie* ('modern' versus 'traditional' forms of education)—the form of the idea of education becomes ever more filtered through the situated lenses of concrete political imaginaries.

However, knowledge of these observable institutions, functions and practices does not necessarily shed light on the underlying relationships, theories, beliefs, interests and emotions which give rise to and legitimise these social functions and practices of education in the first place. The multitude of terms which stand for 'education' in everyday discourse do not exhaustively describe or represent specific institutions or sets of practices, even though they are often discursively employed in this way. Rather, they work as a kind of symbolic shorthand for complex, tacit and often sublimated theories about the relationship between the transformation of subjective consciousness and the future condition of society itself, about the relationship between education and power, and the role of knowledge in social governance and subjective freedom. In addition to thinking about education as a set of institutions and practices, therefore,

---

[7]According to the Kyrgyzstan Ministry of Education, Science and Youth Policy, the state budgeted 7.6% of its GDP to education in 1990, fluctuated thereafter with an all-time low of 3.5% in 2000, rose to 4.6% in 2005 and 8.7% in 2003 (Shagdar 2006, p. 521). In 2007, the United Nations reported that between 2002 and 2005 an estimated average of 4.4% of the GDP was directed towards education (United Nations Development Programme 2007, p. 267). To put this in some international context, during the same period Iceland (ranked first on the UNDP's 'human development' indicators, or HDI) spent an average of 8.1% of GDP, Sierra Leone (ranked last on the HDI) an estimated 4.6%, and Russia (ranked 67th of 177 countries/territories) an estimated 3.6% (United Nations Development Programme 2007, pp. 266–68).

[8]I am grateful to Madeleine Reeves for clarifying this terminology in Kyrgyz.

we can also consider it to be an idea. The 'idea of education' refers to any situated constellation of representations, images, values, relationships, memories and imaginations—and to the expectations and anxieties—that are embodied in and expressed through particular educational discourses and practices.

While an idea of education may thus share some elements of an ideology of education, the two concepts should not be confused. The first implies more fluid and less intentionalist relationships between reason and affect, signifier and signified, fact and imagination, and past and future. In particular, it extends theories of the materialist origin of knowledge and belief to explain how the meaning of any cultural practice emerges through symbolic constellations, in which 'one moment sheds light on the other, and the figures that these individual moments form together are specific signs and a legible script' (Adorno 1994, p. 109). The concept of an idea of education also allows us to recognise that emotions and practices of emancipatory consciousness (such as hope and fear) work to orient social action; in this case, shaping the character of educational practices and the outcomes of educational reform (Amsler 2008b; Anderson 2006; Rorty 1999; Zournazi 2002b). These affective dimensions of the idea of education are not necessarily conscious elements of self-understanding or ideology, but apprehensible as what Raymond Williams once called 'structures of feeling' (Williams 2001, p. 64), and what Ben Anderson has more recently referred to as 'affective cultural politics' (2006, p. 749).[9] The concepts of the idea of education and of the constellation therefore enable us to map the diverse and often conflicting ways that the idea of education is instantiated in personal identity projects, struggles for cultural influence and contests of political authority in contemporary Kyrgyzstan.

The cultural politics of educational reform in historical perspective

In order to understand these cultural politics, however, it is important to recognise that they are not uniquely post-Soviet phenomena. Education has been linked both symbolically and practically to the politics of technological and social progress throughout the history of modernist development projects in Central Asia, from Tsarist to Soviet and through to capitalist interventions (Amsler 2007; Thompson 2008). It is precisely because the idea of education can continue to (re)signify a range of competing political interests and visions of the future, and not because it marks a departure from them, that it remains as a key site for symbolic struggle.

As Kyrgyzstan began its geopolitical ascendance in Soviet space during the mid-twentieth century, the institutionalisation of formal education symbolised progress in both technological and cultural modernisation, thus legitimising Russian colonisation of the region and providing an orientation for the society's Westward-looking development. In the official (Communist Party) narratives of this time, it was argued that prior to the October Revolution 'the Kirghiz people were in number the most severely deprived, in the sense of education, enlightenment and knowledge, with only the elementary trappings of civilisation, and without a national written language' (Tabyshaliev 1984, p. 161). From this barren memory of humble beginnings, the enlightenment of the imperial borderlands could be clearly mapped through the

[9]See also Ahmed (2004).

progress of formal education itself, and particularly of linguistic and scientific literacy: first as the population encountered 'Russian and Western' travelling scholars, and finally 'during Soviet rule, when, among other socialist transformations, the culture of revolution was realised in the periphery' (Tabyshaliev 1984, p. 162).

Some decades later, as the Soviet state struggled to contain growing forces of regionalisation within the non-Russian republics, this idea of education was criticised as having legitimised anti-democratic centralisation, and it was rearticulated to frame new localised visions that were linked to new projects of regional and republican autonomy—or as one Kyrgyz social scientist put it, to the 'revolutionary renewal of Soviet society on the whole and in the union republics in particular' (Isaev 1991, p. 32). In some ways, these ideas of education were integral parts of wider nationalising discourses across the non-Russian Soviet republics during *perestroika*. In another sense, however, they may also be interpreted through the lens of more subjective desires for recognition, self-determination and resource control from subordinated members of an unequal society. As DeYoung and Valyayeva argued of teachers in Kazakhstan, 'reform-minded professional educators tied many of their hopes for educational change to the national movement for *glasnost*' as well' (1997, p. 23). However, these hopes submerged soon after they surfaced, with the disappearance of the Russian 'other' of power and the emergence of new sites of economic power and cultural authority in the global North.[10]

Following independence, the horizon of social imagination about what education was, what it was for and how it ought to be accomplished in Kyrgyzstan became embedded in a meta-narrative of post-Soviet—and primarily neoliberal—educational and social reform. By the mid-1990s it was possible for once communist-identified educators to argue that 'the paradigm of the new global thinking today is the assertion that the fate of humanity is becoming more dependent on the individual resources of the person...human capital, personality, its value orientations and morality' (Arzymatova & Artykbaev 1995, p. 79). As one Kyrgyzstan-based social scientist wrote more explicitly,

> the fact that Kyrgyzstan obtained an independent political status, the transformations occurring in society, the transition to a market economy and the democratisation of social life have created fundamental changes in the educational system ... As our and foreign experience shows, the system of education requires constant improvement. In the history of our education, we also have had efforts to reform it. However, in the conditions of a totalitarian state and ideologicised society, they could not objectively bring to fruition the renewal of education in the spirit of the times... The new conceptions of education maintain the

[10]The 'global North' refers to the world's wealthiest and most industrially advanced societies, particularly in North America, Europe and Oceania. In a broader definition it also includes the economically strongest countries in Asia, and replaces both discursively and geographically earlier concepts of 'first' or 'developed' world. The analytical use of such spatial classifications is increasingly questionable, due to the deterritorialisation and globalisation of capitalism, the emergence of politico-economic alliances such as the G-7, G-8, G-20 and G-33, categories such as 'BRIC' (Brazil, Russia, India and China) and 'emerging economies'. However, for the purposes of this argument and in the context of late-Soviet and early post-Soviet international relations, it remains useful. For more on the concept, see Therien (1999).

independence of educational institutions from ideological institutions, creates the conditions for competition in the sphere of education and the free development of educational institutions in all forms of property, gives the legal foundations for the creation of ties with state and non-state institutions and also for the gradual decentralisation of state administration and the imagination of educational institutions with wide independence. (Kakeev 1995, pp. 6–7)

At first glance, none of these claims seems particularly remarkable. However, a closer reading suggests that the idea of education that is articulated here operates as a something of a symbolic shibboleth. To understand education in this particular sense, to accept the values and practices which underpin these programmes of reform, also communicates an acceptance of and at least formal commitment to the simultaneous affirmation of the economic, political and social values of liberal democracy and neoliberal capitalism. What it does not communicate, however, is an invitation to critically unpack all the symbolically pregnant and politically powerful references to 'independence', 'transformation', 'the market economy', 'totalitarianism', 'ideology', 'competition', 'free development' and 'decentralisation', or to interrogate the particular way that they are woven together into a particular constellation of what education is and is for.

The neoliberal idea of education in Kyrgyzstan

From this example, we can better understand how the idea of education in Kyrgyzstan functions as what Bourdieu described as 'a myth in the strong sense of the word, a powerful discourse, an *idée-force*, an idea which has social force, which obtains belief'; or more simply, as a complex idea or discourse that is imbued with performative social and political legitimacy, authority and power (2001, p. xx). As I have argued elsewhere (Amsler 2008a), many teachers, students and policy makers in the post-communist world—including some who are sceptical that this particular economic and political 'transition' is desirable or even occurring—maintain faith in the power of formal higher education to enable both individual and social progress within a global capitalist system. The rhetorical promises of a de-Sovietised, de-ideologicised and liberalised education might even be said to have assumed the character of a new 'education gospel'. Grubb and Lazerson define the 'Education Gospel' as a globalised discourse of education which 'stresses the failures of schools and universities and then proceeds to reform them with more economic and utilitarian goals' (2006, p. 295), in which teaching and learning are viewed 'as central to national competitiveness in the global knowledge economy' (Lauder *et al.* 2006, p. 3).

Many of the new ideas of education that have emerged since independence indeed resonate with hegemonic discourses of economic liberalism, democracy, development, global citizenship and civil society. Early on in its career of educational reform, the Kyrgyz state adopted elements of a neoliberal vocabulary, issuing a succession of laws and decrees on the necessity of 'marketising', 'democratising', and creating competition in (mainly higher) education. These included a Law on Education (1992), a national Education Doctrine (2000), an educational Development Plan (2002), adoption of the 'Education for All' goals specified in the Dakar Agreement

(2002), constitutional revisions (2003), and a second new Law on Education (2003).[11] In another development, academics and managers at a small number of *vuzy* (higher educational institutions) in Kyrgyzstan have also worked since 1994 to 'take an active part in [the] global project of the creation of [a] European–Asiatic space of higher education' through implementing principles of the Bologna Process in particular fields (Dzhaparova 2006; Resolution 2007).[12] National government bodies such as the UK's Department for International Development continue to monitor Kyrgyzstan's achievements in basic and tertiary education as part of a wider 'development' framework (Robertson *et al.* 2007).

However, the idea of education in Kyrgyzstan is obviously considerably more diverse than this, and neoliberal imaginaries of reform are far from hegemonic in practice (Amsler 2007, 2008a; Liu 2003). In the first instance, the hope that education promises brighter individual and societal futures often coexists awkwardly with educators' and students' lived experiences. Many schools and universities located outside the elite centres of cultural capital and economic privilege remain extremely deprived (DeYoung 2007, p. 243; Niyozov 2006; Tiuliundieva 2006; Toursunov 2008). Within the elite centres themselves, educators speak of subordination to gender, ethnic and cultural 'superiors', constraints on intellectual autonomy, and physically and financially impossible workloads (Amsler 2007). Perhaps unsurprisingly, in recent years admiration for some of the educational achievements of the Soviet past has increased (Reeves 2005, p. 10), as has interest in localised theories of moral and cultural education, such as those based on the redefined 'seven precepts of Manas' (DeYoung 2007). DeYoung has highlighted the significant differences between the effort to 'build open societies' in the region, as according to the Soros Foundation's mandate, and the banking and finance initiatives to create 'future participants in the world capitalist economy', according to the Asian Development Bank (2002, p. 14). There are also now pockets of more radical creative development in education, such as the introduction of the Theatre of the Oppressed for use with rural communities and vulnerable young people,[13] and critical research projects are routinely undertaken by the Social Research Center at the American University in Kyrgyzstan. One such study, funded by the Aga Khan Development Network, is particularly interesting here as it reveals the complex symbolic politics of work now being undertaken by a dizzying number of national and international organisations in order to construct definitions and pedagogies of 'civic education' in secondary, higher and adult education (Social Research Center 2007).

In other words, the idea of education can only be articulated in particular terms by reading it through other symbolic discourses, social practices and material realities. Saying that education promises futures is not equal to saying that learning creates opportunities, or that progress in knowledge contributes to personal emancipation or social improvement. The idea of education can be symbolically reappropriated and

[11]See Amsler (2008a) and Ministry of Education (2006, p. 6).
[12]For details about initiatives to align Kyrgyzstani higher education with the Bologna agreement, see http://www.bolognakg.net/, accessed 20 March 2009.
[13]Theatre of the Oppressed Project in Kyrgyzstan and Central Asia main website available at: http://www.toprojectcentralasia.org/page2.php, accessed 23 May 2009.

reassigned to mean, represent and signify contradictory things. As Ghassan Hage recently argued, we therefore 'need to look at what kind of hope a society encourages rather than simply whether it gives people hope or not' (Zournazi 2002c, p. 152). In the words of Chantal Mouffe, 'the desire for hope is ineradicable, but if democratic political parties and democratic systems do not provide a vehicle for this then we are in the situation where other forms of hope are articulated' (Zournazi 2002b, p. 125). It is in this sort of symbolic space that an idea of education can assume mythological status as an inherently transformative and progressive practice precisely because no other futures are imminently imaginable.

It is against this concern that it becomes important to explore the ways that particular ideas of education are articulated, legitimated and challenged through educational practices. This is necessary not only in order to illuminate the relationship between politics and education, but also because such an understanding can help educators clarify the possibilities of advancing alternative visions of education and, by extension, of society. Whilst acknowledging the complex diversity of experience and activity in everyday practice, my point of departure for this argument is that a neoliberal idea of education either dominates or frames many discourses of educational reform in Kyrgyzstan, and that everyday educational practices are connected both symbolically and materially to wider processes of economic and cultural globalisation. This, of course, does not assume that all international educational organisations working in Kyrgyzstan are monolithic instruments of cultural imperialism.[14] I rather would like to make the basic observation that within the society, and indeed globally, the horizon of imagination about possible approaches to economic organisation, political process and educational activity is not limitless or even very diverse. Few educators, students, governmental bodies, non-governmental organisations or international organisations now working in Kyrgyzstan are developing theories and practices of education which draw on any philosophical or political traditions in socialism, participatory economics, anarchism or other alternatives to capitalism. While this observation may be received as absurd in the 'post-socialist' context, the fact that it is so obvious and yet so seldom made or considered legitimate is significant. There may be no paragons, but there are certainly some clear parameters. In fact, the symbolic naturalisation of this historical conjuncture is one characteristic of a form of discourse that French sociologists Loïc Waquant and Pierre Bourdieu once called 'neoliberal newspeak'—in their definition, a globalising 'form of symbolic violence' that works through 'universalizing the particularisms bound up with a singular historical experience by making them misrecognized as such and recognized as universal' (Wacquant & Bourdieu 2001, p. 2).

Teaching for the transition: pedagogical form as symbolic politics

But how does a particular social value become interpreted and performed as a universal one? How do everyday activities—in this case, the choice of approaches to classroom teaching—function as sources of symbolic power? And how can we learn to

---

[14]Thanks to one of the anonymous reviewers for highlighting that the argument might be read in this clearly reductivist manner.

see the cultural politics of education critically in situations where these politics themselves are interpreted as resources of personal and social hope? To answer these questions, I will consider the symbolic politics of 'lectures' and 'seminars'—or in other words, 'teacher-expert' and 'student-centred' approaches to teaching (de la Soblonnière 2009)—in contemporary Kyrgyzstan. In recent years, particularly in those immediately following independence, the classification of these pedagogical forms into competing sets of political values has been a major activity for reformers from international organisations, the Ministry of Education, and the ranks of professional educators. This is, of course, not particular to Kyrgyzstan: the infamous thousand-strong student lectures in European higher education, late twentieth-century debates about the necessity for more 'student-centred' learning in Britain and the United States, the debate between the 'banking model of education' and 'critical pedagogy' in Latin America, and new developments in 'active learning' more internationally are sufficient evidence of a general (if not generalisable) trend.

In Kyrgyzstan, however, the debate has a heightened symbolic dimension, as it

> becomes especially pronounced in societies experiencing fast paced political, economic and social changes, because the question of what should be taught and how it should be taught becomes a matter for the very future survival of the society. (de la Soblonnière *et al.* 2009)

Furthermore, in addition to (or rather than) being a technical choice about the value of different approaches to pedagogy, the normative classification of lectures and seminars in Kyrgyzstan 'requires teachers and students to respectively modify their thinking and actions towards education' (de la Soblonnière *et al.* 2009). For de la Soblonnière *et al.*, this is primarily a problem of teachers relinquishing authority over knowledge production and students assuming responsibility for it. The authors argue that in Western societies, 'teachers and students have been exposed to both the teacher/expert and student-centred approaches from public debates and real-life experiences in classrooms', and that a 'variety of approaches have been developed under the umbrella of the student-centred approach' (de la Soblonnière *et al.* 2009). They contrast this to the more teacher-expert focus of teachers in Central Asian societies, most of whom had little exposure to this debate or to 'the alternative way to conceptualise education' (de la Soblonnière *et al.* 2009). The result is that 'in spite of all the changes in the educational system in the region during the last decade, we cannot say that there has been a significant shift toward a student-centered approach where the learner plays a more active, constructionist role' (de la Soblonnière *et al.* 2009).

The authors then offer four inter-related explanations for why a majority of educators may resist adopting new student-centred approaches to teaching: 'the lack of motivation, the reluctance to compromise their privileged position, the need for facilitating conditions, and the paucity of resources' (de la Soblonnière *et al.* 2009). However, they also argue that the normalisation of student-centred pedagogies is a normative struggle for influence:

> Because the minority... of people promoting the student-centered approach do not have the benefit of widespread support, they have to be acutely aware of their message compared to

those favouring the traditional teacher/expert approach who try to exert influence on them.... In order to be persuasive, the minority proclaiming the student-centered approach must be doggedly vocal, unified and consistent in their arguments. Faced with such a determined minority, the majority who may feel no pressure to comply, may begin to engage in what theorists label a 'validation process'. (de la Soblonnière *et al.* 2009)

If this is successful, they argue, it will give 'Kyrgyzstan's educational system ... increased hope for applying a student-centred approach' (de la Soblonnière *et al.* 2009). The question is, what is it exactly about this particular educational philosophy that promises hope for a better future for teachers, students and the wider society, and why? What is the political and economic content of this hope? Why would it require a social movement to legitimise and normalise it in the educational community? And how is the 'validation process' referred to above dependent on the transformation of symbolic power; of what Bourdieu called 'symbolic capital', or the resources of authority to interpret and define the world?

Here, individual and institutional preferences for teacher-expert pedagogies rather than for student-centred ones are interpreted as a sort of wilful resistance to progress, a lack of motivation to try something new, ignorance about the possibilities of the primary alternative, and a war of position waged to maintain professional status and hegemonic authority within the system. However, the debate may also be interpreted as a practical example of a more generalised 'struggle for the production and imposition of the legitimate vision of the social world' (Bourdieu 1989, p. 22). This is thus not simply an attempt to shape teaching practices, but a political project to change the world by changing the way that people make sense of it, by altering the distribution of value and esteem within existing social classifications, and thereby altering the distribution of power amongst classes themselves (Bourdieu 1989). Disagreements about the pedagogical merits of authoritative, positivist, behaviourist philosophies of teaching and constructivist and participatory ones (de la Soblonnière *et al.* 2009) are also struggles to establish new collective identities and 'beliefs about the very nature of what it means to be human, to dream, and to name and struggle for a particular future and way of life' (Giroux 1985, p. xiii).

To clarify how this is articulated with wider political and economic projects in practice, it is instructive to examine how teacher-expert and student-centred approaches are classified in relation to one another in a dualistic way, and how they function as normative 'signs of distinction' (Bourdieu 1989, p. 20). Figure 1 lays out, in schematic fashion, some common normative connotations of the concepts of 'the lecture' and 'the seminar' in educational discourses in contemporary Kyrgyzstan. These terms represent, respectively, the teacher-expert and student-centred approaches, and in practice are used to signify a diverse range of actual teaching practices.[15] Each approach occupies a different location within the broader culture and political economy of post-Soviet educational reform. The 'lecture' is associated primarily with the old society and ways of being, which must be overcome in order to

[15]For further reading on semiotic theories of denotation (the literal or intended meaning of a sign) and connotation (a sign's symbolic, affective and ideological meanings), see Barthes (1977), Hall (1980) and Panofsky (1970).

Lecture	Seminar
→ 'transition' →	
didactic	interactive
passive	active
authoritarian	democratic
illiberal	liberal
dogmatic	critical
domination	autonomy
power	freedom
backward	progressive
traditional	modern
old	new

FIGURE 1. SYMBOLIC CONNOTATIONS OF TEACHER-EXPERT AND STUDENT-CENTRED PEDAGOGIES IN EDUCATIONAL DISCOURSES IN KYRGYZSTAN

make room for new and more progressive possibilities in both the classroom and society. It is thus symbolically marked not only as pedagogically inferior but also politically dubious, and articulated as being antithetical to the new idea of education itself, or related only to its distorted or dysfunctional form. The 'seminar', on the other hand, is a space in which students are invited and expected to engage in 'active learning' and critical thinking, and is routinely associated in affirmative ways with the progressive idea of education. This dualism is schematised in Figure 1.

These normative connotations are not merely legitimised through reference to alternative but recognisable traditions of educational theory (for example, those of John Dewey, Lev Vygotsky and Paulo Freire), but also affirmed through their homologous affinity to dominant discourses of capitalist development and liberal democracy. The political character of this dualism is hegemonic rather than dialectical in character; the aim being to define a unidirectional 'transition' in educational identities and reforms that can reflect and serve the wider 'transition' from state to market in the society's geopolitical economy. The symbolic politics of teacher-expert and student-centred education is strikingly homologous to the cultural connotations of the ideas of 'the state' and 'the market', which Wacquant and Bourdieu proposed in their 'summary table of the elementary forms of neoliberal thought' (Figure 2). This set of oppositions, they argued, rests on a series of oppositions and equivalences which support and reinforce one another to depict the contemporary transformations advanced societies are undergoing, economic disinvestment by the state and

State	Market
→ globalisation →	
constraint	freedom
closed	open
rigid	flexible
immobile, fossilised	dynamic, moving, self-transforming
past, outdated	future, novelty
stasis	growth
group, lobby, holism, collectivism	individual, individualism
uniformity, artificiality	diversity, authenticity
autocratic ('totalitarian')	democratic

Source: Wacquant & Bourdieu 2001, p. 5.

FIGURE 2. SUMMARY TABLE OF THE ELEMENTARY FORMS OF NEOLIBERAL THOUGHT

reinforcement of its police and penal components, deregulation of financial flows and relaxation of administrative controls on the employment market, reduction of social protection and moralising celebration of 'individual responsibility', as in turn 'benign, necessary, ineluctable or desirable' (Wacquant & Bourdieu 2001, p. 5).

The homologies between these two otherwise unconnected sets of symbolic oppositions—the connotations of educational philosophies on the one hand and of 'neoliberal newspeak' on the other (Wacquant & Bourdieu 2001)—suggest that even the most seemingly technical debates about pedagogical practice in Kyrgyzstan may be inflected with a wider cultural politics of capitalist globalisation.[16] It is, therefore, important to recognise the explicitly political role that such signifying concepts and systems of classification play in naturalising a neoliberal idea of education within the organisation of everyday teaching practices, and ultimately into the governance of self, esteem and social hope.

Conclusion

The notion of 'symbolic politics' can evoke a rationalised image of individuals, often in elite positions of social power, instrumentally creating and using ideas, representations and symbols in conscious and deliberate ways in order to accomplish particular political objectives. In this instrumentalist view, symbolic representation is

---

[16]This, of course, does not preclude their simultaneous articulation with other discourses, such as that of post-Soviet 'democratic transition' as described by Chad Thompson (2008, pp. 23–25), or of cultural struggle between 'East' and 'West' (DeYoung 2002).

conceptualised as a mechanism of political manipulation, of representing constructed things—or in some cases as constructing imaginary things—which are then transformed into cognitive and affective objects that can be externalised and appropriated to unify conflicting groups, crystallise a collective emotional experience, or reduce complex and ambiguous political situations into simplified narratives or images for mass conversion. The purpose of studying symbolic politics from this perspective is to understand how the dysfunctions of language, knowledge and cultural imaginaries work to construct representations of 'social reality' which serve and extend the interests of the powerful. The attraction of this approach is that if we can decode these signs we can see through them, perhaps catching a glimpse of the 'real' political reality.

Without doubt, in cases of wilful propaganda this intentionalist theory of meaning offers a useful, if partial, framework for analysis. In this essay, however, I have attempted to present a different relationship between the symbolic and the political— namely, that these forms of power are mutually constituted and constituting. To illustrate this, I have attempted to explore how and why the idea of education— particularly the neoliberal idea of education—has assumed particular subjective meanings and action-orienting potentials for educators in Kyrgyzstan. Despite widespread acknowledgement amongst many that the official narrative of Soviet-led educational progress was frequently deployed as a blatant ideology to legitimise economic, cultural and political control, and amongst many others that developmentalist views of education may be equally as ideological, there are also deep, lasting, emotional attachments to both ideas which cannot be explained away through blunt concepts like false consciousness, or by dismissive accusations of 'uncritical thinking'. It is important to understand 'why certain forms of truth come to prevail, and be challenged, at different historical moments' (Popkewitz 1991, p. 43), and what particular hopes the idea of education enables that education itself may not.

Taking this theoretical suggestion seriously does not require a direct critique of either teacher-expert or student-centred teaching. It does not mean that we should adopt an uncritical position towards uninspired and disempowering forms of education, much less towards undemocratic or anti-democratic politics; indeed, far from it. My personal preferences for dialogical learning are themselves informed by critiques of the 'banking concept of education' and philosophies of a more 'critical pedagogy', which aspires to the co-construction of meaningful knowledge for social transformation through the democratic organisation of educational relationships (Freire 2000). The point is rather to de-fetishise these concepts and to be aware that they are affective and political signifiers as much as they are descriptors or prescriptions of lived realities. The aim of such analysis is to enable educators to become more reflexively and collectively conscious of how our most taken for granted ideas of education are shaped through discursive constellations, and how they in turn acquire what Bourdieu defines as 'world-making power', which enables certain people to establish a 'legitimate vision of the social world and its divisions' (Swartz 1997, p. 89). The problem is not that we construct the future in a particular way, for cultural philosophy tells us this is a necessary condition of our existence. The problem is rather that if we mistake our symbolic representations of the world for the world itself, we might miss important political opportunities to imagine and shape it otherwise.

Aston University

References

Adorno, T. (1994) *Hegel: Three Studies* [translated by S. W. Nicholson] (Cambridge, MA, MIT Press).

Ahmed, S. (2004) *The Cultural Politics of Emotion* (London, Routledge).

Amsler, S. (2007) *The Politics of Knowledge in Central Asia: Science between Marx and the Market* (London, Routledge).

Amsler, S. (2008a) 'Higher Education Reform in Post-Soviet Kyrgyzstan: The Politics of Neoliberal Agendas in Theory and Practice', in Canaan, J. & Shumar, W. (eds) (2008) *Structure and Agency in the Neoliberal University* (London, Routledge).

Amsler, S. (2008b) 'Hope', in *The Blackwell Encyclopaedia of Sociology Online*, available at: http://www.sociologyencyclopedia.com/public/, accessed 3 December 2008.

Anderson, B. (2006) 'Becoming and Being Hopeful: Towards a Theory of Affect', *Environment and Planning*, 24, 5.

Anderson, K. & Heyneman, S. (2005) 'Education and Social Policy in Central Asia: The Next Stage of Transition', *Social Policy and Administration*, 39, 4.

Antonio, R. (2007) 'The Cultural Construction of Neoliberal Globalization', in Ritzer, G. (ed.) (2007) *The Blackwell Companion to Globalization* (Oxford, Blackwell).

Arzymatova, A. & Artykbaev, A. (1995) 'Nekotorie problem v prepodavanii sotsial'nykh nauk v novom obrazovatel'nom i informatsionnom prostranstve', in *Obrazovanie i nauki v novom geopoliticheskom postranstve: nauchno-prakticheskaya konferentsiya* (Bishkek, International University of Kyrgyzstan).

Asanova, J. (2006) 'Emerging Regions, Persisting Rhetoric of Educational Aid: The Impact of the Asian Development Bank on Educational Policy Making in Kazakhstan', *International Journal of Educational Development*, 26, 6.

Baker, N.J. & Thompson, C. (2009) 'Ideologies of Civic Participation in Central Asia: Liberal Arts in the Post-Soviet Democratic Ethos', *Education, Citizenship and Social Justice*, 4, 3.

Balci, B. (2003) 'Fethullah Gülen's Missionary Schools in Central Asia and their Role in the Spreading of Turkism and Islam', *Religion, State and Society*, 31, 2.

Barthes, R. (1977) *Image–Music–Text* (London, Fontana).

Berryman, S. (2000) *Hidden Challenges to Education Systems in Transition Economies* (Washington, DC, World Bank, Europe and Central Asia Region, Human Development Sector).

Bokonbaev, K.J. (1995) 'Krizis nauki i obrazovaniya Kyrgyzstana: chto delat?', *Obrazovanie i nauki v novom geopoliticheskom postranstve: nauchno-prakticheskaya konferentsiya* (Bishkek, International University of Kyrgyzstan).

Bourdieu, P. (1989) 'Social Space and Symbolic Power', *Sociological Theory*, 7, 1.

Bourdieu, P. (2001) *Acts of Resistance* (Cambridge, Polity Press).

Briller, V. & Iskakova, S. (2004) 'University Ranking in Central Asia: The Experience of Kazakhstan', in Heyneman, S. & DeYoung, A. (eds) (2004).

de la Soblonnière, R., Taylor, D. & Sadykova, N. (2009) 'Challenges to Applying a Student-Centered Approach to Learning in the Context of Education in Kyrgyzstan', *International Journal of Educational Development*.

Demir, C., Balci, A. & Akkok, F. (2000) 'The Role of Turkish Schools in the Educational System and Social Transformation of Central Asian Countries: The Case of Turkmenistan and Kyrgyzstan', *Central Asian Survey*, 19, 1.

DeYoung, A. (2002) 'West Meets East in Central Asia: Competing Discourses on Secondary Education Reform in the Kyrgyz Republic', Report, ERIC documentED465476.

DeYoung, A. (2007) 'The Erosion of *Vospitaniye* (Social Upbringing) in Post-Soviet Education: Voices from the Schools', *Communist and Post-Communist Studies*, 40, 2.

DeYoung, A. & Valyayeva, G. (1997) 'The Views of 149 Classroom Teachers', *Central Asia Monitor*, 3.

Drummond, T. & DeYoung, A. (2004) 'Perspectives and Problems in Education Reform in Kyrgyzstan: The Case of National Scholarship Testing', in Heyneman, S. & DeYoung, A. (eds) (2004).

Dzhaparova, R. (2006) 'On Whether Kyrgyzstan Should Join the Bologna Process', *Russian Education and Society*, 48, 10.

Freire, P. (2000) *Pedagogy of the Oppressed* (New York, Continuum).

Freyberg-Inan, A. & Cristescu, R. (2007) *The Ghosts in Our Classrooms, or, John Dewey Meets Ceausescu: The Promise and Failures of Civic Education in Romania* (Germany, Verlag).

Giroux, H. (1985) 'Introduction', in Freire, P. (1985) *The Politics of Education: Culture, Power and Liberation* [translated by D. Macedo] (CT, Greenwood Publishing Group).

Giroux, H. (2005) *Schooling and the Struggle for Public Life: Democracy's Promise and Education's Challenge* (Boulder, CO, Paradigm Publishers).

Grubb, W. & Lazarsen, M. (2006) 'The Globalization of Rhetoric and Practice: The Education Gospel and Vocationalism', in Lauder, H. et al. (eds) (2006).

Hall, S. (1980) 'Encoding/Decoding', in Hall, S., Hobson, D., Lowe, A. & Willis, P. (eds) (1980) *Culture, Media, Language* (New York, Routledge).

Harvey, D. (2005) *A Brief History of Neoliberalism* (Oxford, Oxford University Press).

Heyneman, S. (1998) 'The Transition from Party/State to Open Democracy: The Role of Education', *International Journal of Educational Development*, 18, 1.

Heyneman, S. & DeYoung, A. (eds) (2004) *The Challenges of Education in Central Asia* (Greenwich, CT, Information Age Publishing).

Isaev, K. (1991) 'Sotsiologiya v Kyrgyzstane: sostoyanie i perspektivy', *Obshchestvennye nauki, Akademiya Nauki Respublikoi Kyrgyzstana*, 2.

Isaev, K. (1993) 'O meste i roli sotsiologii v sisteme sotsial'nykh predmetov vuzov Kyrgyzskoi Respubliki', *Kut Bilim*, 28 May.

Kakeev, A. (1995) 'Obrazovanie v Kyrgyzstane: problemy i perspektivy', *Obrazovanie i nauki v novom geopoliticheskom postranstve: nauchno-prakticheskaya konferentsiya* (Bishkek, International University of Kyrgyzstan).

Lauder, H., Brown, P., Dillabough, J. & Halsey, A. (eds) (2006) *Education, Globalization and Social Change* (Oxford, Oxford University Press).

Lisovskaya, E. & Karpov, V. (1999) 'New Ideologies in Postcommunist Russian Textbooks', *Comparative Education Review*, 43, 4.

Liu, M. (2003) 'Detours from Utopia on the Silk Road: Ethical Dilemmas of Neoliberal Triumphalism', *Central Eurasian Studies Review*, 2, 2.

Mannheim, K. (1991) *Ideology and Utopia: An Introduction to the Sociology of Knowledge* (New York, Harcourt and Brace).

Ministry of Education, Science and Youth Policy (2006) *Education Strategy of the Kyrgyz Republic, 2007–2010* (Bishkek, Ministry of Education, Science and Youth Policy).

Niyozov, S. (2006) 'Trading or Teaching: Dilemmas of Everyday Life Economy in Central Asia', *Inner Asia*, 8, 2.

Panofsky, E. (1970) *Meaning in the Visual Arts* (Harmondsworth, Penguin).

Popkewitz, T. (1991) *A Political Sociology of Education Reform: Power/Knowledge in Teaching, Teacher Education and Research* (New York, Teachers College Press).

Popkewitz, T., Franklin, B. & Pereyra, M. (eds) (2001) *Cultural History and Education: Critical Essays on Knowledge and Schooling* (New York, Routledge).

Reeves, M. (2004) 'Academic Integrity and its Limits in Kyrgyzstani Higher Education: A View from the Margins', *International Higher Education*, 37, Fall.

Reeves, M. (2005) 'Of Credits, *Kontrakty* and Critical Thinking: Encountering "Market Reforms" in Kyrgyzstani Higher Education', *European Educational Research Journal*, 4, 1.

Resolution (2007) 'Resolution: Quality and Renovation of the Kyrgyz Republic Higher Education', *2007 Scientific-Practical Conference*, 15–16 November, available at: http://www.bolognakg.net/doc/resolution.pdf, accessed 20 March 2009.

Robertson, S., Novelli, M., Dale, R., Tickly, L., Dachi, H. & Alphonce, N. (2007) *Globalisation, Education and Development: Ideas, Actors and Dynamics*, Educational Paper produced for the UK Department for International Development, available at: http://www.dfid.gov.uk/pubs/files/global-education-dev-68.pdf, accessed 23 March 2009.

Rorty, R. (1999) *Philosophy and Social Hope* (New York, Penguin).

Sabloff, P. (1999) *Higher Education in the Post-Communist World: Case Studies of Eight Universities* (New York, Garland Press).

Shagdar, B. (2006) 'Human Capital in Central Asia: Trends and Challenges in Central Asia', *Central Asian Survey*, 25, 4.

Silova, I. & Steiner-Kamsi, G. (2009) *How NGOs React: Globalization and Education Reform in the Caucasus, Central Asia and Mongolia* (Sterling, VA, Kumarian Press).

Social Research Center (2007) 'Civic Education in the Kyrgyz Republic: Achievements, Problems and Prospects for Development', Final Report, available at: http://src.auca.kg/images/stories/files/final_report_eng_AKDN_SRC_KBS.pdf, accessed 20 March 2009.

Svi Shapiro, I. (ed.) (2009) *Education and Hope in Troubled Times* (New York & London, Routledge).

Swartz, D. (1997) *Culture and Power: The Sociology of Pierre Bourdieu* (Chicago, IL, University of Chicago Press).

Tabyshaliev, S. (1984) 'Razvitie obschestvennykh nauk v Kirgizstane', *Velikii Oktiabr' i obrazovanie SSSR v sovremennoi ideologicheskoi bor'be* (Frunze, Ilim).

Therien, J. (1999) 'Beyond the North–South Divide: The Two Tales of World Poverty', *Third World Quarterly*, 20, 4.

Thompson, C. (2008) *Epistemologies of Independence: Technology and Empire in the Post-Soviet Borderlands*, PhD dissertation, York University, Toronto, Ontario.

Tiuliundieva, N. (2006) 'The Accommodation of Children and Young People in Kyrgyzstan by the System of Education, and the Problem of Gender Inequality', *Russian Education and Society*, 48, 1.

Toursunov, M. (2008) 'Kyrgyzstan: Still Waiting?', *Transitions Online*, 29 April, available at: http://www.soros.org/initiatives/esp/articles_publications/articles/kyrgyzstan_20080429, accessed 19 January 2009.

United Nations Development Programme (2007) *Human Development Report* (New York, UNDP).

Wacquant, L. (2005) 'Symbolic Power in the Rule of the "State Nobility"', in Wacquant, L. (ed.) (2005) *Pierre Bourdieu and Democratic Politics: The Mystery of Ministry* (Cambridge, Polity).

Wacquant, L. & Bourdieu, P. (2001) 'Neoliberal Newspeak', *Radical Philosophy*, 105, January.

Williams, R. (2001) *The Long Revolution* (New York, Broadview Press).

Zournazi, M. (2002a) *Hope: New Philosophies for Change* (Annandale, Pluto Press).

Zournazi, M. (2002b) '"Hope, Passion, Politics"—with Chantal Mouffe and Ernesto Laclau', in Zournazi, M. (2002a).

Zournazi, M. (2002c) '"On the Side of Life": Joy and the Capacity of Being—with Ghassan Hage', in Zournazi, M. (2002a).

Identity, Symbolism, and the Politics of Language in Central Asia

WILLIAM FIERMAN

THIS ARTICLE IS DEVOTED TO THE SYMBOLIC ASPECTS OF language and power in the four Turkic-speaking republics of Central Asia—Kazakhstan, Kyrgyzstan, Turkmenistan and Uzbekistan. Much of the discussion will analyse what I will refer to as 'reference points' of identity represented in language. These include 'Islam', 'Turkicness', 'Persian culture', 'nationality', and two 'international' reference points—'world international' and 'Soviet international'. In the very first years after the Bolshevik Revolution, 'international' referred to parts of the world beyond the former Russian Empire, especially the industrial states of Western Europe. In the 1930s, however, 'international' came to mean the USSR, and in particular, Russia. In the post-Soviet world, 'international' is once again acquiring a much broader and more global meaning. Following a brief discussion of these reference points, the essay will illustrate some of the ways in which they were embodied in Soviet language policy and language change during the Soviet era, especially the early years. This is critical background to understanding the manipulation of language since the late 1980s, the topic of the remainder of the essay. This essay will examine only a few of the most easily studied domains of language use, primarily education, mass media and government records. The analysis below will be limited to questions of alphabet, orthography, vocabulary and language status.

It is critical to keep in mind that the Central Asian republics were themselves created by Soviet power. None of them existed as distinct entities until the 1920s. Likewise, the Communist Party supervised the creation of the nationalities that were associated with the established republics, as well as the standardised languages assigned to the republics and their titular inhabitants. This was a natural product of the Soviet approach to nationality issues which linked territory, population and language. The widespread popular belief in this link was an important element in Soviet policy, but it is arguably even more important as the underpinning for language policies in all post-Soviet states, including those in Central Asia.

The development of literary norms for Central Asian Turkic languages in the early years was far from smooth. Rather open debates about the languages continued until the end of the 1920s, and in some cases even into the early 1930s. In these years many of the voices that expressed conflicting views about language came from within Central Asia. From the mid-1930s onward, however, it was Moscow, with a very heavy hand, that determined language policy. This has important implications for the analysis below. Whereas the debates in the 1920s offer us insights into Central Asians' own conflicting views of language and identity, from about 1935 until near the end of the Soviet era we are left primarily to observe policy shifts that in large measure reflected decisions made in Moscow. Under Gorbachev, thanks to *glasnost'*, there were more clues about language and identity from Central Asians' own voices.

During the period that decisions on language policy were nearly monopolised by Moscow, there were relatively minor shifts in language corpus. The Gorbachev era, however, saw the reappearance of debates about the nature of the Central Asian languages; these would continue into the era of independence. A similar pattern applies to language status. The trajectory of Central Asian status development from the late 1930s until the 1980s, though not unilinear, did not reflect the magnitude of policy shifts that was characteristic of the 1920s and early 1930s. From the mid-1980s onward, however, debates on fundamental issues of language status reappeared. Both in the case of language corpus and status, these debates took on particular importance after independence in 1991.

In order to appreciate the differences between language as symbol under the mature Soviet system and after independence, it is worth noting the powerful levers in the hands of the Communist Party to control language during most of the Soviet era. The regime's ability to control the mass media, the educational system, political and economic mobility, and movement of information and people across borders also endowed it with powerful means to control language and the symbols it represents.

'Reference points' of identity

The 'reference points' concerning language and identity are, of course, over-simplifications of very complex phenomena. However, this scheme will allow us to trace the broad dynamics of change in language policy and identity both during the Soviet era and beyond.

A key reference point for early Soviet language policy (including in Central Asia) was what I have labelled 'international'. The early 'internationalism' was rooted in Marxist ideology and the Bolshevik vision of an international proletarian revolution. Because Marxist theory suggested that industrialised capitalist societies were the most advanced on the road to socialism and communism, the reference point for 'international' culture was situated outside the former Russian Empire, in Western Europe. Over time, in Soviet ideological tracts, 'international' would come to mean something quite different. The change would occur as it became clear that a world proletarian revolution was not imminent, and that, therefore, for the foreseeable future, socialism would have to be built in only one country. As the Communist Party leadership recognised this, it eschewed the 'internationalism' with its reference points in the West. It would not be until the mid-1930s, though, that 'international' in Soviet parlance came to be synonymous with 'Russian'.

Islam was a second reference point important for Soviet language policy, especially in Central Asia. Among the reasons that Bolsheviks opposed Islam (as well as other religions) was that it directed individuals away from the material world and secular sources of authority. Naturally, Bolsheviks were hostile to the conservative Islamic *ulama* and their followers, who opposed the Bolshevik attempt to curb activities of religious institutions. Although Pan-Islam was not a political threat to the Bolsheviks, the Party was eager to seize on opportunities to place distance between peoples in their emerging state and the influence of an 'obscurantist' faith. For tactical reasons, Bolshevik policy towards Islam remained relatively moderate until the last years of the 1920s. Nevertheless, it demonstrated early on that the Party rejected any claim that Russia's Muslims might organise based on their common religion.

Although the overwhelming majority of all Turkic populations in the Russian Empire and beyond were Muslim, 'Turkicness' was a separate reference point of identity with critical relevance to Soviet language policy in Central Asia. Jadid Muslim reformers from Central Asia, many of whom had studied in Istanbul, emphasised common roots and bonds with Turkic peoples, links which they sought to embody in language. Despite the importance of this current of thought among Central Asia's early twentieth-century intellectual elite, there is little evidence that a sense of 'Turkicness' was strong among the masses of Central Asian speakers of Turkic dialects. Furthermore, even among the intellectuals who felt a strong attachment to Turkicness, there was far from unanimity that this should be reflected in political forms that would unite those who called themselves 'Turks'. Some Central Asians, for example, harshly criticised what they perceived as attempts by Tatars to be the arbiters of what constituted 'Turkicness'. The Tatars' major role in language reform in Central Asia was linked to their prominent role in education, press and other aspects of culture in Central Asia in the early twentieth century.

Although this article deals only with Central Asian Turkic languages, it is important to mention 'Persianism' as another reference point relevant to language policy in the region.[1] Despite the presence of speakers of Persian languages in other countries outside the Russian Empire and the Central Asian vassal states of Bukhara and Khorezm (most immediately, of course, in Afghanistan and Iran), the Bolsheviks expressed much less anxiety about a 'pan-Persian' than a pan-Turkic threat. Among other reasons, this was likely because the Persian-speaking world was divided between Shi'a and Sunni Islam, and because in the case of Persian culture there was no equivalent of a Tatar 'pan-Turkic' intelligentsia in the Russian Empire. Furthermore, links between Iran and Persian-speaking regions of what became Soviet Central Asia had been quite tenuous for centuries, and even in the case of populations in Central Asia, speakers of Persian and other Iranian languages were geographically scattered. The greatest centres of Persian culture—Bukhara and Samarkand—were 'islands' largely surrounded by territories inhabited by Turkic speakers who did not know Persian or any other Iranian language. The danger of any pan-Persian sentiment in Central Asia was all the more remote because the largest territory with a dense population of Persian speakers—eventually designated as Tajikistan—contained no major urban cultural centres in the early twentieth century.

The critical reference point for Soviet nationality and language policies, especially in the period beginning in 1933, was 'Soviet International' or 'Russian'. As noted above, in the years immediately following the Bolshevik Revolution, the reference point for 'international' was west of the former Russian Empire. The word 'international'

[1] I use this term, parallel to Turkicness, to indicate the links to 'Greater Iran', to Iranian culture, including Iranian languages.

remained in the Soviet lexicon, but its meaning altered. This became clear during the 'Great Retreat' from cultural revolution, when Stalin adopted more traditional policies towards non-Russians, granting them far fewer concessions in developing their cultures in ways that distinguished them from Russian culture. Although the meaning of 'international' had begun to shift already in the early 1920s (as the Bolsheviks recognised that the world revolution was not imminent), it was during the 'Great Retreat' of the 1930s that Soviet, 'international' and 'Russian' became tightly bound.

Finally, with regard to reference points, we should note the individual nationality labels established by Soviet power. Thus, although the content of nationality and national language may have been empty until its contents were assigned by Soviet-appointed elites, the labels 'Kazakh', 'Kyrgyz', 'Turkmen' and 'Uzbek' came to represent orientations in their own right. As we will see below, this was particularly true in the case of language status, where the greatest tension in orientation was between Russian and the titular nationality language.

The list of reference points above is, of course, not comprehensive. For example, early twentieth-century Kazakhs viewed their relations based on blood ties signifying membership in a particular lineage, clan, tribe or horde. In contrast to nomadic groups such as the Kazakhs, local territorial identities were more important to sedentary populations, including in the great cultural centres of Bukhara and Samarkand. Despite the importance of the blood ties and links among the people living in a particular territory, these local territorial designations and blood relations do not appear to have become significant reference points in public debates over language policy in Central Asia to the extent of the categories introduced above.

Symbolic aspects of Soviet language policy in Central Asia

Establishment of standard languages

In accordance with Leninist–Stalinist theory, national delimitation necessitated the creation of distinct literary languages. The Bolshevik regime established norms and designated precisely which dialects belonged to which language. In the case of Kazakh, despite the vast territory in which it was spoken, there were relatively minor dialect differences. Uzbek and Tajik, on the other hand, were established as literary standards for a wide variety of dialects. The choice of dialect base was often contentious and in certain cases it shifted. For example, initially the Uzbek standard was based on dialects considered more 'pure Turkic' (not 'spoiled' by Persian elements). However, as described below in the section on alphabet and orthography, this changed after just a few years.

Although the establishment of literary norms for each Central Asian language did not mean that people stopped using their local speech varieties with their families, neighbours and co-workers, it did mean that all who attended the schools in the same language would eventually use identical textbooks, and their consumption of mass media would also be according to the same newly developing standards. This was to be true in languages both with relatively little dialect variation (notably Kazakh), as well as those (like Uzbek) which subsumed a wide variety of dialects.

After the national and linguistic delimitation of the region, there does not appear to have been any serious discussion in the Soviet era of a re-division of the Turkic dialects into a different set of 'languages'.[2] Under the influence of Marxist theories, Soviet linguists claimed that Central Asian (and other) languages were moving towards unification into a single world language, and certain 'international' elements were cited as evidence of this process. A discussion of this, however, never went beyond general talk of long term processes.

Alphabet and orthography

The alphabet shifts in Central Asia are the most easily identifiable element based on the shift of Soviet policies reflecting identities. The Arabic alphabet, closely associated with Islam, was replaced by the Latin alphabet for all Central Asian languages at the end of the 1920s. This was the most prominent (though very short-lived) move that represented the selection of a symbol that represented a 'world international' identity. Indeed, in 1930 Soviet Commissar of Enlightenment Anatoly Lunacharsky published an article in which he revealed that Lenin himself had recognised that Russian would eventually shift to Latin letters; that same year a plenum of the All-Union Committee of the New Turkic Alphabet declared Latin the 'alphabet of October'. Just a decade later, however, the Latin alphabet was replaced by the Cyrillic alphabet. This latter shift, which brought the writing systems of Central Asian languages very close to that of Russian, also served to separate them from the languages of Western Europe that not long before had been the reference points for 'international' identity.

Aside from embodying a shift from 'international' in its earlier meaning, the change to Cyrillic letters also signified a shift away from a Turkic identity. One reason is that it separated the Central Asian Turkic languages from Turkish which had shifted from the Arabic to the Latin script in the 1920s. Furthermore, unlike the relatively uniform version of the Latin alphabet that was used for Central Asian Turkic languages, the Cyrillic alphabets they adopted were not coordinated. For this reason, different letters were used for the same sound in different languages. This impeded communication among writers and readers of closely related Turkic languages.

Though not as obvious as the alphabet shifts from Arabic to Latin to Cyrillic, orthographic changes within each of these scripts also demonstrate the ways in which language change reflects realignment in accordance with new reference points. The jadid-supported reforms of the Arabic alphabet in the 1920s represented a distancing from a form of Islam their proponents considered backward and irrelevant. In an attempt to modernise spelling, Uzbek language reformers eliminated a number of letters whose presence in their language had kept Uzbek spelling consistent with Arabic; however, the letters complicated Uzbek writing because the 'foreign' letters had no phonetic meaning in Uzbek which differentiated them from other letters.

[2]It is worth noting that the Central Asian Turkic cases are somewhat different than the case of language in Azerbaijan. In the earlier years after independence, Azerbaijani was referred to as 'Turkic' or 'Turkish' (*türk dili*). This same term was used in Azerbaijan to refer to the local language during the rule of the National Front in 1992–1993. A somewhat analogous situation exists in Tajikistan. Although not supported by the political authorities in Dushanbe, some intellectuals in Tajikistan speak about Tajik in a way that creates a very fuzzy line dividing it from Persian.

(The reforms were opposed by those *ulama* members who maintained that the alphabet and orthography of words used in the holy Koran must not be changed.)

An attempt to emphasise Turkic identity was clearly manifest in Central Asian reformers' approach to the orthography of words in their languages that were borrowed from non-Turkic languages. This was true both in the case of the Arabic as well as the Latin alphabets, and was closely related to the Turkic linguistic property of 'vowel harmony'. According to this phonetic principle, all vowels of a single word are of the same type (such as rounded or unrounded, front or back). The resolution of the 1926 Baku Turcological Congress, which formalised the forthcoming shift to Latin letters, affirmed this principle, and it was reiterated at a number of other forums in the years immediately following.

Applying this principle was very complex, above all because it was extremely difficult to determine principles that applied to languages that were just being codified; this was especially true for languages with a large number of dialects. Furthermore, all Central Asian Turkic languages included very common borrowed words that did not follow the rules of vowel harmony. (Many of these had been borrowed from Arabic or Persian.) Were they to be changed so that they could be written and pronounced with new rules? Or would they constitute exceptions to the 'rules' of a particular language?

Uzbek provides perhaps the best example of the complexity in determining a new language's rules. One of the major dividing lines among the dialects that Soviet linguists labelled 'Uzbek' was between dialects that maintained vowel harmony and those, primarily urban, that did not. Proponents of observing Turkic principles in orthography insisted on representation of vowel harmony in orthography; they considered the 'Persianised' urban dialects that had lost vowel harmony to be 'corrupt'. The Uzbek Latin alphabet adopted at the end of the 1920s maintained letters which had made it possible to represent vowel harmony; however, in 1933, the All-Union Committee of the New Alphabet announced in Moscow that several letters that had allowed representation of vowel harmony in Uzbek were to be eliminated. This change and certain other spelling modifications were implemented the following year (Fierman 1991, p. 130).

Although the problem of establishing a norm was especially problematic in a language with so many dialects as Uzbek, spelling problems due to unclear 'principles' plagued other languages as well. Thus, for example, despite the creation of detailed rules, one account states that in Kazakh the word 'communist' was rendered with 16 different spellings (Zhubanov 1935). Such problems were no doubt one of the reasons that a special congress of Kazakh cultural workers in 1935 adopted a resolution mandating that the Russian spelling be maintained for 'international' terms in Kazakh (Printsipy 1935). In 1936, a Turkmen linguistic congress adopted an analogous decision, mandating that Turkmen orthography of 'international' also preserve the original Russian form, even if this violated Turkmen vowel harmony (Edgar 2004, p. 163).[3]

---

[3]According to Grenoble (2003, p. 53), a 'common rule' was eventually adopted in the 1940s mandating that the spelling of loan words in non-Russian languages throughout the USSR be subordinated to the Russian version.

In addition to ignoring vowel harmony, the unification with Russian spelling during the 1930s meant that, contrary to Turkic phonetic rules, borrowed words with initial consonant clusters were to be written with the cluster intact. Thus, this meant, for example, that Uzbek spelling of *Stalin*, *traktor* and *stol* would be identical with Russian (rather than, for example, *Istalin*, *istol* or *tiraktor*). Additional letters were added to the Latin alphabets of some Central Asian languages to allow them to render spellings closer to Russian. This was the reason for adding the three letters f, x and v to the Kazakh Latin alphabet.[4]

Despite the overwhelming trend to bring orthography of borrowed words into line with Russian spelling, a few exceptions were allowed. In particular, spelling continued to reflect the local pronunciation for a small class of words that Central Asian languages borrowed from Russian before the Bolshevik Revolution. Thus, for example, even after the shift to Cyrillic writing, the Russian words *samovar* (самовар) and *krovat'* (кровать) (bed) continued to be written samauyr and kereuet in Kazakh.[5]

Vocabulary and terminology

In the case of alphabet and orthography it is relatively easy to point to specific turning points that represent changes in policy towards representation of identity. The situation is more complex in the case of lexical items. One reason is that two ways of expressing a concept continued to exist, sometimes with only a slight difference in meaning or tone. Nevertheless, it is clear that the same general pattern described above concerning alphabet and orthography also applied to vocabulary. The main difference appears to be that vocabulary never reflected a 'world international' orientation in such an unambiguous way as alphabet did (through the adoption of Latin letters). The most discernible pattern in the case of vocabulary in the 1920s was the replacement of Arabic and Persian words with 'world international' and Turkic ones. However, as in the case of alphabet and orthography, in the middle of the 1930s many of the Turkic words (as well as some of those representing Arabic, Persian and 'world international' orientations) were expelled, and replaced with 'Soviet international' (Russian) ones.

It is possible to illustrate these trends with examples of words to represent political and social concepts that were adopted in Central Asian Turkic-language public discourse in the early post-revolutionary years. Initially, many were taken from Arabic and Persian sources. Thus, authors who wrote in what we can call 'Uzbek' frequently used words from Arabic to represent such concepts as revolution (*inqilob*), party (*firqa*), and communist (*ishtirokiyun*); likewise, they used words taken from Persian to mean capital (*sarmoya*), and soviet or council (*sho'ra*). Although Kazakh (and Kyrgyz) authors appear to have adopted fewer Arabic and Persian terms, vocabulary for concepts in education and political life in the early years (which were later 'expelled') were also drawn from these languages. Among these were *daris* (Arabic) for

---

[4]The sounds 'f' and 'v' occurred only in borrowed words (Razvitie 1980, p. 127).

[5]In the early 1950s, however, there were discussions about unifying the spelling of these words with the Russian orthography (see Sauranbaev *et al.* 1952). For whatever reason, it appears that far fewer Uzbek than Kazakh words maintained a distinct spelling that reflected the local pronunciation.

lesson and *basuazir* (the first element from Turkic and the second from Persian) for prime minister (Isaev 1965, p. 104).

Many of the prominent Turkic-minded language planners sought to cleanse their languages of such 'alien' terms and replace them with words from Turkic roots. Thus, for example, in 1923 the Uzbek newspaper *Turkiston* carried a series of articles with lists of words borrowed from Arabic and Persian that it suggested should be removed from Uzbek. They included *mehnat* (labour), *tashkilot* (organisation), *nashriyot* (publisher) and *fikr* (thought); the proposed respective equivalents were the Turkic *ish, uyushma, tarqatish* and *uy*.[6]

The question of sources for vocabulary figured prominently at the 1926 Baku Turcological Conference. The resolution of that gathering still strongly favoured Turkic words, but it was far from absolute. It suggested that a language which lacked certain terms created from Turkic roots might borrow them from other Turkic languages. However, it conceded that in cases where no Turkic equivalent existed and where Arabic or Persian terms had already been assimilated, the foreign terms need not be purged. This represented a relatively relaxed stance towards Arabic and Persian terms (Fierman 1991, p. 155).

Some of these Arabic and Persian words, and even Turkic ones, were to remain in the Central Asian Turkic languages only until the Russification of the mid-1930s. For example, in Turkmen '*sovet*' replaced '*shura*' to mean council; '*ministr*' replaced '*vezir*' to mean 'minister'; and '*respublika*' replaced '*jemkhuriyet*' (Zakonomernosti 1969, p. 31). A Russian–Uzbek dictionary published in 1934 still gave the translation of the Russian words '*sovet*' and '*respublika*' as '*shora*' and '*zhumhuriyat*'. The dictionary, however, provides insights into the beginning of a shift: '*revolyutsiya*' is given 'in Uzbek' first as '*revolutsija*', but is still followed by *inqilab* (derived from Arabic) and *ozgerish* (derived from Turkic).[7] Soon after the dictionary's appearance, however, such words as *ozgerish* and *inqilab*, as well as *shora* and *zhumkhuriyat*, would totally disappear from the Uzbek publications.

It goes without saying that terminology in all Central Asian languages grew exponentially with the expansion of education, political mobilisation and economic development. The overwhelming share of new terms created from the mid-1930s until the end of Soviet power, especially in technical fields, were Russian borrowings. According to one account, on the eve of the Bolshevik Revolution, the Turkic languages which were spoken on the territory later to become the USSR each had between 25 and 50 Russian loanwords;[8] by 1940, a number of the languages had 500 such words; by the late 1960s, the figure is said to have reached into the thousands, with over half of those words consisting of commonly used vocabulary (Zakonomernosti 1969, p. 32). This calculation is in line with a study of the Kyrgyz literary language, which asserts that in the early 1980s, 80% of terminology in the 'Kyrgyz literary language' consisted of loans either from Russian or from West European languages through Russian (Akhmatov 1984, p. 146).

---

[6]*Turkiston* various issues between 5 September 1923 and 21 November 1923.

[7]The entry for '*revolyutsionnyi*', however, gives only the Arabic-derived equivalent *inqilabiy*.

[8]In a strict sense, of course, this predates the creation of these 'languages', since by and large standards had not been established.

It should be emphasised that despite the changes in vocabulary discussed here, all Central Asian Turkic languages contain (and still contain) a large number of common assimilated words that came from Arabic and Persian, but which most speakers of the languages do not recognise as alien. The share of such words, however, varies among the languages and across time. (Uzbek probably has the largest share.) For all of the languages, however, it is clear that terminology became highly politicised in the Soviet era, and that the sources that provided much of the terminology in the early years after the Bolshevik Revolution—Arabic, Persian and Turkic—lost substantial ground from the 1930s onward, with the vast majority of the new words coming from Russian.

Language status

Although language corpus issues lend themselves to the kind of analysis of a larger number of symbols of identity and power as presented above, language status—despite its extraordinary importance as a symbol of power and an instrument for exercising it—does not offer the same opportunities to examine the same set of reference points. The focus in this section will therefore be on the changing dynamics between the newly established nationalities' titular languages and Russian. However, considering status more broadly, we should keep in mind the radical diminution in the status of Arabic language and those who knew it at a time when the Bolshevik regime closed mosques, Islamic schools and other religious institutions. We should also recognise that in each of the republics the tension was not merely between Russian and the titular nationality language, but rather also included other minority languages.

In the early years of Soviet power, the Bolshevik regime's 'world internationalism' obliged it to attempt to demonstrate that it would not continue the Russian chauvinist policies of its tsarist predecessors. In line with this, it carried out a programme of '*korenizatsiya*' ('nativisation'). Under this initiative, which began in the early 1920s, the Bolshevik regime encouraged the preparation and promotion of local cadre to work in administration in all non-Russian areas of the emerging USSR. As part of *korenizatsiya*, administrative institutions were required to work in the local languages (Martin 2001, pp. 75–77). Among other things, this meant that non-locals were supposed to learn these languages.

Korenizatsiya was especially difficult to implement in Central Asia. Among the main reasons were the low levels of education and literacy, the lack of standard writing systems, and the constant changes outlined above. Furthermore, and related to this, many Russians and other members of non-local ethnic groups resisted learning the local languages, which they considered backward. The Soviet regime never publicly rejected *korenizatsiya*. Furthermore, some of the activities related to this effort—such as the development of primary and secondary education and a mass press in the local languages—survived throughout the Soviet regime. Indeed, even higher education (especially teacher training) was to develop in Central Asian languages; however (depending on the republic and the era) a much broader range of subjects and a higher quality of teaching was usually available in Russian than in the local languages.

From the mid-1930s onward, Soviet policy generally encouraged asymmetrical bilingualism, with non-Russians obliged to learn Russian, but Russians and other minorities having little need to learn the local languages. Russian was officially introduced as a mandatory subject in all schools of the USSR in 1938. In the 1950s Russian began to be called the 'second mother tongue' of all non-Russians of the USSR.[9] Party First Secretary Nikita Khrushchev adopted this characterisation in his speech at the 22nd CPSU congress in 1961. Russian language was closely linked with what was called 'international upbringing', a kind of 'internationalism' clearly rooted in Russian culture and language. At various times in Soviet history, pupils in Russian-medium schools of Central Asia were offered opportunities or even obliged to study the local language; however, anecdotal evidence overwhelmingly indicates that the teaching of Central Asian languages to non-native speakers was poor and frequently viewed with disdain.

Demographic patterns in urban areas were an important factor supporting the dominance of Russian in Central Asia. The policies that produced these patterns, though adopted for a wide variety of reasons, nevertheless constituted part of the Soviet policy to create a single 'Soviet people'. Soviet ideological literature praised migration, which made Soviet cities more ethnically diverse, as 'international'. In the case of Central Asian urban areas, the Slavic dominance was largely a matter of Slavic in-migration. True, in rural areas and even provincial towns the Central Asian ethnic groups were often dominant; there, for local purposes, Russian might occupy a secondary position. However, the Soviet Union was ruled by a hierarchically organised party that radiated power from Moscow, and transmitted it through republic capitals. In no Central Asian capital city did the titular nationality during the Soviet era achieve a majority share of the population and, indeed, as of 1970, Russians alone outnumbered the titular population in every case; combined with other Slavs, they continued to outnumber the titular nationality in every capital in 1979 (Guboglo 1990/91). In capital cities and other urban areas with a large non-titular population, Russian was overwhelmingly the language of communication between or among members of different nationalities. This was usually the case even in settings where Russians were a small minority and members of the local nationality an overwhelming majority. The dominant language in urban factories and other enterprises, not to mention the Communist Party, was Russian. By the 1970s and 1980s, even in informal situations in Slavic-dominated large urban areas, Central Asians were often obliged to communicate in Russian, even if they did not have a good mastery of it. Although the most important Central Asian language in each republic during the Soviet era was the titular language of that republic, the Soviet system in some ways supported the status of non-titular Central Asian languages in neighbouring republics. Uzbek primary and secondary schools operated, for example, in all Central Asian republics, and some graduates of those schools entered higher education in Uzbekistan. Local Uzbek-language media (such as *raion* newspapers) were also published in the other republics of Central Asia. Likewise, Uzbekistan's schools for its minorities received some textbooks from neighbouring republics.

---

[9]Simon (1991, p. 246) notes a 1958 reference by Bobojon Gafurov in a *Kommunist* article as one of the earliest demands to declare Russian the 'second mother tongue' (Gafurov 1958). Until he left to direct the Institute of Oriental Studies in Moscow in 1956, Gafurov had served for a decade as head of the Tajik Communist Party.

Symbolic aspects of language policy in Central Asia since Gorbachev

Since the late Soviet era the overall shift in language as a symbol of power throughout Central Asia has been away from Russian (representing 'Soviet internationalism') and towards symbols representing the titular 'nationality' promoted by the elites of the newly independent states. The shifts, however, especially in the case of corpus, are quite complex; furthermore, they vary from country to country. Unlike in the Soviet era, since 1991 there has been no central party apparatus in Moscow dictating uniform principles. Instead, individual leaders, attempting to foster a basis for national development, have opted for diverse policies. One extreme is represented by Turkmenistan, where the late President Niyazov conducted a bold policy of Turkmenisation and de-Russification. Uzbekistan's president has also pursued 'nationalisation', glorifying Uzbeks above other nationalities in his country. On the other hand, due above all to demographic and geographic factors, the nation-building projects in Kazakhstan and Kyrgyzstan have been less exclusive, and they have allowed more prominent representation of non-titular groups and their languages.

Throughout Central Asia governments generally have less control over important domains of citizen's language behaviour than did Soviet leaders prior to Gorbachev, in particular Stalin. Part of the reason for this is that, even though they may have crossed republic borders with ease, most Soviet Central Asians as a rule did not travel beyond local towns or perhaps their own republic's capital city. Only in the rarest of circumstances did they cross a Soviet border. Today, most often due to economic necessity, many live for extended periods outside their home country. The situation is quite different for those who live at home, too. Under Stalin, Central Asians, even urban residents, had no access to mass media except programmes broadcast by local stations (perhaps rebroadcast from other Soviet cities) or newspapers sold at local kiosks. Today, even in Turkmenistan, many have access to electronic media from beyond their country's borders. The language of the mass media within Central Asia, particularly in Kazakhstan and Kyrgyzstan, is not subject to the kind of control that it was in the Soviet era. Furthermore, in some parts of Central Asia, new sorts of norms may be developing for 'the same language'. Uzbek textbooks in Kyrgyzstan, for example, are being published in the Cyrillic script while those in Uzbekistan have long ago shifted to Latin.

Language status

Gorbachev's policies of *glasnost'* and *perestroika* permitted and even encouraged citizens to express their views in a more open fashion. 'National fronts' formed throughout the USSR during the Gorbachev era; their memberships were comprised mostly of the titular nationality in each republic. One of their primary goals almost everywhere was to raise the status of the titular languages of the republic. Over the course of 1989–1990, all Soviet non-Russian republics whose constitutions did not already identify a state language adopted new laws which raised the status of their titular languages in such areas as education, media, public services and administration. Importantly, the laws adopted in Central Asia in this period still referred to Russian as the language of 'interethnic communication'.

Since 1989, the main thrust of laws and other regulations concerning language throughout Central Asia has been to expand the domains for the titular language and reduce the domains for Russian. This has been pursued most harshly in Turkmenistan. Niyazov's regime marginalised all non-Turkmen languages in public spaces, including Russian. Almost all non-Turkmen schools were closed or turned into mixed schools (with some classes using Turkmen, and others Russian or Uzbek as the language of instruction), and there was a shift in higher education to the exclusive use of Turkmen. Russian language was removed as an obligatory subject in the school curriculum. Although many Turkmens accessed foreign television through satellite broadcasts, subscriptions to print media published outside Turkmenistan were severely limited. This, in combination with the end of most Russian-language broadcasts within Turkmenistan, also contributed to the country's linguistic nationalisation.

Kazakhstan also raised the status of the titular language, but to a much lesser extent than in Turkmenistan and through much less severe measures. Besides the nature of the political leadership, another reason for this is that Kazakhstan became independent not only with a minority titular population (especially in urban areas), but even among ethnic Kazakhs, only a minority in urban areas were literate in Kazakh. Overall, as of 1991, probably only about one third of the country's total adult population was literate in Kazakh, whereas 90% were literate in Russian (Fierman 2006, p. 101). Although legislation in Kazakhstan has promised a shift of all government office work to the state language, a number of deadlines for this have passed with limited results. The country's electronic mass media have proven adept at finding ways around laws which require that at least 50% of broadcasts be in Kazakh. A new language law adopted in 1997 stripped Russian of its role of 'language of cross-national communication', but introduced an equally ambiguous status for it as the language 'used officially on a par with Kazakh in state organisations and organs of local self-government' (Fierman 1998, p. 179). Despite these and many other problems, Kazakh has begun to occupy a more prominent place in the country's cities. This has been supported in part by the growing proportion of Kazakhs among urban residents, many of whom are former rural residents with strong Kazakh language skills. (Many of them have replaced Slavs who have emigrated to Russia.)

The extent of linguistic nationalisation in Uzbekistan and Kyrgyzstan has been somewhere between the pole of Turkmenistan on the one hand and Kazakhstan on the other. Although the role of Russian in Uzbekistan has sharply declined since 1991, the regime has pursued linguistic 'Uzbekisation' much less vigorously at those times it has sought improved relations with Russia. The greatest pressure inside Uzbekistan, it appears, has been on the Tajik language, particularly in its traditional areas of strength, Bukhara and Samarkand. Kyrgyzstan's government, due to demographic factors and less abundant resources, has promoted change in language status in ways that are more like those employed in Kazakhstan than Turkmenistan. Thus, it has continued to permit extensive use of Uzbek through all levels of education in the country's south. However, it has refused to yield to demands to raise Uzbek to a regional official language. By contrast, and despite the sharp decline of the ethnic Russian population, Kyrgyzstan has made Russian an 'official' (but not state) language.

Alphabet and orthography

At least to some extent, the Latin alphabet has replaced Cyrillic for writing Turkmen and Uzbek. In both cases, the shift to the Latin alphabet has been a powerful symbol of rejection of the 'Soviet international' (Russian) identity. Prior to the 1993 announcement of the impending shift in Uzbekistan, the country's press had carried extensive discussions of alphabet, including a possible shift from Cyrillic to the Arabic script. This choice, which was quickly rejected, would have represented a stronger tie to Islam and to the literature written before the adoption of Latin letters in the 1920s. Because the script is also used for such languages as Persian, Dari and Pashto, not to mention for Uzbek in Afghanistan, Uzbek's adoption of Arabic letters would also have reinforced cultural links with neighbours to Uzbekistan's south.

Turkmenistan, the only Central Asian state that has completed the transition to Latin letters, announced plans to shift from Cyrillic in a 1993 presidential decree. Although for several years the shift proceeded slowly, on 29 December 1999, Turkmenistan's parliament adopted a resolution mandating that beginning in the new millennium, Turkmen would be written in Latin letters. Within days, all central newspapers began to appear only in Latin. Aside from this delayed but eventually rapid shift, the Turkmen case is particularly interesting because of the choice of symbols. The initial version of the Turkmen Latin alphabet included Ññ, $¢, ¥ÿ and £ſ.[10] In January 2000, however, three of these symbols—Ññ, ¥ÿ, and £ſ—were replaced with Ňň, Ýý and Žž (Postanovlenie Khalk Maslakhaty 1999).[11] Anecdotal reports indicate that authorities originally selected symbols representing international currency (dollar, yen and pound) because they were often on standard typewriter keyboards. If true, the choice of such 'international' symbols might best be interpreted as a symbolic turning away from Russia.

Although poor coordination and various economic factors also played important roles, the slower pace of shift from Cyrillic to Latin for Uzbek is also probably linked to the frequent shifts in relations between Uzbekistan and foreign countries, most importantly Russia and Turkey, and perhaps the 'West' represented by Western Europe and the USA. Uzbek's projected shift to Latin that was originally announced in 1993 was supposed to be completed by 2000. The deadline was later pushed forward to 2005, but in 2002 it was moved back another five years, to 2010. Elementary school textbooks began to be changed, one year at a time, beginning with 1996. This process was completed on schedule in 2005. However, in late 2008, the final instalment of a five-volume Uzbek language Cyrillic-based dictionary appeared, and as of spring 2009, most Uzbek newspapers continued to be published in Cyrillic; according to a report from 2007, 80–85% of Uzbek book production was still in Cyrillic (Sharifov 2007).

Aside from its rejection of symbols associated with Russian, initially Uzbek's adoption of the Latin alphabet could be interpreted as both a move bringing them

---

[10]'Report on the Current Status of United Nations Romanization Systems for Geographical Names', available at: http://www.eki.ee/wgrs/rom2_tk.htm, accessed 7 January 2009.

[11]The symbols (upper case) $ and (lower case) ¢ were apparently replaced at some earlier date with Ş and ş, respectively.

closer to a more 'world international' orientation as well as one that emphasised Turkic bonds. But later developments downplayed the link with Turkic, particularly as represented by Turkish. The first version of the Uzbek Latin alphabet, promulgated in 1993, adopted the Turkish convention of representing the sound 'sh' with the letter 'ş'. Two years later, however, along with some other changes, 'ş' was replaced with 'sh'. This change meant that, except for the reverse apostrophe, Uzbek writing did not require any special letters beyond those used for the world's most 'international' language, English.[12]

Kazakhstan's President Nazarbaev has spoken on several occasions about a possible shift to Latin letters, and in 2006, a commission was established to study the question. No firm decision has been announced, and the president has emphasised that if Cyrillic is abandoned for the Kazakh language, this will be a very gradual process. Such a shift is a particularly sensitive issue in Kazakhstan, where ethnic Russians still constitute at least a quarter of the population, and about 20% of ethnic Kazakhs still receive their education in Russian-medium classes. In spring 2008 Nazarbaev seemingly backtracked on a course leading towards adoption of Latin. In an interview with Kazakh-language media, he took pains to note that Kazakh in fact did not use the Cyrillic alphabet as such, but a 'Kazakh alphabet' developed on the basis of Cyrillic. He further pointed out that the Cyrillic used for Russian 'is not a Slavic form of writing, but represents a modified form of Latin' (Velikii put' 2008). Although the possibility of a change of alphabet has been discussed in Kyrgyzstan, to date there have not yet been any official moves to indicate a shift is likely in the near future.

Orthographic changes in the region have been relatively modest, but some are clearly tied to questions of identity. For example, even before Uzbek began to shift to Latin from Cyrillic, it dropped the ь (soft sign) from the end of the names of the nine months written with that letter in Russian. Personal and place names have also brought changes in orthography. Indeed, in some cases the authorities in Central Asian countries have insisted that the Russian language spelling of place names conform not to standards established in Russia, but to those of the language of origin. Consequently, whereas Russian-language newspapers in Russia use 'Kirgizstan' or 'Kirgiziya' to denote the now independent country of Kyrgyzstan, the official Russian language norm that is widely (but not universally) followed inside the Central Asian country itself is 'Kyrgyzstan'. (This violates the usual phonetic and spelling rules for Russian.) Likewise, Russian-language publications issued in Moscow consistently spell the name of Kazakhstan's largest city and former capital 'Alma-Ata'. This is the name that was used throughout the Soviet era in Russian-language publications. Today, however, Kazakhstan's Russian-language publications generally write it as 'Almaty', in conformance with the Kazakh orthography.

This differentiation according to country of publication underlines the changed meaning of borders in the post-Soviet era, both the very porous borders that once separated Soviet republics, and the much more formidable ones that once separated Soviet citizens from those abroad. In the Soviet era, with political power concentrated in Moscow, it would have been inconceivable for separate alphabets or orthographies

[12]According to Sharifov (2007), the adoption of the Latin alphabet itself was not so much a step reflecting a desire to Westernise as a rejection of Russia and a 'gift presented to Turkey'.

to be used for what was recognised as the same language in different republics. Thus, Uzbek in formal communications of Tajikistan or Kyrgyzstan (such as mass media or education) used the Uzbek standard promulgated in Tashkent; the same applied in other languages in more than one republic, such as Tajik in Uzbekistan's cities of Samarkand and Bukhara, and in Tajikistan. Due to poor relations between the USSR and China, however, Kazakhs in Xinjiang generally used a script that did not coincide with the norm set in Kazakhstan, just as Soviet Uyghurs, who began to use Cyrillic in the 1940s, generally used a different alphabet than Uyghurs in Xinjiang.

The barriers among the Central Asian countries that are represented by the new borders have created situations where, as noted above, distinct norms may be starting to develop within the former Soviet space. This seems to apply in particular to Uzbek: all Uzbek language schools in Uzbekistan are supposed to be using Latin-alphabet textbooks, whereas those in Kazakhstan, Tajikistan and Kyrgyzstan continue to use Cyrillic. Part of the reason for continued use of Cyrillic books, especially in Tajikistan and Kyrgyzstan, may relate to the financial burden of shifting to a new form of writing. However, the reluctance to shift to Latin also seems to represent a continued greater orientation in those countries towards Russia than in the case of Uzbekistan.

Meanwhile, Kazakhstan has made prominent overtures to ethnic Kazakhs living beyond the borders of Kazakhstan, including outside the former USSR. Despite the fact that Kazakhstan has announced no decision about whether Kazakh will shift to Latin, beginning in April 2004, the Kazakhstan National Information Agency (Kazinform) began disseminating news in Kazakh for Kazakhs living abroad in the Latin alphabet along with that in Cyrillic-version Kazakh (as well as Russian and English) (Akanbai 2004).

Vocabulary

Since the late 1980s the Soviet 'internationalisation' ('Russianisation') of vocabulary in Central Asian languages has been somewhat reversed. Indeed, in the last 20 years all Central Asian Turkic languages have been 'internationalised' primarily through the incorporation of words from English. Although many of these same words are probably also being adopted in Russian, today they represent a link to a broader world than the 'international' world once defined in Moscow in the 1930s. Not surprisingly, many of these new 'international' words relate to such fields as economics and business.

The pace of replacement of 'Soviet international' words (borrowed from or through Russian) accelerated during the Gorbachev era and probably reached its height in the last months of Soviet power or the early years of independence. At least initially, the 'new' replacement words were not primarily English, but rather lexical items based on Arabic, Persian and Turkic roots. Often these were the same words that had been purged from the standard literary languages in the 1930s. Some of these words had begun to reappear in limited domains in the 1960s and 1970s in particular genres, especially historical fiction.

Before looking at the broad trends, it should be noted that the picture of the shift in lexical items since 1991 is very complex, varying from country to country, and across time, genre, author and publication. In some countries, such as Kazakhstan, due to

less political control of the media, authors have had more discretion to choose either
'Russian' vocabulary or 'new' equivalents drawn from other sources. In other
countries, such as Turkmenistan and Uzbekistan, because the government regulates
public domains of communication more tightly, it also has greater power to influence
the language they use. With this caveat in mind, we can say that in the last 20 years the
general trend has been de-Russianisation. Thus, for example, Kazakh has rejected the
Russian names of months and adopted new ones based on Turkic and Persian roots.
In Turkmen the Russian word for system (*sistema*) has been replaced by *ulgam*; the
Russian *klas*, which had been used to mean 'class' both in terms of a 'social class' or a
'school class', has entirely been displaced in the latter sense by *synp*.

More often, the shift is one of degree, meaning that there has been a shift in the
relative roles of two or more lexical items that co-existed in the Soviet era. Very often,
in the Soviet era the Russian loan word was dominant, with the other form restricted
to a narrow set of genres, such as historical fiction, or to very specific and limited
meanings. Both variants may exist today, though with a shift in the balance and a
broadening of the meaning of the word that had been more limited in the Soviet era. In
Uzbek, for example, during the Soviet era both *avtor* and *muallif* were used to mean
'author'. The word from Arabic, *muallif*, which was bookish in the Soviet era, today is
used more broadly than *avtor*; the latter has almost disappeared from formal
discourse. Likewise, the common Uzbek words for 'secretary' and 'reform' in the
Soviet era were the same as in Russian (*sekretar'* and *reforma*), whereas the words
kotib and *islokhot* with much the same meaning were classified as archaic. The balance
has now changed: *kotib* and *islokhot* have largely displaced *sekretar'* and *reforma* in
the mass media.[13] In some cases, the 'new' word was almost or totally absent during
the Soviet era. To the best of my knowledge, only the borrowed Russian word *samolet*
was used to signify aeroplane in Kazakh. Today this word coexists with the Turkic-
derived term *ushaq*. It is too early to tell whether both of these terms will remain,
whether *samolet* will again become the only word used, or if *ushaq* will displace it.

What does this tell us about the importance of the 'Turkic', 'Iranian' or 'Islamic'
points of reference discussed at the beginning of this article? There seem to be no
consistent ideological guidelines which require the selection of new words only from
particular sources, such as only Turkic or only Persian. For example, although the
'new' Uzbek word for 'ticket' (*chipta*) is Turkic, the new words cited above for
secretary and reform are Arabic. Uzbek also has many 'new' old words from Persian,
such as *hiyobon* ('park' or 'lane'). Although many Russian borrowings in Kazakh have
partially or entirely been displaced by words of Turkic origin, such as *kalendar'*
(calendar) with *kuntizbe*, *privatizatsiya* (privatisation) with *zhekeshelendiruw*, and
suvernitet (sovereignty) with *egemendik*, other 'new' words are based on Arabic and
Persian roots such as *quqyk* (law) for *pravo*, *matn* (text) for *tekst*; and *ziyapat*
(banquet) for *banket*. These examples suggest that although Central Asian speakers of
Turkic languages may be aware in some vague sense of linguistic bonds that they share
due to their Turkic roots, language planning in post-Soviet Central Asia has not been
guided by the kind of ideological orientation to Turkey that many language planners
of the 1920s sought to observe, and there is no sign that selection of vocabulary has

[13]Umida Khikmatillaeva kindly provided help on these changes in Uzbek.

. been guided by a desire to underline links with Persian culture or bonds with other Islamic peoples. Rather, the main trend has been 'de-Russianisation'.

Despite this, all of the Central Asian languages continue to use many lexical items borrowed from Russian, both for everyday concepts and (especially) for terminology. Furthermore, it should also be noted that many 'new' words that were revived or invented to replace those that had been borrowed from or through Russian have failed to take root. Some have disappeared, or else are used rarely. Thus, in the early 1990s some authors used such 'Uzbek' words as *dorilfunun* (from Arabic) and *tayeragoh* (with Arabic and Persian elements) in place of the Russian words for university and airport (*universitet* and *aeroport*), but the Russian words have remained, and 'new words' have now practically disappeared. In Turkmen, there also appears to be a return to lexical items borrowed from or through Russian. In this regard the newly invented Turkmen names of the months (created under President Niyazov) have been abandoned, and the Russian-based names are again being used.

Conclusion. Regional variation of language and power across time

The deliberate attempts of the Soviet regime and the post-Soviet leaders in Central Asia to manipulate language behaviour clearly demonstrate their recognition of language as a powerful symbol. Of course it is impossible entirely to separate the regimes' symbolic concerns from more practical ones. Thus, for example, Soviet leaders certainly viewed the adoption of the Latin alphabet in the 1920s as a measure that would facilitate literacy; this was a very practical objective. On the other hand, the shift away from Arabic letters no doubt appealed to Stalin as a symbolic blow to Islam. Analogous points about a balance of symbolic and instrumental concerns apply to the changes in vocabulary of the 1930s described above. Thus, Stalin no doubt favoured the unification of vocabulary through the Russification of the terminology of Central Asian languages for instrumental reasons: it facilitated translations from Russian. However, the symbolism which this unification represented was also certainly a reason for the policy. It is natural, then, that when Central Asian Turkic authors in the last decades of Soviet power began to use words or terminology that were barely acceptable, they were engaged in a symbolic demonstration of power that challenged representations promoted by Moscow. The adoption of language laws in the waning years of the Soviet era had many practical ramifications. However, at the time of their adoption their greatest significance was as a symbol of the changing dynamics of power between Moscow and the individual republics, and changing balance among competing world views.

We must see the language and language policy changes of the post-Soviet era in this context: the regimes in post-Soviet Central Asia make decisions about script, orthography and status with an acute sense of the symbolic significance of their decisions. However, it is also clear that they take account of instrumental goals and non-symbolic political realities in devising language policies. Both in the Soviet and post-Soviet eras, political control over language has varied both over time and across domains. As for the Soviet period, Moscow's influence over language policy and language behaviour consolidated during Stalin's terror in the 1930s. Later, urbanisation probably facilitated Moscow's control over the language used by a larger cohort of individuals; however, the changed atmosphere during Khrushchev's thaw and Brezhnev's 'stagnation' allowed members of the intelligentsia to use language in ways that were difficult for Moscow to control. Space does not permit an exploration of the fluctuations in level of control in each of the countries in the post-Soviet era; however, it is critical to note that, unlike in the Soviet era when the CPSU dominated decisions about language policy, in the post-Soviet era each of the countries of Central Asia has moved on its own trajectory.

Among the domains most controlled by the CPSU were mass media and public signs in the capital cities, and documentation in the republic party records. Certainly the regime's power over the language used in the classroom by remote village school teachers was far less, not to mention communications between grandparents and grandchildren or between spouses in the privacy of their own homes. True, especially over time, Party policy affected even some of these exchanges, so that, for example, parents (even if they spoke seriously flawed Russian) used only Russian with their offspring. Parallels no doubt exist throughout post-Soviet Central Asia. Thus, for example, even in Turkmenistan, where the government has sharply curtailed the number of pupils receiving primary education in languages other than Turkmen, we can assume that Uzbek and Russian (not to mention local dialects of Turkmen that differ from the official standard) are widely used among certain populations.

Although since 1991 the status of Russian has declined greatly throughout Central Asia, with the possible exception of Turkmenistan, Russian has continued to maintain a high symbolic niche everywhere. This is indicated, for example, by the fact that many of the most prized slots in primary, secondary and higher education are still in Russian-language tracks or institutions. Unlike Russian, languages of Central Asian nationalities outside their 'titular home' lack such a high symbolic niche. Therefore, for example, no high prestige is attached to Uzbek-language tracks or institutions in Tajikistan, Kyrgyzstan or Kazakhstan, let alone to Tajik, Kyrgyz or Kazakh tracks or institutions in Uzbekistan. This is certainly the case, for example, of Uzbek in Turkmenistan, Kazakh and Tajik in Uzbekistan, or even Uzbek in Kyrgyzstan.

Kazakhstan continues to support primary and secondary education in Uzbek, Uyghur and Tajik, but pupils attending these schools account for only a few per cent of enrolments. Unlike in Turkmenistan, Kyrgyzstan or Uzbekistan, their share is dwarfed by that of Russians and other Slavs. The reluctance to grant concessions or decentralise power over language in Kazakhstan thus is largely not about the languages of other Central Asian nationalities; it is, rather, about symbolic and real power in the hands of a very large share of Russians and other *russkoyazychnye*, including many Kazakhs whose dominant language is Russian. The tight central control over language policy is no doubt related to a worry that decentralisation of language policy could be exploited for other forms of political autonomy, which to Kazakh nationalists is the first step on a slippery slope that might lead to secession of 'Russian-speaking' areas of the country. Analogous comments may be made about Uzbekistan, Kyrgyzstan and Turkmenistan, but the potential major claimants of power in those cases are members of co-ethnic groups of neighbouring Central Asian countries, not representatives of the former colonial power. The largest geographically concentrated non-Russian minorities in Uzbekistan are the Tajiks and Kazakhs; both in Kyrgyzstan and Turkmenistan the largest minority is Uzbeks.

Contacts with the 'outside world' are a key factor affecting the Central Asian governments' control of language as a symbol as well as the salience of the symbol in power relations within the country. Today, communications and movement across certain former Soviet internal borders are problematic; yet communications and movement across former Soviet external borders are generally much easier than in the Soviet days. Uzbek speakers of Tajikistan are quite isolated from those in Uzbekistan. Moreover, the governments of Kazakhstan, Kyrgyzstan and Tajikistan have demonstrated their 'power' over their ethnic Uzbek citizens by refusing to follow Uzbekistan's lead in adopting Latin letters to write Uzbek.

The nature and intensity of interaction with the outside world appear to be one reason that in every Central Asian country many non-titular citizens lack enthusiasm for the state language. Thus, for example, despite government policies to promote Uzbek, many non-Uzbeks in Uzbekistan prefer to invest their time in learning English (not to mention Russian) rather than the state language. The reasons for this include the perceived and real advantages in employment conferred by knowledge of English or Russian. Such phenomena suggest that (with the possible exception of Turkmenistan) not only do the Central Asian regimes generally have fewer effective levers than Moscow once did to control language policy and behaviour, but also that many citizens of Central Asia may be far less affected than their parents were by the symbolic value of the state language that the government promotes.

Variation across Central Asia demonstrates a great variety in regimes' political styles, willingness or ability to manipulate linguistic symbols, and the way in which they balance symbolic aspects of language with economic and social realities. This is apparent, for example, in the respective patterns of shift to the Latin alphabet in Turkmenistan and Uzbekistan. Given the nature of Uzbekistan's political system, it would seem that the reason for the lack of progress on Latinisation is not the leadership's inability to implement change, but the fact that it is carefully balancing the economic and social costs and benefits.

In this regard, the decision-making process concerning language in Kazakhstan reflects power relations that are quite different from those in Uzbekistan. As long as he leads Kazakhstan, President Nazarbaev will undoubtedly play a crucial role in the decision of whether Kazakh will adopt Latin letters. Nevertheless, with the president's blessing, Kazakhstan's mass media launched a very public debate on the desirability and feasibility of a shift to Latin. It is hard to imagine a public debate about any linguistic issue with such great symbolic meaning in Uzbekistan, let alone Turkmenistan.

Given the relevance of language to power, it is particularly significant that in some cases language as a symbol of power appears to have been manipulated particularly against members of the titular nationality who do not know 'their own' language. Such individuals are almost always the products of Russian-language schools, whose student body contained a disproportionately large share of children of the elite. This has made many of the Central Asian nationalities' most highly educated individuals, who lack a firm grounding in 'their own' language, vulnerable to attacks from their more 'truly national' co-ethnics.

The environment for such attacks is particularly favourable in the light of the fact that Soviet ideology, despite its promotion of Russian as a 'progressive' phenomenon, produced a widespread belief that an individual's 'native language' should match his or her 'passport nationality'. This belief was reflected in the 2005 legislation proposed to the Kazakhstan parliament that would have required candidates to demonstrate a knowledge of Kazakh. However, this was to apply only to Kazakhs, and not to Russians or any other minorities (Absalyamova 2005).

In Kazakhstan, Kyrgyzstan and Uzbekistan (but not Turkmenistan), the constitution gives a high symbolic status to the titular language in another way—through requirements that the president be fluent in the state language. Indeed, during the run-up to presidential elections in 2000 in Kyrgyzstan, a number of candidates were eliminated from the race because they could not pass the language test.

For the future, one of the most salient domains for power is language in higher education. Barring political change that would result in a reconfiguration of the political geography of Central Asia, it is virtually certain that the future leaders of Central Asian countries will pass through their respective higher educational institutions. In Turkmenistan today, virtually all higher education is in the Turkmen language.[14] Even though the value and quality of higher education have seriously deteriorated in Turkmenistan since independence, a university diploma is a highly prized document. In that country, it is almost inconceivable that a student could complete the courses of a higher educational institution without knowing Turkmen.

The situation with regard to language and access to higher education in Uzbekistan and Kyrgyzstan is very different. True, as part of the secondary school curriculum, a graduate of a Russian-language secondary school in either of these countries is required to complete courses in the state language. However, in these countries, lack of knowledge of the state language is not a barrier to higher education: graduates of Russian-medium schools need not take an exam of the state language if they intend to enter Russian-medium groups in higher education.

The situation in Kazakhstan is unique, and reveals an attempt to promote Kazakh as a symbol, along with a realisation that its promotion may involve consequences with (at least for the time being) an unacceptably high cost. Until 2008, similar to the situation in Uzbekistan and Kyrgyzstan, those taking the 'Unified National Testing' (UNT) higher educational entrance exam were not required to take a test of their Kazakh language skills if they intended to study in the Russian medium. In 2007, however, it was announced that in 2008 a test of Kazakh language would be made a major UNT component for those seeking to enter Russian language sections in higher education (Nachinaya 2007). This created anxiety among families of many pupils in Russian primary and secondary schools. As a result, the original plans were abandoned. Although the exam remained mandatory, a decision was made not to take it into account as a part of the total entrance exam grade.

These four cases illustrate quite distinct styles of promoting the state language in the respective countries. In Turkmenistan, where virtually all higher education is in Turkmen, the state has obviously made knowledge of Turkmen a condition for higher education. In Kyrgyzstan and Uzbekistan, the state has not required that students

---

[14]Among the exceptions are certain classes in Turkish or English at the International Turkmen Turkish University and certain non-Turkmen instructors who deliver lectures at other institutions in Russian to students whose education is mostly in Turkmen.

entering higher education know the state language. In the case of Kyrgyzstan, this would have contradicted the policy which made Russian that country's 'official' (but not 'state') language. Such a policy would also have contradicted the interests of many members of the political elite and would have been very costly. These latter reasons also likely apply in Uzbekistan, but in that country there seems to be a greater sense that over time the Uzbek language will in any case become dominant.

As for Kazakhstan, the initiative to introduce the Kazakh language exam was a step of potentially enormous importance. As it turned out, however, as a concession to 'linguistic nationalisers' an exam which did not seriously penalise anyone was left as a symbol. The retreat on this policy suggests that the regime was not yet ready to accept the consequences of obliging all students entering the university to know the state language. Whether this might happen in the future is an open question. The answer will shed light on the extent to which Kazakhstan's leadership intends to link the Kazakh state to the Kazakh language, as well as the extent to which this policy is tolerable to broad segments of the country's population.

Indiana University, Bloomington

References

Absalyamova, N. (2005) 'Parlamentarii prinyali paket popravok k konstitutsionnomu zakonu 'O vyborakh v RK'', *Kazakhstanskaya Pravda*, 9 April.

Akanbai, E. (2004) 'About Advantages of the Latin Alphabet', *Kazinform Report*, 16 April, available at: http://www.inform.kz/showarticle.php?lang=eng&id=75040, accessed 4 January 2009.

Akhmatov, T. (1984) 'K voprosu o razvitii i obogashchenii kirgizskogo yazyka', in Orusbaev, A.O. & Sheiman, L.A. (eds) (1984) *Russkoe slovo v yazykovoi zhizni Kirgizii* (Frunze, Mektep).

Edgar, A. (2004) *Tribal Nation. The Making of Soviet Turkmenistan* (Princeton, Princeton University Press).

Fierman, W. (1991) *Language Planning and National Development: The Uzbek Experience* (Berlin & New York, Mouton de Gruyter).

Fierman, W. (1998) 'Language and Identity in Kazakhstan: Formulations in Policy Documents, 1987–1997', *Communist and Post-Communist Studies*, 30, 2.

Fierman, W. (2006) 'Language and Education in Post-Soviet Kazakhstan: Kazakh-Medium Instruction in Urban Schools', *The Russian Review*, 65, 1.

Gafurov, B. (1958) 'Uspekhi natsional'noi politiki i nekotorye voprosy internatsional'nogo vospitaniya', *Kommunist*, 11.

Grenoble, L. (2003) *Language Policy in the Soviet Union* (Boston, Kluwer).

Guboglo, M. (1990/91) 'Demography and Language in the Capitals of the Union Republics', *Journal of Soviet Nationalities*, 1, 4.

Isaev, S. (1965) 'O roli russkogo yazyka v formirovanii kazakhskoi terminologii', in Kenesbaev, S.K., Isengaliev, V.A., Sarybaev, Sh.Sh. & Nurkhanov, S. (eds) (1965) *Progressivnoe vliyanie russkogo yazyka na kazakhskii* (Alma-Ata, Nauka).

Martin, T. (2001) *The Affirmative Action Empire: Nations and Nationalism in the Soviet Union, 1929–1939* (Ithaca, Cornell University Press).

Nachinaya (2007) 'Nachinaya s 2008 goda, s perekhodom na 12-letnyuyu sistemu obucheniya, kazakhskii yazyk stanet obyazatel'nym predmetom pri sdache ENT', 24 April, available at: http://www.zakon.kz/our/news/printt.asp?id=30099280, accessed 6 March 2009.

Polivanov, E. (1926) *Kratkii russko-uzbekskii slovar* (Tashkent & Moscow, Turkpechat').

Postanovlenie Khalk Maslakhaty (1999) 'Postanovlenie Khalk Maslakhaty Turkmenistana 'O navechnom utverzhdenii turkmenskogo yazyka i turkmenskogo natsional'nogo alfavita v deyatel'nosti organov gosudarstvennogo upravleniya, vo vsekh sferakh zhizni nezavisimogo Turkmenistana', *Neitral'nyi Turkmenistan*, 30 December.

Printsipy (1935) 'Printsipy terminologii kazakhskogo literaturnogo yazyka, primenyaemye gosudarst-vennoi terminologicheskoi kommissiei Odobreno s''ezdom kul'turnykh rabotnikov' (Alma-Ata, 1935 g.). [Reference is to the version reproduced in Zhubanov (1999).]

Razvitie (1980) *Razvitie kazakhskogo sovetskogo yazykoznaniya* (Alma-Ata, Nauka).

Sauranbaev, N., Iskakov, A., Makhmudov, Kh., Musabaev, G. & Balakaev, M. (1952) 'K itogam diskussii po nekotorym voprosam kazakhskogo yazykoznaniya', *Vestnik Akademii Nauk Kazakhskoi SSR*, 6, 87. [Reference is to version reproduced in *Akademik Nyghmet Sauwranbayevtyn enbekteri. III tomdyk*, Vol. 3 (2000) (Almaty, Kenzhe Press).

Sharifov, O. (2007) 'Latinizatsiya alfavita. Uzbekskii opyt', 28 April, available at: http://www. ferghana.ru/article.php?id=5092, accessed 4 January 2009.

Simon, G. (1991) *Nationalism and Policy toward the Nationalities in the Soviet Union* (Boulder, Westview Press).

Velikii put' (2008) 'Velikii put' proidem v edinstve', available at: http://www.titus.kz/?type=polit& previd=5943, accessed 7 January 2009.

Zakonomernosti (1969) *Zakonomernosti razvitiya literaturnykh yazykov narodov SSSR v sovetskuyu epokhu* (Moscow, Nauka).

Zhubanov, Q. (1935) 'Qazaq tilinin emlesin ozgertu zhayly', *Memlekettik terminkomnyn biulleteni*, 4. [Reference is to the version reproduced in Zhubanov (1999).]

Zhubanov, Q. (1999) *Qazaq tili zhonindegi zertteuwler* (Almaty, Ghylym).

The Invention of Legitimacy: Struggles in Kyrgyzstan to Craft an Effective Nation-State Ideology

ASEL MURZAKULOVA & JOHN SCHOEBERLEIN

DASTAN SARÏGULOV, THE FORMER STATE SECRETARY under the current President of Kyrgyzstan, Kurmanbek Bakiev, agreed to set aside time in his schedule to meet with us.[1] He had clearly prepared himself enthusiastically for the meeting, ready with a small pile of books and brochures, all of which he had written himself. 'Do you know what these are?' he asked, producing one of his props. He seemed a little surprised when this pair of researchers, a foreign man and a young, very modern Kyrgyz woman, quickly recognised them as the knuckle bones of sheep, used for divining the future. He nevertheless went on to explain with precision how they are used and he then produced an illustration in one of his books, showing that such bones were found in burial mounds in the Altay Mountains dating from sometime about 3,000–4,000 years ago. His point was that the Kyrgyz, which he identified with what archaeologists refer to as the Andronovo Culture inhabiting a huge span of the interior of Eurasia, have a very ancient and enduring culture characterised by a unique spirituality and a harmony with nature, among other things.[2] Thus began his two-hour long account, into which we inserted our questions, about the reasons why there has been such a prolific discourse around the issue of developing an ideology for the new state of Kyrgyzstan. In the context of the broader debates in Kyrgyzstan, Sarïgulov appears as a rather idiosyncratic figure, but his interest in history, moral values, and what makes the Kyrgyz people special and potentially strong are all themes that resonate in the discussions of ideology.

This article addresses the puzzle of why the leaders of Kyrgyzstan, a country beset by one economic or political crisis after another over the nearly two decades since

The article is based on research supported by the Open Society's Central Asia Research and Traning Initiative (CARTI) Programme.

[1]Interview with Dastan Sarïgulov (Parliamentary Deputy, 1995–2000; State Secretary, 2005–2006), Bishkek, 19 November 2008; interviews for this article were conducted primarily by A. Murzakulova, though a minority of them were conducted jointly by both authors.

[2]Sarïgulov's account did not take into consideration the generally accepted view among archaeologists and historians that the Andronovo Culture is associated with the Indo-Iranian peoples—the Saka/Scythians—who inhabited this region before the arrival of Turkic groups, the linguistic heritage of which the Kyrgyz are associated with.

independence, have devoted considerable attention to things like sheep bones, mythical heroes, slogans and flags. What has it all been about?

> Why do we need ideology? The main function of ideology is to stimulate positive changes both in mass and individual social consciousness. Ideology unites the nation; it explains the meaning of the processes taking place in society, and helps to conceptualise the goals and tasks of developing the country. A society, when it possesses a strong ideology, itself becomes strong. The people, united by a single idea, are capable of a great deal in their enthusiasm. But before this is possible, we must create such an ideology that would find resonance in the hearts of millions, and would awaken the dormant potential of the nation. (Rakïmbay uulu 2005)

> The goal of ideology is to mobilise the citizens to achieve the happy present and future, to secure reliable prospects for the generation that is coming of age, and to preserve moral values. (Nazarov 2006)

> At first we were the periphery of the Russian Empire, and then we became the Soviet provinces. The cattle farm of USSR, with an educated population, whereon, by-the-by, they produced torpedoes and cartridges. And what are we now? (Beshimov 2008)

Problem orientation and methodology

As Kyrgyzstan embarked on the project of state building following the collapse of the USSR in 1991, this has been accompanied by broad discussions of the role of state ideology in this process. Ideology is held to be a key to successful state building, which sometimes seems to be more important than any more practical area of policy. Often, the failures of state building are blamed on the absence of a suitable state ideology. Political and ideological leaders generally express their dissatisfaction with previous iterations of post-Soviet ideological programmes, but they remain engaged in the project trying to produce a better one. One might be tempted to explain this as sheer inertia of a belief—inherited from Soviet times—in the crucial role of ideology in the functioning of the state. Or perhaps instead that ideology is deployed as a sort of smokescreen to turn public attention away from more practical issues such as rebuilding a failing economy or combating corruption.

We will argue that it is most useful to analyse these debates as a key feature of the post-Soviet political environment which helps to reconstruct relations between the state and society. Central Asian regimes are usually conceptualised in authoritarian terms, in a system where agency is concentrated in the regime. Thus, ideology is analysed as something that emanates from the political elite and acts on a passive population (Akbarzadeh 1996, 1999; Marat 2008; Adams 2004, p. 94). But the fact that the discourse about ideology is permeated with notions of its mobilising power points to the need for considering the agency of the population in this framework. This study suggests that the system from which discourse about ideology emerges is not solely driven by elite concerns but also by those of other social actors. Thus, we should not consider ideology as subterfuge and empty symbolism, but as the idiom in which concepts of freedom, responsibility, and a just social order—the concepts which give shape to the relationship between the state and the society—are formulated and contested in a process which involves actors 'from below' as well as policies issued 'from the top down'.

Furthermore, studies of ideology in Central Asia generally assume a relatively simple process, wherein ideology is viewed as a homogeneous product, the impact of which is assumed to be contingent mainly on its message (Hegarty 1995; March 2002, 2003). In our study, we go further, to analyse the changing manifestations of ideology as they relate to the changing political context, noting that it is impossible to understand the meaning of the specific ideological initiatives and debates that occur at a given time without reference to the political context from which they emerge. The variegated post-Soviet period, now almost two decades long, provides the possibility for such an analysis, in contrast to previous work treating ideology as largely a product of what is imagined as a static political environment. And we consider the way that the ideological message is interpreted in the political process based not only on the message itself, but also on the context in which it is produced, and specifically, on the roles played by people who are charged with producing it, presenting it, and interpreting it in the public discourse.

The project is formed by some of the basic assumptions which underlie Antonio Gramsci's concept of 'cultural hegemony' (1971), and Michel Foucault's concepts of power (1975) and 'discursive formation' (2002). With Gramsci, we recognise that state power is enacted, not only through coercion, but also through persuasion. The state ideology is thus a means by which a vision of the relationship between state and society is promoted, such that loyalty to the state is attained among the population. However, we do not see this process as exclusively serving the interests of the elite ideology producers. Rather, with Foucault (1975, 2002), we see a more dynamic process whereby the ideological system is formed by processes that mediate the engagement of a wide variety of social actors. What comes out of this—the formulations of ideology—must be understood as a product of multiple actors' engagement.

This study is based on three main sources of information: our interviews, published texts by contributors to the ideological debate, and sources on the general political context in which the ideological process is played out. In the period from September 2007 to December 2008, we conducted 12 in-depth interviews of members of the ideological elite, selected for their prominence either in the process of formulating state ideology or in the public discourse in which these debates have been articulated.[3] We were particularly interested in those who lead or otherwise are influential in the state institutions that are responsible for promoting ideology, morality and culture among the population—the ministries of education and culture, universities, the state agencies responsible for Islam (the State Committee on Religion and the Muftiyat). Meanwhile, we were also interested in those who contributed substantially to public discourse, promoting positions that were sometimes counter to those of state actors. We did not particularly try to embrace the full diversity of views, but rather concentrated on views that were integral to the wider debates. The interviews were semi-structured, working from a list of 14 questions asking for assessments of the specific features of post-Soviet state ideology and the debates about them.

---

[3]Most interviews were conducted primarily in Russian, although Kyrgyz was also used.

We also draw on textual materials including speeches, publications, press interviews and other materials, containing the views of key figures in the ideological debates, many of whom we also interviewed. The prolific debates on ideology have been played out at numerous conferences, policy round-tables, press interviews and editorials which have contributed to a wealth of relevant textual materials. For these purposes, we made a thorough survey of the Kyrgyzstan newspapers with the largest and widest circulation—*Slovo Kyrgyzstana*, *MSN*, *Obshchestvennyi reiting* and *Vechernyi Bishkek*—as well as the internet-based information agencies Tazar, AKIpress and Kabar. We complemented this with a survey of scholarly and media sources for analysis of the political context in which the ideological debates are situated.

The producers of ideology whom we focused on represent a diversity of social positions: government ministers, university rectors, teachers, journalists, NGO staff, Islamic leaders, and so on. Some were central figures in the official initiatives to produce state ideology. For example, Kusein Isaev (a prominent university professor) and Muratbek Imanaliev (a former Foreign Minister and current head of a think-tank) were members of the group charged by the current president with elaboration of the official ideological programme for Kyrgyzstan (Razvitie cherez edinstvo 2007). Alibek Jekshenkulov, another former Foreign Minister (2005–2007), and leader of an opposition political bloc, had initiated the adoption of an ideological frame for external politics aimed at promoting an image of the state projected outward on the world arena. Jolbors Jorobekov twice headed the State Commission on Religion (1999–2002, 2006–2007). In 1992–1993, Askar Kaikeev held the post of State Secretary (head of President Akaev's administration) and was the Minister of Education from 1993 to 1998. Muratalï ajï Jumanov has served as Mufti of Muslims of Kyrgyzstan since 2002.

Other interviewees were in roles outside of state-sponsored institutions: Tashmambet Kenensariev is a prominent member of the opposition party *Erkindik*, alongside his role as rector of Jalal-Abad State University in southern Kyrgyzstan, and he also played an active role in the so-called 'Tulip Revolution' which led to President Askar Akaev's ouster. Denis Toichiev, leader of the NGO Youth Parliament of the Kyrgyz Republic, was associated with the politics of 'new internationalism' during the Akaev period, and he was also a member of the governing council of the Assembly of the People of Kyrgyzstan. Turat Akimov, Editor-in-Chief of the newspaper *Obshchest-vennyi reiting* (2007–2008) was an initiator of a special rubric in the newspaper dedicated to questions of national history, genealogy (*sanjïra*), and the search for an appropriate ideology.

In Kyrgyzstan, there has been a wide array of ideological initiatives which range from appeals to the multi-ethnic character of the state to claims about the moral heritage and the ancient roots specifically of the Kyrgyz people and their special role in the Kyrgyz Republic. Though our analysis is not comparative, it is nevertheless instructive to consider Kyrgyzstan in the context of other Central Asian countries, where there has also been a tremendous emphasis on the production of national ideologies. The year 2009 in Tajikistan, for example, has been dedicated to the legacy of the founder of the Hanafi Islamic legal school which predominates in the region. Turkmenistan's national ideology has featured such symbols as Makhtumkuli (a seventeenth century Turkmen poet), the melon, the horse, and the ideological text, the

Ruhnama, attributed to President Niyazov whose eccentric rule ended with his death in 2006. Historical state-builders feature prominently in these ideological initiatives, such as Timur in Uzbekistan and Ismāil Sāmāni in Tajikistan, both of whom founded empires and dynasties.

If we characterise the trends in ideological debates from 1991 onwards, all across the region the early 1990s saw relatively coherent, if hurriedly formulated discourse focused on the idea of independence and 'national self-determination'. However, already by the mid-1990s, changes occurred regarding the character of public discourse, and in many countries the matter of state ideology became the exclusive purview of the heads-of-state. Hence, in Turkmenistan, Uzbekistan and to a lesser extent in Kazakhstan, the debate turned into a monologue coming from the institution of the presidency.

In this regard, the case of Kyrgyzstan is not typical, for though the presidents have remained engaged in initiating ideological programmes, it is not their exclusive domain, and the discussions are still very open. Where other Central Asian states, like the Soviet state that preceded them, have been relatively successful in maintaining a monopoly over the production of symbols, in Kyrgyzstan this constitutes a field of competition and negotiation in which the state is only one among a variety of actors, and often not a particularly decisive one. As a result, we consider that the state-centred analysis that has dominated scholarship on Central Asian states is inadequate— certainly for the study of Kyrgyzstan, and undoubtedly for the study of other Central Asian countries, as well.

Kyrgyzstan's 'ideological space'

The 'ideological space' in Kyrgyzstan is characterised by a diversity of positions as well as actors. This is in contrast to what existed during Soviet times, when ideology was produced and disseminated by a set of central institutions under the control of the Communist Party of the Soviet Union.[4] In Kyrgyzstan since independence, there is no analogous centralised process or institutions. This creates the opportunity for a wide-ranging political field of contention, encompassing actors who are making appeals and critiques not only from above. There is even the possibility to promote alternative rules and values, by which state ideology should be defined. New conditions in access to information make the field of ideas a highly competitive one. There are the traditional institutions of ideology, such as state-run schools and universities, and the state sources of information (including press offices and government-friendly information agencies), while there is also a range of new actors, such as private schools and universities, mosques, independent media, NGOs, and independent scholarly centres and think-tanks.

A significant role in the discussions has been played by the Kyrgyz intelligentsia, whose independence has greatly increased following the collapse of the USSR, although their social status has declined. Their engagement in this process allows them to aspire to a role close to the authorities, as a sort of court intellectual. Whether or

---

[4]For an analysis of how Soviet ideology was propagated, see Kara-Murza (2006) and Voslenskii (2005).

not they curry favour with the regime, their authority on issues of ideology—such as their knowledge of history or ability to assert positions on moral issues—enables them to reclaim some of the social role that had been accorded to them through high salaries and privileged status during Soviet times.[5] The role that the intelligentsia plays is understood simultaneously as meeting the needs of the state and fulfilling a demand from society. Understood in these terms, both the intelligentsia and ideology play a role in mediating relations between state and society, which, despite the social and economic shocks of the 1990s, maintains continuity with rules and procedures familiar from Soviet times, as well as with concepts such as 'the Soviet people'. Ideology thus provides a framework for understanding both past and future, and the intelligentsia, adapting to new political conditions, provides a connecting link with traditions established in Soviet times. Chinghiz Aitmatov (1928–2008), the author who spoke in many ways for the late-Soviet generations, described it thus in an interview with a journalist:

> Given that behind us we have a common life that was difficult and complex, we all derive from the Soviet system. From the USSR. Yes, Soviet ideology was decisive. But during all those years, we got to know each other. Culture and scholarship penetrated and enriched one another. In just such a context we were formed. Remember that the first priority at that time was to define oneself as a Soviet individual. Only after that came the question of who one was by nationality. (Karlyukevich 2003)

Our interviewees also stressed the way that ideology is firmly rooted in the Soviet past. For example, one respondent declared:

> We are a society with a strong ideological past, educated on the ideology of the USSR. It is difficult for our generation to think of itself outside of a framework, in which ideology is necessary both as a kind of projector, and as that which can unite.[6]

According to another, 'We need to live out the consequences of the communist ideology. Many people are thinking according to this stereotype. The attempt to create a new ideology for Kyrgyzstan comes precisely from this'.[7]

So a particular attitude seems to be a part of the Soviet legacy, involving the assumptions that every state needs an ideology, that it is the job of the political leadership to develop and promote that ideology, and that the intelligentsia has a special role to play in this. This assumption operates all across Central Asia, and is articulated implicitly or explicitly, though what unfolds based on it varies greatly. In Turkmenistan, it takes the form of a personality cult, which even three years after President Niyazov's death, still reverberates in the country. In many places, it takes the form of historical claims of continuity with a great past, such as in Tajikistan, where a

---

[5]Concerning post-socialist elite formation in Kyrgyzstan and the role of the intelligentsia in it, see Koichuev (2007) and Nogoybaeva (2007).

[6]Interview with Maksat Begaliev (Instructor at Bishkek Humanities University), Bishkek, 7 October 2007.

[7]Interview with Askar Chukutaev (State Secretary, 1992–1993; Minister of Defence, 1993–1998, 2000–2005; current Rector of Kyrgyz National University), Bishkek, 18 December 2008.

'kinship' is claimed between current President Rahmon and the founder of the great 'Tajik' Sāmānid dynasty of a millennium ago. Even though Uzbekistan, Kyrgyzstan and other Central Asian countries are politically quite different in many ways, including the basis on which they have sought to legitimise the regimes (in Kyrgyzstan, as supporting democracy; in Uzbekistan, as developing their own special model), in all of these countries, ideology is a major component of state building programmes (Akaev 2002; Karimov 2001; Turkmenbashy 2005).

In our view, an important key for the understanding of post-Soviet ideology is recognition that the process of new state formation in the aftermath of the state reconfiguration, such as in the case of the break-up of the Soviet Union and the end of the monopoly of communist ideology, is conceptualised as a liminal condition, wherein the old order no longer holds and a new order is ultimately introduced (Turner 1967). The major trope in conceptualising this liminal condition is the notion of an 'ideological vacuum', which allows the perception of a radical break with the old order, and an unstable interim condition which requires specific operations—here, measures to establish a new ideology—in order to usher in the new order. The procedures that aim to achieve this include renaming: all across Central Asia 'non-national' names—especially 'communist' names such as 'Leninabad' or 'Marx Street'—were traded for names marking out a landscape of personalities and events that make up the new national ideology. Ritualised events also play a major role in this, such as anniversary celebrations in Uzbekistan of figures such as Timur (the empire builder whose 660th anniversary was in 1996) and Baha-ud-Din Naqshband (founder of a major Sufi order whose 675th anniversary was in 1994). Ideology producers are thus bridge-builders, constructing a connection between the past, the present and the future. The image of a vacuous present or recent past serves as justification for the need to create an ideology. Ideology creation thus becomes a part of the rules and procedures in the process of state building. This is simultaneously necessitated by the legacy of ideologised statehood in the region, and by the imperative of providing strong ideology to ensure stability in the process of state building. Furthermore, the discourse about ideology becomes the focus of the elites' ideas about the available means for communicating with the population, and it becomes a mechanism for linking social groups from top to bottom and for mediating relations between state and society.

In analyses of the political systems of contemporary Central Asia the state ideology is also understood as a resource that is capable of providing for elite legitimacy (March 2003; Cummings 2006; Marat 2008). Ideology reinforces a narrative about discontinuity with the past, representing a radical break, via the 'ideological vacuum' with the de-legitimised Soviet past. At the same time, it is precisely in their continuity with the authoritarian state of Soviet times that leaders appeal to ideology for bolstering legitimacy, because ideology is a familiar idiom of state legitimacy inherited from Soviet times.

The political context of ideological production

In the period since independence in Kyrgyzstan, ideological debates have continued unabated. Sometimes they have been tightly linked with political events, such as the discussions of 1993–1994, or the debates which followed the so-called 'Tulip Revolution', while at times they have gone by the wayside of broader public opinion. There have been a large number of ideological initiatives put forward on an even larger number of themes. On two occasions, these ideological initiatives had a comprehensive character and were adopted as formal state ideological programmes: during Askar Akaev's presidency, there was the 'Ideological Programme of Kyrgyzstan: Charter for the Future' (Ideologicheskaya programma 2003), while the second was adopted under President Kurmanbek Bakiev, entitled 'Development through Unity: The Comprehensive National Idea of Kyrgyzstan' (Razvitie cherez edinstvo 2007). These programmes were devised to provide ideological underpinnings for the state-building process. They were accompanied by the publication of various books and brochures, as well as the performance of state-organised celebrations, such as the 1,000 year anniversary of the Manas epic, Osh-3000 (marking the antiquity of Kyrgyzstan's 'southern capital'), and 2,200 years of Kyrgyz statehood.[8] On one level, these events led to a certain public apathy in relation to the project of building ideology. At the same time, they stimulated the participation of different actors in public discussions, including criticism of projects promoted from above and articulation of alternative approaches.

In an analysis of this field of ideological competition, the prominent themes that can be identified include nationalism, 'new internationalism', Islam and '*Tengirchilik*'.[9] These themes are not necessarily well-articulated, and do not represent discrete, mutually opposed concepts, but rather they are intertwined components of various initiatives and programmes. Indeed, typically, these themes are articulated as inter-related components of ideological campaigns; for example, *Tengirchilik*, criticism of Islam, and a history-oriented nationalism often go hand in hand. Each of these themes entails a core set of values, which serves to justify the orientation as a moral imperative. In Islam, this core is 'Muslim values' (rules and procedures of behaviour and social justice); in the new internationalism it is a substitution of Soviet values (of patriotism, solidarity, and the key role of Russian culture); and in Tengirchilik it is notions of prosperity, heritage and social justice, based on the Kyrgyz culture and language. The rhetoric of nationalism is present in virtually all of the discussions of state ideology, and hinges on the necessity of a coincidence of the cultural and political borders, as well as the role of the state in preserving that culture. In asserting one or another position, there is always a subtext regarding the issue of who may legitimately define the directions of state building. Also always present is an assumed threat of a loss of identity, statehood and social cohesion.

---

[8]Manas is an epic hero, to whom the Manas epic—the largest epic text recorded anywhere—is devoted. Celebration of the anniversary of the epic revolved around extracting from the epic story such elements as could be useful for promoting a national state with moral values rooted in tradition.

[9]*Tengirchilik*, sometimes referred to in English as Tengriism (in Russian, as *tengryanstvo*) is an ideology of post-Soviet origins, also enjoying some interest on the part of the political elite in other Turkic regions of the former Soviet Union (Laruelle 2007), which appeals to '*Tengri*', a supposedly monotheistic, pre-Islamic concept of a deity, as well as other customs and beliefs which are supposed to be pre-Islam. *Tengirchilik* is also related to a concept of '*Kyrgyzchilik*', designating the essence of being Kyrgyz. See for example Aitpaeva and Molchanova (2007).

Changes in the balance between these different orientations have accompanied changes in the political context. The projects which were promoted during the 1990s, following the agenda largely set by President Askar Akaev, put the emphasis on a vision of ideology which was on the whole consistent with the values of the Soviet intelligentsia. The rhetoric of Islam as opposed to *Tengirchilik* as alternative foundations for national-state ideology began to gain force in the late Akaev period, and especially following the 'Tulip Revolution'. The common thread that unifies all of the orientations is a notion of the imperative to achieve national unity as a necessary condition for prosperity and stability.

In general, the themes raised at various times under the Akaev administration have continued to set the agenda for ideological strategies of the main actors, even after Akaev's demise in March 2005. These themes are represented in slogans which were promoted under Akaev: 'Kyrgyzstan—our common home', 'Kyrgyzstan is a state of human rights', 'The seven commandments of Manas', '2,200 years of Kyrgyz statehood', among others. The concepts which Akaev proposed have been interpreted differently by different groups. On the positive side, there was agreement, whatever the intrinsic merits of the symbolism, that it was aimed at strengthening statehood. Others, meanwhile, dismissed these initiatives as intended to distract attention from the country's economic and political problems. Muratbek Imanaliev, a Foreign Minister under Akaev, told us, 'I supported the idea to celebrate 2,200 years of Kyrgyz statehood, not because I also share it, but because for the future this idea will have an important effect and significance for statehood'.[10]

The components of Akaev's ideological programme ranged from short slogans, for example, 'Kyrgyzstan—our common home', to much more elaborate formulations, such as the 'Charter for the Future', various book-length publications and public celebrations (for example, those associated with the 2,200 years anniversary of Kyrgyz statehood, and the Manas epic). It should be noted that the slogan of the common home, which found institutional expression in the Assembly of the People of Kyrgyzstan (APK), remains today one of the principal elements of the policy of new internationalism not only in Kyrgyzstan, but also in Kazakhstan.[11]

The ideology of civic nationhood, proposed by Akaev and embodied in the Assembly of the People of Kyrgyzstan, serves today as the main focus of criticism on the part of those promoting ideologies of Islam and Kyrgyz nationalism. Meanwhile, many other features of Akaev-era ideology have received such criticism, such as the 'Seven commandments of Manas' and '2,200 years of Kyrgyz statehood'. This criticism came to a head with the 'Tulip Revolution' in March 2005. Almazbek Atambaev, one of its leaders, said 'All this foolishness, such as the seven commandments of Manas, which the previous regime was constantly harping on about, is a load of rubbish, Putin is not endlessly talking about the commandments of

---

[10]Interview with Muratbek Imanaliev (Foreign Minister, 1997–2002; current president of Institute for Public Policy), Choq-Tal village, Isïq-Köl Province, 16 August 2008.

[11]The APK was created in 1994, and an analogous structure has existed in Kazakhstan since 1992. With the constitutional reform in 2007, the APK in Kazakhstan was assigned the role of selecting nine deputies to the parliament. In Kyrgyzstan, there were also attempts to enhance the status of the APK; after the constitutional reform in 2002, the status of the APK was upgraded as a deliberative body under the President of the Kyrgyz Republic.

Ilya Muromets!' (Kabar Kyrgyz National Information Agency 2006). Immediately on coming to power, then Acting President Bakiev proclaimed, 'We should stop rushing for historical leadership. The Kyrgyz are an ancient nation, living among and together with other ancient nations'.[12] The Mufti of Kyrgyzstan, Muratalï ajï Jumanov, also can be heard making criticisms in a nationalist spirit: 'I think that the idea of Akaev, "Kyrgyzstan—our common home", did not take account of the interests of Kyrgyz people; that's why this idea will not meet with approval'.[13]

Although by the time of our interviews, the Akaev regime was already a thing of the past and the Bakiev regime had already begun to assert ideological positions, most of our interviewees tended to focus overwhelmingly on the concepts proposed under Akaev. From this, one may conclude that the Akaev-era notions, whatever shortcomings were seen in them, nevertheless set the agenda for later debates, and subsequent efforts were often focused on improving these ideas. The following statement by Tashmambet Kenensariev, a prominent intellectual, is typical:

> In order to unite the people, Akaev was trying to create a pivot and was searching for it in history. He was trying to create a basis on which the Kyrgyz would be proud of their past, but he left out the unifying elements. The role of Manas as a factor of ideology is more suitable for the northern Kyrgyz, while in the south, for example, in Batken or Osh Provinces, it is not really so important. Manas is important for Kyrgyz spirituality, but it cannot be accepted as a substitute for national ideology, because it is a type of folk creation, not an ideological one.[14]

The echoes of Soviet 'internationalism' were strong in Akaev's ideology, appealing to the vision of a civic nation in the good traditions of the Soviet intelligentsia. Early on, Akaev put forward the concept of 'Kyrgyzstan—our common home', appealing to the idea of the nation as a family:

> I would propose the following philosophy. Your country is your home. Thus, our Kyrgyzstan is our common home. Indeed, it has been built by all of us, including Kyrgyz, Russians, Uzbeks, Germans, Jews, Uyghurs, Koreans, and Karachays. They built it without any doubt that they will live in this home as a single family in friendship and harmony, for eternity. (Akaev 1995, p. 97)

The same theme continued to reverberate through the late Akaev period: 'We are a consolidated and stable nation of the Central Asian region, where the ideology of an amicable home inhabited by a united family became a firm foundation of the unified interethnic community of the Kyrgyz people' (Ideologicheskaya programma 2003).

The Assembly of the People of Kyrgyzstan is a clear example of how Akaev's ideology aimed to create a connection between images of the Soviet and post-Soviet societies of Kyrgyzstan. However, at the same time, Akaev clearly felt it important to

[12]K. Bakiev, 'Obrashenie ispolnyayushego ob yazanosti Presidenta Kyrgyzstana Bakieva narodu Kyrgyzstana', 30 April 2005, Bishkek, Kyrgyz Television and Radio. See also Bakiev (2005).

[13]Interview with Muratalï ajï Jumanov (Mufti of Kyrgyzstan), Bishkek, 16 January 2008.

[14]Interview with Tashmambet Kenensariev (at the time of the interview, Prorector of the Kyrgyz–Russian Slavic University; Rector of Jalal-Abad State University; candidate for deputy from the Erkindik party in the 2007 parliamentary election), Bishkek, 17 December 2007.

appeal to the Kyrgyz nationalism of those who were becoming the elite of the new country. Hence, in parallel with promoting this internationalism, Akaev rolled out a campaign promoting the symbol of Manas, which clearly was in a degree of tension with the new internationalism. In 1995 the Akaev government organised a celebration of the 1,000th anniversary of the Manas epic. Although planning for this celebration had already begun in Soviet times, the new symbol was claimed for Akaev in his effort to strengthen the Kyrgyz elite and the rhetoric of nationalism. Such appeals to nationalism have clear resonance:

> [The policy of] 'Kyrgyzstan—our common home' aimed to consider the interests of the non-titular population. I consider this to be wrong, because—since this is the state of the Kyrgyz people—it is necessary to put first and foremost the interests of the Kyrgyz people. Think about it: in France, the Arabs must learn French in order to be French citizens.[15]

Even one of those most engaged in the institutions of internationalism offered this ambiguous assessment of their social effect: 'I do not think that the Assembly [of the People of Kyrgyzstan] plays a role for preserving interethnic harmony; however, it is important as an element of popular democracy'.[16] The apparent utility of the Assembly is not in its institutional functioning, but in its symbolic value. The Assembly paints an image of multicultural Kyrgyzstan sustained by an ideology of 'interethnic harmony'. Even after Akaev's demise, the Assembly retains its importance. After his rise to power, President Bakiev also aligned himself with the Assembly, and it is apparent that the Assembly is treated as a resource for dealing with the deficit of legitimacy that widely affects politics in Kyrgyzstan. According to Askar Chukutaev, a prominent former Akaev government official, 'The Assembly, in general, is a successful idea, and that explains why it still exists. It is another matter that the Assembly has come to pursue pro-authority politics. It has come to be used for achieving certain goals'.[17] The two divergent concepts, 'Kyrgyzstan—our common home' and 'Manas', were intended for different audiences. These messages must necessarily be considered as parts of a single strategy; where one piece does not work, the other is deployed. Their common objective is to obtain the solidarity and loyalty of different groups within the society. In explaining the ideological dilemma, some people try to map their experience onto that of a country like America, where the nation concept does not have a strictly ethnic character. For example: 'Kyrgyzstan as a country inhabited not only by the Kyrgyz; or a state where the Russians, Tatars, Uzbeks and others call themselves the Kyrgyz people—here we ought consider what sort of future we imagine and what we aspire to'.[18]

While the Akaev regime's ideology focused on these two polar themes, other themes have also competed in this field and increasingly have come to the fore—most

---

[15]Interview with Kuseyn Isaev (professor at Bishkek Humanities University; president of the Sociological Society of Kyrgyzstan; member of the working group for the development of the state ideology in 2007), Bishkek, 16 December 2008.

[16]Interview with Denis Toychiev (head of the Youth Parliament NGO, 2000–2001; member of the Council of the Assembly of the People of Kyrgyzstan), Bishkek, 3 November 2007.

[17]Interview with Askar Chukutaev, Bishkek, 18 December 2008.

[18]Interview with Denis Toychiev, Bishkek, 3 November 2007.

prominently, Islam and *Tengirchilik*, both of which also are put forward as the potential basis for state building.

Islam, as an ideology, presents the problems of the development of the state in the light of a moral lapse in society. With the help of Islam, the Kyrgyz—or indeed, society more widely in Kyrgyzstan, among which Islam is considered naturally to play a pre-eminent role—will overcome their current problems, which are primarily conceptualised as having a moral character. Appeals to Islam are contingent on the expectation that the religion will provide a set of guidelines—rules and procedures— for addressing society's ills. As Kyrgyzstan's Mufti put it, 'Missionaries come to us from foreign countries, and mass culture fills up our screens, and this has a negative influence on Kyrgyz morals, traditions, and culture'.[19] This position is articulated, not only by the traditional Islamic leadership, but also by young voices with a more secular appeal:

> Ideology must possess the power of suggestion . . . to influence people's behaviour through an impact on their consciousness. . . . The time has arrived to make up our minds, for with every day there is an increasing risk of repeating the same mistakes of the Mayram-Akaev epoch of poetic Manas commandments.[20] Furthermore, we are being asked to return to the very sources of dark ignorance of the archaic stage of paganism.[21] For what purpose? . . . The majority of the population historically associate themselves with traditional Islam. Is it not here that we should seek the possibility for . . . active work of the state? . . . Is it not here that we have the possibility to create our counterbalance as a more modernized, progressive traditional Islam of an orthodox orientation? . . . It is necessary to create under the government a committee for state (national) ideology and propaganda. This can involve and make use of the resource of religion in work among the population, especially the rural population. (Malikov 2005)

Here, there is a high degree of contrast with Uzbekistan, where the discourse in opposition to Islam is the concept of a secular society and a strict isolation of Islam from the state, education and other domains.[22] In Kyrgyzstan, there is also a sharp competition between Islam and appeals to an image of the Kyrgyz people's primordial, pre-Islamic condition in '*Tengirchilik*'. The central concern of this ideology is to formulate a version of Kyrgyz culture which is free of Islam. From the perspective of *Tengirchilik*, Islam is dismissed as exogenous to Kyrgyz identity, and as fundamentally at odds with the essence of Kyrgyz character. In the words of Dastan Sarïgulov,[23] the most prominent proponent of the *Tengirchilik* ideology:

> We need to return from Islam to the ideology of *Tengirchilik* . . . . Islam is a system with the help of which it is easy to control people, and which came here through the migration of Tatar mullahs. Islam is the death of the spirits of nomads . . . .[24]

[19]Interview with Muratalï ajï Jumanov, Bishkek, 16 January 2008.

[20]Reference here is to Mayram, the unpopular wife of the former president.

[21]This reference is to *Tengirchilik*.

[22]For example, Adeeb Khalid's concept of 'secular Islam' (2003).

[23]The most prominent proponent of the *Tengirchilik* ideology, Dastan Sarïgulov held the post of State Secretary of the first presidential administration of Bakiev in 2005, during which time he devoted considerable public attention to the cause. For an exposition of his views, see Sarygulov (2001, 2007).

[24]Interview with Dastan Sarïgulov, 19 November 2008, Bishkek.

Kusein Isaev, who was also involved in developing the official state ideology under Bakiev, further argued: 'The activisation of Islam in our social conditions is wrong. Among the Kyrgyz, the holy fire, water, stones, moon, and many "holy sites" are sacred even today, and they are still revered by the Kyrgyz'.[25]

Concern with the loss of identity is a theme that runs through discourses about Islam and *Tengirchilik*, as well as nationalism more generally. The discourses are filled with parallel processes of 'loss' and 'searching'. Globalisation and other attributes of modernity are viewed as threats to identity, and the loss of historical and cultural memory is a persistent motif in the *Tengirchilik* narrative: 'We have no immunity that would answer the challenges of globalisation, since we have lost ourselves and our past'.[26] Those who appeal to *Tengirchilik* also see in the Kyrgyz past their period of greatness, as typified by the great Manas—in contrast to the poor and marginal position of Kyrgyzstan in the world today.

At the core of all of the ideology projects—including even the project of new internationalism—is the problem of how to preserve what is essential to the Kyrgyz identity. In all cases, it is backward looking, appealing to the morality of a previously prevailing social order, whether it be a primordial Kyrgyz essence, as in *Tengrichilik*, a focus on issues of language and culture preservation, as in nationalism, a focus on Islamic morality and just social order, or a focus on the respect and appreciation for other cultures from Soviet times in the more civic and secular orientation of internationalism. Assumptions about the role of Kyrgyz identity as a principal object of 'protection' to be provided by the state ideology, define the field of ideological competition. Kyrgyzstan's vulnerable position in the face of powerful global forces is a common refrain: 'It is vitally important to realise and to understand that we are the part of a modern, interconnected world, and not the isolated provincial corner' (Ideologicheskaya programma 2003). As Chinghiz Aitmatov put it in a newspaper interview:

> We are choosing the path of our involvement to the modern system. It is simply absurd to close ourselves into our shell, while the world is being shaken by the processes of globalization. I don't dispute that at one time such isolation was necessary and retreating into our shell did save us from destructive outside forces. But not so today.... (Karlyukevic 2003)

It is important to emphasise that these concerns with loss and with the need for finding the right path for society today are not the exclusive domain of leaders trying to claim a following through ideological tropes. Rather, these concerns occupy a substantial part of the intellectual energies of the country. Manas is not simply a state ideology; there are people learning to recite the Manas epic and they are honoured by their communities. *Tengirchilik* may have been devised as an ideology in a rather deliberate way to offer a basis of identity in opposition to Islam, but it has found resonance, at least among a part of the elite who were formed by the Soviet experience and who are deeply concerned with what they view as the danger of Islam as a de-modernising force. Even those on various levels of society who are attracted to

[25]Interview with Kusein Isaev, 16 December 2008, Bishkek.
[26]Interview with Dastan Sarïgulov, 19 November 2008, Bishkek.

nationalism also feel a need to temper that with an affirmation of the value of a society which accommodates multiple cultures, especially the Russian culture which still retains a strong appeal in a great many realms. Furthermore, there is a broad social consensus that it is appropriate for a state to have an ideology, and indeed, that if lacking a good ideology, their state cannot flourish. There are many aspects of Kyrgyzstan society today which feed into the belief in this search for an ideology. The familiarity of the concept and role of ideology from Soviet times is no doubt a part of this, but this is not a matter of sheer inertia. There is also tremendous disorientation caused by the collapse of the Soviet Union, post-Soviet turmoil, and the country's uncertain future:

> Ideology emerges only when the people face desparation [sic]. Desparation is a situation in which it is impossible to resolve one's problems with the help of available resources and means. It seems to me that we are in this very situation, and it results in very large activeness in life. For instance, Kazakhs are better off; they have a lot of money and they do not want to change anything, whereas we want to change many things. All these talks [sic] about ideology, searching for a national idea—all of this means that finally there is a need in the society to answer the question: what should we do next? (Bogatyrev 2006)

In contrast to Soviet times, public discourse is filled with a huge diversity of positions, and individuals are faced with finding their own sense of the right path for their society. Ideology may not hold the answers to many questions that bedevil the future of Kyrgyzstan, but it has become the idiom in which possible paths to the answers are articulated.

Part of the turmoil which strengthens appeals to ideology is the crisis of leadership. There was general disappointment with Akaev, who as well as being seen as increasingly corrupt, authoritarian and weak as a leader, was also viewed as having failed to produce an adequate ideology. Those whom we interviewed were in almost every case eager to criticise the failings of Akaev's ideological projects, but they also almost invariably retained the conviction that ideology is vital. Perhaps even more surprisingly, some of those who had been involved in producing the Bakiev-era ideological programmes have not shown much confidence that they have devised the right formula. Thus, we see that the ability to provide leadership specifically in the realm of ideology is considered to be a key attribute of the good leader:

> We cannot find ourselves; we cannot find the leader who would lead us to our ideals. Our country is in search of an alternative leader. Today, pure chance is a characteristic feature of the Kyrgyz leaders (as in the rise to power of both presidents). We need a person with a heightened sense of what are state attributes. Today, in place of landmarks of the state, religious ones are appearing. The crisis comes from the fact that market values do not reflect our spiritual values, and they stand in conflict. That's why we need not just a leader, but the spiritual leader to serve as a landmark.[27]

[27]Interview with Turat Akimov (Editor-in-Chief of the newspaper *Obshchestvennyi reiting*), Bishkek, 17 December 2008.

Thus, ideology is seen as providing the social order—the rules and procedures—that define the moral and practical relationships between state and society, between leader and population, between intellectuals and the political order, and ultimately, between members of the society in general. A successful search for a state ideology is expected to yield a congruence of identity between the state and the members of the society.

Ideology as a key feature of state building

A curious measure of the explicit importance of ideology in post-Soviet Kyrgyzstan can be seen in a survey that was conducted by the Ministry of Education to assess the state of ideology in the country in the aftermath of the 'Tulip Revolution'. It was a huge study in which 15,000 respondents were surveyed. An overwhelming 92% 'supported the idea of the creation of the national ideology' (Malikova 2006). It is indicative of the circumstances peculiar to Kyrgyzstan that such a study would be conducted, and that the results would be so definitive—people in Kyrgyzstan believe in the idea of ideology. What is more, although the results of the survey were not made available in full to the public, this definitive role for ideology is one thing that the ministry was keen for the public to know. Belief in the idea of ideology is also quite evident in Kyrgyzstan's opinion-leaders, who affirm that it is important for a national-state ideology to provide a set of values and a basis for power and solidarity.[28]

It is noteworthy that while Kyrgyzstan society, even nearly two decades after independence, has not become disillusioned with ideology, at the same time, there have been times when ideological debates are particularly active. Our survey of ideological debate in the Kyrgyzstan press yielded a clear picture: the most active periods of debate were in the periods 1993–1995 and 2005–2006, during the periods when important changes were taking place in the political system. In 1993, constitutional reforms took place which changed the principle of checks and balances in the relationship between the parliament and the presidency. In that reform, the unicameral parliament was replaced with a bicameral one. Then, in 2007 a new constitutional reform further weakened the position of the parliament, this time by means of a transformation from the bicameral system back to a unicameral one.

The first years of independence were characterised by enthusiasm for democratic reforms, and Akaev not only presided over a relatively pluralistic system in which power was only moderately concentrated in the presidency, but he also oriented his appeals for legitimacy to the commitment and success of political reforms. The constitutional reforms were an effort to reconcentrate power in the hands of the executive branch. This required a new relationship between the state and society, and efforts to work out that new relationship are mediated through ideological debates. A similar crisis emerged following President Akaev's ouster in March 2005. During this period, issues came to the fore regarding the roles in government of northern and southern regions of the country. Furthermore, the Bakiev regime was struggling to

---

[28]For example see the contribution to a newspaper discussion by Sultan Raev (Malikova 2006), Sarygulov (2005), Aliev (2006) and Togoybaev (2006). Such views were also expressed in our interview with Muratalï ajï Jumanov, Bishkek, 16 January 2008.

gain legitimacy in the wake of its coming to power by non-constitutional means. This was followed by the parliamentary reform mentioned above.

It is interesting to juxtapose excerpts from the presidentially sponsored ideological programmes that followed each of these periods of rapid political change. Examples include the following: 'We need a new national self-consciousness, based on the idea of state independence, on the principle of democracy, human rights and liberty, a new conscious economic philosophy and applicable code of behaviour of everybody and each person individually' (Ideologicheskaya programma 2003); 'The state without its own ideology cannot be powerful. Because every state must rely upon its own national foundation, and its own common national values, without this, there cannot be clear social development and the ability to provide guidelines for the future' (Razvitie cherez edinstvo 2007, p. 39).

The new round of political uncertainty surrounding the ouster of Akaev, followed by Bakiev's consolidation of his position, for example, led to the creation of a working group on ideology, which produced Kyrgyzstan's second major ideological programme, as cited above. Meanwhile, the work of this group has not been distinguished by 'new thinking', and in essence it repeated the appeal for legitimacy already familiar from the Akaev period, using the same kinds of appeals for legitimacy.

Our analysis of the state ideology programmes of the Akaev and Bakiev regimes has shown a fundamental similarity of their positions. However, our interviews demonstrate that the programmes are interpreted differently: the programme put forward by Bakiev is presented as more oriented to the Kyrgyz in contrast to Akaev's programme. In our view, this does not reflect a difference of programme content, but is more related to the post of State Secretary in Bakiev's administration.[29] Two of the previous State Secretaries in the Bakiev administration, Madumarov and Sarïgulov, have played particularly strong roles in the ideology realm, and both have been perceived as using nationalistic rhetoric.

As we noted previously, the field of ideological competition is in some ways not typical for the region. The state in Kyrgyzstan is not an all-pervasive institution, penetrating all aspects of the society with strong vertical linkages in the system of power and with tight bureaucratic control. The state's role is in many ways as a mediator rather than a system of control. Ideology must be seen then as playing a crucial role in the state's ability to mediate with the society.

> Kyrgyzstan is weak state, first of all intellectually and spiritually. Our people has lost itself in self-identification. Some are southerners, while others are northerners, a third group includes ardent Muslims, while others are atheists. We also have the *Tengirchilik* people [*tengryantsy*], democrats, autocrats, right-wingers and left-wingers, Bugus, Bostons,[30] and so on. Who don't we have? Accordingly, there are many different ideas. Mainly they are small and personal. There is no sober, united view on the principles for development of the country. Correspondingly, everyone is weak: the authorities, the opposition, and ordinary people.

---

[29]Key roles of the State Secretary include public relations duties and what in American terms might be called the 'Ideology Czar'.

[30]Bugu and Boston are names of Kyrgyz lineage groups.

Weak ideas mean weak spirit. That's why we aren't taken seriously. They will do with us whatever they want. (Junusov 2007)

This refrain of dissatisfaction with the quality of Kyrgyzstan's ideology is striking, especially when most of the critics also remain convinced that effective ideology is crucial to successful state building. What is it that is lacking, then? How is the success of ideology to be assessed?

The current stage of the development of Kyrgyzstan has put on the agenda the objective of a search for our own national identity and its elaboration of basis of national ideology and statehood. One way this has taken form since 2006 is in the armchair format for work on writing 'national ideology'. This chosen approach has no prospects and has been exhausted. This was confirmed by the discussion of the latest 'document', which no one takes seriously. The reason is simple: the ideologies should not be written in offices ... They are born in the boiling of daily life, crystallizing themselves in concrete ideas, which are understood and shared by the majority. (Omarov 2007)

This vision of the 'natural' development of ideology, of course, has nothing in common with the way that ideologies are in fact formulated in the political process of Kyrgyzstan. Here ideology is always characterised by abstract formulations, self-consciously put forward in the form of public discourse. This critique of ideology in Kyrgyzstan is characteristic of the ideological environment overall: there is a broad consensus that ideology is needed as the glue to hold Kyrgyzstan society together, but there is an equally strong sense that attempts to date to create a state ideology have been unsuccessful. There is a sense that ideology should be something 'natural' for a people—something that grows out of their history and moral qualities—but with all forms of ideology under heavy debate and critique, there is a sense that everything that is on the table is somehow 'artificial'. Thus, it may be that the Soviet-style vision of ideology is not compatible with a society such as Kyrgyzstan where it is possible to debate things so extensively.

If we consider ideology as a system, one thing that is most striking about the debates in Kyrgyzstan is how little the vision for ideology has changed since Soviet times, despite the dramatic changes that the society has undergone. The object that ideology is meant to impact for all ideology-producers is the same: the 'hearts and minds' of the population. And the main tools to which they appeal for achieving this effect are the same: ideological production is to be carried out by government committees with the participation of ideological specialists among whom the intelligentsia plays a special role; the ideological initiatives thus devised are to be propagandised via education and the mass media (Malikov 2005; Malikova 2006; Toygobaev 2006). There is great continuity with the vision of the 'mechanism of ideology' from Soviet times.

At the moment, we are in a relative lull as regards ideological debates, following the most recent burst of activity in 2005–2007. This reflects the fact that the political system has for the moment stabilised, following Bakiev's consolidation of his position. However, we can expect that if there is a new contestation of the balance of political forces in society, there is likely to be a renewed focus on ideology. Furthermore, we may observe a strong tendency to return to the same ideological symbols, thanks to the fact that Kyrgyzstan inherited from Soviet times a set of concepts of nation, ideology and social consensus which continues to give form to the ideological debates. Thus, for example, Manas is a theme which was first promoted in a context where Islam was being played down, and Manas as a mythic hero was traced to pre-Islamic times. But more recently, he is being reinterpreted in the context of Muslim values, and has already been transformed into a sort of 'believer hero'.[31]

The persistence of appeals to ideology is explained by the fact that ideology is considered to be a fundamental element of statehood—a means for achieving regime legitimacy and effective state building. As such, ideology is understood as having concrete and vital effects in providing coherence in state and society. It is also understood as the space in which social consensus can be achieved, especially in periods of political destabilisation such as 1993 and 2005. Those who make appeals to ideology view it as a mechanism by which it is possible to meet the deficit of political trust and to provide for social justice and solidarity.

The fact that ideological debates in post-Soviet Kyrgyzstan have revolved around the themes of nationalism, internationalism, Islam and Tengirchilik is not incidental. These themes capture many of the issues that are at play in the definition of relations between the state and society in Kyrgyzstan today. The debates about ideology are thus not a disconnected elite discourse, but rather an integral part of the process of seeking social consensus. The fact that there is so much dissatisfaction with state ideology in Kyrgyzstan today—but still a conviction that state ideology is needed— reflects the severe lack of social consensus that characterised the post-Soviet period in Kyrgyzstan, as well as the resilience of Soviet concepts and practices aimed at achieving that consensus.

Kyrgyz–Russian Slavic University
Harvard University

References

Abdurazakov, I. (2006) 'The National Ideology: The Choice of Direction', *Round Table Materials*, Institute of Public Policy, available at: http://ipp.kg/files/roundtables/RTFeb22_2006_ENG.pdf, accessed 14 May 2009.

Adams, L. (2004) 'Cultural Elites in Uzbekistan: Ideological Production and the State', in Jones Luong, P. (ed.) (2004) *The Transformation of Central Asia: States and Societies from Soviet Rule to Independence* (Ithaca, Cornell University Press).

Aitpaeva, G. & Molchanova, E. (2007) 'Kyrgyzchylyk: Searching between Spirituality and Science', in Aitpaeva, G. (ed.) (2007) *Mazar Worship in Kyrgyzstan: Rituals and Practitioners in Talas* (Bishkek, Aigine Cultural Research Center).

Akaev, A. (1995) *Kyrgyzstan: na puti stanovleniya nezavisimosti: Izbrannye vystupleniya i rechi Prezidenta Kyrgyzskoi Respubliki Askara Akaeva* (Bishkek Uchkun).

Akaev, A.A. (2002) *Kïrgïz mamlekettüülügü zhana 'Manas' eldik eposu* (Bishkek, Uchkun).

Akbarzadeh, S. (1996) 'Nation-Building in Uzbekistan', *Central Asian Survey*, 15, 1.

Akbarzadeh, S. (1999) 'Nation Identity and Political Legitimacy in Turkmenistan', *Nationalities Papers*, 27, 2.

Aliev, A. (2006) 'Kakaya ideologiya nam nuzhna?', *MSN*, 28 March, available at: http://www.msn.kg/ru/news/13439/, accessed 26 April 2009.

---

[31]Interview with Muratalï ajï Jumanov, Bishkek, 16 January 2008.

Bakiev, K. (2005) *Ölkönü rekonstruktsiyaloo: Kïrgïz Respublikasïnïn Prezidentinin mildetin atkaruuchu Kurmanbek Bakievdin uluttuk telekörsötüü zhana radio arkïluu kairïluusu (2005–zhïldïn 30-apreli)* (Bishkek, Uchkun).

Beshimov, B. (2008) 'Kyrgyzstan: top-problemy natsii i Realpolitik', *Politika, Institut obshchestvennoi politiki* (Bishkek), 28 March, available at: www.ipp.kg/ru/analysis/621/, accessed 26 April 2009.

Bogatyrev, V. (2006) 'National Ideology: Choosing the Direction', Round Table held on 22 February, Institute of Public Policy, available at: http://ipp.kg/files/roundtables/RTFeb22_2006_ENG.pdf, accessed 26 April 2009.

Cummings, S. (2006) 'Legitimation and Identification in Kazakhstan', *Nationalism and Ethnic Politics*, 12, 2, pp. 177–204.

Foucault, M. (1975) *Discipline and Punish: The Birth of the Prison* (New York, Random House).

Foucault, M. (2002) *The Archaeology of Knowledge* (London, Routledge).

Gramsci, A. (1971) *Selections from the Prison Notebooks* (New York, International Publishers).

Hegarty, S. (1995) 'The Rehabilitation of Temur: Reconstructing National History in Contemporary Uzbekistan', *Central Asia Monitor*, 1.

Ideologicheskaya programma (2003) *Ideologicheskaya programma Kyrgyzstana: Khartiya budushego. Prilozhenie k Ukazu Prezidenta Kyrgyzskoi Respubliki ot 15 maya 2003 goda No. 152* (Bishkek, Tipografiya Administratsii Prezidenta).

Junusov, B. (2007) 'Pravila kozlodraniya', Informational Agency Tazar, available at: http://www.tazar.kg/news.php?i=8463, accessed 7 April 2008.

Kabar Kyrgyz National Information Agency (2006) 'A. Atambaev o razgovorakh po natsional'noi idee: Vse eti gluposti tipa 7 zavetov Manasa o kotorikh taldychili prezhnie vlasti—eto polnaya chush", available at: http://rus.gateway.kg/news/analytics/3477, accessed 26 April 2009.

Kara-Murza, S.G. (2006) *Manipulyatsiya soznaniem,* revised edition (Moscow, Algoritm).

Karimov, I.A. (2001) 'Predislovie', in *Ideya natsional'noi nezavisimosti: osnovnye ponyatiya i printsipy* (Tashkent, O'zbekiston).

Karlyukevich, A. (2003) 'Chingis Aitmatov: Ya yavlyaus kosmopolitom…(interv'yu)', Rossiiskaya gazetaprilozhenie 'Soyuz: Belarus'-Rossiya', 7 August, available at: http://www.centrasia.ru/newsA.php?st=1060556400, accessed 26 April 2009.

Khalid, A. (2003) 'A Secular Islam: Nation, State, and Religion in Uzbekistan', *International Journal of Middle Eastern Studies*, 35, 4.

Koichuev, T. (2007) 'Elita postsotsialisticheskogo obshchestva: Kogo k nei otnosit'?', *Obshchestvo i ekonomika*, 5/6, June.

Laruelle, M. (2007) 'Religious Revival, Nationalism and the "Invention of Tradition": Political Tengrism in Central Asia and Tatarstan', *Central Asian Survey*, 26, 2.

Malikov, K. (2005) 'Gotovy li my segodnya prinyat' ideologiyu? I esli da, to kakuyu?', *Slovo Kyrgyzstana*, 5 August.

Malikova, B. (2006) 'Zhelezobeton dlya natsii' [Discussion with S. Raev, Minister of Culture of the Kyrgyz Republic, K. Chyganov, Acting Chairman of the Assembly of the People of Kyrgyzstan, and E. Baisalov, Chairman of the Coalition NGO 'For Democracy and Civil Society'], *Vechernyi Bishkek*, 6 January.

Marat, E. (2008) *National Ideology and State Building in Kyrgyzstan and Tajikistan*, Silk Road Papers, January (Washington, DC & Stockholm, Central Asia–Caucasus Institute/Silk Road Studies Program).

March, A. (2002) 'The Use and Abuse of History: "National Ideology" as Transcendental Object in Islam Karimov's "Ideology of Independence"', *Central Asia Survey*, 21, 4, December.

March, A. (2003) 'State Ideology and the Legitimation of Authoritarianism: The Case of Post-Soviet Uzbekistan', *Journal of Political Ideologies*, 8, 2.

Nazarov, S. (2006) 'O gosudarstvennoi natsional'noi ideologii', *MSN*, 1 February, available at: http://www.msn.kg/ru/news/12825/, accessed 26 April 2009.

Nogoybaeva, E. (2007) 'Kyrgyzstan: formirovanie i vzaimodeistvie politicheskoi elity', *Tsentral'naya Aziya i Kavkaz*, 1, 49.

Omarov, N. (2007) 'Razmyshleniya nakanune dnya nezavisimosti Kyrgyzstana', *Informatsionnoe agentstvo 24.kg*, available at: http://www.24.kg/glance/2007/08/30/60693.html, accessed 26 April 2009.

Rakïmbay uulu, N. (2005) 'Novaya natsional'naya ideya dlya Kyrgyzstana: Nuzhna? Kakaya?', *Obshchestvennyi reiting*, 3 January, available at: http://rus.gateway.kg/news/analytics/946, accessed 26 April 2009.

Razvitie cherez edinstvo (2007) *Razvitie cherez edinstvo: Obshchenatsional'naya ideya Kyrgyzstana* (Bishkek, Tipografiya Upravleniya delami Prezidenta).

Saadanbekov, J. (2005) 'Ideologiya formiruetsya ne zavisimo ot nas', *Slovo Kyrgyzstana*, 10 February.

Sarygulov, D. (2001) *Bespametstvo potomkov razrushet budushee i unichtozhaet proshloe* (Bishkek, 'S-B-S').

Sarygulov, D. (2005) *Kyrgyzy: proshloe nastoyashee i budushee* (Bishkek, 'S-B-S').

Sarygulov, D. (2007) *Ubienie natsional'noi pamyati ili SPID* (Bishkek, TAS).

Toygobaev, J. (2006) 'Problemy gosudarstvennoi ideologii', *Obshchestvennyi reiting*, 2 February.

Turkmenbashy, S. (2005) *Ruhnama* (Ashgabat, State Publishing Service Turkmenistan), available at: http://www.turkmenistan.gov.tm/ruhnama/ruhnama-index.html, accessed 26 April 2009.

Turner, V. (1967) 'Betwixt and Between: The Liminal Period in Rites de Passage', in Turner, V. (1967) *The Forest of Symbols* (Ithaca, Cornell University Press).

Voslenskii, M.S. (2005) *Nomenklatura* (Moscow, Zakharov).

Mass Spectacle and Styles of Governmentality in Kazakhstan and Uzbekistan

LAURA L. ADAMS & ASSEL RUSTEMOVA

Styles of governmentality in Central Asia

MOST ACCOUNTS OF POLITICS IN CENTRAL ASIA ARE variations on a theme: former Soviet apparatchiks usurped state power and became authoritarian leaders in their respective states (Bunce 1998; Collins 2006; Gleason 1997; Jones Luong 2002; Olcott 2005). Authors often point to the basic similarities between Kazakhstan and Uzbekistan, which both score as 'not free' on indexes of political and civil liberties published by organisations such as Freedom House (Collins 2006, p. 6; Olcott 2005, p. 148; Rumer 2005; Smith *et al.* 1998, ch. 7; Spechler 2008, ch. 5). In spite of rather dramatic differences in the economic policies they have pursued, President Nursultan Nazarbaev of Kazakhstan and President Islam Karimov of Uzbekistan are indeed similar: both leaders have remained in power for more than 17 years by manipulating formal political institutions and by becoming increasingly repressive of societal institutions. Rather than fostering the development of civil society and implementing democratic political reforms, both leaders have perpetuated inefficient and corrupt bureaucracies and encouraged a view among their population that they alone have the ability to take care of their people. But in this last point the leaders again diverge: each president takes a rather different role in relation to his citizens, and thereby cultivates differences in the ways that their respective states relate to their populations and vice versa.

In this article we explore this relationship between state and population that Michel Foucault (1991) termed governmentality, in order to highlight what we find to be important differences between the two countries that larger political analyses might overlook. We do not attempt to theorise or explain as much as we seek to interpret the differences, sometimes subtle and sometimes not, in what techniques and practices are enacted, what forms of knowledge are produced, and what kinds of subjects are constituted in each country. While a strictly Foucaultian approach would require us to investigate everyday micropolitics, our research is grounded instead in relations of power that are typically cast in the state–society paradigm (Jones Luong 2003; Migdal 2001; Mitchell 1991). De-centring the state from its stereotypical functions (such as repression, taxation, welfare provision) to the realm of celebration provides us with interesting insights into how power relations are produced in the two countries. Rather than examining political campaigns, social movements or official policies for evidence of differences in governmentality, we devote most of our attention in this article to a realm that is particularly rich in symbolic content: the mass spectacles orchestrated by the state on national holidays, which enable us to look at how states attempt to channel power through ritual action and carefully selected symbols of the nation, as well as how citizens experience their relationship with the state through such rituals and symbols.

We argue that despite their commonalities in the realm of formal politics and the fact that stability is the primary end towards which both governments direct their behaviour, Kazakhstan under President Nazarbaev and Uzbekistan under President Karimov have developed distinct styles of governmentality. In Kazakhstan, state actors see the primary role of the state as managing society via incentives and arms-length regulation within the framework of market competition.[1] State initiatives emphasise this idea with slogans such as 'a competitive nation' and 'competitive products' (Nazarbaev 2006, 2007). The citizens in turn are encouraged to pursue self-enrichment projects whose success is credited to Nazarbaev's policies. In Uzbekistan, however, the state has a very different relationship to its population. Karimov's regime promotes a strong state that penetrates and intervenes in all social realms, a state that asks for unconditional support, patience, and obedience among its citizens.[2] Its argument for legitimacy is based on the uniqueness of the 'Uzbek way' whose success is long term and incremental in nature. As a result, the lived experience of these states is very different and characteristic of a managerial style of governmentality in Kazakhstan and a paternalistic style of governmentality in Uzbekistan. Table 1 summarises our argument.

Uzbekistan has a strong, paternalistic state that aims to shape its population through discourses about nationhood and moral order that are crafted by the government itself. The Uzbek government portrays itself as the guarantor of the good in society, as well as the arbiter of what constitutes the good. Broadly speaking, enemies of the state are those who threaten to disrupt the moral order, which flows from the person of President Karimov himself. This threat comes not just from challenges to the state, but even from non-compliance with the state. In fulfilling the roles of economic and moral arbiter, the state penetrates extensively into society and relies on hierarchical forms of social organisation to control the population. The particular models of the good that the government has chosen rely heavily on a backward-looking national idea that draws on essentialist discourses about ethnic and

---

[1]This point is reflected repeatedly in various government programmes such as the Government of Kazakhstan (2001, 2003).

[2]'Uzbek Leader: Corrupt Officials "My Enemies"', *BBC Summary of World Broadcasts*, 11 September 2001, available via: www.lexisnexis.com, accessed 2 December 2008; 'Uzbek President Visits Home Region, Appoints New Governor', *BBC Summary of World Broadcasts*, 17 December 2003, available via: www.lexisnexis.com, accessed 2 December 2008; 'Uzbekistan: President Karimov Says He Will Shoot Islamic Fundamentalists', *BBC Summary of World Broadcasts*, 1 May 1998, available via: www.lexisnexis.com, accessed 2 December 2008. Among the most recent ones 'Uzbek Leader Rebukes Central Region's Top Officials for Low Efficiency', *BBC Summary of World Broadcasts*, 17 April 2008, available via: www.lexisnexis.com, accessed 2 December 2008; 'Address by the President Islam Karimov at Festive Ceremony Dedicated to 14th Anniversary of Independence of Uzbekistan, Tashkent, 1 September 2005', available via: www.uza.uz, accessed 2 December 2008.

TABLE 1
STYLES OF GOVERNMENTALITY IN UZBEKISTAN AND KAZAKHSTAN

	Paternalistic governmentality (Uzbekistan)	Managerial governmentality (Kazakhstan)
Government's view of its population	Passive, malleable, collective, hierarchical	Individuals driven by desire in a system of exchange
Techniques of power	Impose models of the good, state is strong and omnipresent	Provide broad economic models with little content, manage exchange through incentives
Forms of knowledge	Right/wrong; problems caused by disruption of the moral order	Cost/benefit; problems caused by an imbalance in the system
The 'national idea'	Essentialist and backward-looking national idea	Contextual and forward-looking national idea

national identity, leaving little room for a specific vision of what would constitute success in fulfilling the goal of becoming a 'great state in the future' (O'zbekiston kelajagi buyuk davlat).

Kazakhstan also has a strong state, but rather than put forth specific models of the good, the government focuses on broad models of efficiency and progress that only superficially propagate ethno-national and historical content. Instead, the 'national idea' of Kazakhstan is defined differently in different contexts and discourses of the nation are comparatively forward looking. The government views its population not as a dangerous mass to be rigorously policed but as a network of individuals who act based on their needs and desires, and the government sees its task as facilitating the exchanges that will meet those needs and desires by providing incentives and corrections to problems that crop up in the system. Threats to that system come from inaccurate data or from disruptions, such as political upheaval. President Nazarbaev guarantees order not through moral authority but through beneficence and efficiency. The success of the nation is linked to its management of diversity and its integration into the global economy.

In this analysis, we are not trying to discern the causes of these different styles of governmentality as much as to provide a textured description of how power relations are expressed in each country, and to interpret how these differences in style play out in various symbols and practices. Specifically, we focus on holiday celebrations as a particular regime of practices, where we can clearly see the productive aspect of power, how power 'induces pleasure, forms knowledge, produces discourse ... [rather than just] as a negative instance whose function is repression' (Foucault 1980, p. 119). Although we do not focus our empirical attention here on the everyday experience of this particular regime of practices, we do explore disciplinary relations of power. Both governments made the creation of new holidays (and the 'revival' of old holidays) a high priority in their nation building process, continuing the Soviet tradition of seeing holidays and festivals as key opportunities to shape the subjectivities of their citizens (Binns 1979/80; Chatterjee 2002, ch. 6; Lane 1981; Petrone 2000). Despite the common Soviet legacy, today there are differences in degree, and sometimes in kind, between the styles of governmentality that show up in the holiday spectacles of the two countries.

National holidays in Kazakhstan and Uzbekistan, as in many countries, take the form of mass spectacles, of outdoor concerts attended by thousands in the capital cities on the day of the holiday. Mass spectacles are a rather rarefied object of study, but one where the state strives for maximum influence over the perceptions of its population.[3] Mass spectacles in particular are an interesting form of power relations to study because they have properties that enable elites to close opportunities for input from below, but they do not make the masses feel left out like closed-door proceedings or official decrees do. These kinds of spectacles enchant and persuade, and their audiences feel included without feeling responsible for action. Spectacles tend to monopolise discourse by privileging the definition of truth and reality belonging to elites, and by using technology such as the mass media to create a one-way flow of communication. As Lisa Wedeen noted in her excellent analysis of the cult of Hafez al-Assad in Syria, political spectacles also 'help to foreclose possibilities for political thought and action, making it hard either to imagine or enact a truly democratic politics' (Wedeen 1999, pp. 155–56). Ideology, when cloaked in spectacle, takes on a vibrant quality of democratic participation, even though there is nothing democratic or participatory about it. Mass spectacles produce a hum of excitement and physiological arousal that, as Durkheim noted, binds us more closely to the group sharing the experience and fixes in our minds the ideas and symbols portrayed therein (Durkheim 1915, pp. 236–45). In Foucault's terms, spectacle restricts the field of possible actions that agents can take, but the restriction is disguised by spectacle's aesthetically and psychologically pleasant properties.

Our argument about holiday spectacles is structured by Mitchell Dean's framework for studying governmentality (Dean 1999). We start with Dean's category of 'telos', the 'ultimate ends and their utopian goals', that direct and legitimate actions (Dean 1999, p. 33), which also encompasses the 'national idea' (*natsional'naya ideya*) of each country, a term that has become popular in Central Asia as the solution to the so-called 'ideological vacuum' left by the collapse of communist ideology.[4] The second dimension of Dean's framework that we explore is the 'fields of visibility', or 'diagrams of power' that characterise a particular government: how does it illuminate what it wishes to expose and how does it hide what it wants to obscure? We explore the visual representations of government and the governed in holiday spectacles, the spatial portrayal of relations of authority and the aesthetic mapping of relationships between different categories of people within and outside of the nation state in the second section of our argument.

In our third section, we explore ways of doing and ways of knowing, the dimension that Dean calls the '*techne*' and '*episteme*' of government. *Techne* is the power dimension that entails the 'means, mechanisms, procedures, instruments, tactics, techniques, technologies and vocabularies [by which] authority [is] constituted and rule [is] accomplished' (Dean 1999, p. 31). The *episteme* of government is a dimension of practices of government that is, in the Foucaultian tradition, closely intertwined with

[3]On these kinds of mass spectacles, see Adams (forthcoming), Falasca-Zamponi (1997), Macaloon (1984) and Roche (2000).

[4]'Komu nuzhna natsional'naya ideya?', available at: http://www.ferghana.ru/article.php?id=5874, accessed 24 March 2009.

techne and entails how we understand truth and how knowledge is constructed (which we also touch on in the telos section). This dimension examines how governance is accomplished through practices that constitute truth, expertise and rationality (Dean 1999). We explore how relations of power are constituted through the spectacle production process, how the role of the audience for holiday concerts expresses relationships between the state and the population, and how authority is constituted in the person of the president through cults of personality by proxy. In our conclusion, we revisit Dean's framework and provide some analytical tools which might help provide an explanation for the differences between Kazakhstan and Uzbekistan.

Telos: utopia and governmentality

Official discourse in both Kazakhstan and Uzbekistan emphasises the goals of stability and prosperity, but the difference is in the way that these goals are to be achieved. We commence our introduction to the two cases by providing an overview of each government's portrayal of its ultimate goals, which Dean labels the 'telos'. Telos is the utopian element of governmentality that lays out 'the type of person, community, organization, society or even world which is to be achieved' (Dean 1999, p. 33). In the 1990s, the two governments adopted different logics of transition: Uzbekistan took a gradual path to a market economy, leaving the state as a major owner and distributor of economic resources, whereas Kazakhstan turned sharply away from the 'old system' and implemented extensive market reforms. President Karimov has emphasised the idea of the 'Uzbek Path' (to independence, to development, to civil society) (Karimov 1993), while President Nazarbaev has focused on a programme called 'Kazakhstan-2030', a development plan dedicated to 'prosperity, security, and the improvement of living conditions for all Kazakhstanis'.[5] The ideal goals of Kazakhstan and Uzbekistan diverge most fundamentally in the principles that guide state intervention into economy and society, that is, the specific role that the state envisions for citizens in its economy. But there are also important differences in terms of how goals are set and progress is defined (that is, how accountability works in each country), and in the role of ethnic heritage in the utopian vision.

Essentially, the 'Uzbek path' of reform sees the role of the state as ensuring social protection and redistribution and looks to an ethnic past for models of utopia. Karimov's conception of Uzbekistan's own 'authentic' path to independence was initially characterised in ethnic terms: the Uzbek path 'first and foremost follows from the national–historical way of life of the population, the style of thought, the folk traditions and customs', namely collectivism, respect for elders, duties to family and children, friendliness to all nationalities, interdependence and compassion for those less fortunate (Karimov 1992, p. 10). Karimov's rhetoric has shifted in the last two years, away from issues of culture and heritage (among the main themes of the 1990s and early 2000s), away from fierce anti-Western rhetoric about Uzbekistan's own

---

[5]'Kazakhstan-2030: Prosperity, Security, and the Improvement of Living Conditions for All Kazakhstanis, Message of the President of the Country to the People of Kazakhstan', available at: http://www.akorda.kz/www/www_akorda_kz.nsf/sections?OpenForm&id_doc=DD8E076B91B9CB 66462572340019E60B&lang=ru, accessed 10 January 2009.

variant of democratisation and civil society (themes of the mid-2000s), to a rhetoric in 2008 and 2009 that emphasises economic development. Karimov's holiday speeches have moved from being litanies of the ethnic virtues of the Uzbek people to recitation of economic statistics, reflecting a change not in substance but in style, an interest in appearing more managerial, perhaps inspired by Kazakhstan's economic success. During his speech before the 2008 *Navro'z* holiday spectacle, President Karimov stated that

> one of the principles of the 'Uzbek model', recognised around the world, is the provision of a strong social policy. In 2007, 53.8% of the government's budget went to the social sphere, and in 2008, that number will hit 54.6%. Such figures are rare in other countries.[6]

However, the principle of the Uzbek path is still paternalism: the guiding hand of the state (rather than the supposedly invisible hand of the market) controls the economy.

In the first years of independence, Kazakhstan's telos also seemed more oriented towards ethnic heritage and vague hopes for reform, but that began to change in the late 1990s after the economic crisis of 1998 and the relocation of the capitol to Astana. This new neoliberal vision of the future came together with Kazakhstan-2030, 'a model, an ideal goal, a dream' of a society where individual citizens and families prosper economically and are able to achieve self-actualisation, where ethnic heritage is respected, and where the state's role is to ensure stability and maintain the country's independence from outside powers.[7] This ambitious programme consists of seven priority areas, including the expected (such as economic growth and development), and the somewhat surprising (professionalisation of the state and the limitation of its functions). In terms of the role that the state envisions for citizens in its economy, one of the main features of Kazakhstan-2030 is a break with 'the old system' by fostering a liberal market economy based on principles of efficiency and utility: 'the new role of the government now consists not in making decisions for the people, but first and foremost in creating the conditions under which free citizens and the private sector can undertake effective measures for themselves and their families'.[8] The plan envisions the state's role as providing the conditions for a decent standard of living, such as being able to provide for one's family, own a home, get a good education and health care, and accumulate funds for retirement. But above all, is economic development:

> Entering fifty [sic] most competitive countries of the world is to be made a national idea ... I should think about the future. I do not think of the next elections, I should think of far

---

[6]'V Uzbekistane otmechaetsya prazdnik Navruz', Uzbekistan National News Agency, available at: http://uza.uz/ru/society/2445/, accessed 15 January 2009.

[7]See 'Kazakhstan-2030: Prosperity, Security, and the Improvement of Living Conditions for All Kazakhstanis, Message of the President of the Country to the People of Kazakhstan', available at: http://www.akorda.kz/www/www_akorda_kz.nsf/sections?OpenForm&id_doc=DD8E076B91B9CB6 6462572340019E60B&lang=ru, accessed 10 January 2009.

[8]See 'Kazakhstan-2030: Prosperity, Security, and the Improvement of Living Conditions for All Kazakhstanis, Message of the President of the Country to the People of Kazakhstan', available at: http://www.akorda.kz/www/www_akorda_kz.nsf/sections?OpenForm&id_doc=DD8E076B91B9CB6 6462572340019E60B&lang=ru, accessed 10 January 2009.

prospects of the country and people, how our children and grandsons will live, that is why I was elected.[9]

In contrast to President Karimov's 'national idea', based on ethno-national values and the conservation of a strong welfare state, President Nazarbaev has a forward looking, development-oriented telos. Although both leaders paternalistically portray themselves as personally responsible for the common good, Nazarbaev, unlike Karimov, allocates both the responsibility and accountability for fulfilling these goals; individual citizens to a large degree are responsible for their own success or failure.

In contrast, the extreme state control over economic development in Uzbekistan allows the government to define a vision of the future divorced from economic reality. The government is not interested in the evaluation of actual material conditions, in the market value of enterprises for sale, or in economic efficiency, but rather in performing the 'Uzbek path to reform'. The government performs, on the ideological level, what Karimov says ought to be true about the 'Uzbek path', and on the material level, what will benefit the oligarchs. Given this performative economy, anything that shatters the illusion of the official truth is considered subversive, whether it be the non-compliance of cross-border trade in the face of official declarations of self sufficiency, or the unwelcome news of harsh reality that accurate economic statistics would bring. In this style of governmentality, non-compliance is seen as a challenge to the existing regime, an impediment to security, and a detriment to its population. The directive nature of Uzbekistan's *telos* disregards the horizontal accountability and genuine reporting that is so common to states that employ economic rationality. Uzbekistan alone among the post-Soviet states has yet to conduct a census of its population. Its economic indicators are widely disregarded for their unreliability, and international organisations such as the International Monetary Fund (IMF) and Organization for Economic Cooperation and Development (OECD) have chastised the government for its lack of interest or inability to conform to international standards for statistical reporting (Saidazimova 2007; Spechler 2008).

In addition, unlike the plan of Kazakhstan-2030 that sets benchmarks and concrete goals with timetables, the definition of progress in Uzbekistan is set year-to-year by the president and his advisors, who designate an annual campaign that targets a particular social group or problem for state support, such as 'The Year of Mothers and Children' (2002), 'The Year of Health' (2005), 'The Year of Youth' (2008), and 2009 'The Year of Rural Development'. These sorts of campaigns reflect a style of governmentality that is paternalistic (the state decides what is best for the 'family' this year), but one that is also spectacular in that social policy is conducted through campaigns rather than through bureaucratised and regularised policy development and programme implementation. This paternalistic style of governmentality envisions a citizenry that is

[9]'The Head of State, Chairman Nursultan Nazarbaev of the Assembly of the Nations of Kazakhstan took part in the XII Session of the Assembly, which was Held in the Peace and Accord Palace in Astana', Official Site of the President of Kazakhstan, available at: http://www.akorda.kz/www/ www_akorda_kz.nsf/news-open?OpenForm&idn=1&idno=D3DCBAE766E725F14625725200336893& lang=en, accessed 3 May 2009.

passive and malleable, a citizenry not of individuals but of groups formed by government categorisation: mothers, pensioners, peasants, youth. In contrast, in Kazakhstan effective social support targets not the entire population, or entire categories of the population (such as 'health workers' or 'youth'), but those who need it most on an individual or family basis. So, for example, rather than seeing unemployment as a social problem and fighting unemployment by creating jobs, the government keeps its distance, creating the economic conditions for job creation and making sure that the system is balanced so that unemployment does not threaten the system itself. If the effects of an imbalance in some part of the system are significant enough that they threaten stability, the state avoids intervening directly, instead providing incentives for the kinds of actions that will correct the imbalance. The proliferation of these kinds of market principles into politics, the forms of knowledge that prioritise assumptions of the market as a superior reflection of reality, is one of the hallmarks of governmentality, where the task of the government is aimed at the development of ever wider circuits enabling and ensuring the circulation of people, merchandise and clean water (Foucault 2007, pp. 51–64). It constantly integrates new knowledge about production, human psychology and economics in order to better integrate the country with the world market.

In addition to embracing this sort of neoliberal vision of state–society interaction, another major difference between the styles of governmentality in Uzbekistan and Kazakhstan is the latter's interest in governing its own conduct. The professionalisation of government, the implementation of benchmarks for progress, the regularisation imposed by statistics, and the openness to assessment are all norms to which the government of Uzbekistan does not even pay much lip-service. As a teleological statement, Kazakhstan-2030 lays out general priorities, but in its implementation, it has specific short-term goals for every two or three years that are based on a rational, managerial approach to policy making: analysing the problems the government would like to target, evaluating the government's own capacity for solving the problem, analysing threats that might prevent the problem from being solved, and only then proposing strategic actions to resolve the problem. The language of description is crucial here: like the government of Uzbekistan, Kazakhstan's government is also performing, but in this case, it is not that the government sets out a vision and pretends that reality is complying. The government is performing its managerial style of governmentality by setting informed targets that are constrained by existing conditions.

None of this is to say that neoliberalism and managerial governmentality have anything to do with political freedom. Kazakhstan's style of governmentality encourages self-discipline, and the acquisition of competitive skills, but only allows people to have the freedom to prosper and improve themselves based on their own capacities. Indeed, in such a system where politics is dominated by economic ideology, democratisation is seen as a threat to the system that Kazakhstan's technocrats have so carefully set up. The government of Kazakhstan maintains the necessary institutions and discourses that 'perform' basic democratic freedoms (such as the racy newspaper *Vremya*, a Nazarbaev family-owned tabloid that performs the role of free press by criticising the government), but the priority of economic growth and development allows the regime in Kazakhstan to depoliticise genuine political problems as technical, managerial and a matter of skill. As a result, democratisation is perceived as a challenge that threatens economic stability and is presented as bringing poverty to the countries that attempt it.

Holiday spectacles as 'diagrams of power'

How do the teloi of Uzbekistan and Kazakhstan translate into the regime of celebration practices?[10] Uzbekistan has two main national holidays that are celebrated with spectacular concerts: Independence Day on 1 September (celebrating the official declaration of independence after the coup of August 1991) and *Navro'z*, the traditional New Year, a spring equinox holiday, on 21 March. Independence Day features a wide variety of cultural elements that characterise the country as a civic nation, while *Navro'z* focuses almost exclusively on an ethnic definition of the nation. Kazakhstan has three main national holidays that entail mass spectacle: Day of the Republic (25 October, the day the Kazakh SSR declared its sovereignty in 1990), Independence Day (16 December, the official declaration of independence, timed to coincide with the date in 1986 when demonstrators fatally clashed with police in Almaty) and *Nauryz* (22 March). Independence Day tends to focus on civic nationhood and international high culture, while Day of the Republic and *Nauryz* tended to have more folk and popular culture symbols, and are focused somewhat more on ethnic Kazakh heritage. All of these holidays (with the exception of Kazakhstan's Independence Day, due to the cold) are celebrated with outdoor concerts and street fairs (*narodnoe gulyan'e*), where the people can stroll from venue to venue, buying food and children's toys from concessions along the way.

These holiday concerts are not simply musical performances, however. In form, they are similar to the internationally recognisable genre associated with the Olympics opening and closing ceremonies. The holiday spectacles of both countries involve many similarities of genre: 'theatricalised' elements illustrating historical or mythical figures or performing everyday folklife activities; fireworks, fancy lighting or other special effects (such as hot air balloons); youth in national costume performing group

---

[10]The research was carried out over the course of four trips to Uzbekistan (six weeks in 1995, 10 months in 1996 and one month each in 1998 and 2002), in which Laura Adams (hereafter LA) conducted in-depth (between one and three hours) interviews with 32 cultural elites, several of whom were interviewed more than once. Seventeen of these elites were involved in the creative aspects of culture production, 10 were academics or critics, and five were bureaucrats. Additionally, she conducted about 35 shorter interviews with other cultural elites from Tashkent and various regions of Uzbekistan, as well as a few in-depth and several shorter interviews about culture and national identity with people who did not fit the definition of cultural elite. She was present at holiday planning meetings and rehearsals on a nearly daily basis in February–March and July–August 1996. She also viewed videotapes of the *Navro'z* Independence Day celebrations from 1994–1998 and saw parts of the broadcasts of the holiday concerts from 1998–2008. The evidence on Kazakhstan is very different, and comes from LA's viewing of the television broadcasts of 16 holiday concerts and nine other holiday spectacles from 1989–2008, archived at the Khabar Television station or in the collection of one of the directors who worked on some of these spectacles, as well as on Assel Rustemova's (AR) personal experience growing up in Kazakhstan. Additionally, one holiday celebration (the tenth anniversary of Astana) was observed by both authors. Only two interviews were conducted with members of cultural elites involved with holiday concerts in Kazakhstan (one by each author).

dances; musical dance performances by amateur folk groups from the ethnic minority's local cultural centre; children singing pop songs in the national language; large-scale depictions of national symbols (such as a large group of young men carrying a football-field sized national flag); well-loved pop stars singing patriotic tunes (often in ensemble); aestheticised military performances (e.g. military bands and choreographed drill moves); and all of it pre-recorded on a soundtrack. These holiday spectacles are both a mirror and a medium of governmentality in the two states, allowing periodic, limited mobilisation of society to take place without the politicisation of everyday life characteristic of more party-states such as the Soviet Union.

One of the differences between these spectacles in the two countries is in degree: the shows in Uzbekistan cost about \$2 million to produce, run up to two hours long, and involve 6,000–10,000 performers, while the Kazakh concerts are less expensive, shorter in duration, and involve somewhat fewer people. There are also differences in genre: the production values of Kazakhstan's concerts more closely resemble Soviet style spectacles of the 1980s (parades, 1980s Olympic-style stadium events) while Uzbekistan's concerts strive to come as close as they can to the aesthetic and technological values of contemporary Olympic ceremonies. Kazakhstan's concerts more often have a parade element to them and their thousands of performers are often arrayed in geometrical formations strung out across a stadium field. Uzbekistan's concerts, on the other hand, take place almost entirely on stages and they make use of masses of performers to perform dances more often than athletic moves.

In the early 1990s, the shows in Uzbekistan were much more similar to those in Kazakhstan than they are today; over time they have evolved from being mere concerts to real extravaganzas. In Kazakhstan, however, the celebrations in Almaty and other cities have stayed largely the same in scale and genre over time; only in the celebrations now held in Astana do we begin to see some of the more flamboyant production values that now characterise Uzbekistan's holiday spectacles. One possible interpretation of these differences is that the importance of these mass spectacles is greater in Uzbekistan than in Kazakhstan. The government of Uzbekistan has put more effort in general into the development of symbolic expressions of the nation, and this is reflected in the greater resources devoted to increasing the technological and aesthetic sophistication, including the appointment of lead directors from the world of theatre (as opposed to from the world of music or sports) to take charge of holiday spectacles.

In terms of content, these holidays did not seem to change much between 1989 and 2008, with the exception of the replacement of communist with nationalist ideology in the early 1990s and, in Kazakhstan, the gradual increase in emphasis on economic prosperity and 'friendship of the peoples' from the early 2000s to the present. There are four main areas of content we use to explore 'diagrams of power', the visual representations the government uses to 'make it possible to "picture" who and what is to be governed, how relations of authority and obedience are constituted in space, [and] how different locales and agents are to be connected with one another' (Dean 1999, p. 33): ethnic diversity, sub-ethnic and regional diversity, history and heritage, and patriotism.

Ethnic diversity

The theme of 'friendship of the peoples' is probably the dominant theme in Kazakhstan's concerts where depictions of Kazakh folk rituals are followed by Ukrainian *chastushki* or beloved Caucasian dances such as *Lezginka*. Presentations from Russians, Ukrainians, Koreans, and so on, play a large role as representatives of their ethnic group in all of Kazakhstan's holiday celebrations, which stands in contrast to Uzbekistan, where 'friendship of the peoples' is typically performed only in the civic holiday concert programme and occupies a much smaller proportion of the programme than in Kazakhstan. Like in Kazakhstan, most of Uzbekistan's Independence Day holiday concerts contain a 'block' of songs and dances by members of Tashkent's ethnic cultural centres, serving as both an index for Uzbekistan's ethnic diversity and a performative declaration of the ideology of civic nationalism. Unlike in Kazakhstan which incorporates these organisations in the governmental structure via the Assembly of the People of Kazakhstan, these cultural centres in Uzbekistan receive only nominal governmental support and are reluctant to devote their time and energy to the holiday concerts. Also, after 1994, the theme of 'friendship of the peoples' was rarely included in Uzbekistan's *Navro'z* holiday concert. In Uzbekistan, the divide between civic and ethnic holidays is much sharper than it is in Kazakhstan, where the show of support for a multi-ethnic civic-national identity in the public sphere is clearly a high priority. The former May Day holiday on 1 May, honouring workers of the world, is now Unity of the Peoples Day in Kazakhstan, which has become the official day to celebrate multiculturalism with, for example, pop concerts featuring bands playing rock music with an ethnic twist appropriate to the band members' heritage.

This emphasis on multiculturalism in Kazakhstan also shows up in the way holiday concerts use language: where in Uzbekistan, the narration, dialogue and lyrics of the spectacle are almost always Uzbek, Kazakhstan's are bilingual. The narration is often in both Kazakh and Russian, so, for example, when historical figures on horseback march down the parade alley, all viewers will be able to identify them. When President Karimov gives a speech at these events, it is always in Uzbek, whereas President Nazarbaev often gives his speech first in Kazakh, then in Russian. Thus even though there is a large component of ethnic nationalism to these spectacles in both countries, in Kazakhstan the narration serves to include citizens who do not speak Kazakh in the 'national idea', while in Uzbekistan citizens who do not understand Uzbek are missed targets of the state's propaganda and rightly feel excluded from the *esprit de corps* of the nation building being done on national holidays. Kazakhstan is much more ethnically heterogeneous than Uzbekistan and seems to have embraced diversity as one of its strengths. This may be related to the managerial style of governmentality, in that it corresponds with the idea that diversity enriches the nation through complimentary exchanges of skills, knowledge and practices. Any citizen participating in these spectacles is forced to acknowledge Kazakh culture but also to experience multi-ethnicity, as well. As other scholars have argued, the government of Kazakhstan does not see ethno-nationalism as a practical, rational strategy (Cummings 2005; Dave 2007; Schatz 2004). For the government to overemphasise Kazakh culture could trigger disruptions to the economic machine they have worked so hard to build.

Sub-ethnic and regional diversity

During holidays in Kazakhstan, regional differences were rarely emphasised,[11] but in Uzbek spectacles, the 'regions' block of song and dance take up more time than any other segment of Uzbekistan's concerts (in Kazakhstan's concerts, the *estrada* singers take up the most time). The regions are emphasised more in Kazakhstan's street fairs, such as a festival held in a park during Astana's tenth anniversary celebration, where the government paid the way of groups from each of Kazakhstan's regions to come and set up a yurt with traditional household items, and to send local performers (but not to the main concert).[12] Uzbekistan has 12 provinces (*viloyatlar*) and an 'autonomous region' inhabited largely by the Karakalpaks, who are considered a distinct nationality separate from the Uzbeks but are included in the regions block because their 'native territory' is within the borders of Uzbekistan. This block serves as a *tableau vivant* of Uzbekistan's cultural cartography: amateur and professional ensembles from each province of Uzbekistan perform a snapshot of folk culture representing their region. The elements of these snapshots include distinctive costume, musical and dance styles, patriotic lyrics that mention the region's accomplishments, and bits of theatrical business representing the way of life in the region, such as baking bread or churning butter.

While Kazakhstan has perhaps swept regional and sub-ethnic differences under the rug in favour of an ethno-national identity defined by central elites (Cummings 2005, pp. 94, 154), Uzbekistan has chosen to highlight regional differences, but only in order to incorporate them into the broader category of Uzbek ethno-national identity. The government of Uzbekistan sees its diversity as an unavoidable deviation from the way things 'should' be: heritage should be united with territory, but Uzbek ethnic identity comes from a history of hybridity, of Persian and Turkic, of sedentary and nomadic, and these complexities are exactly what nationalism demands be glossed over. Furthermore, during the Soviet period, regional elites in Uzbekistan were played against each other by Moscow, solidifying sub-ethnic regional identities in a way that fractured national-level allegiances (Roy 2000). This lack of centre–periphery integration posed an ongoing problem for the nation-building project of independent Uzbekistan. Likewise, the emphasis on the Uzbekness of these regions was an attempt to downplay the country's significant Tajik minority and the Persian roots of much of what is labelled Uzbek national heritage. At a 1996 seminar for directors of regional folk groups who would be participating in the *Navro'z* concert, a director from Bukhara proposed a Tajik song for his group's performance, but was brusquely told that speaking Tajik would not be allowed and that he should just have them sing it in Uzbek. The director replied that this was ridiculous and in the end his group performed an Uzbek song.[13] Regional colour was encouraged by the director in charge of the 1996 Independence Day concert's regions block, but Tashkent choreographers

[11]One notable exception was the extensive, multi-day news coverage of the gifts (statues and the like) given to Astana, on the occasion of its tenth anniversary, by each *oblast'* of Kazakhstan.

[12]LA conversation with a participant in the tenth anniversary celebration and observations of the celebration, Astana, 5 July 2008.

[13]LA, observations of a training seminar for directors from the regions, Tashkent, 27 February 1996. We will return to this point in the next section.

were allowed to shape the performances to their stereotypes of what a Khorezmi or Bukharan dance should be, thereby keeping even the expression of regional diversity under central control.[14] In these ways, the unity of heritage and territory was depicted on stage as well as enacted behind the scenes, though not without conflict between artists representing both centre and periphery.

History and heritage

Kazakhstan devotes a few minutes in each spectacle to pre-Soviet history and heritage. Holiday parades have historical figures, defenders of the nation, such as *batyrs* and Ablai Khan riding their horses, and most shows depict the *Zolotoi Chelovek* (the 'golden man' archaeological find dating from the third century BCE Scythian-Saq civilisation) either in pictorial or dramatised form. More backward-looking symbolic elements are more often found in *Nauryz* (a 'traditional folk holiday') than in the civic holidays. Often *Nauryz* concerts depict Kazakh rituals such as *tusau-kesu* (cutting a ribbon wrapped around a child's legs to symbolise the independence of the child learning to walk) or *shashu-toi* (the farewell a family bids to their daughter on the occasion of her wedding). Uzbekistan's holiday spectacles, however, devote more time to heritage than to any other theme. These spectacles are elaborate, aesthetic explorations of medieval history and ethnic heritage that aim to strengthen the population's identification with historically significant states located on the territory of Uzbekistan, as well as with the tradition that was institutionalised during the Soviet period as Uzbek national culture. This heritage is a pastiche of elements from a variety of cultures: the Zoroastrian holy book Avesta, mediaeval Persian writings and classical Chinese scholarship have all been claimed by Uzbek academics as parts of a repressed cultural legacy that belongs to the Uzbek people. Even the state's appropriation of Islam is framed not as living religious practice but as heritage, as in 2008 when *Pravda Vostoka*'s account of the *Navro'z* concert featured commentary on the state-sponsored reconstruction of sacred sites as the 'ongoing development of our rich cultural heritage ... [and the] study of the scientific and cultural legacies of our great ancestors' (Mirzo 2008). The particular symbols of heritage featured by the government varied some over time for, as with social policy, cultural policy in Uzbekistan is conducted by campaign, with different years featuring a different hero or concept. So while the emphasis changes over time (state building concerns in the mid-1990s were addressed with the fourteenth-century symbol of empire builder Amir Timur, while concerns about religious extremism ten years later were addressed with the fourteenth-century symbol of the founder of the Naqshbandi Sufi order), the symbols themselves are selected at the top for political purposes.

In stark contrast with Uzbekistan's concerts, which focus on a distant past, Kazakhstan's spectacles frequently devote time to remembering the Soviet past, most frequently by dramatising the sacrifice and suffering of World War II, but occasionally (in 1998 and 2001) by performing pieces about tragedies visited on Kazakhstan's citizens by the Soviet government: the famine, Stalin's deportations and the testing of

---

[14]LA, observations of rehearsals and staff meetings for the Independence Day concert, Tashkent, August 1996.

nuclear and biological weapons. This appears to be a fairly standard framing device for the Soviet past in Kazakhstan, one that is a part of the government's emphasis on strength in diversity: the people who were here before (mostly Kazakhs) were decimated by famine, many of the people who are here now were victims of deportation, but we are all in this together. For example, in the spectacle celebrating Astana's first anniversary, there was a whole thematic block depicting 'the tragic history of the people of Kazakhstan'. There are even rare references to the still-touchy issue of Zheltoqsan, the December events of 1986 in which members of the current government are implicated. The government seems to walk a thin line with Zheltoqsan, commemorating the conflict with renamed streets and monuments as another tragedy suffered by Kazakhstani citizens, but avoiding producing any official discourse about the event (apparently there is still no official statement on what really happened or how many were killed). Although a museum in Tashkent is dedicated to these kinds of reflections on the Soviet past, references to historical events of the twentieth century (even World War II) are nearly absent from holiday concerts in Uzbekistan, and there is certainly no trope in Uzbek discourse about the country's 'tragic' history. Instead, holiday concerts overlook several centuries of 'inconvenient' history and attempt to link contemporary Uzbekistan directly to the greatness of a long-ago past.

Patriotism

In both countries, patriotic themes relate to the natural landscape as well as to vague ideas of greatness. Uzbekistan's spectacles contain patriotic platitudes such as 'Greatness is in store for you, Uzbekistan', and 'Uzbekistan, my homeland, my spring flower'. Other themes of patriotism in both countries' spectacles are simply a checklist of the features of a modern nation state: Olympic athletes, military bands, an 'international block' that depicts something about the country's foreign relations. References to Uzbekistan as a 'cradle of civilisation' and to the contributions of Uzbekistan's 'great ancestors' to the spiritual heritage of the Muslim world also underline the outward orientation of this discourse which defers to the judgment of 'the world' in determining greatness. However, vague patriotism in Kazakhstan's spectacles also has a future-orientation tied closely to Kazakhstan-2030, which is a symbol that is not sung about or enacted in performance as often as it is depicted in letters and numbers (for example on billboards, on top of buildings, and in pictorial backgrounds behind the spectacle). The symbolism of this framework for national ideology points to the emphasis on economic development as the government's main priority. In contrast to Uzbekistan's ethno-historical patriotism, Kazakhstan's self image is multi-ethnic and united not by a historical narrative but by a vision of economic prosperity. The holiday spectacles of both Uzbekistan and Kazakhstan have patriotic elements that look outward—projecting an image of a normal nation state to the rest of the world, but in their inward-looking patriotism, they are projecting very different national ideas to their citizens. The corollary to these national ideas is the way that 'diagrams of power' map out the population in each country: as a more-or-less homogenous collective in Uzbekistan, and as a diverse but united group of self-interested actors-in-the-making in Kazakhstan.

Ways of doing and ways of knowing

Viewing holiday spectacles through the lens of 'diagrams of power' gives us insight
into the ways that holiday spectacles draw boundaries and constitute identities.
Boundaries are drawn and relations of power are reproduced in the way that the
concerts are organised and structured, as well. This is where the *techne* and *episteme*
dimensions of Dean's framework intersect: the governmentality approach 'attends to
all the more or less explicit, purposive attempts to organise and reorganise
institutional spaces, their routines, rituals and procedures, and the conduct of actors
in specific ways' (Dean 1999, p. 32). Not just the content, but also the production of
mass spectacles serve as diagrams of power, forming identities and directing how
individuals and groups are 'made to identify with certain groups, to become virtuous
and active citizens' (Dean 1999, p. 32). By analysing the production of holiday
spectacles in Uzbekistan and by making comparisons with Kazakhstan when
adequate evidence is available,[15] we can see how culture production in these two
countries mirrors broader relations of power. Uzbekistan's relations of power are
structured by hierarchy and centralisation which facilitates the government's
monopolisation of meaning, whereas Kazakhstan's relations of power are
somewhat more localised, with a greater degree of initiative, resources and input
being expected from ordinary people and groups in the periphery. The way that
people, from the lead director to an audience member, concretely interacted with these
spectacles also dramatises the relationship people have with the state and the way that
the state enacts, rather than just symbolising their national idea through these
spectacles.

Spectacle production and relations of power

In Uzbekistan, *Navro'z* and Independence Day are, at the highest level, the
responsibility of the state organisational committee for the production of holidays
(the Orgkom, for short). The head of the committee is the prime minister and the
committee is comprised of the cabinet ministers of Uzbekistan, with auxiliary
members from the cultural elite such as poets laureate. A few months in advance of the
holiday, the broad concept of the spectacle is sketched out by a scriptwriter and the
holiday's lead director (who was the same person for most of the concerts throughout
the 1990s through the mid-2000s, indicating one of the main reasons for so much
continuity in Uzbekistan). The rest of the details are delegated to a team of senior
choreographers, directors and composers, but all their decisions are subject to the
approval of the *Orgkom* upon their viewing of a dress rehearsal. The hierarchical
structure of holiday production imposed more general constraints on the creative
collective, since it operated as a command system of cultural production, a particular
'*techne*' of power that characterises governmentality in Uzbekistan. During the process
of preparing for Uzbekistan's holidays, artists are pulled from their regular jobs as

---

[15]We can say considerably more about the production side of Uzbekistan's holiday concerts since
this was a focus of LA's research from 1995 to 2004 (see Adams 2010).

composers or theatre directors by orders from the festival producers, whether they want to contribute to the holiday or not.

Thus, the people who experience a relationship to power through these spectacles most concretely are the performers who participate, ranging from professional singers to students who sit in a section of the stadium making mosaics by holding up coloured panels of fabric. There are literally thousands of extras in these holiday spectacles, many of whom are employed as part of the background effects. In one sense, this is a literal demonstration of the power of the state to mobilise bodies, but it also has a psychological effect on the participants as well as the viewers. The sheer mass character (*massnost'*) of these spectacles results in a sense of overwhelming activity: in addition to the main stage in Uzbekistan's concerts, there are often side stages where dancers perform; during the show, props such as 20 metre-high inflatable buildings emerge along the sides of the main stage; there are hundreds of students sitting in bleachers forming the above-mentioned pictorial backgrounds; young men carrying banners and young women in costumes cycle through the area behind the stage forming patterns and giving a sense of fluidity to the background; and technical effects such as laser lights and glow sticks come into play towards the end of the show. The overall impression of these concerts is that the state commands the bodies of a joyful public as well as the material resources and technological know-how to produce a show worthy of a Las Vegas casino.

But it is not just the fact that the state can mobilise bodies; it is also important how these bodies are mobilised. State power is not experienced by these performers as an abstract force acting upon them, but via the places that shape their everyday life experiences in an intimate way. Government ministries are put in charge of recruiting performers through their workplaces and schools, and bosses and teachers become the immediate agents of state power that coerce or persuade individuals to participate. As Table 2 shows, in Uzbekistan performers are requisitioned in a manner similar to other supplies that the spectacle producers must acquire.

For some of these performers, their participation in these spectacles was experienced, in Wedeen's terms, as an occasion 'for the enforcement of obedience, [inducing] complicity by creating practices in which citizens are themselves "accomplices", upholding the norms constitutive of [the state's] domination' (1999, p. 6). Regimes that rely on 'disbelieving obedience' do not need legitimacy because complicity is what guarantees an act of conscious submission to the state (Wedeen 1999, pp. 69–74). Other performers, however, related their participation in these events as normal or even as pleasurable (Adams 2003). As in the Soviet Union, there is a 'hegemony of representation' in Uzbekistan, which is so taken for granted, that it is not significant enough to merit resistance or even to consider whether one believes or not (Yurchak 1997, p. 163). While there are some true believers, especially among the ranks of the directors of the spectacle, for many, participating is simply

> an act of recognition of how one must behave in a given ritualistic context in order to reproduce one's status as a social actor … To analyze this act only for its truth conditions— as 'real' support or 'dissimulation' of support … —is to miss the point. (Yurchak 2003, pp. 485–86)

TABLE 2

'PRELIMINARY PLAN OF ASSIGNMENTS' ISSUED BY THE MINISTRY OF CULTURAL AFFAIRS DELEGATING
RESPONSIBILITIES TO VARIOUS ORGANISATIONS INVOLVED IN UZBEKISTAN'S 1996 INDEPENDENCE DAY
CELEBRATION (EDITED VERSION)

Ministry name	Provided what	For what purpose
Public education	1,200 technical high school girls	Background—placard mosaics
	150 each boys/girls in grades 3–4	Children's block
	180 young athletes	Sport block
	150 young dancers	Theatrical performance, misc.
	Exhibits, athletic exhibition, contests, performances	Children's festival on plaza in front of Navoiy Theatre
Higher/middle education	2,500 young women and 400 young men	Theatrical performance, misc.
Internal affairs	400 cadets	Flag bearers
	100 cadet-firemen	Construction, stagehands
	Orchestra	Performance during street fair
Public health	2,500 young women and 400 young men	Theatrical performance, misc.
	Medical and sanitation services	Rehearsals
Communication	Megaphones, television transmitters, telephone lines, cell phones	Rehearsals, communication among organisers, transmission of broadcast
Defence	300 cadets	Flag bearers
	Musicians, soldiers	Military block
	20 pyrotechnicians	Fireworks display
	Musicians, etc.	Concert during street fair
Commerce, local industry	Necessary goods and materials	Costumes, props, etc.
Cultural affairs	All Tashkent's theatre troupes, professional and regional artists' collectives, and students of the choreography school, the technical school and institute of culture	Theatrical performance, misc. and supply of costumes, props, etc.
	Professional directors and choreographers	Organising the theatrical performance
	Entertainment of various sorts	Performances during street fair

A mixed-ethnicity (Koreans, Russians and Uzbeks) group of older students participating in the 1996 *Navro'z* concert said they were participating because 'it's a national holiday, the biggest', and 'we are proud to show off our national traditions', but on further questioning, said things like 'they force us to do it', 'we get a bonus in addition to our [student] stipend', 'it's a break from studying'.[16]

Anecdotal evidence suggests that performers are recruited in a similar manner in Kazakhstan, but with a few differences. An interviewee involved in the production of these spectacles in Kazakhstan indicated that the participation of students was entirely voluntary, whereas in Uzbekistan, interviews with the student performers indicated that they felt they could not say no. The interviewee also claimed that schools and other organisations in the Kazakhstani concerts are given some autonomy over

[16]LA, conversations with student participants in the *Navro'z* concert during rehearsals, Tashkent, 16 March 1996.

deciding their own costumes and choreography, but are expected to pay for those costumes themselves.[17] Finally, the MC or narrator of concerts in Kazakhstan will often give credit to the school or organisation sponsoring the group by announcing which school is performing to the music of which composer. Interestingly, none of this is the case in Uzbekistan. Even though the concerts are put together in a very similar way, in Uzbekistan the direction comes from the lead directors, choreographers and composers (none of whom receive credit in the performance), and much of the financing comes from the holiday's main budget. Performers are not officially recognised in the performance as anything but bodies, they represent not their schools or locality, but nothing more than the meaning that is given to them by the spectacle directors.

Similarly, as we mentioned above, meaning was imposed from the top-down and from the centre outward on the performers who came from Uzbekistan's regions to represent their own local culture in the Tashkent concert, and Tashkent experts attempted to impose uniformity on regional celebrations through 'training seminars' for people from the regions responsible for putting on their local spectacle.[18] Thus, what might be an opportunity for an act of regional autonomy ends up reinforcing vertical power relations and the dominance of the centre. In theory, the amateur ensembles that perform in this block are selected by the regional department of culture as being the best representative of the region, but in reality, the regional government sends the ensemble whose director has an arm that can be twisted. For many of the ensembles from the provinces, participation in the performance and in the month of rehearsals preceding it is seen as a hardship. 'It's hard, especially for people who have to leave their families for a month', said a director from another region, 'but it goes through the channels of authority [po linii]. We can't refuse. It's our debt we owe to the government, to our country'.[19] This ambivalence about participation was also evident in the representatives of the ethnic cultural centres, who felt coerced into performing in the 1996 Independence Day concert.[20] Participants in these spectacles feel a patriotic loyalty to the principle of the national holiday, but feel resentment towards the actual agents of state power and the way that the channels of authority work.

In Kazakhstan, the direction of spectacle content from above is much less intense and the government takes a more *laissez-faire* attitude towards holiday production. There are still hierarchical power relations, to be sure, but there are also vertical relationships that are not often evident in Uzbekistan. Kazakhstan's cities and regions seem to be allowed greater latitude in determining the content of their local

---

[17]LA, interview with a director of various holiday spectacles, Almaty, 19 July 2008.

[18]LA, observations of rehearsals, seminars, and staff meetings for *Navro'z* and Independence Day, Tashkent, February, March and August 1996. Mary Doi in her book (2002) on dancers in Uzbekistan found that this process of experts and professionals defining regional cultures goes back to the very beginning of the development of Soviet Uzbek culture. She also found that this resulted in a standardisation and homogenisation of dance styles.

[19]LA, conversation with an ensemble director from Syrdarya Viloyat at rehearsals for Independence Day, Tashkent, 9 August 1996.

[20]LA, observations during staff meetings for Independence Day, Tashkent, 16 July, 1 August and 6 August 1996.

celebrations, or even the date of the celebration: Mangistau celebrates *Nauryz* on 14 March, which local elders say is their traditional date of celebration.[21] Kazakhstan seems to foster a greater degree of delegated responsibility in its culture production process (and in other realms, as well), as opposed to Uzbekistan's hierarchical 'lines of authority'. Local authorities in Kazakhstan are delegated more responsibility and given more autonomy than their counterparts in Uzbekistan, and not just in the realm of holidays (Cummings 2005; Jones Luong 2002). For example, the participation of ethnic dance groups in *Nauryz* celebrations is dependent on the groups showing initiative and self-reliance: the funding is directly related to the number of successful activities their national cultural centre managed to organise in the past. In other words, if minority groups continuously obtain private financial resources and attract people to their events, then the state allocates money for their participation in national celebrations.[22]

Furthermore, the move of the capital from Almaty to Astana has created a multipolar political world in Kazakhstan, and that is reflected in holiday celebrations. For many years, President Nazarbaev attended Almaty's holiday concerts, but now he tends to attend *Nauryz* in Almaty and the civic national holidays in Astana. This split makes sense because in Kazakhstan's episteme Astana is seen as the cultural centre that is oriented towards the world, while Almaty is the cultural centre oriented more towards Kazakhstan's past. Kazakhstan's holidays are also not as neatly split between civic and ethnic holidays, as the featuring of 'friendship of the peoples' in *Nauryz* demonstrates; Kazakhstan is more pluralistic than Uzbekistan because of its demography, as well.

Spectacle audiences and the relationship of people to the state

Of course, these holiday spectacles are also part of their audience's lived experience of the state. In both Uzbekistan and Kazakhstan, these concerts are viewed by more than 10,000 spectators live, and by millions of people on television. In terms of the live audience, there are some interesting differences between the holiday concerts of Uzbekistan and Kazakhstan that enact rather different kinds of boundaries between the state and the people. The live audiences at mass spectacles are stand-ins for the citizenry at large and the way that audiences are constituted and 'conducted' is shaped at these concerts and has symbolic meaning both for the audience's understanding of itself and for the audience's relationship to the president, about which we go into more detail in the next section. The concerts also come across very differently to the broadcast audiences in the two countries and these differences reflect some of the points made above about the state's monopolisation of meaning.

In Uzbekistan up until the mid-1990s, holiday concerts were rather informal affairs for their audiences, much like they are in Kazakhstan. By 1996, however, security perimeters were set up around the parks where the concerts were held,

---

[21]'V Mangistau otmechayut novyi god', Channel 31, 15 March 2005, available at: http://www.31.kz/ 31channel/index.php?uin=1103077523&day=15&month=03&year=2005, accessed 2 April 2009.

[22]AR, interview with the chairman of an ethnic minority centre, Almaty, 3 July 2008.

spectators were required to have a ticket or pass to pass through the perimeter. This security perimeter does not allow ordinary people to get close enough to get a good view of the fireworks on Independence Day and creates a spatial barrier between the concert and the street fair, which is open to the public. In the case of Independence Day, there is a temporal barrier between the official concert and the street fair, as well, in that the latter does not happen until the next day. What was once a temporary staging area taken down between concerts (as is the case in Kazakhstan) became a permanent set of stages and stadium seating for just 10,000 invitation holders. There is a divide in the staging area between the audience and the performers, the latter of whom usually stay on the raised stage and do not interact directly with the audience.

In Kazakhstan, the way the staging area is set up is much more fluid: the general public is allowed to attend, though kept standing behind a barrier. The (temporary) stage is much lower, sometimes with a ramp leading to the area where the audience is standing, so performers can get close enough to have at least minimal interactions with the audience (e.g. by making eye contact). There is also temporary seating set up, but a special invitation is not required and people are free to come and go during the performance. The *narodnoe gulyan'e* part of the holiday festivities is also more closely integrated with the concert itself than in Uzbekistan. In Kazakhstani public squares, both kinds of activities are happening in close proximity to one another. Also, the structures of the staging areas are different, in that the Kazakhstani concerts are organised so that a parade alley can run between the stage and the audience, allowing for floats and other large, mobile pieces for the performance (such as the parade of fancy sport cars in one concert). Like Karimov, President Nazarbaev attends these spectacles himself, but unlike Karimov, Nazarbaev (sometimes to the dismay of his security personnel) is not afraid to climb down from his viewing spot, cross the parade alley, and reach out across the barriers to shake some hands. Clearly there is a difference between the way that mass spectacles diagram the relationship between the people and the leader in these two countries. Compared to holidays during the Soviet era and during the first few years of independence, today's holidays in Uzbekistan involve fewer people overall. Perhaps this was in part an aesthetic decision and in part out of Karimov's concern for his own safety, but it was also due to the willingness of the government-led Organisational Committee to produce a more elitist form of performance that dramatised new political boundaries.

The broadest potential impact these spectacles have is on their television viewing audiences, which are in the millions. This is not to say that the viewing audience at home watched these broadcasts with rapt attention or even retained much of what they saw. It may very well be the case that, except as part of a larger symbolic universe, these spectacles had little direct effect on those not directly participating in them and we did not do any formal research on audience reception of holiday concerts, but questioning of our acquaintances indicated that few of them paid much attention to any part of the concerts except for the performances of the famous singers and musical groups.

The differences between the ways the government-owned television stations of each country crafted their broadcasts of these spectacles also supports the idea that the state in Uzbekistan claims its role as arbiter of the good through monopolising not just meaning, but in a way, by monopolising agency and voice, as well. In Uzbekistan, the holiday concerts are broadcast in their entirety from start to finish without interruption, indicating that they are to be interpreted as a narrative and aesthetic whole, much like a play or a film. In Kazakhstan, while some concerts are broadcast as performance pieces, others are treated more like the Macy's Thanksgiving Day Parade in the United States; that is, snippets of performance are interspersed with interviews with politicians and cultural figures.

The difference results in different impressions of the role of prominent individuals in these spectacles: in Uzbekistan, only the president (who gives a speech at the start) and the pop stars are recognisable as individuals, but only the president is allowed to speak as himself; the singers are restricted to songs with pre-vetted patriotic content. Furthermore, all other performers are either subsumed in a role (famous actors are recognised but are playing a part; they are not representing themselves) or are part of an anonymous mass. In contrast, the president plays a proportionally smaller role in Kazakhstan's holiday broadcast; the broadcasters of Kazakhstan's holiday concerts spread the recognition around to a number of individuals who not only appear on television as themselves, but are allowed to speak, to comment on the concert and the holiday, illustrating the somewhat more diffuse nature of power in Kazakhstan's public sphere. For example, in Kazakhstan's 1997 *Nauryz* broadcast, reporters conducted interviews with the head of the Writers' Union, the Mayor of Almaty, with an ethnic Azeri philologist who spoke perfect Kazakh, and with ethnic Russian veterans of World War II. These individuals certainly were not giving voice to radically different sentiments or opinions that challenged the overall ethos of the celebration in any way, but not all power was channelled via the spectacle directly to the president.

Spectacles and cults of personality by proxy

When asked why the regional ensembles mentioned above bothered coming to Tashkent if it was so inconvenient for them, one of the members of the creative group replied without irony, 'because the president can't travel to all those places himself'.[23] Just as the focal point of the Soviet parade was the point where the marchers passed the platform upon which the leadership was standing, the focal point of the Tashkent spectacle is the place where President Karimov sits. For example, during the *Navro'z* spectacle of 1996, cups of *sumalak* (the special dish of the holiday) were handed out to audience members, beginning with Karimov. As in most authoritarian states, quotes from the speeches of the country's respective leader are found on billboards: one found all over the country in the summer of 2008 (the tenth anniversary of Astana) was 'From Astana, with love' written in Nazarbaev's own handwriting in Russian, Kazakh, and sometimes in English. News articles and broadcasts typically begin with a connection between the event being reported on and the president. So, a report on *Nauryz* often begins: 'President Nursultan Nazarbaev observed the *Nauryz* holiday with residents of Almaty today'. One typical broadcast went on to highlight the

---

[23]LA, conversation with a director working on Independence Day, Tashkent, 23 July 1996.

placement of quotes from Nazarbaev in the parade props, the fact that the president was not bothered by the heavy rain, and his interaction with the viewers along the parade alley, congratulating them on the holiday and 'telling the residents of Almaty [*Almatintsy*] about the new national idea'.[24] If we are to examine the styles of governmentality in Kazakhstan and Uzbekistan, we cannot avoid an analysis of the spectacular cults of the leader in both countries because the state is personified in everyday life by the figure of the president. In nearly every official speech at every kind of ceremonial event, the president is thanked for bringing the country independence, for their wise decisions in guiding the economy and for restoring their (ethnic) nation to greatness.

In other personality cults, the role of national patriarch demands obedience but also implies 'responsibility to provide for the material needs of citizen-children' (Wedeen 1999, p. 51). If the president is the root of all good, the ultimate authority, how can he not be to blame when something goes wrong? In such a cult, a sceptic will blame Karimov for everything from bad roads to low salaries, while a true believer retorts that the president is being shielded from the truth by his toadies and if he only knew how bad life was for his people, he would most certainly do something about it. Both the sceptic and the true believer are taken in by the cult's tendency to portray the leader as omnipotent and thus deserving of all praise or blame. But the cults of Nazarbaev and Karimov themselves perform a sleight of hand in that, unlike Asad or their former comrade Sapurmurat Niyazov in Turkmenistan, the president displaces part of his cult onto another symbol, creating a cult of personality by proxy. The creation of a proxy serves to somewhat stabilise the deligitimising features of the cult of the president by providing an object of admiration that is associated closely with the president but more or less immune from criticism.

The choice of this proxy was closely related to the style of governmentality of each regime: President Nazarbaev made the new capital city, Astana, his proxy, emphasising an orientation to the future, to development, to global managerial ideas of 'best practices', and to aesthetics not based on an ethno-national idea (Bissenova 2007). President Karimov, on the other hand, chose the fourteenth-century ruler, Amir Timur (Tamerlane) as his proxy. For most of the late 1990s, Karimov related almost everything about himself or his actions to Timur, leading to a common discourse about Timur as a patron of the arts and sciences, as a strong leader and caretaker of his people, and as a pious but worldly Muslim. The cult of Timur in Uzbekistan emphasises glories of the past, a strong leader (and the steel of Stalin is echoed in the name Timur, which means iron), a programmatic vision of the good that draws on *The Institutes of Timur* (such as *kuch adoloatda dir*—strength in justice), cultural and scientific accomplishments of the Timurid rulers, and an attempt (not completely successful) to emphasise the Turkic, rather than Persian, essence of Tamerlane's state. In this last section, we will look at a couple of brief examples of how celebratory spectacles work to create these proxy cults.

The tenth anniversary of the founding of Kazakhstan's new capital, Astana, took place on 6 July 2008 preceded by several days of lavish festivities and months of propaganda unlike any campaign previously mounted by the Kazakhstani

[24]Broadcast of 'Pyatichasovoi', Channel 31, 23 March 2006.

government.[25] Nazarbaev's writings propagate slogans such as 'Independence created Astana, Astana develops independence' (Nazarbaev 2008b), and official documents proclaimed the political, spiritual and philosophical meaning of Astana as a symbol of rebirth, renewal and independence that embodied the hopes and dreams of all Kazakhstanis.[26] In previous years, the anniversary had been celebrated on 10 December, but the date had been moved to coincide with President Nazarbaev's birthday (yet when a member of parliament suggested that the city be renamed Nursultan, the president said that was going too far!). In July of 2008, the celebration was everywhere in the mass media, ranging from short interviews with citizens, full-blown high-production value music videos featuring songs with words about Astana, video montages showing picture-postcard perfect scenes of the city, and special reporting on events going on all over the country to celebrate the capital's first decade. The music videos, in particular, were striking for the way that they portrayed the city as an idyllic destination for domestic tourists. The videos were pictures of ordinary Kazakhstani citizens getting their pictures taken in front of Astana's fountains, strolling through the city's parks, driving at night past the new centre's hyper modern architecture, sailing down the river on a picturesque boat ride, or shopping at one of the city's mega malls. The tourist gaze was complimented by the president's gaze, as cameras followed him around the city, viewing the sculptures and monuments sent by Kazakhstan's various regions to honour the capital city's celebration, visiting the newly opened buildings, listening to a multi-ethnic choir singing him a song in Kazakh outside the Central Mosque, attending concerts and cultural events, the culmination of which was a birthday concert for Nazarbaev that featured internationally known opera singers and an embarrassingly deranged performance from Whitney Houston. State television also paired a documentary film about this history of Astana with biographical documentary about Nazarbaev, further cementing the association of the president with the nation's premier symbol of its future-oriented model of economic prosperity.

   Although both presidents started their proxy cults at about the same time, Karimov's cult peaked quickly in 1996–1998 and then abated somewhat as Karimov himself loomed even larger as a symbol of the state. Amir Timur made an appearance in both the *Navro'z* and Independence Day spectacles in 1996 because it was his 660th jubilee year and then, very close to the celebration of Independence Day, there was also a mass spectacle celebrating Timur on Samarkand's Registan plaza. In October of 1996, the Amir Timur Museum opened in Tashkent, featuring a mosaic in the entrance hall that soon became infamous because it portrayed the sweep of Uzbekistan's official history, from ancient times to Amir Timur to the present, with a picture of Islam Karimov at the very top, higher even than the picture of the Koran. Visual and verbal equivalencies were created between Karimov and Timur everywhere in the public realm during these years. For example, in his speeches in the mid-1990s, Karimov

[25]Leading up to the holiday, LA was in Karaganda while AR was in Almaty, and both spent the holiday itself in Astana. This paragraph is based on our observations during late June and early July 2008.
   [26]'Astana is Destined to Be the Capital', *Astana Akimat*, available at: http://www.astana.kz, accessed 5 January 2009.

often referred to the policies of Timur in one sentence and current state policies in the next. The growing discourse about Timur emphasised a picture of him as a patron of the arts and sciences, as a strong leader and caretaker of his people, and as a pious but worldly Muslim. In contrast to Nazarbaev's cult of the knowledgeable manager plotting out a future where prosperity is an end in itself, Karimov's cult drew on past models of good governance emphasising patronage and a worldly spirituality in which prosperity is not an end in itself, but rather a means to cultural achievement. In recent years, however, it seems that Karimov may be taking a cue from Nazarbaev, with the increased emphasis on economic rhetoric and a lessening of the emphasis on heritage as the source of Uzbekistan's greatness.

Conclusion

As these strong cults of the leader indicate, a wide range of policies in both Kazakhstan and Uzbekistan are attributed to the talent, the wisdom and the benevolence of the leader himself. But to what extent do the capabilities and personality traits of Nursultan Nazarbaev and Islam Karimov contribute to the kinds of state–society interactions we have examined here? It is clear that many of the differences between Kazakhstan's and Uzbekistan's styles of governmentality stem from decisions made in the early 1990s, when President Nazarbaev's administration made a commitment to reform Kazakhstan's economy in accordance with the recommendations of international institutions, while President Karimov's administration committed to the Uzbek model and largely rejected both input from outside sources and internal pressures to change the course of reform. Kazakhstan's *episteme*, the practices that constitute truth, expertise and rationality, has therefore embraced neoliberal forms of governance and assumes accountability in the form of professionalisation and benchmarks. Uzbekistan, on the other hand, constitutes truth from the top-down, leading to a situation where avoiding the state can be construed as working against the state, and where power and truth are made to seem as if they flow directly from the person of the president. But is it the case, as some Uzbeks argue, that they were just 'unlucky' to end up with stubborn and dogmatic Karimov instead of flexible and pragmatic Nazarbaev? On one level this explanation may be somewhat frivolous, but what is interesting about this contingent argument about 'luck' is that it shows that from a local perspective, it is possible to reject some of the more deterministic arguments that Western scholars have put forth to explain differences between the two countries, such as sweeping generalisations about differences between nomadic and sedentary societies. Thus far, we have mostly avoided causal arguments about Kazakhstan and Uzbekistan's differing styles of governmentality because we have chosen to take a more idiographic approach in this essay. However, we can suggest some lines of reasoning that the reader might want to consider in trying to answer the question of why Kazakhstan experiences a managerial style of governmentality while Uzbekistan's governmentality is so much more paternalistic.

Earlier, we briefly referred to demographic explanations for why Uzbekistan's 'national idea' is much more rooted in ethnicity than Kazakhstan's, and this focus on backward-looking ethnic identity may also tell us something about Uzbekistan's lack of openness to the rest of the world. During the Soviet era, a series of historical events such as the famine, the forced settlement of ethnic minorities, and the influx of ethnic Russians into the country created a demographic situation that limited the ability of independent Kazakhstan to establish a nation-state based on an ethnic 'national idea' in the way that Uzbekistan has. Kazakh nationalism is relatively weak due to the fuzzy boundaries between Kazakh and Russian culture, and the 'negative identity' of many Kazakh elites at the time of independence (Cummings 2005, p. 78; see also Schatz 2004; Dave 2007). For these reasons, Kazakh culture may have been less useful as the basis for a 'national idea' than Uzbek culture was. Furthermore, Kazakhstan's economic development was closely tied to Russia, perhaps leading Kazakhstan to be more open than Uzbekistan to international influences in determining its policies (Gleason 2003, p. 37; Olcott 2005, p. 148), and shaping its more neoliberal 'ways of doing and ways of knowing'. Soviet Uzbekistan did not experience the extreme demographic shifts that Kazakhstan experienced. Economic development in Soviet Uzbekistan was less associated with an influx of Europeans, keeping economic power during Soviet times was much more firmly kept in the hands of ethnic Uzbeks. Because of this greater cultural homogeneity in Uzbekistan, the prospect of ethnic, as opposed to civic nationhood, gave greater guarantees of stability to those in power in the short term at the time of independence.

The salience and legitimacy of ethnicity can tell us something about the telos in the two countries, but we have also noted differences in techniques of power, specifically hierarchy and centralisation. In providing historical background to the current political situation, authors often point out that the nomadic Kazakhs had loose governmental structures that required consensus among various leaders, thus permitting them considerable autonomy, whereas sedentary societies such as that of the Tajiks and Uzbeks in Transoxiana required strong central control, rewarding submission to the needs of the group, which leads to monitoring and control over individual behaviour (Gleason 1997; Olcott 1994, p. 22; Yalcin 2002). This kind of historical argument to explain contemporary political differences is problematic because it neglects the more recent Soviet past and is usually based on a cultural determinism that precludes a possibility of real social change. However, in as much as the leaders themselves refer to these cultural legacies to legitimate their political decisions, the social constructs of 'Kazakh culture' and 'Uzbek culture' may have an effect on the differences in governmental styles. Cultural tropes such as 'Uzbeks need a strong hand' and 'Kazakhs are clannish' can have political effects, even if they are 'just' stereotypes. The invocation of 'Uzbek culture' had resonance and gave Karimov a kind of legitimacy that Nazarbaev could not get with a similar invocation of 'Kazakh culture', for precisely the reason that much of the Central Asian elite buys into this kind of cultural essentialism.

State centralisation in Kazakhstan may also be hampered by the vastness of the territory and low density of Kazakhstan's population, combined with 'too many different populations whose interests are not shared' and who could simply move elsewhere (Olcott 1994, pp. 43–44). This led to an elite at the time of independence that was divided ethnically and regionally fragmented, pulling the state in various directions and resulting in a greater diversity of policy and greater pragmatism (Cummings 2005). Several scholars have also pointed to opposite structural reasons for the greater centralisation of power in Uzbekistan, including the way that the Soviet method of balancing the power of regional elites was taken over by Karimov's regime (Roy 2000; Ilkhamov 2003), and an argument that proposes that Uzbekistan's dense rural population and the distribution of water for the irrigation-dependent agriculture that makes up a large part of Uzbekistan's economy make it a 'hydraulic economy', a type of society that lends itself to a despotic political system (Gleason 2003; Pomfret 2006). However, recent research on one of Uzbekistan's agricultural regions challenges this kind of deterministic explanation, showing that local relations of power have changed quite a bit since the demise of the *kolkhoz*, and that local elites flexibly manipulate policies and practices that ostensibly demonstrate the domination of the centre over the periphery (Trevisani 2007).

In the end, neither luck nor structural determinants fully explain the differences we have explored here. In general, ahistorical or essentialist explanations, or country-level explanations grounded in generalisations about material conditions, miss much of what is important in understanding governmentality, which is the micro level interactions that constitute relations of power in the everyday lives of individuals. Indicators of political freedom in Kazakhstan and Uzbekistan show strong similarities between the authoritarian practices of the two governments, but these generalisations disguise what can be felt on the ground as very different styles of governmentality. Our task in this essay has been to explore how these styles differ and to show what those differences mean for the relationship between the state and society, specifically in the realm of holiday celebrations. We explicated the differences by treating mass spectacles not only as a tool of national propaganda, but as a symbolic realm of the regime's representation of itself in society. These kinds of details about the ways that relationships of power produce symbolic representations, practices and forms of knowledge have many implications for the ways that citizens experience their state in their daily lives. Broad indicators of democratisation and freedom create their own forms of knowledge and power that allow us to see very diverse situations as being comparable, thereby leading to a homogenisation of both analysis and prescription.

Harvard University
Rutgers University

References

Adams, L.L. (2003) 'Cultural Elites in Uzbekistan: Ideology Production and the State', in Jones Luong, P. (ed.) (2003).

Adams, L.L. (2010) *The Spectacular State: Culture and National Identity in Uzbekistan* (Durham, NC, Duke University Press, forthcoming).

Binns, C.A.P. (1979/1980) 'The Changing Face of Power: Revolution and Accommodation in the Development of the Soviet Ceremonial System: Part I & II', *Man*, 14/15.

Bissenova, A. (2007) 'The Roles of the State and Capital in the Construction Boom in Kazakhstan', Conference Presentation, *Association for the Study of Nationalities*, New York, 12–14 April 2007.

Bunce, V. (1998) 'Regional Differences in Democratization: The East versus the South', *Post-Soviet Affairs*, 14, 3.

Chatterjee, C. (2002) *Celebrating Women: Gender, Festival Culture, and Bolshevik Ideology, 1910–1939* (Pittsburgh, University of Pittsburgh Press).

Collins, K. (2006) *Clan Politics and Regime Transition in Central Asia* (New York, Cambridge University Press).

Cummings, S.N. (2005) *Kazakhstan: Power and the Elite* (London & New York, I.B. Tauris).

Dave, B. (2007) *Kazakhstan: Ethnicity, Language and Power* (Abingdon & New York, Routledge).

Dean, M. (1999) *Governmentality: Power and Rule in Modern Society* (Los Angeles, SAGE Publications).

Doi, M.M. (2002) *Gender, Gesture, Nation: Dance and Social Change in Uzbekistan* (Westport, CT & London, Bergin & Garvey).

Durkheim, E. (1915) *The Elementary Forms of the Religious Life* (New York, The Free Press).

Falasca-Zamponi, S. (1997) *Fascist Spectacle: The Aesthetics of Power in Mussolini's Italy* (Berkeley, CA, University of California Press).

Foucault, M. (1980) *Power/Knowledge: Selected Interviews & Other Writings 1972–1977* (New York, Pantheon Books).

Foucault, M. (1991) 'Governmentality', in Burchell, G., Gordon, C. & Miller, P. (eds) (1991) *The Foucault Effect: Studies in Governmentality* (Chicago, University of Chicago Press).

Foucault, M. (2007) *Security, Territory, Population: Lectures at the College De France, 1977–78* (London, Palgrave MacMillan).

Genkin, D.M. (1975) *Massovye Prazdniki* (Moscow, Prosveshchenie).

Gleason, G. (1997) *The Central Asian States: Discovering Independence* (Boulder, CO, Westview Press).

Gleason, G. (2003) *Markets and Politics in Central Asia: Structural Reform and Political Change* (New York, Routledge).

Government of Kazakhstan (2001) 'The Strategic Plan for Development through 2010', adopted by the Decree of the President of the Republic of Kazakhstan, 4 December, available at: www.akorda.kz, accessed 1 December 2008.

Government of Kazakhstan (2003) 'The Strategy of Innovative Industrial Development of Kazakhstan for the Years 2003–2015', adopted by the Decree of the President of the Republic of Kazakhstan, 17 May, available at: www.akorda.kz, accessed 1 December 2008.

Ilkhamov, A. (2003) 'The Limits of Centralization: Regional Challenges in Uzbekistan', in Jones Luong, P. (ed.) (2003).

Jones Luong, P. (2002) *Institutional Change and Political Continuity in Post-Soviet Central Asia: Power, Perceptions and Pacts* (Cambridge, Cambridge University Press).

Jones Luong, P. (ed.) (2003) *The Transformation of Central Asia: States and Societies from Soviet Rule to Independence* (Ithaca, NY, Cornell University Press).

Karimov, I. (1992) *Uzbekistan: The Road of Independence and Progress* (Toshkent, Uzbekiston).

Karimov, I. (1993) *Building the Future: Uzbekistan—Its Own Model for Transition to a Market Economy* (Toshkent, Uzbekiston).

Karimov, I. (2007) 'Our General Goal—to Steadily Follow the Course of Building the Free Society and Prosperous Life', Address of the President Karimov at the Festive Ceremony Dedicated to the Constitution Day, Tashkent, 10 December, available at: http://www.uzbekistan.org/news/archive/516/, accessed 2 December 2008.

Lane, C. (1981) *The Rites of Rulers: Ritual in Industrial Society—The Soviet Case* (Cambridge, Cambridge University Press).

MacAloon, J.J. (1984) 'Olympic Games and the Theory of Spectacle in Modern Societies', in MacAloon, J.J. (ed.) (1984) *Rite, Drama, Festival, Spectacle* (Philadelphia, Institute for the Study of Human Issues).

Migdal, J. (2001) 'The State-in-Society Approach: A New Definition of the State and Transcending the Narrowly Constructed World of Rigor', in Kohli, A. & Shue, V. (eds) (2001) *State in Society: Studying How States and Societies Transform and Constitute One Another* (Cambridge, Cambridge University Press).

Mirzo, G. (2008) 'Prazdnik vesny, molodosti i dobra', *Pravda Vostoka*, available at: http://www.pv.uz/?inc=60&snd=&news=4247, accessed 24 March 2009.

Mitchell, T. (1991) 'The Limits of the State: Beyond Statist Approaches and Their Critics', *American Political Science Review*, 85, 1.

Nazarbaev, N. (2006) 'Kazakhstan's Strategy of Joining the World's 50 Most Competitive Countries', Address of the President of the Republic of Kazakhstan to the People of Kazakhstan, Astana, March, available at: www.akorda.kz, accessed 2 January 2009.

Nazarbaev, N. (2007) 'New Kazakhstan in a New World', Address of the President of the Republic of Kazakhstan to the People of Kazakhstan, Astana, 28 February 2007, available at: www.akorda.kz, accessed 2 January 2009.

Nazarbaev, N. (2008a) 'Growth of Welfare of Kazakhstan's Citizen is the Primary Goal of State Policy', Astana, 6 February, available at: www.akorda.kz, accessed 2 December 2008.

Nazarbaev, N. (2008b) 'Vystuplenie Prezidenta N. A. Nazarbaeva na torzhestvennom sobranii po sluchayu 10-letiya perenosa stolitsy', available at: www.akorda.kz, accessed 2 December 2008.

Olcott, M.B. (1994) 'Ceremony and Substance: The Illusion of Unity in Central Asia' , in Mandelbaum, M. (ed.) (1994) *Central Asia and the World: Kazakhstan, Uzbekistan, Tajikistan, Kyrgyzstan, and Turkmenistan* (New York, Council on Foreign Relations Press).

Olcott, M.B. (2005) *Central Asia's Second Chance* (Washington, DC, Carnegie Endowment).

Petrone, K. (2000) *Life Has Become More Joyous, Comrades: Celebrations in the Time of Stalin* (Bloomington, Indiana University Press).

Pomfret, R. (2006) *The Central Asian Economies since Independence* (Princeton & Oxford, Princeton University Press).

Roche, M. (2000) *Mega-Events and Modernity: Olympics and Expos in the Growth of Global Culture* (London & New York, Routledge).

Roy, O. (2000) *The New Central Asia: The Creation of Nations* (New York, New York University Press).

Rumer, B. (2005) 'Central Asia: At the End of the Transition', in Rumer, B. (ed.) (2005) *Central Asia at the End of the Transition* (Armonk, NY, M.E. Sharpe).

Saidazimova, G. (2007) 'Uzbekistan: Economic Hardships Belie Official Growth Figures', *RFE/RL*, available at: www.rferl.org/content/Article/1079058.html, accessed 24 March 2009.

Schatz, E. (2004) *Modern Clan Politics: The Power of 'Blood' in Kazakhstan and Beyond* (Seattle, WA, University of Washington Press).

Smith, G., Law, V., Wilson, A., Bohr, A. & Allworth, E. (1998) *Nation-Building in the Post-Soviet Borderlands: The Politics of National Identities* (Cambridge, Cambridge University Press).

Spechler, M.C. (2008) *The Political Economy of Reform in Central Asia: Uzbekistan Under Authoritarianism* (New York, Routledge).

Trevisani, T. (2007) 'After the Kolkhoz: Rural Elites in Competition', *Central Asian Survey*, 26, 1.

Wedeen, L. (1999) *Ambiguities of Domination* (Chicago, University of Chicago Press).

Yalcin, R. (2002) *The Rebirth of Uzbekistan: Politics, Economy and Society in the Post-Soviet Era* (Reading, Ithaca Press).

Yurchak, A. (1997) 'The Cynical Reason of Late Socialism: Power, Pretense, and the Anekdot', *Public Culture*, 9, 2.

Yurchak, A. (2003) 'Soviet Hegemony of Form: Everything was Forever Until it was No More', *Comparative Studies in Society and History*, 45, 2.

Materialising State Space: 'Creeping Migration' and Territorial Integrity in Southern Kyrgyzstan

MADELEINE REEVES

Behind the beautiful façade of independence and the loud, sombre pronouncements of 2,200 years of Kyrgyz statehood, an ugly reality is concealed. Kyrgyzstan as a state does not even have its own borders, and the borders that we do have more often have just an administrative character, so our neighbours can move them about just as they like. And yet—territorial integrity and borders—aren't these supposed to be the very foundation of any state? (Kalet 2006, p. 1)

Places... are always imagined in the context of political-economic determinations that have a logic of their own. Territoriality is thus reinscribed at just the point it threatens to be erased. (Gupta & Ferguson 1997, p. 40)

THIS ESSAY IS CONCERNED WITH THE MATERIALITY OF STATE SPACE in a rural region of post-Soviet borderland. It examines the institutional forms and mundane practices through which a juridical boundary between Kyrgyzstan and Tajikistan is materialised; the work involved in inscribing territoriality (Gupta & Ferguson 1997, p. 40), and the social consequences of these interventions. Such processes, it argues, are more extensive, complex and disjointed than the mounting of barbed wire or the building of border posts. Territorialising the state is never merely a technical exercise; it is disparate, contentious, temporally extensive, symbolically loaded and, as Kyrgyzstan's recent past has shown, politically consequential.[1] The intense political

Research for this article was generously supported by a postgraduate training award from the Economic and Social Research Council and a RCUK Research Fellowship. I would like to thank Dacia Viejo-Rose, Edmund Harzig and Alexander Morrison for the opportunity to present earlier versions of this paper in seminars at Cambridge and Oxford, to Dastan Nadyrov and Gulnara Aitpaeva for responding generously to my questions; and to Sally Cummings, Peter Gatrell, Maja Petrovic-Steger, Montu Saxena and two anonymous E-AS reviewers for their detailed and helpful comments on an earlier draft.

[1]The revelation of concessions of land to China by former President Akaev during closed-door negotiations fostered public outrage and was the catalyst for popular demonstrations that led to political violence in Aksï in 2002. See ICG (2002, pp. 17–18), Khamidov (2001), Plenseev (2002) and Sydykova (2003) for contemporary analyses of these events, and Lewis (2008, pp. 127–33) on the significance of the allegations of 'treacherous' land sales for Akaev's political demise.

and material investment that is entailed in producing 'territorial integrity' is particularly striking in the area of the Kyrgyzstan–Tajikistan borderland in the Isfara valley that is the focus of concern here: a region where borders have historically been of little popular relevance and where they remain poorly demarcated and weakly institutionalised.

Yet if this essay seeks empirically to explore some contemporary practices of 'state-fixing' in rural Kyrgyzstan it also harbours a second aim, one that speaks directly to the volume's broader concern with understanding the place of the symbolic in our analyses of Central Asian politics. This is to understand the politics and pathos of territorial integrity in Kyrgyzstan: the anxieties around territorial 'unboundedness' that ring through Kalet's article above, written in the aftermath of political crisis and a moment of intense public debate about being an 'integral' state. The essay argues that 'territorial integrity' has become an issue of public and political significance in contemporary Kyrgyzstan for two main reasons. First, the very material consequences of having an undemarcated border directly affect the livelihoods of thousands of people along the country's southern perimeter, and the future dynamics of inter-communal relations. Secondly, the 'border' has come to figure in public discourse—a fantastical border that is contingent, resistant to inscription, vulnerable to the whims of neighbours and liable to shift—and to articulate much broader concerns about the correlates of independent statehood and the integrity of the body politic.

The point of entry for this analysis is a particular empirical phenomenon known as 'creeping migration' (*polzuchaya migratsiya* in Russian; *jïlma migratsiya* in Kyrgyz) that is occurring along parts of Kyrgyzstan's southern border with Tajikistan. In contemporary official and popular usage 'creeping migration' refers to the illegal purchase, or leasing, of property and land plots from citizens of Kyrgyzstan by citizens of neighbouring Tajikistan. It is a process that has gained increasing prominence in Kyrgyzstani public and political debate in recent years: the object of internationally sponsored roundtables, policy documents and law-making initiatives aimed at preventing Kyrgyzstan's (ethnically Kyrgyz) border populations in parts of Batken *oblast'* from selling up and moving north.[2] The discourse enacts a particular—and productive—equation: between the sale or leasing of land in a border village, and the 'creep' of the state border itself.

The essay draws on ethnographic fieldwork in the Isfara valley between 2004 and 2008,[3] as well as an analysis of newspaper discourse and official documentation pertaining to the issue of 'creeping migration'.[4] It seeks to illuminate both the

---

[2] Several local and international organisations working in the Ferghana valley have examined the phenomenon in published analyses. See, for example ICG (2002), Kuehnast and Dudwick (2008), Passon and Temirkulov (2004), UNDP (2006) and most systematically, FTI (2008). For an important recent contribution which situates 'creeping migration' within the broader context of regional 'delimitation politics' see Bichsel (2009, pp. 114–6).

[3] All translations are my own.

[4] The main period of field research was between March 2004 and September 2005 in Batken and Sokh raions, supplemented by two shorter return visits in 2008. This research was primarily qualitative, and involved participant observation and extended ethnographic interviews with dozens of people whose livelihoods involved crossing, guarding or 'working' Batken's southern borders, including traders, herders, students, border guards, children, teachers, grandparents, customs officers, NGO employees and bus drivers. I have used pseudonyms throughout the essay unless requested otherwise by my informant. All translations are my own.

dynamics of such land sales in one densely populated area of borderland along the Isfara valley (see Figure 1), and the political reaction that it has fostered. This reaction is both discursive and material: that is, there has emerged a particular account of

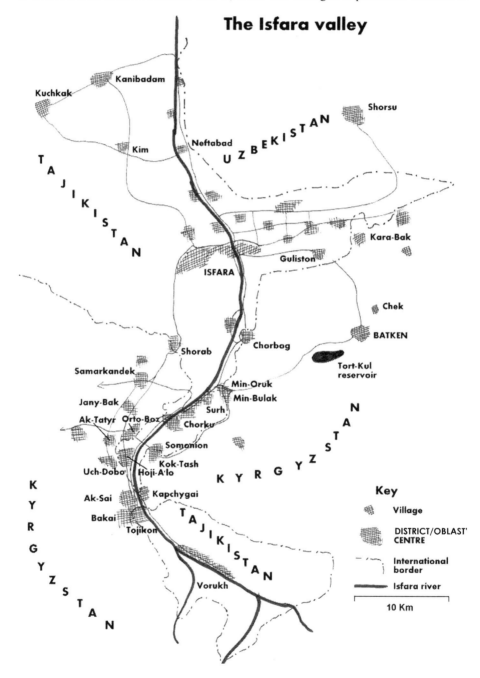

FIGURE 1. MAP OF THE ISFARA VALLEY, SHOWING PLACES REFERRED TO IN THE TEXT. BOUNDARIES
SHOULD NOT BE TREATED AS AUTHORITATIVE

threat posed by 'creeping migration' which has tangible material effects. The articulation of risk to the state's territorial integrity is used to mobilise resources and to fix state infrastructure such as roads, water-channels and border-posts; and it has been used to determine the kinds of state benefits (*l'goty*) that border populations are able to access and the areas to be policed by border guards. Such infrastructure, in turn, leads the 'border' to be experienced and imagined in new ways: it shapes the kinds of everyday paths through the landscape that are walked and driven along; the kinds of exchange that are encouraged or deemed illegal; the sites where collecting firewood or grazing cattle are to be either ignored or subject to a fine; and the places that come to be learned and lived as 'shared' and those that are separate.

Through this analysis, the essay makes two broader interventions of relevance to the study of symbolic politics in Central Asia. The first is to argue for a more nuanced analysis of the dynamics of coexistence and conflict in the Ferghana valley, alert to the lived history of a landscape and the diverse spatial visions that it animates. The region of borderland on which the essay focuses has come to be identified, in scholarly and policy discourse alike, as one where a particular conjunction of resource shortage, geographic complexity and ethnic diversity has rendered it unusually vulnerable to cross-border conflict.[5] As such it has been the site of numerous interventions aimed at 'preventive development': that is, state and donor-driven projects aimed at mitigating inter-ethnic conflict through a combination of 'community mobilisation' and the fixing of material infrastructure including water pipes, irrigation canals, schools, markets, health clinics and 'bypass roads'.[6]

In making a critique of the logic of some of these interventions, the essay does not seek to question the considerable threats to inter-communal relations posed by acute shortages of land and water. The Tajikistan–Kyrgyzstan borderland in the Isfara valley has been a site of periodic stress from at least the 1930s, since when the region's population has grown dramatically, creating considerable tension over land today (Bushkov & Mikul'skii 1996; Faizullina 2007; FTI n.d.; Ikromov 2006). At the time of writing, informal labour migration to the markets and construction sites of urban Russia remains the major source of livelihood for people on both sides of the border, and there is considerable anxiety about the potential for tensions to rise as Russia's construction sector contracts and the volume of money remitted home declines. Yet this is also a landscape which, since at least the middle of the twentieth century, has been subject to attempts to render ethnic and administrative boundaries isomorphic. Soviet Socialist Republic (SSR) borders have been shifted to accommodate *de facto*

---

[5]See, indicatively, Lubin and Rubin (1999), Passon and Temirkulov (2004), Satarbaev (2006), Slim (2002), Tabyshalieva (1999), UNDP (2006) and Young (2003).

[6]During my period of research in the mid-2000s, interventions with the aim of conflict prevention or mitigation were being conducted, amongst other agencies, by the UNDP through its 'Preventive Development in the South' programme (UNDP 2001); the German Organisation for Technical Cooperation (GTZ); Mercy Corps, through its Peaceful Communities Initiative (PCI); the Swiss Development Cooperation, through its project on Regional Dialogue and Development; and through programmes on poverty alleviation and cross-border co-operation in the Ferghana valley and peace promotion in the Ferghana valley, as well as several local donor-funded NGOs. In some border villages, these agencies have occasionally been working at competing purposes (interview with Gerald Gunther, GTZ, Batken, July 2005). See also Passon and Temirkulov (2004, p. 51) and Maasen *et al.* (2005, p. 21).

shifts in population, maps have been written and rewritten, and the establishment of new 'planned' border villages has been justified in terms of ethnic 'defence' against migratory pressures.[7] It is a region, in other words, in which territory and ethnicity are both symbolically linked and discursively over-determined. Leasing a home to someone from a neighbouring village who happens to have different ethnic identification and a different colour passport enters discourse today not as an instance of administrative violation, or as an unremarkable and legal transaction within the same federal state, as was the case in Soviet times, but rather as an act of gross symbolic transgression: selling a home as selling the border.

In this context, delimiting the border—establishing its location categorically as a preliminary to physical demarcation—is an intensely contentious process, and that contention is unlikely to diminish if local populations are not actively involved—or do not perceive themselves to be actively involved—in its determination. The essay thus argues against the claim, widespread in Kyrgyzstani public discourse and in much of the policy literature concerning peace and conflict potentials in the Ferghana valley that territorial delimitation—'fixing' the border categorically to determine its 'true' spatial correlates—will necessarily act as a guarantor of peace; a technical solution to social complexity and competing claims upon the land.

Second, and linked to this, the essay examines the ambiguous and at times contradictory effects of interventions aimed at territorialising the state. Many of the most prominent and costly of recent development initiatives on the Kyrgyz side of the border have sought, literally and metaphorically, to create 'detours' around neighbouring Tajikistan; that is, to obviate the need to enter the neighbouring territory through the building of alternative roads and infrastructure, and the fostering of separate paths and channels through the landscape. This is true of recent road-building projects in Batken *oblast'*, which create detours around Uzbekistan's Sokh enclave and the Tajikistani settlements of Chorku and Surh, respectively.[8] But it is also reflected in other initiatives, such as the establishing of separate 'national' markets instead of the existing cross-border bazaars; in the location of new school buildings in such a way as to prevent schoolchildren from needing to cross the border on their way to and from classes, and in the posting of border guards to police contested territory.[9] By drawing attention to the importance of everyday cross-border contact—the mundane sociality that tends to fall under the radar of 'community building'

---

[7]Such is the case, for instance, with Ming-Örük, a border village established in 1991 to accommodate ethnic Kyrgyz 'returnees' from Tajikistan. The most striking example of such strategic village-building is in the case of Maksat, in Batken's western-most Leilek district. This village was created in 1996 with Kyrgyzstani state funds with the explicit aim of limiting the unregulated occupation of land in the Maksat *massiv* since the late 1980s by ethnic Tajiks from the much larger village of Qalacha (Tajikistan) (FTI 2008, p. 4). In the words of one recent newspaper article, the village was conceived to act as an 'outpost [*forpost*] in the way of unwanted migration' (Khamidov 2006).

[8]The bypass road around the Sokh enclave was commenced in 2006 using unpaid voluntary labour [*ashar*], later supplemented with state funding (Urumbaev 2007). Construction of the detour around Chorku and Surh was commenced in 2007 (Anarkulov 2008b).

[9]For example, recent school-building initiatives in the border village of Tashtumshuk (bordering Taijkistan) and Charbak (bordering Uzbekistan in the Sokh valley), have been explicitly conceived to obviate the need for children to pass through the neighbouring state on their way to school (FTI 2008, p. 18).

initiatives—this essay questions the assumption that fostering separate 'routes' through borderland space will minimise the likelihood of inter-communal conflict.

Symbolic politics and 'state effects' in the study of Central Asia

As Cummings argues in her introduction (Cummings 2009), understanding the 'politics of the spectacular' in Central Asia demands an inter-disciplinary approach— one alert to the symbolic dimensions of social life. My essay argues specifically for the potential of an anthropological perspective to enrich our understanding of the political—or, put differently, the need to attend to the affective dimensions of the 'symbolic' beyond the domains of formal institutional politics. This is in part a methodological claim: that an ethnographic analysis, alert to the ways in which technical interventions are encountered, subverted, contested and appropriated in specific sites, can enable a more nuanced and less teleological account of political transformation in the region. This is an argument that has been well made before, and informed a number of insightful critiques of triumphalist narratives of 'transition' (Kandiyoti & Mandel 1998; Liu 2003; Megoran 2006; Sahadeo & Zanca 2007). However, my concern in this essay is not simply with the need for the study of political processes from the 'bottom up', or to couple 'macro-analyses' with attention to the lived worlds of ordinary people. It is also, more substantively, to explore the significance of two anthropological insights for an analysis of political transformation in Central Asia.

The first is to question an easy separation between 'the material' and 'the symbolic' in analysing the political process. If we start from a recognition that human beings are creatures who make meaning and are constantly engaged in symbolising the world to themselves and others, then 'the symbolic' is integral to political life, not simply an epiphenomenon or a tool for political manipulation. Moreover, the domain of the 'symbolic' should not be confined to those iconic markers of self-representation of the state that make their way onto flags, school books and national currencies, such as the figure of Manas in Kyrgyzstan, or the architecture of the yurt. From an ethnographic perspective, the most mundane of objects can come to 'stand for' something else—that is, they can come to do symbolic work. A water pipe, or road; an apricot tree or a stretch of pasture can be the locus of enormous affective and symbolic investment, just as a flag or a statue can.

The tendency to treat the 'material' and 'symbolic' as separate domains (with the 'symbolic' epiphenomenal to 'real' material interests) is analytically consequential. It reflects, as Joyce (2008, p. 5) puts it, a 'basic western epistemological distinction between the subject and the object, the material and the non-material, the concrete and the abstract', one that can limit our capacity to recognise the enormous significance of interventions that would appear to be 'purely' technical (Barry 2001; Harvey 2005). But it is also significant for the way it constrains our analysis of the political. Politics, as moments of upheaval remind us, is messy; it is radically unpredictable; and it tends to exceed the institutional bounds within which state officials and analysts would try to contain it (Gupta 1995; Navaro-Yashin 2003, 2002, pp. 155 203, Spencer 2007). An anthropological perspective can help us gain some conceptual and theoretical purchase on what Spencer (2007, p. 17) has called 'the dynamic force of the political': the political that overspills institutional bounds and animates everyday life. Attending to this dimension, I argue, is crucial for developing a non-reductionist account of cross-border contention in southern Ferghana.

The second insight which this essay draws from recent anthropological literature concerns the study of the nation state, and specifically the importance of attending, ethnographically, to what Timothy Mitchell calls 'state effects': the practices, institutions, technologies and material objects through which the state comes to appear bounded, integrated and connected; as well as separate from the domain of 'society' and authoritative over it (1999). Mitchell draws on governmentality theory to emphasise the activity and techniques involved in producing what he calls 'two-dimensional effects'; that is, the practices that

> contribute to constructing a world that appears to consist not of a complex of social practices but of a binary order: on the one hand individuals and their activities, on the other an inert 'structure' that somehow stands apart from individuals, precedes them and contains them and gives a framework to their lives. (Mitchell 1999, p. 89)

Like other governmentality theorists, Mitchell is concerned with the constitution of the state through representational practices such as statistics and mapping (Mitchell 1988). But he also seeks to move beyond a Foucauldian concern with discourse to explore the concrete mechanisms and material technologies through which 'the state' comes to be produced as something outside and 'above' society (Mitchell 1999, 2002). State effects, in other words, are not simply the outcome of discourse, but are rather 'consolidated' in 'visible everyday forms, such as the language of legal practice, the architecture of public buildings, the wearing of military uniforms, or the marking and policing of frontiers' (Mitchell 1999, p. 81).

Mitchell's concern with the materiality of state effects is useful here in that the imagined unity of the state and the search for an ordered world are outcomes not only of ideological investment, but are also the product of specific technological possibilities and material interventions. Moreover, it follows from Mitchell's argument that we should not accept easy distinctions between the 'material' and the 'conceptual'; between particular logics of rule and the technological forms that enable certain kinds of social and political organisation to become imaginable and possible. The 'imagined' state is always already materially mediated:

> A construct like the state occurs not merely as a subjective belief, incorporated in the thinking and actions of individuals... The cultural forms of the state are an empirical phenomenon, as solid and discernable as a legal structure or a party system. Or rather, I argue, the distinction between a conceptual realm and an empirical one needs to be placed in question if we are to understand the nature of a phenomenon like the state. (Mitchell 1999, p. 81)

This kind of theoretical move is helpful in focusing our attention on how it is that 'stateness' comes to be produced and consolidated—a dimension that has tended to receive little attention in studies of the former Soviet space.[10] Specifically, in the case of

[10]However, see Collier (2001, 2004).

the poorly demarcated, weak sovereign borders of the Ferghana valley, it allows us to approach the production of state territoriality ethnographically: to explore how it is that the state comes to be produced as something bounded, integrated and protective of its citizens, bearing both authority and 'territorial integrity'; how space comes to be turned into territory.

Mapping the Ferghana valley

The region where this study is focused lies on the southern perimeters of the Ferghana valley, a large, fertile basin that is the most densely populated region of Central Asia. Ethnically and politically diverse, this region has nonetheless been part of a single polity for most of its history, and residents often speak of a distinct 'Ferghana' identity that coexists with other forms of ethnic, regional and religious identification (Abashin & Bushkov 2004). Today the Ferghana basin is divided between independent Kyrgyzstan, Uzbekistan and Tajikistan, with the Isfara valley, where my research was concentrated, marking an ecologically transitional, irrigation-dependent region between the fertile Ferghana basin to the north and the Turkestan mountain range which rises steeply to the south.

The cartographic divisions that now mark international boundaries in the Ferghana valley were drawn up between 1924 and 1927 as part of the 'national-territorial delimitation of Central Asia'. This was a critical event in the region's history, for whilst it was not the first instance of territorial boundary making in the Soviet Union, or the only one to be conducted upon 'national' lines (Brown 2003; Haugen 2003; Hirsch 2005; Martin 2001), it was the first in which a process of national delimitation was conceived as an explicitly modernising move, one that would overcome backwardness and the 'perversions' of previous Tsarist policy by propelling nations (*natsii*) into being. As one commentator put it during celebrations to mark the tenth anniversary of delimitation in 1934, the creation of 'national' republics on the territory of former Turkestan had allowed the populations of Central Asia to 'become closer [*priobshchitsya*] to the family of soviet nations who are building socialism' by enabling 'tribe, an ethnographic category, to be transformed into nation, a historical category' (Shteinberg 1934, p. 53).

Western Sovietology (and now, in an interesting twist, contemporary Uzbekistani historiography) has tended to depict the national-territorial delimitation of 1924 as an arbitrary, indeed wilfully malevolent, act of artifice designed to thwart a nascent pan-Turkism in late colonial Central Asia.[11] This view, which has received sustained critique in recent years from scholars who have made use of recently opened archival materials (Haugen 2003; Hirsch 2005; Karasar 2008; Khalid 1998, 2007; Koichiev 2001) misses much of the complexity of the dynamics of delimitation and its aftermath, for it occludes the detailed, minutely calibrated and positional languages of identification that characterised pre-modern Central Asia; and ignores the extent to

[11]See, for example Carrère d'Encausse (1987). For critical analyses of Western historiography of the delimitation, see Byrbaeva (2005, pp. 73–84) and Haugen (2003, pp. 9–29). For an analysis of the divergent reinterpretations of the delimitation in contemporary Uzbekistani and Kyrgyzstani scholarship, see Reeves (2008, pp. 51–52).

which the articulation of the 'nation' (*halq*) and the 'country' (*watan*) were the subject of intense debate amongst the local reformist elite prior to the delimitation (Khalid 1998, pp. 184–215). Crucially, moreover, this narrative obscures the extent to which a logic of national delimitation, premised upon the possibility of creating coherent 'proto-national' republics, coexisted with a quite different rationale throughout much of the Soviet period: that of producing an integrated, centralised system of transport, provisioning and agricultural production that would propel a 'backward' region into socialist modernity.

Although the delimitation had invoked 'nationhood' as the organising category of Soviet administration, the realities of Soviet modernisation often undermined the coherence of these newly national republics from within. From the 1930s onwards, resettlement policies, building programmes, mine workings, roads, railway lines and often quite utopian irrigation projects were built with little regard for the republican boundary lines. State policies often tended to alter the border line *de facto* through the leasing of land from collective farms on one side of the border to those on the other, or the exchange of land in return for the provision of irrigation water. Pastoralist Kyrgyz populations from the high Turkestan mountains were resettled into 'planned villages' (*planovye sela*) further down the valley well into the 1970s, such that summer migration patterns now traversed the land of the neighbouring republic.[12] Reservoirs and canals were built ignoring the republican boundary line (Bichsel 2006; Thurman 1999, pp. 203–59); tractor stations nominally under the jurisdiction of one republic were built on the land of the neighbouring one (Mamaraimov 2007); new Tajik *mahallas* (neighbourhoods) that were subordinate to state farms in the Tajik republic were built on the outskirts of villages that were themselves administratively part of the Kyrgyz SSR. This has created a border that is often hard to determine today. The village of Kök-Tash, for instance, administratively part of Kyrgyzstan, contains within it the *mahalla* of Somonion, which is administratively part of Tajikistan's Chorku *jamoat* (district). The two schools in the village, 300 metres apart, operate on different time-zones and celebrate different independence days, though no-one in the village is able to say with any confidence where the territorial border lies—the assumption is that 'if it's a Tajik house, then it is probably Tajikistan' (see Figure 1).

Such arrangements, often provisional, and sometimes occurring without formal ratification at the republican level, were consistent with the broader logic of Soviet state-formation, in which nominally 'sovereign' republics were involved in multiple and complex relations of mutual inter-dependence. This was not, *pace* Slim (2002), a case of the 'deliberate' creation of enclaves to ensure dependency on Moscow. Indeed, early Soviet maps reveal that the borders of the Ferghana valley were initially contiguous with the enclaves visible on maps today that emerged as a result of the development of collective farms from the 1930s and the expansion of territory under cultivation (Koichiev 2001, pp. 88–89; CECCP 1928; Alamanov 2008).

---

[12]According to Osh historian Zairbek Ergeshov (personal communication, Workshop on Nationhood and Narrative in Central Asia: History, Context, Critique, Issyk-Kul, January 2009), the fact that the initial process of delimitation occurred in the summer months, when Kyrgyz herders tended to be in the summer pastures (*jailoo*) meant that many Kyrgyz pastoralists found that their winter settlements and summer grazing grounds were located on the territory of different Union republics. See also Dzhunushalieva (2006, pp. 9–10) and Koichiev (2001, pp. 48–77).

FIGURE 2. CHILDREN PLAYING IN THE AK-TATĪR/MACHAI CANAL ON THE KYRGYZSTAN–TAJIKISTAN BORDER

The case of the Kyrgyz–Tajik Ferghana valley boundary is particularly instructive here. As early as 1949, a parity commission was established to try to resolve conflicts that were emerging over *kolkhoz* lands, which decreed that the boundary of the Union republics should be shifted to coincide with *de facto* land use of the respective collective farms. Continuing disputes over collective farm boundaries led to a second parity commission in 1958, which determined the line of the border that is today considered authoritative by Kyrgyzstan. However, whilst the document was ratified by both Kyrgyz and Tajik *oblast'* administrations, it was only ratified by the Kyrgyz (and not the Tajik) Council of Ministers. Consequently it is disputed as the basis for current interstate negotiations (Alamanov 2005, pp. 82–84; Faizullina 2007). For this reason, when the process of delimitation of this border was initiated by independent Kyrgyzstan and Tajikistan in 1997, it was interrupted a year later because of disagreement over the principles by which to proceed and the maps to use as a point of reference. (The issue was whether to take the parity commission of 1959 as authoritative, or to return to the original agreement on the location of borders between the Uzbek SSR and Kyrgyz Autonomous *Okrug* from 1925.) Talks recommenced in 2002 but have proceeded slowly. Consequently, to date only 237 km of the 674 km of the Kyrgyzstan–Tajikistan border have been delimited, and these overwhelmingly in uninhabited mountainous regions (FTI 2008, p. 5).

Contemporary cartographic and political complexity is not, then, simply the result of a shift in status as Soviet-era republican boundaries became international frontiers. It arises, rather, from the conjunction of multiple logics—with 'national' borders overlaid upon kinship networks, trade routes, grazing patterns, pilgrimage circuits, canal systems and memories of historical landholdings that follow entirely different spatial patterns and social logics. It was never assumed, for instance, that a long-term land lease from one Union republic to its neighbour would result in the creation of what are now, juridically, enclaves of one independent state inside another, or that it would leave officials from neighbouring republics arguing over which Soviet map is to be treated as historically authoritative (Urumbaev 2008).

Materialising independence

The conjunction of these logics has been particularly consequential in the last decade. The first years of independence were characterised by relatively open borders between the three Ferghana valley republics of Kyrgyzstan, Uzbekistan and Tajikistan (Liu 2002, pp. 31–67; Megoran 2004, p. 732). None of the three states was politically, economically or militarily prepared for 'independence' and for those living in the border regions there were few material traces of state territoriality in the form of patrolling border troops, manned border-posts or barbed wire. Indeed, as Salamat Alamanov, the head of Kyrgyzstan's commission on delimitation and demarcation noted in a recent 'open lecture', he and other Central Asian officials responsible for conducting delimitation with China in the early years of independence 'never imagined that we would have to undertake the same task [of delimitation] with our other neighbours—with Kazakhstan, Tajikistan and Uzbekistan'. This assumption set the tone for the early discussions:

> If you leaf through the documents from those early meetings of the heads of state at that time, it is written there that we wouldn't have any borders, we won't bother with any of that business [of changing borders], that we would keep the same community [*obshchnost'*] that we had in the Soviet Union. (Alamanov 2007)

The continuation of relatively open cross-border movement that characterised the early post-Soviet period deteriorated dramatically from 1999, when Uzbekistan unilaterally closed its border with Kyrgyzstan, destroying a symbolically resonant 'bridge of friendship' across the canal border in Kara-Suu on the eastern side of the valley, mounting barbed wire and laying land-mines along stretches of the border deemed particularly vulnerable to 'terrorist' incursion. As Megoran (2002, 2004) has argued, this was the first moment at which the border came to be experienced as a 'concrete reality' by many of those who found themselves living at the new state edge, and it precipitated a series of reciprocal interventions from Uzbekistan's neighbours, in the form of fixed and mobile customs units, the closing of previously cross-border bus routes and restrictions upon cross-border trade.

The result has been a qualitative shift in the everyday experience of 'living at the border' over the last decade, one profoundly mediated by a stately optic of finite, bounded, homogenous space (Scott 1998; Yeh 2003). Yet it would be an oversimplification to assume that the process of materialising the state has been straightforward, unidirectional or uncontested. It entails considerable effort: creating 'homogenous space' demands improvisation; manning the border, as much as crossing it, demands negotiation and an ability to 'read the land'. Moreover, state practices of inscription never entirely erase other readings of that landscape. Memories of seasonal migration and of pilgrimages to sacred sites, myths about land that was worked and watered by ancestors, experiences of obligatory resettlement to lower-lying 'planned villages', practices of place-making through ritual visiting, and claims about land that was unjustly taken or distributed during Soviet times are not simply deleted by technologies of control (Verdery 1994). This multiple spatiality is materialised today in the scattered private land plots and the rusting remnants of collectively owned infrastructure which create a 'chessboard border' (*shakhmat chek arasi*), the precise spatial correlates of which are often indistinct. They are present in the stretches of so-called 'contested land' (*talash jer*), and in the thousands of hectares of undemarcated border which sustains cross-border livelihoods. Above all, they are present in the contestation over the historical legitimacy of 'illegal' land seizures, as logics of contemporary state territoriality collide with memories of pre-war spatial perimeters and the location of grandparents' fields.[13]

The villages that lie along the length of the Isfara valley, which tacks back and forth between the jurisdiction of Kyrgyzstan and Tajikistan, provide a particularly vivid illustration of the issues at stake. Landscapes and livelihoods here are shot through with reminders of intertwined pasts and the simultaneity of claims upon the land and its history. Many villages, sacred sites and informal landmarks bear both Kyrgyz and Tajik names;[14] many people have held—and often continue, informally, to hold—citizenship of both states; many others have built homes and gardens and raised families on land allocated in the 1980s whose status is today contested. In the contiguous villages of Hoji-A'lo/Machai (Tajikistan), Üch-Döbö (Kyrgyzstan) and Tashtumshuk (Kyrgyzstan), it is common for families to receive electricity from one state and to collect water from the other. The minibuses that run the route along the valley between Isfara and Vorukh are used to accepting two currencies and the conversations onboard, the gestures of respect and recognition, the greetings and subtle demarcations of space according to age and gender speak of such public transport as shared space. The pervasiveness of Kygyz–Tajik bilingualism among the older generation attests to a past in which ethnic boundaries were much less firmly marked, and in which inter-marriage between the settled and semi-nomadic populations of today's Vorukh enclave was much more common that it is today.[15]

---

[13]Such appeals are common. In a recent instance when the Kyrgyz authorities sought to deport a Tajik farmer from Chorku who had started to lay the foundations for a home on contested territory, the farmer justified his actions by reference to the fact that he had helped his grandparents farm that land immediately after the war (interview with Mansur-aka, Ak-Sai, August 2008).

[14]Examples of villages in the Isfara valley that have both Tajik and Kyrgyz variants include Govsvuar/Orto-Boz, Tojikon/Poselok, Tangi/Kapchïgai and Hoji-A'lo/Machai/Oktiabr'.

[15]According to one elderly informant from Ak-Sai, due to extreme poverty during the Second World War, Tajik girls from Vorukh would often be married at a young age to Kyrgyz men, who were prepared to pay higher bride-price (interview with Tolib-aka, Ak-Sai, August 2008). Certainly, until the resettlement of Kyrgyz herders in the 1970s and 1980s, the village of Vorukh, today considered ethnically 'Tajik', had a significant Kyrgyz-speaking and identifying minority, and ethnic inter-marriage, mutual visiting and ritual celebrations seem to have been much more common than they are today (author's informal conversations with elderly residents of Ak-Sai, Vorukh and Tojikon villages, June–July 2005). Kyrgyz–Tajik inter-marriage in the Isfara valley is today extremely rare. When I asked young people from Ak-Sai and Ak-Tatïr in 2004–2005 whether they condoned inter-ethnic

This is not to romanticise a past or present of harmonious coexistence. The Isfara valley has been the site of considerable tension over land and water since at least the 1930s; and these resources remain contentious today. There is an indigenous discourse on 'conflict' and contention (*konflikt, talash*) which cannot be reduced simply to the politicisation of difference by outsiders; and the contours of perceived difference are often articulated in unambiguously ethnic terms. As everyday 'categories of practice' (Bourdieu 1992; Brubaker 1996), the ethnic identifiers 'Kyrgyz' and 'Tajik' are locally salient and understandings of ethnic difference structure social life, patterns of social visiting and the dynamics of friendship and marriage in significant ways. Nigora, a teacher from Hoji-A'lo, who had recently started working in the Kyrgyz village school across the border as a teacher of Russian, was typical in speaking of the 'nervousness' she felt if she departed from the main roads and into side streets on her way to and from work. It is important not to underestimate the sense of relations under strain, or the potential here for conflict to be structured along lines that actors themselves perceive in terms of ethnic difference.[16]

But it is equally important that recognition of this contemporary reality does not lead us to ignore those mundane spaces of 'everyday getting along' which are crucial to the production and experience of a space as shared: the kind of borderland sociality that develops in markets, at bus stops, on public transport, at water pumps, walking to fields, in medical clinics, or to and from school (Flynn 1997). As one Ak-Tatïr school teacher put it to me, in the context of a long interview in which he expressed frustration at several of the 'tolerance building' projects that had been initiated to improve relations between schoolchildren in Ak-Tatïr and neighbouring Hoji-A'lo, the important thing was to sustain the mundane forms of cross-border connection, rather than in a few symbolic displays of 'toleration':

> During the [Soviet] Union there were all sorts of things. Then we really met! Today, we only get together when [U] or [A] comes along and starts to organise something.[17] They have their goals, definitely, they want to develop friendship between our communities, tolerance, but now when they leave the friendship goes with them... Someone should make sure that after holding all these kinds of events that people really do make a point of starting to visit each other every day. Now when they come along and hold some volleyball match they can hardly wait until it is over. They come along and before the match is even over they come up and go 'gently, gently, thank-you, thank-you. Well done. Remember to stay friends'. They have that kind of volunteer, kind of... without a sense of responsibility. If I were organising that kind of thing I would make sure that they met up with each other every day. That's the most important thing. It shouldn't be a one-off meeting.[18]

marriage, the response was almost uniformly negative. '*Tukhum buzulup baratat*' ('the lineage would be broken') was how one eighth-grade schoolgirl put it.

[16]This is not, of course, the same as according some ontological status to ethnicity, or assuming it to be the 'driver' of conflict. As Brubaker has demonstrated, the conceptual challenge is to understand how and when social life comes to be structured in terms of ethnicity—when ethnicity 'happens'—without taking it to be a self-explanatory analytical category, or according ontological status to 'ethnic groups' (Brubaker 2005; Brubaker *et al.* 2006).

[17]Tursun-agai mentioned here two international organisations, the names of which I omit.

[18]Author's interview with Tursun-agai, Ak-Tatïr, July 2005.

It is in such contexts, I suggest—of simultaneous claims upon the landscape; of intransigent infrastructure; of a history in which borders were felt to move, often quite arbitrarily; and of the exigencies of daily getting along—that we need to understand both the dynamics of 'creeping migration', and the considerable local ambivalence that surrounds interventions aimed at materialising the state border. In villages such as Ak-Sai and Üch-Döbö there is, on the one hand, a real concern that the boundary be 'fixed' and a fear of 'enclavement': a desire, as Temirbek, a middle-aged father of two put it in an interview in September 2004, that the authorities in Bishkek 'delimit and give us' the border (*taktap berish kerek*); but there is also a real concern that 'fixing' the border without recognising the degree of mutual interdependence risks being counterproductive. 'When you are only given [irrigation] water for half an hour every two weeks', this same man told me later in the interview, referring to the summer distribution cycle for irrigation water 'you know what harmony [*ïntïmak*] is; you don't need to be taught toleration [*tolerantnost'*]. You know what we need more than anything? More than toleration? A bath-house!!'

The contexts of 'creeping' migration

As we have seen above, 'creeping migration' refers, in contemporary public discourse in Kyrgyzstan, to the illegal purchase of homes and land plots on Kyrgyzstani territory by citizens of Tajikistan. Typically, the homes or land in question are sold by Kyrgyzstani citizens who wish to leave their village and move to Batken town or to the more fertile and land-rich Chui valley in the north of Kyrgyzstan. In this strict sense, 'creeping migration' is a relatively sporadic and isolated phenomenon that, according to my informants in the Kyrgyz border village of Ak-Sai, was much more common in the early 1990s than it is today.[19]

However, as the term has gained political currency in recent years, it is used to refer to the broader social and spatial transformation of border villages that is less about the juridical exchange of land than it is about their perceived 'Tajikisation' (*Tadzhikizatsiya*). Precisely this term, which collapses citizenship and ethnicity into a generic 'Tajik' threat, was used by the authoritative 'Expert Group' of Bishkek's International Institute of Strategic Studies in its 2008 'analytical reference' on creeping migration along Batken's borders (Ekspertnaya gruppa MISI 2008). In this much looser sense, the term is used to refer to a variety of processes whereby people of Tajik

---

[19]My informants often mentioned the considerable social and legal sanctions that inhibit people today from selling land to citizens of Tajikistan, even in those instances where the latter could offer a larger sum for the purchase of the land than a citizen of Kyrgyzstan. According to Salamat Alamanov, director of the Institute for Regional Problems under the President of the Kyrgyz Republic, and the geographer responsible for chairing Kyrgyzstan's commission on demarcation and delimitation, there are few contemporary instances of illegal land sales, but there were many historical instances of such sales, and it is precisely because these families are now well established and cultivating the land in question that they 'create headaches for us today' (Alamanov 2007; see also 'Batken: Prokuror oblasti Ryskul Baktybaev oproverg soobshcheniya o sluchayakh zakhvata kyrgyzskikh zemel' grazhdanami Tadzhikistana', *KyrgyzInfo*, 28 April 2005).

ethnicity from villages on the Tajikistani side of the border enter into informal long term lease agreements with Kyrgyzstani citizens to rent or otherwise come to occupy abandoned homes or to lease land for their own cultivation; a process that has been accelerated by growing differentials in the cost of land on the two sides of the border and the scale of Kyrgyz out-migration. This arrangement can involve a variety of procedures to ensure that land is still formally owned by a Kyrgyzstani citizen, including the (informal) purchase of Kyrgyz citizenship by the person wanting to lease or purchase the property; the registering of what is *de facto* a land purchase as a loan or rental agreement; the registering of property under the name of a relative who already has Kyrgyzstani citizenship; or, more commonly, the registering of the property in the name of some other real or fictive Kyrgyzstani citizen. It can also refer to the cultivation of un-demarcated, so-called 'contested' territory (*spornaya territoriya/talash jer*) lying between the jurisdiction of the two states, and some observers have used the term to characterise the documented or illegal use of Kyrgyzstani pastures by citizens of Tajikistan as a source of grazing land or firewood.[20]

What is at stake at one level, therefore, is an issue of informal, and technically illegal, sales and leases of land and property between citizens of neighbouring states, brought about by changes in the juridical status of land that accompanied independence.[21] But as the anxieties about 'Tajikisation' suggest, the reason for the considerable political and public debate around the issue is less to do with the juridical validity of land sales in this particular region of Batken than with two much more emotive processes: the cultural transformation of villages that are understood to be

[20]In the Isfara valley, pastures are a particular source of local contention. There are barely any Tajikistani pastures, and as foreigners on Kyrgyzstani pastures, citizens of Tajikistan have to pay a land tax of 200 som per month (c. $5), plus 50 som ($1.5) per head of livestock to the shepherd who looks after them (figures from 2005). Citizens of Kyrgyzstan pay a land tax which entitles them to use the pastures, and the rates per head of livestock are considerably lower (25–30 som) which is a source of some resentment (author's fieldnotes from Ak-Tatyr and Orto Boz villages, July 2005; UNDP 2006, p. 19). This has led to widespread illegal pasture use, a source of concern to the Batken border authorities (Aiypova 2008).

[21]According to Kyrgyzstan's 1999 Land Codex (*Zemel'nyi kodeks*), foreign citizens do not have the right to purchase land in Kyrgyzstan, though they do have the right to purchase property. In practice, however, the procedures involved, which demand presenting a packet of documents to the Ministry of Justice in Bishkek for authorisation, mean that virtually none of the property in question is exchanged in a juridically authorised way. See *Poriadok priobreteniya inostrannymi grazhdanami zhilykh, nezhilykh pomeshchenii i zemel'nykh uchastkov*, available at: http://www.kg.spinform.ru/articles/bvv004.htm, accessed 11 January 2009. Further complicating the legislative environment in Batken is the coupling of statewide legislation with locally issued 'orders' (*rasporyazheniya*), some of which are in tension with statewide legislature. In March 2006, for instance, the local administration of Batken *oblast'* issued its own order forbidding the sale of houses and land to foreign citizens (*O zaprete na prodazhu domov i zemel'nykh uchastkov inostrannym grazhdanam*). This gave the regional administration and the mayors of towns the authorisation to conduct investigations amongst border settlements to determine whether there had been instances of illegal land sales to citizens of Tajikistan, and authorised the state security agencies to invoke 'strong measures' against those found violating Kyrgyzstan's land codex (FTI 2007b, 2008, pp. 8–9). Land and property sales are also affected by a bi-party moratorium on land sales in contested areas between Kyrgyzstan and Tajikistan, and by the law on the state border of the respective states (Imanaliev 2006a, 2006b).

'historically' Kyrgyz; and the spatial movement of the state's own boundary line and associated 'sapping' of sovereignty. In a context where borders are poorly demarcated, and where in everyday practice (and political discourse), the border is understood to follow the spatial contours of 'Tajik' and 'Kyrgyz' homes and land plots, leasing a house and garden to somebody from a neighbouring state, or allowing an area of un-demarcated borderland to be cultivated by a citizen of Tajikistan is understood to be tantamount to 'moving the border'. As 'creeping migration' has come to enter political and academic discourse, therefore, it is as much the border that is felt to 'creep' (*polzat'*)—a term that gestures at once to stealth, invisibility and deception—as it is with the movement of people. 'Land' and 'motherland' are collapsed in this discursive move: selling a house transformed into a threat to the very integrity of the state.

To understand the dynamics of such cross-border arrangements, and the intense political debate that they have served to fuel, it is therefore important to examine the historical and political contexts in which they occur. First and most striking is the enormous difference in the relative population density of Kyrgyz and Tajik villages. This reflects, in part, historical differences in patterns of settlement, sources of livelihood and social organisation of space. But it also, crucially, reflects the legacy of Soviet delimitation and subsequent exchanges of land between Kyrgyz and Tajik SSRs, some of them as late as the 1960s. This has created along this valley a situation where the population of Tajikistan is concentrated into settlements, such as Vorukh, that are today either *de jure* enclaves, entirely enclosed within the territory of a neighbouring state (see Figure 1), or which, whilst not enclaves in a juridical sense, are experienced and spoken of as such by their residents, surrounded on three sides by the territory of the neighbouring state, and on the fourth by mountains, or connected to the state's 'mainland' by only a thin finger of territory.

The conjunction of these cultural and environmental factors is socially consequential. Tajik family life has historically been organised around a high-walled courtyard, and married sons are expected to remain close to the parental home and within the latter's *mahalla* (Bushkov & Mikul'skii 1996). The *mahalla* in this sense is more than simply a neighbourhood or administrative district: it denotes a moral community and a finite geographical space; one which contains and animates senses of historical connectedness, and in which a 'moral self' is able to develop (Rasanayagam 2002, pp. 75–102). As Liu argues in his account of Uzbek sociality in Osh, *mahalla* space is experientially and discursively a 'realm of distinct manners', one in which, for Osh Uzbek men, a sense of distinct ethnic identity can be articulated in a Kyrgyz majority state (Liu 2002, p. 10). In the villages along the Isfara valley, ethnic boundaries are similarly indexed and 'read' through distinctly different socio-spatial organisation. Walking between Üch-Döbö, a Kyrgyz-majority village, and its more populous Tajikistani neighbour, Hoji-A'lo, my interlocutors would often point out the otherwise unmarked state border through shifts in building style and the organisation of communal space. In Hoji-A'lo, high courtyard walls, metal gates, narrow streets and the concentration of homes into discrete, contiguous groups demarcate distinct realms of 'courtyard' and 'public' life. In Üch-Döbö, by contrast, it is often difficult to tell where a family land plot ends and a path or short-cut begins. Walls, if they exist at all around a domestic land plot, are usually well under human height; with single-storey homes both visible from the road and a site from which to observe what is going on around.

We should be wary, of course, of extrapolating in any simple way from such obvious spatial distinctions to the kind of social life they foster: to read the presence of high walls and metal gates as a sign of less 'openness'; or to assume that architecture dictates the organisation of social life. This, indeed, is how the *mahalla* has often been portrayed in the policy literature (and spoken of by many of my Kyrgyz informants): as a potential barrier to the rational organisation of space, just as it has been a vehicle for institutionalising projects aimed at 'preventive' development.[22] Yet if we should be cautious about identifying attachment to place as a 'source of conflict', or dismissing as 'irrational' the concern of those who have grown up in Chorku and Surh to remain in the area that they consider ancestral lands, we should also not underestimate the degree to which transformation of a lived landscape can come to stand for much more than itself—can signal a threat to sources of livelihood and act as a trigger for open antagonism (Bichsel 2009, p. 117). In Ak-Sai (Kyrgyzstan) in 2008, for instance, the appearance in the last year of a row of high-walled homes and a large, brick-built wedding-hall (*toikhana*) on the road that marks the border with neighbouring Vorukh (Tajikistan) was a source of considerable local comment. Although these buildings are not on contested land, the wealth which they evidence; the wedding music that regularly punctures the evening calm (this, too, 'heard' in ethnic terms by the Kyrgyz family with whom I was staying); and the transformation of previously open fields into homes and garden plots, fuels anxieties about being 'hemmed in' by a much larger, and apparently wealthier, population—of Ak-Sai itself 'becoming an enclave'.

The point, then, is that we need to recognise the symbolic resonance of such changes, whilst refusing to read them simply in 'cultural' terms. To understand the striking differences in population density on either side of the border and the concomitant pressure on land, we need to attend to the political economy of its allocation. The Tajik *jamoats* of Chorku, Surh and Vorukh sustain levels of population density that are some of the highest in Central Asia: in the enclave district of Vorukh, over 40,000 people derive a living from the enclave's 64,000 hectares of land; whilst Chorku and Surh have populations of over 30,000 and 12,000, respectively (FTI 2008). These three large villages (for, in the administrative system of contemporary Tajikistan, this is indeed how they are categorised) exceed the total population of the whole of Batken *raion*, which had an estimated population in 2001 of 80,800 (UNDP 2002). When one considers that much of this land in these enclaves and semi-enclaves is mountainous and thus unsuitable for cultivation; and that despite the size of population, people here rely on agriculture for their livelihood, this makes

---

[22]A 2004 report analysing peace and conflict potential in Batken *oblast'*, for instance, identifies the '*mahalla* concept' as one among a series of 'sources of conflict' in its discussion of inter-ethnic relations in the Isfara valley: 'Because people are strongly attached psychologically to their communities (the "*mahalla* concept"), they are reluctant to migrate permanently to other places. They fear not being accepted by residents of other regions if they leave their homes. The demographic pressure combined with a perceived need to remain close to one's place of birth forces Tajiks to migrate to nearby disputed areas and Kyrgyz territory rather than to less controversial land further away. However, neither land shortage nor demographic growth is currently having a practical impact on their *mahalla* concept' (Passon & Temirkulov 2004, p. 50).

FIGURE 3. THE KYRGYZSTAN–TAJIKISTAN BORDER BETWEEN AK-SAI AND VORUKH IN 2004

FIGURE 4. THE KYRGYZSTAN–TAJIKISTAN BORDER BETWEEN AK-SAI AND VORUKH IN MARCH 2008,
SHOWING NEW CONSTRUCTION UNDERWAY

for levels of rural population density on a par with southern China and Bangladesh (Imanaliev 2006a, p. 7). In practice, it creates a situation where several married sons and their families will continue to live in the parental household, since there is no further land available for new domestic developments; and a land pressure which means that the price of property can come to exceed that in Dushanbe. It also creates a local, cross-border economy which is ripe for informal, illegal cross-border sales and leases. According to the Foundation for Tolerance International (FTI), for instance, on the Kyrgyz side of the border in 2007, a *sotok* of land (0.1 hectare) cost between $240 and $450, whilst in Chorku and Vorukh it cost between $4,000 and $4,500 in the same period. The same contrast characterises the cost of houses on both sides of the border. In the mid-2000s, a house on the Tajik side of the border cost between $25,000 and $30,000—considerably more than in neighbouring villages of Kyrgyzstan (Kozhomkulova 2008), and considerably exceeding the cost of a house on the outskirts of Bishkek or in the fertile Chui valley.

The pressures created by this local difference in the cost of real estate are compounded by the extent of irrigation dependence and the way in which this limits the possibilities for the cultivation of new lands. Other than in the narrow alluvial plane of the Isfara river, where rice and other irrigation-dependent crops are grown, the region relies upon artificial irrigation for the watering of fields and land plots. This irrigation is either electricity-dependent, as in the village of Ak-Sai where a pumping station pumps water from the Isfara river; or it is generated mechanically from the Ak-Tatïr and Törtköl canals. The opening of these irrigation canals during late socialism transformed this formerly barren 'stony land' (*tashtyk jer*) into an area sustaining the cultivation of tobacco, rice and apricots. It also enabled the creation of new, so-called 'planned villages' where Kyrgyz herders who had continued to lead a semi-nomadic lifestyle on the high pastures above Vorukh were resettled in the 1970s and 1980s. Such irrigation systems, however, were never intended to sustain the volume of domestic garden plots which, with the end of state socialism, have become a primary source of family livelihoods. This irrigation-dependence means that land without access to water is of little use; and it has also served to transform a finite resource that has historically been pumped, piped and channelled with little regard to international borders, into a 'national' resource with enormous social consequences if it is withheld, diverted or siphoned off by upstream homes. This situation also helps to explain the continued pressure on land in upstream Tajik villages, despite the formal allocation of land plots lower down the valley.[23]

Local pressures on cross-border sales are complicated by the political economy of land. On the Tajik side of the border, land is not only in considerably shorter supply but the majority of arable land also remains the property of the state, farmed collectively with crops that are not of the individual farmer's choosing. The privatisation of land in Kyrgyzstan has not been without profound social consequences: one of the most

[23]In densely populated Chorku and Surh, for instance, many young families have been allocated land in the Shorab, a mining town that formerly enjoyed 'Moscow provisioning' (*Moskovskoe obespechenie*). Shorab has lost the majority of its population through out-migration and its dependence upon pumped water for irrigation and drinking has made domestic cultivation virtually impossible. Many of the families allocated land there only reside during part of the year, returning downstream to Chorku during the spring planting season.

painful shocks of a relentless programme of neoliberal 'shock therapy' (Pelkmans 2005; Pétric 2005). When the lands of the former collective were privatised, many families found that the land to which they were nominally entitled was several dozen kilometres away on the other side of Batken town, making it too costly for all but the best-resourced families to farm. Most of my Kyrgyz informants were extremely nostalgic for a time of collectively farmed land. Yet despite the failings of Kyrgyzstan's land privatisation, for Tajiks living at the border, the presence of large tracts of Kyrgyz land that are left uncultivated (often for want of fertiliser, diesel fuel and now, given the scale of out-migration to Russia, human labour) is interpreted less as a sign of the failure of land privatisation in Kyrgyzstan, than a further insult to their own land poverty (Kuehnast & Dudwick 2008; UNDP 2006; Urumbaev 2008).

Zukhro, a Tajik woman from Hoji-A'lo in her early forties who scraped a living from her small domestic plot and the remittances sent by her husband in Novosibirsk, echoed a view that I often heard when she remarked, tracing a line across her neck in a gesture of abundance that she and her four children would 'live like this [in plenty] if we had been given the same amount of land to farm as the Kyrgyz'. Like the three-storey wedding hall that is a source of rumour and speculation in Ak-Sai, what is significant here is the capacity of a piece of uncultivated land to mediate much bigger concerns about unequal distribution. Both of these objects are symbolically resonant, just as they are materially important to lives and livelihoods.

Perhaps the most significant local factor for understanding contemporary tensions over land, however, concerns the role of memory, and the way in which different groups of people differently remember place and its rightful ownership. The significance of these divergent spatial visions was expressed vividly by Jamshed-aka, a Tajik doctor from the village of Tojikon, when he gestured to the surrounding pastures—pastures that my 'reading' of the landscape, based on contemporary maps of the valley, told me were unambiguously Kyrgyzstani territory—and recalled a time when these were, as he put it, 'all Tajik lands'; and when the planned, 'Soviet' villages that we could see from where we stood had never existed. His account of how the surrounding pastures came to be 'lost' to the neighbouring republic—one that I have heard versions of from several interlocutors from Tojikon and Hoji-A'lo—claimed that they were given informally on long term lease to the neighbouring Kyrgyz collective farm to avoid unnecessary taxes on swathes of unused pastureland. This was, as other interlocutors also reiterated, the result of a misguided decision by a lowly collective farm official, one that should never have been taken as politically authoritative and which was never ratified by the Constitutional Council of the USSR.[24]

---

[24]This sense of 'betrayal' comes through vividly in a comment made by the head of the Vorukh farmers' cooperative, Validjon Nozirov, to a local Tajik journalist: 'The will of one local Soviet official cannot carry authority for the population . . . However, precisely because of this betrayal on the part of local officials during the life of the Soviet Union, Tajiks now find themselves caught in a vice [*zazhati v tiski*]. Today we are forced to reap the fruits of that tolerance and internationalism, which was drummed into our heads in Soviet years. Judge for yourself: the Tajik villages today are deprived of pastures, of water, of any kind of land reserve [for distribution to new families]. Each year the population is growing and people need to find homes for young families, and yet the borders of Vorukh village cannot in any way be moved. Is there any logic in the fact that all the land surrounding this settlement should belong to the neighbouring state?' (Mirsaidov 2008).

FIGURE 5. VIEW FROM JAMSHED-AKA'S ROOF, SUMMER 2005: 'THESE USED TO BE ALL TAJIK LANDS'

Stabilising space: 'creeping migration' in Kyrgyzstani political discourse

These, then, are the contexts in which land is bought, sold, leased and used along Batken's borders, and which frame contemporary political debate. The paradox here is that 'creeping migration' in the strict sense of the term was largely a phenomenon of the 1980s and 1990s. It occurred at a time when the borders along the Isfara valley were not only un-demarcated (as they remain today) but were also comparatively little policed. This was also a time of considerable population growth and population movement, when many Kyrgyz families sold up and moved north. The more recent and relatively isolated instances of creeping migration since 2000 have tended to be on uncultivated, 'contested land' between Kyrgyz and Tajik settlements, where there is a moratorium on new construction.

Yet despite this, it is in the last few years that creeping migration has become a significant political issue. Newspaper searches through the Integrum database going back to the early independence period suggest that the term first entered public discourse in 2001, when outspoken governor Mamat Aibalaev headed the Batken *oblast'* administration; and there has been a proliferation of references since 2006.[25] In

[25]Integrum database, available at: http://www.integrumworld.com, is a database of print and online media reports from Russia and the CIS. See, indicatively, Abdullaev (2006), Aiypova (2008), Anarkulov (2008a), Kozhomkulova (2008), Omuraliev (2008), Pozharskii (2008), Skorodumova (2007) and Urumbaev (2005, 2006, 2007). For a critique of the tenor of some of this reporting, see Mirsaidov (2008) and Alamanov (2008).

the last two years, illegal exchange of land and property in border areas has become the object of newspaper and online debate, NGO-sponsored roundtables investigating the potential for violence and threats to the integrity of the state, and analytical reports predicting the expansion of neighbouring states onto Kyrgyzstani territory and urging restrictions upon freedom of movement to prevent, as the title of one report put it, the 'loss of the south' (*Poteryannyi yug?*) (Ekspertnaya gruppa assotsyatsii politologov Kyrgyzstana 2007). This has been coupled with legislative initiatives seeking to accord 'special status' to border regions and a notable concentration of resources to institutionalise and enforce a *de facto* international border through the construction of bypass roads, the allocation of land in newly formed border villages for the construction of homes, and the expansion of territory under the ownership and control of border units (FTI 2008, pp. 7–8).

Perhaps most significantly, it has turned the 'defence' of border villages into an issue of political capital. In 2008 President Bakiev visited the border village of Tashtumshuk promising that he would sort out the village's electricity shortages, a visit that was soon followed by a raid by regional officials to determine the number of properties that had been illegally sold to citizens of Tajikistan.[26] A few months later, at a meeting for the heads of *raion* and *oblast'* administrations, Prime Minister Chudinov insisted that the government was 'devoting all its strength' to prevent, as he put it, the 'further depopulation [*ogoleniya*] of border regions'.[27] Echoing a claim that Bakiev had made when he visited Batken the previous spring, Chudinov insisted that the government itself would purchase the homes of Kyrgyz citizens in border villages who might otherwise be tempted to sell their property to citizens of the neighbouring state:

> To halt this process [of illegal sales of property] I invite the residents of these regions to inform me personally, so that the government of Kyrgyzstan can buy these houses from its citizens. It is better that we buy these houses than that they are bought by citizens of neighbouring states. Given the current rate of development of this process of latent migration, I wouldn't be surprised if in one of the border districts of Kyrgyzstan there will soon appear the school of one of the neighbouring states. And then just try moving it or bringing it to the other side of the state border.[28]

The concern with territorial integrity that such initiatives evince is not in itself new. The 1999–2000 'border crisis' with Uzbekistan (Megoran 2004) thrust questions of state spatiality into the public domain, and concerns about the vulnerability of the state borders to pressure from neighbouring states gained momentum in the new millennium with revelations over secret exchanges of land with China. Throughout the spring and summer of 2005, in the euphoria and chaos following Kyrgyzstan's so-called 'Tulip Revolution' in March of that year, television bulletins and newspapers

---

[26]'V Batkenskoi oblasti 8 zemel'nykh uchastkov pereshli na balans Tadzhikistana', *Obshchestvennyi reiting*, 12 September 2007.

[27]'Igor' Chudinov: Pravitel'stvo vystupaet za pridanie osobogo statusa prigranichnym raionam strany', *Gazeta.kg*, 27 February 2008, available at: www.gazeta.kg/image/2008-02-27/4252, last accessed 17 January 2009.

[28]'I. Chudinov obespokoilsya zaseleniem prigranichnykh raionov yuga respubliki grazhdanam sosednikh stran', *Obshchestvennyi reiting*, 27 February 2008.

were full of accounts of disgraced President Akaev's 'secret sales' of land. The border issue (*chek ara maselesi*), then, has been a staple of opposition discourse throughout the new millennium. What appears to be new in the current moment, however, is the extent to which issues of territorial integrity have gone from being a discourse through which the political opposition mobilised, and through which the 'treachery' of President Akaev was discursively sealed, to becoming much more thoroughly embedded in government rhetoric and official state policy: a vehicle for 'stabilising' the state after the ousting of Akaev.

Mitchell's concept of 'state effects' is helpful in exploring why this is so. Mitchell draws attention to the way in which certain 'novel practices of the technical age' allow the categories 'state', 'society' and 'economy' to come to appear to be both ontologically and conceptually distinct. His critique of existing state theories is precisely that they fail to problematise how it is that the state comes to appear as an entity 'outside' of society and authoritative over it. Once we turn attention to the permeability of the state–society boundary and the 'political significance of maintaining it' (Mitchell 1999, p. 82), then the spatiality of the state comes into view not as an *a priori* attribute, but as the outcome of technical interventions and social practices that are accessible to empirical exploration.

It is in the realm of such 'effects' that we need to locate the 'creeping migration' that has taken on life in political discourse. For whilst the term denotes an empirical process—one that is indeed socially and economically consequential for people living at the border—it is also, crucially, a generative site for the elicitation of state effects. That is, it allows a proliferation of assertions to territorial integrity; it legitimises quite draconian interventions to keep populations 'in place', and it rationalises these through reference to acute, existential threat to the continuity of the nation and the integrity of the state. Two recent responses to the phenomenon of creeping migration illustrate such state effects particularly vividly: the designation of 'special' status to border villages, and the building of bypass roads. Like the raft of official visits, neither of these has done much to address the acute underlying sources of tension over water and land; and yet, like the 'dropping in' of the president to a border village, the sudden raid by local migration officials to determine who of the village's residents 'turned out' to have been living there illegally, or the promise by a prime minister that the state would buy up property that might otherwise be sold to neighbour-foreigners, these are important vehicles for enacting territorial integrity.

'By whatever means we must keep people in the south of the country': the draft law on 'special' border villages

In March 2008, Batken parliamentary deputy Marat Juraev drafted a law that would grant special status to those Kyrgyz border villages most at threat of creeping migration.[29] This followed an earlier legislative initiative in 2006 to give 'special legal

---

[29]Draft law, 'On Special Border Settlements of the Kyrgyz Republic' [*Ob osobykh prigranichnykh naselennykh punktakh KR*] initiated by Deputy Juraev, available at: http://www.kenesh.kg/.f/98ccf0fe-c839-46ef-ab45-2495d24aeb16/Проект%20закона%20о%20пригр.пунктах.doc, accessed 1 May

status' to border regions of the Kyrgyz Republic, which would accord material benefits to residents of border regions in return for their active involvement in civic border defence.[30] As Juraev explained in an interview with the Russian-language *Vechernii Bishkek*, the 2008 draft was motivated by a quite personal sense of threat at the lost of familiar lands in his native Leilek district:

> In the 1970s I remember as a boy helping the adults to collect cotton on the fields. And these same fields now belong to others. As children we loved climbing up in the mountains. We considered them ours. Now there are claims on them by residents of the neighbouring states. I see that little by little we are giving away our own areas [*uchastki*] to other republics. (Temir 2008a)

The law was debated in parliament and received the support of the parliamentary speaker and presidential party member, Adakhan Madumarov.[31] It was ultimately returned to the committee for constitutional affairs for reworking, however, because of the excessive costs that would be entailed in its implementation. The draft listed a series of so-called 'special' (*osobye*) border villages, all but one of them in Batken *oblast*',[32] in which citizens of Kyrgyzstan would be forbidden from leasing, selling or giving away any land to any foreigners or stateless persons; or to the spouse or business partner of any foreigner or stateless person (Article 1).[33] This would be accompanied by a special system of entry and exit (*ustanovlenie kontrol'no-propusknogo rezhima*) to regulate movement in and out of border villages, and would punish those deemed to be selling or leasing land illegally (Article 2).

The same law also outlined a series of provisions which sought, quite explicitly, to keep the border population 'in place'. These included preferential rates in applications for state loans; increased wages, the provision of 110 free university places for students applying to become doctors, teachers or military officers, and 'the provision of ... drinking water, food, irrigation systems, electricity, transport, [telephone] connections and educational facilities in a manner to be determined by the Government of the Kyrgyz Republic' (Article 4). As Juraev explained in a newspaper interview at the time of the parliamentary debate, 'the most important thing is that by whatever means we keep people in the south of the country'. This entailed 'creat[ing]

2009. The parliamentary debate was widely covered in the print and online media. See Akmat uulu (2008), Anarkulov (2008a), Erkin uulu (2008), Karimov (2008), Kozhomkulova (2008), Nurakun uulu (2008), Temir (2008a, 2008b) and 'M. Dzhuraev: Na granites s Tadzhikistanom bole 3 tysyach gektarov territorii Kyrgyzstana zakhvatili grazhdane sosednei strany', *Obshchestvennyi reiting*, 4 March 2008.

[30]Draft law, 'On the Special Legal Status of Border Settlements of the KR' [*Ob osobom pravavom statuse prigranichnykh naselennykh punktov KR*], initiated by Deputies Imanaliev, Tekebaev, Juraev and Shernyazov in 2006, see FTI (2007b).

[31]A figure, as one of the reviewers of this article correctly noted, regarded with fear by minority groups in Kyrgyzstan for his outspoken nationalist statements.

[32]The one village that was not in Batken *oblast*' was Barak, a small enclave of Kyrgyzstan with a population of 700, in the territory of Uzbekistan.

[33]Draft law, 'On Special Border Settlements of the Kyrgyz Republic', Article 1, available at: http://www.kenesh.kg/.f/98ccf0fe-c839-46ef-ab45-2495d24aeb16/Проект%20закона%20о%20пригр.пунктах. doc, accessed 1 May 2009.

the conditions for people living in border regions, so that they do not leave and abandon their homes' (Pozharskii 2008). The draft law was accompanied by a document outlining the rationale (*obosnovanie*) for these changes, which stressed that the protection of border populations in 'strategic' areas was not simply a matter of social concern but an issue of national security:

> It is important to note that the majority of residents of the above-named border settlements are obliged to leave their settlements because of the absence of suitable living conditions. This leads to the abandoning of homes and land, which become the target of creeping migration from neighbouring states. This represents a threat to the safety and integrity [*tselostnost'*] of the state. The guaranteeing of state security and the integrity of the state border represent one [sic] of the strategic directions of state policy.[34]

Juraev accompanied his proposed law with a series of strongly worded newspaper interviews, in which this sense of 'threat' was spelt out all the more vigorously. In an article published in the independent newspaper *Delo Nomer* under the headline, 'Is Kyrgyzstan a country without territory?' (*Kyrgyzstan—strana bez territorii?*), Juraev detailed the 'take-over' (*zakhvat*) of land and property in particular border villages by citizens of the neighbouring state:

> Tajikistanis are building huge mansions with fountains and then live there under Kyrgyz surnames. At the same time the [northern Tajik] city of Khujand is literally twenty kilometres away and they can travel to Tajikistan without obstacle. In this way the line of the border is moving, and the speed is not letting up … The paradox is that if for the Kyrgyzstanis the districts bordering Tajikistan are contested, for the Tajiks these same lands are no longer contested, since they have already appropriated this land and constructed buildings on it. On the contrary, they increase the territory that is contested by dint of the fact that Kyrgyzstanis from Batken *oblast'* abandon their lands, sell their homes, or lease them to citizens of Tajikistan, and themselves migrate to the Chui valley, to Kazakhstan or to Russia. (Pozharskii 2008)

To stress this growing threat, the article was accompanied by a map showing large swathes of contested territory along Batken's borders and a village plan on which were highlighted the land plots that had been illegally sold to citizens of Tajikistan: a stark visual representation of the border under threat.

Juraev's law, together with the official rationale that was debated in parliament and accompanying public interviews, articulated a particular conception of the threatened state—one that in turn was used to justify a series of interventions: economic, military and technical. It is striking for the conceptual elisions that it makes between state territory and an (ethnic) national body; between human movement and the creep of the border. But it is also remarkable for the particular kind of state that it is used to effect—a state that controls and regulates, but which also provides materially for its

---

[34]'Obosnovanie k proektu Zakona Kyrgyzskoi Republiki 'Ob osobykh prigranichnykh naselennykh punktakh Kyrgyzskoi Republiki', available at: http://www.kenesh.kg/.f/98ccf0fe-c839-46ef-ab45-2495d24aeb16/Проект%20закона%20о%20пригр.пунктах.doc, accessed 1 May 2009.

borderland population so as to ensure that people remain 'in place'. As James Ferguson notes in his analysis of contemporary topographies of power, such gestures of stately provision are as important to spatialising the state as the mounting of a border post: 'state benevolence as well as coercion must make its spatial rounds' (Ferguson 2006, p. 110).

State effects

In analysing these effects, three features of the emergent discourse around creeping migration deserve particular note. The first is the suggestion that the fact of illegal land sales at the border was less a natural, if lamentable, response to the acute land shortage in the neighbouring state than a deliberate policy, which had the blessing of the authorities in Dushanbe. Juraev was at pains to contrast the relative peace of Kyrgyzstan's much more vigorously militarised border with Uzbekistan, and the 'openness' that allowed the Tajik 'creep' to persist: 'The Uzbek authorities have already put up border posts and barbed wire along the areas of contested territory', he argued. 'That's why there are no attempts there to settle and appropriate Kyrgyz territory' (Pozharskii 2008). By contrast, the Tajik authorities had allowed, as he put it in a meeting of the parliamentary committee on constitutional affairs on 4 March 2008, the 'systematic occupation [*planomernyi zakhvat*] of our territory'.[35]

This emphasis was echoed in a report, widely discussed in Kyrgyz online forums and extensively reproduced on the internet, which was prepared for official use by the International Institute for Strategic Studies under the President of the Kyrgyz Republic. Entitled 'On the policy of Dushanbe concerning the "Tajikization" of border territories of Batken *oblast*' of the Kyrgyz Republic and possible measures in response', the report started from the premise that creeping migration was an intensely political issue, of more than merely local significance. The situations of conflict (*konfliktnye situatsii*) that had occurred in Batken *oblast*' during the preceding two years, the report argued, 'witness to the single-minded policy of Dushanbe for the further appropriation of Kyrgyzstani territories bordering Tajikistan in areas still awaiting delimitation'. The report went on to elaborate the population differentials in border regions that gave Tajikistan an advantageous position (*preimushchestvennoe polozhenie*) in negotiations. Recognising its advantage, it argued,

> Dushanbe secretly supports the borderland Tajik population in putting psychological pressure on Kyrgyz, with the goal of forcing them to move. The tactical instrument in this policy is ... the illegal purchase and building of homes, and likewise the sowing of crops in areas located very close to the border or on the very territory of Kyrgyz villages.

---

[35]'Grazhdane Tadzhikistana uzhe zakhvatili bole 2 tysyach gektarov kyrgyzstanskoi territorii', *Gazeta.kg*, 4 March 2008, available at: http://www.gazeta.kg/news/2008-03-04/4382, accessed 1 May 2009.

> The departure of Kyrgyz families to different regions of the KR creates for the Tajik side a 'precedent of success' in its tactic of psychological pressure, it shows the relative closeness and the ease of reaching their goals. (Ekspertnaya gruppa MISI 2008)

Striking in the vigorous online response to this report, and in much of the subsequent newspaper coverage, was a sense of shock and offence that *Tajikistan*, the weakest and poorest of all Kyrgyzstan's neighbours, should be acting in such a way. In an article published in April 2008, shortly after a local conflict over water between upstream and downstream communities in the Isfara valley made national headlines, Kubanichbek Omuraliev, a prominent public figure, responded angrily to the incident by asserting that the dynamics of 'expansion' of citizens of Tajikistan into Kyrgyzstani territory represented 'an example of grave violation of land, belonging by right of historical ownership [*po pravu istoricheskogo vladeniya*] to another people' (Omuraliev 2008). Omuraliev's report completely ignored the complex dynamics of the conflict in question, which had little to do with 'creeping migration' and was in fact triggered by the unannounced closure of the waterway during the spring planting season. Instead he went on to make a critique of the 'long-standing silence, excessive patience and indecisiveness' of the Kyrgyz authorities, which had allowed this situation to develop:

> This position [of inaction] is more or less understandable when, in the question of contested border territories with China, Bishkek demonstrated a certain willingness to concede. However, such concessions are simply shameful [*postydny*] in relation to Tajikistan, where the authorities are unable even to provide their citizens with light and heat, and where the basic source of monies entering the state budget is the army of illiterate guest-workers, with a solid reputation as narco-traffickers. Bishkek is obliged, come what may, to finally stand by the rights of its citizens, and ensure the inviolability of its own territory. (Omuraliev 2008)

The tenor of Omuraliev's critique points to a second striking effect of the developing public debate: to demand a more assertive policy in regard to its neighbour, Tajikistan. 'Creeping migration' was taken as a sign of state weakness: the 'moving' borders less a reflection of the overlapping territorial claims bequeathed by 70 years of coexistence than the symbol of a much broader failure of state sovereignty. Juraev, for instance, responded to a question about why this was happening with the response, 'if we were a strong state [*sil'nym gosudarstvom*], of course [Tajikistan] wouldn't treat us like that'. He then went on to list Kyrgyzstan's territorial concessions, with the 'creeping migration' from Tajikistan the last in an ongoing drama of disappearing territory: 'First it was China, now talks are going on about us giving land to Kazakhstan; then in turn Uzbekistan will want something or other. And then Tajikistan will join in this process' (Pozharskii 2008).

The third striking effect of the discourse that emerged around 'creeping migration' was the way in which it transformed a phenomenon of state territoriality into a cultural threat. Speaking to the parliamentary committee on constitutional legislation, for instance, deputy Juraev began by outlining the danger to the state's territorial integrity posed by illegal occupation and lack of border controls. This, however, was immediately followed by a rather different kind of threat—less the moving of the border than a process of cultural domination: what Juraev calls a 'Kosovo scenario':

We are witnessing a classic 'Kosovo' scenario. We may well reach a moment, when this territory will be inhabited by citizens of other nationalities [*grazhdane drugikh natsional'nostei*]. Who would have thought that Kyrgyz citizens would have to take their passport with them to fetch water? Or that girls would have to be accompanied to school by several lads, so that they weren't attacked? Or that our [*oblast'*] governor would be beaten up by the border guards of the neighbouring state![36] Whatever next? (Karimov 2008)

Juraev's 'citizens of other nationalities' is telling here. For it suggests that it is less the fact of different citizenship that is the issue in the illegal land sales, or their illegality *per se* than the cultural integrity that is at stake when those purchasing the land are perceived to be linguistically, culturally and ethnically 'other'. Asked several days later in interview to explain what he meant by this 'Kosovo scenario', Juraev responded by describing how the gradual migration of ethnic Albanians had led to a declaration of independence in a 'Serbian *oblast'*', leading to the splitting apart of a previously integral state: 'When [Yugoslavia] fell apart, it turned out that in Serbia one *oblast'* [sic] had become predominantly Albanian. The Albanians conducted a referendum on their *oblast'*, announcing the independence of Kosovo, and Serbia was split apart [*raskololas'*]' (Pozharskii 2008). Quite apart from its rather scant regard for historical, demographic or juridical accuracy, Juraev's comment is striking for the parallel that he immediately went on to draw with the situation in southern Kyrgyzstan, in which the real threat—that of cultural and ethnic domination by ostensibly 'minority' groups—comes to the fore:

In the South of Kyrgyzstan, there are about one million Kyrgyz people living, 600–700,000 Uzbeks and 100–120,000 Tajiks. But many Kyrgyz have left and continue to leave for work abroad. Maybe things will turn out such that in the future the Kyrgyz won't be the ethnic majority. And what if another ethnic group wants to create a South Kyrgyz republic with its capital in Osh? They'll conduct a referendum and there, you'll find that you've got one more Kosovo, only in Asia. Kyrgyzstan will be split in two. (Pozharskii 2008)

It is easy to dismiss such assertions as the rhetorical excesses of a nationalist politician, whose draft law had given him a moment of brief and short-lived attention; but the assumption, implicit or explicit, that informal land sales represent a greater threat when carried out by people of different ethnicity from the majority Kyrgyz is also found in much more sober and informed analyses. FTI, for instance, in its analytical reports, distinguishes between illegal immigrants from Tajikistan on the basis of ethnicity. Ethnic Kyrgyz migrants who are moving to their 'historical homeland' [*iskonno istorcheskuyu rodinu*] are not a source of concern to the local authorities, the reports argue, because alongside a simplified system for acquiring citizenship, such migrants 'have kinship links with the local population [and] the same

---

[36]The event alluded to here referred to a violent outburst that emerged between Batken governor Aijigitov and Tajik border guards posted at a mobile border unit in Surh in January 2007. The mobile post was located on a stretch of Tajikistani road that had been loaned to Kyrgyzstan for 49 years (and therefore should not have any border controls). The event escalated into an open conflict, involving the border units of both states (FTI 2007a).

traditions and habits, enabling them to adapt painlessly' (FTI 2007b, 2008). By contrast, ethnic Tajiks who managed to regularise their status through the acquisition of Kyrgyzstani citizenship, were nonetheless deemed to represent a threat to inter-ethnic peace. It is one of the striking features of borderland migration that many Tajik migrants are quite keen to acquire Kyrgyzstani citizenship, not least because having a Kyrgyzstani passport tends to attract less harassment for labour migrants from the Russian and Kazakh police. Yet in its detailed recommendations to law makers and local authorities, FTI warned about the risks of granting citizenship to those ethnic Tajiks who were already *de facto* permanent residents of Batken *oblast'*. If the Tajik immigrants were granted citizenship and were then to invite their kin and friends, the report argued, it 'could destroy the habitual ethnic balance in the given border villages and eventually lead to interethnic conflicts' (FTI 2008, p. 21).

Whilst very different in tone and rhetorical effect, what links the law-maker's initiative with FTI's empirical analysis is an underlying assumption about the relationship between ethnic 'imbalance' and social risk, whether at the level of an individual village, or of the nation state as a whole. This conception is consequential, because as well as essentialising cultural difference, it also tends to justify policies that are aimed at minimising inter-ethnic contact rather than addressing the underlying sources of tension (Reeves 2005; Bichsel 2009). Attempts to construct a school in the Kyrgyz border hamlet of Tashtumshuk, for instance, have been justified on the grounds that children currently have to walk through the Tajik village of Hoji-A'lo on their way to their current school, and that it is precisely whilst walking there that 'small everyday quarrels and fights [*mel'kie bytovye ssory i stychki*]' are liable to break out (FTI 2008, pp. 17–18).

What this kind of equation misses is that such quarrels occur not because of different ethnicity, nor even, as the FTI report argues, because one village is significantly more populous than the other, but because in a context of acute resource shortage and the political over-determination of ethnic difference, it is hardly surprising that children learn to structure antagonism along 'national' lines. Tashtumshuk, after all, was the scene of a raid to root out 'illegal' residents—hardly an initiative conducive to harmonious inter-communal relations or the depoliticisation of difference.

Allowing the 'taste of independence': bypass roads

If official pronouncements are anything to go by, however, precisely this logic of separation seems to underlie the building of two new 'bypass roads' in Batken region. Roads, as Penny Harvey points out in a South American context, are powerful sites for enacting territorial integrity: they 'materialise state and corporate ambition, and transform particular territorial spaces into sites of fantasy and projection for politicians, planners and local people' (Harvey 2005, p. 131). Moreover, what they materialise is not just any old 'fantasy', but a particular conception of the state as bounded, contiguous and extensive. They are 'immobile material entities yet they draw attention to mobility; they have fixed geographical coordinates yet they extend beyond and exceed named places and thus have an air of the translocal about them' (Harvey 2005, p. 131). The symbolic potential is particularly striking when the roads in question, such as those currently under construction in Batken *oblast'*, are explicitly conceived to bypass a neighbouring state. In the Isfara valley, the 'detour' in question is a 23 kilometre stretch of road that creates a loop to the south of the populous Tajik villages of Surh and Chorku, remaining entirely within Kyrgyzstani territory. Moreover, in a striking reflection of the entanglements of the 'international' in statist construction projects, the road is financed with funding of €6.5 million from the European Commission (Anarkulov 2008b; Urumbaev 2007).

Like other bypass roads, the detour around Surh and Chorku was conceived to enable citizens of Kyrgyzstan to pass with ease between different parts of their own state, without risk of customs and border checks at the point that they crossed the border. The mobile customs posts that appear on market day in Chorku are, indeed, a source of considerable local frustration. Taxi-drivers would often lament how cars with Kyrgyzstani number plates would be selected for checks, and were vulnerable to arbitrary 'fees' simply for transporting potatoes or rice between the market and home. As several of my interlocutors pointed out, however, the bypass road around Tajikistan had a secondary aim, by effectively delineating, in a quite literal and visible sense, the hitherto unmarked contours of Kyrgyzstani territory in a zone deemed vulnerable to the border's 'creep'.

Certainly, the official pronouncements that have surrounded the recent road-building projects in Batken have stressed that these stretches of asphalt are as much symbolic as technical. President Bakiev, at an August 2008 presentation of technical equipment acquired by the Ministry of Transport, announced that in ensuring the country's 'transport independence' (*transportnaya nezavisimost'*), the government was simultaneously resolving 'a most important political task': the future stabilisation of the country, and the 'improvement of relations with neighbouring states'.[37] Prime Minister Chudinov celebrated the Day of Auto Transport Workers by announcing that road building projects in the south of the country would turn Kyrgyzstan 'from a country of geographical dead-ends into one of transit' (*iz tupikovoi strany v tranzitnuyu*),[38] whilst the former governor of Batken *oblast'*, Sultan Aijigitov, celebrated the detour roads as having finally allowed inhabitants of the region to enjoy the 'taste of independence'. He was quoted as saying:

> On the territory of the *oblast'* are five enclaves, and all communication goes precisely through these enclaves. To tell you the truth, it is precisely for this reason that for already fifteen years now the local population has not yet experienced the taste of real freedom [*vkus nastoyashchei svobody*]. The taste of independence. Such problems can be resolved in one way only. We must build detour roads around these enclaves. (Anarkulov 2008b)

Such, then, is the logic of the 'detour': separate roads as a way of fostering, quite literally, separate paths through the landscape—with this the precondition for a sweet-tasting 'independence'. The problem with this logic is threefold: first, it risks

[37]'K. Bakiev prinyal uchastie v prezentatsii tekhniki, priobretennoi Mintransom', *Kabar*, 4 August 2008.

[38]'I.Chudinov prinyal uchastie v torzhestvennom sobranii ko Dnyu rabotnikov avtomobil'nogo transporta', *Kabar*, 10 October 2008.

FIGURE 6. Start of the New 23km Bypass Road around Chorku and Surh, Funded by the European Commission, August 2008

undermining those mundane spaces of borderland conviviality—of which public transport is as important as it is overlooked—that provide the context within which larger, more consequential issues are resolved. Secondly, and related to this, it tends to reduce the incentives to seek collective solutions to pressing issues of land shortage, pasture and water use. As the UNDP noted recently in a cross-border analysis, the tendency to seek solutions 'through more ethnic separation' rather than 'through improvement in interethnic relations' may be popular with domestic constituencies, but is unlikely to address the underlying sources of tension (UNDP 2006, p. 4). Rather than seeking funding for new roads, for instance, the report recommends investing in existing infrastructure and developing mechanisms for shared use (UNDP 2006, p. 38).

Perhaps most significantly, however, the logic of 'separate roads' serves to politicise space in new ways. In a region where the formal, cartographic border is not visibly demarcated, it is the road that serves as the *de facto* site of stately territorial control, at least as far as ordinary border-dwellers are concerned. It is on roads and bridges that the fixed border and customs posts tend to be sited; it is at the side of roads that mobile border units tend to regulate movement; it is the goods that pass, legally and illegally, along roads that allow the extraction of fines and bribes.

A number of recent reports have highlighted the degree of popular resentment of this everyday securitisation of border space—and the extent to which 'border defence' can morph into the extraction of tribute (Dolina mira 2004; Kadyrova 2005; Kuehnast & Dudwick 2008, pp. 10–18; UNDP 2006, pp. 25–26). In the past it has precisely been the fact of 'transport inter-dependence'—the fact that Tajik citizens depend on passing through Kyrgyzstani territory and vice versa—that has tended to act as a constraint upon the degree of everyday border enforcement. 'Transport independence' allows for space to be unilaterally militarised in new ways, with unpredictable consequences. It is too early to say what the effects of this will be, but certainly, the tendency to respond to moments of heightened tension by increasing, or threatening to increase, the number of border and customs controls does not bode well for populations here, for whom border-crossing is a fact of life.

Conclusion

This essay has drawn on a concept of 'state effects' to explore recent attempts to 'stabilise the border' and materialise state space in southern Kyrgyzstan. It has argued that the illegal cross-border sale of land and property in the Isfara valley, whilst an empirical process that is indeed a source of concern to local people, has taken on a dynamic in contemporary political discourse in Kyrgyzstan that is quite unrelated to the actual dynamics of co-existence along Batken's borders. It is a discourse, moreover, which is symbolically charged and politically productive. As the previous section has demonstrated, the threat posed by 'creeping migration' from neighbouring Tajikistan has been used to enact the 'encompassing' state in border regions in various ways—through stately beneficence; through raids on homes now deemed 'illegal'; through the materialisation of stately infrastructure; and through the increasing militarisation of borderland space. If we proceed from a recognition that territorial integrity, rather than an *a priori* attribute of the state, is rather a 'precarious achievement' (Ferguson 2006, p. 11), then such interventions come into view as powerful techniques both for spatialising the state and for asserting a particular conception, in a region of ethnic diversity, of the normative relation between 'nation' and 'state'.

In developing this argument, the essay has made a second claim, relating to our analysis of the Ferghana valley. The essay has echoed recent calls to interrogate the reification of ethnicity as a category of analysis in our study of the region (Megoran 2007). Yet it has also sought to explore why it is that, in this particular part of the Ferghana basin at least, ethnicity has come to be so very salient as an everyday 'practical category'. To understand why, the essay has suggested, we need to attend to the particular history of border drawing and re-drawing in this region; the legacies of spatial settlement which sought to 'fix' populations and in so doing 'fix' the border, and the contemporary political economy of land. These historical and post-Soviet dynamics have created a situation where 'ethnicity' and 'territory' are symbolically over-determined: that is, they have come to be so firmly linked in popular and official understandings of this region that the border is 'read' according to the ethnic distribution of villages and homes. It is in this context of over-determination that selling a home to someone of different ethnicity and different citizenship can become tantamount to 'moving the border'. Attending to this history of 'ethnic-spatial fixing' (Moore 2005) is crucial for understanding the potential future dynamics of co-existence in this region.

This in turn has implications for how we theorise 'symbolic politics' in Central Asia. To reduce political action to questions of instrumentality, the essay has argued, is to occlude much of what gives politics its dynamic force. Specifically, in exploring the dynamics of cross-border relations, an account framed in terms of 'resource shortage' or material needs alone gives us little conceptual purchase on what is at stake at times of heightened tension: why it is that certain people, objects and places can come, quite suddenly and dramatically, to be invested with enormous significance as markers of difference or vehicles for the production of peace.

In exploring the place of the symbolic in Central Asian political life, therefore, we should attend not just to those symbols that adorn school books and public monuments, which are invoked in speeches and reproduced on state regalia to signify national unity, ethnic primacy or state strength. If we proceed, rather, from an expansive account of the symbolic—an approach that recognises our intrinsic competence as humans to represent the world to ourselves through other people and things—then we can begin to attend to the local meanings, including seemingly 'irrational' responses, to interventions that would appear to be purely technical. In the case of the symbolically freighted ribbon of land that lines the Isfara valley, such an approach can help us to grasp something of the dynamic force of the political in everyday life: how it is that a donor-sponsored water pipe can become a symbol of unequal distribution and deliberately targeted in a moment of inter-communal violence (Reeves 2008, pp. 167–96); how a new stretch of tarmac, an apricot tree planted on contested territory, or the appearance of a brightly painted wedding hall at the edge of a village can come to condense otherwise quite diffuse feelings of historical justice and incite talk of ethnic difference; how the sale of a land plot can be transformed into an act of symbolic treachery against the national body; how, under certain circumstances land can transform, suddenly and even violently, into 'motherland'.

It follows from such an approach that we should be wary of the claim that delimitation alone will put an end to ongoing contestation over local assertions of territorial primacy. Bilateral delimitation by Tajikistan and Kyrgyzstan is often held out as a panacea—a technical solution that will stop the border 'creeping' further in the Isfara valley and therefore guarantee peace. The analysis presented here suggests that whilst having a 'clear' cartographic border may indeed help to curb claims upon currently contested territory, delimitation alone will do little to address the pressures that have turned 'creeping migration' into an issue of political capital and will do little to challenge the 'ethnic-spatial' fix that sees nation, territory and state as properly isomorphic. In contexts of acute land and water shortage, the exigencies of daily life are liable to unsettle the logic of state inscription.

University of Manchester

References

Abashin, S. & Bushkov, V. (2004) *Ferganskaya dolina: Etnichnost', etnicheskie protsessy, etnicheskie konflikty* (Moscow, Nauka).

Abdullaev, N. (2006) 'Polzuchaya ekspansiya Tadzhikistana na Kyrgyzkie zemli', *Agenstvo politicheskikh novostei*, 11 November, available at: http://www.apn.kz/publications/print7197. htm, accessed 17 January 2009.

Aiypova, E. (2008) 'Kak okhranyayutsya rubezhi gosudarstvennoi granitsy?', *Kabar*, 3 December.

Akmat uulu, A. (2008) 'M. Juraev: jïlma migratsiyanï chukul toktotuu zarïl', *Azattïk unalgïsï*, 7 March.

Alamanov, S. (2005) *Kratkaya istoriya i opyt resheniya pogranichnykh problem Kyrgyzstana* (Bishkek, Friedrich Ebert Stiftung).

Alamanov, S. (2007) 'Protsess prinyatiya reshenii v uregulirovanii prigranichnykh konfliktov v Kyrgyzstane', Open Lecture, Bishkek Press Club, 25 December, available at: http://www.bpc.kg/publications/information/14, accessed 22 December 2008.

Alamanov, S. (2008) *Protsess prinyatiya reshenii v uregulirovanii prigranichnykh konfliktov v Kyrgyzstane*, Round Table Transcript, Institute for Public Policy, 6 June, available at: http://ipp/kg/files/ks-almanov.pdf, accessed 27 December 2008.

Anarkulov, N. (2008a) 'Pravda o poluzuchikh ekspansiyakh: Obstanovka na tadzhiko-kyrgyzskoi granitse. Ekspansiyam nazlo, ili starye problemy na novyi lad', *Kabar*, 2 July.

Anarkulov, N. (2008b) 'Kirgizskii Batken zakanchivaet stroitel'stvo avtodorog, obkhodyashchikh inostrannye anklavy', *Kabar*, 15 July.

Barry, A. (2001) *Political Machines: Governing a Technological Society* (London, Athlone).

Bichsel, C. (2006) *Dangerous Divisions: Irrigation Disputes and Conflict Resolution in the Ferghana Valley*, PhD Dissertation, Institute of Geography, University of Berne.

Bichsel, C. (2009) *Conflict Transformation in Central Asia: Irrigation Disputes in the Ferghana Valley* (London, Routledge).

Bourdieu, P. (1992) 'The Practice of Reflexive Sociology. The Paris Workshop', in Bourdieu, P. & Wacquant, L. (eds) (1992) *An Invitation to Reflexive Sociology* (Chicago, University of Chicago Press).

Brown, K. (2003) *A Biography of No Place: From Ethnic Borderland to Soviet Heartland* (Cambridge, MA, Harvard University Press).

Brubaker, R. (1996) 'Rethinking Nationhood: Nation as Institutionalized Form, Practical Category, Contingent Event', in Brubaker, R. (ed.) (1996) *Nationalism Reframed: Nationhood and the National Question in the New Europe* (Cambridge, Cambridge University Press).

Brubaker, R. (2005) *Ethnicity without Groups* (Cambridge, MA, Harvard University Press).

Brubaker, R., Feischmidt, M., Fox, J. & Grancea, L. (2006) *Nationalist Politics and Everyday Ethnicity in a Transylvanian Town* (Princeton, NJ, Princeton University Press).

Bushkov, V. & Mikul'skii, D. (1996) *Anatomiya grazhdanskoi voiny v Tadzhikistane (etno-sotsial'nye protsessy i politicheskaya bor'ba, 1992–1995)* (Moscow, Institut etnologii i antropologii RAN).

Byrbaeva, G. (2005) *Tsentral'naya Aziya i sovetizm: kontseptual'nyi poisk evro-amerikanskoi istoriografii* (Almaty, Daik Press).

Carrère d'Encausse, H. (1987) *Le Grand Défi: bolcheviks et nations, 1917–1930* (Paris, Flammarion).

Central Executive Committee of the Communist Party (CECCP) (1928) *Atlas soyuza sovetskikh sotsialisticheskikh respublik* (Moscow, Central Executive Committee).

Collier, S. (2001) *Post-Socialist City: The Government of Society in Neo-Liberal Times*, PhD Thesis, Department of Anthropology, University of California, Berkeley.

Collier, S. (2004) 'Pipes', in Harrison, S., Pile, S. & Thrift, N. (eds) (2004) *Patterned Ground: Entanglements of Nature and Culture* (London, Reaktion Books).

Cummings, S. (2009) 'Inscapes, Landscapes and Greyscapes: The Politics of Signification in Central Asia', *Europe-Asia Studies*, 61, 7.

Dolina mira (2004) *Analiz situatsii po perekhodu granits v Ferganskoi Doline* (Osh, Dolina mira).

Dzhunushalieva, G. (2006) *Evolyutsiya kyrgyzskoi gusudarstvennosti (20-80-e gody XX veka). Avtoreferat*, Candidate of Science Dissertation, Kyrgyz–Russian Slavonic University, Bishkek, Kyrgyzstan.

Ekspertnaya gruppa assotsiatsii politologov Kyrgyzstana (2007) *Poteryannyi yug? Analiticheskii doklad* (Bishkek, Association of Political Scientists of Kyrgyzstan (Assotsiatsiya politologov Kyrgyzstana)), available at: http://www.iadp.kg/iadp/index.php?newsid=76, accessed 30 March 2009.

Ekspertnaya gruppa MISI pri Prezidente Kyrgyzskoi Respubliki (2008) *O politike Dushanbe po 'tadzhikizatsii' prigranichnykh territorii Batkenskoi oblasti Kyrgyzskoi Respubliki i vozmozhnykh otvetnykh merakh (Analiticheskaya spravka)* (Bishkek, International Institute for Strategic Research), available at: http://www.forum.msk.ru/material/fpolitic/462220.html, accessed 17 January 2009.

Erkin uulu, S. (2008) 'Jïlma migratsiyanï mïizam menen toso alabïzbï?', *Azattïk unalgïsï*, 5 March.

Faizullina, G. (2007) '"Ketmennye" voiny', *Oazis*, 3, February.

Ferguson, J. (2006) 'Transnational Topographies of Power: Beyond "the State" and "Civil Society" in the Study of African Politics', in Ferguson, J. (2006) *Global Shadows: Africa in the Neoliberal World Order* (Durham, NC, Duke University Press).

Ferguson, J. & Gupta, A. (2002) 'Spatializing States: Towards an Ethnography of Neoliberal Governmentality', *American Ethnologist*, 29, 4.

Flynn, D. (1997) 'We Are the Border: Identity, Exchange and the State Along the Benin–Nigeria Border', *American Ethnologist*, 24, 2.

Foundation for Tolerance International (FTI) (2007a) *Ezhenedel'nyi Vestnik proekta 'Ranee preduprezhdenie dlya predotvrashcheniya nasiliya'*, 54, 17 January.

Foundation for Tolerance International (FTI) (2007b) *Ezhenedel'nyi Vestnik proekta 'Ranee preduprezhdenie dlya predotvrashcheniya nasiliya'*, 72, 24 May.

Foundation for Tolerance International (FTI) (2008) *Konfliktogennye faktory, svyazannye s nelegal'nym osvoeniem grazhdanam RT ob"ektov v prigranichnykh naselennykh punktakh Batkenskoi oblasti KR: Tematicheskoe issledovanie* (Bishkek, Foundation for Tolerance International).

Foundation for Tolerance International (FTI) (n.d.) *Conflict Analysis in Samarkandek–Chorku–Surkh Area: Project 'Kyrgyzstan–Tajikistan'* (Batken, Foundation for Tolerance International).

Gupta, A. (1995) 'Blurred Boundaries: The Discourse of Corruption, the Culture of Politics and the Imagined State', *American Ethnologist*, 22, 2.

Gupta, A. & Ferguson, J. (1997) '"Beyond 'Culture'": Space, Identity and the Politics of Difference', in Gupta, A. & Ferguson, J. (eds) (1997) *Culture, Power, Place: Explorations in Critical Anthropology* (Durham, NC, Duke University Press).

Harvey, P. (2005) 'The Materiality of State Effects: An Ethnography of a Road in the Peruvian Andes', in Krohn-Hansen, C. & Nustad, K. (eds) (2005) *State Formation: Anthropological Perspectives* (London, Pluto Press).

Haugen, A. (2003) *The Establishment of National Republics in Soviet Central Asia* (London, PalgraveMacmillan).

Hirsch, F. (2005) *Empire of Nations: Ethnographic Knowledge and the Making of the Soviet Union* (Princeton, NJ, Princeton University Press).

Ikromov, B. (2006) 'Fergana—dolina angelov', in Ikromov, B. (2006) *I zvezdy plachut. Publistika* (Kazan', Mir bez granits).

Imanaliev, M. (2006a) *Tsentral'naya Aziya: granitsy na zamke?*, OSCE Academy Research Report on Legal Aspects of Border Regulation (Bishkek, OSCE Academy), available at: http://www.osce-academy.net/uploads/wysiwyg/files/Preface_LABM.pdf, accessed 17 January 2009.

Imanaliev, M. (2006b) *Pravovye aspekty upravleniya granitsamy Kyrgyzskoi Republiki*, OSCE Academy Research Report on Legal Aspects of Border Regulation (Bishkek, OSCE Academy), available at: http://www.osce-academy.net/uploads/wysiwyg/files/Kyrgyz_Republic.pdf, last accessed 17 January 2009.

International Crisis Group (ICG) (2002) 'Central Asia: Border Disputes and Conflict Potential', *Asia Report*, 33, 4 April (Osh/Brussels, ICG).

Joyce, P. (2008) *Postal Communication and the Making of the British Technostate*, CRESC Working Paper 54 (Manchester & Milton Keynes, Centre for Research on Socio-Cultural Change).

Kadyrova, R. (2005) 'Protection of Power in Central Asia: Using Terror as a Pretext? A Kyrgyz NGO's Vision', in Ebnöther, A., Felberbauer, E. & Malek, M. (eds) (2005) *Facing the Terrorist Challenge—Central Asia's Role in Regional and International Co-operation* (Vienna, National Defence Academy).

Kalet, A. (2006) 'Rostki tyulpanov', *Oazis*, 24, December.

Kandiyoti, D. & Mandel, R. (eds) (1998) 'Special Issue on Market Reforms, Social Dislocations and Survival in Post-Soviet Central Asia', *Central Asia Survey*, 17, 4.

Karasar, H. (2008) 'The Partition of Khorezm and the Position of Turkestanis on *razmezhevanie*', *Europe-Asia Studies*, 60, 7.

Karimov, D. (2008) 'Parlament Kyrgyzstana nameren vernut'sya k obsuzhdeniyu zakonoproekta, kazayushchegosya problemy polzuchei migratsii', *24.kg Information Agency*, 6 March, available at: http://www.24.kg/parliament/2008/03/06/78517.html, accessed 15 January 2009.

Khalid, A. (1998) *The Politics of Muslim Cultural Reform: Jadidism in Central Asia* (Berkeley, University of California Press).

Khalid, A. (2007) *Islam after Communism* (Berkeley, University of California Press).

Khamidov, A. (2001) 'Dispute over China–Kyrgyz Border Demarcation Pits President vs. Parliament', *Eurasianet Insight*, 28 June, available at: http://www.eurasianet.org/departments/insight/articles/eav062801.shtml, accessed 1 May 2009.

Khamidov, O. (2006) 'Kishlachnyi renessans', *Vechernii Bishkek*, 26 September.

Koichiev, A. (2001) *Nasional'no-territorial'noe razmezhevanie v ferganskoi doline (1924–1927 gg.)* (Bishkek, Kyrgyz State National University).

Kozhomkulova, N. (2008) 'S nashego pozvoleniya...tadzhikskie "sosedi" perekhodyat granitsy', *Obshchestvennyi reiting*, 4 April.

Kuehnast, K. & Dudwick, N. (2008) *Whose Rules Rule? Everyday Border and Water Conflicts in Central Asia* (Washington, DC, World Bank Group).

Lewis, D. (2008) *The Temptations of Tyranny in Central Asia* (London, Hurst and Company).

Liu, M. (2002) *Recognizing the Khan: Authority, Space and Political Imagination among Uzbek Men in Post-Soviet Osh, Kyrgyzstan*, PhD Thesis, Department of Anthropology, University of Michigan.

Liu, M. (2003) 'Detours from Utopia on the Silk Road: Ethical Dilemmas of Neoliberal Triumphalism', *Central Eurasian Studies Review*, 2, 2.

Lubin, N. & Rubin, B. (1999) *Calming the Ferghana Valley: Development and Dialogue in the Heart of Central Asia* (New York, Century Foundation Press).

Maasen, K., Bagyskulov, B., Bakirov, A., Egemberdiev, A., Eginalieva, A., Karataev, A., Kolesnikova, L. & Mirsangilov, A. (2005) *The Role and Capacity of Civil Society in the Prevention of Violent Conflict in Southern Kyrgyzstan* (Bishkek, Foundation for Tolerance International).

Mamaraimov, A. (2007) 'Salamat Alamanov: Granitsa mezhdu Kirgiziei i Uzbekistanom napominaet sito', *Ferghan.ru*, 27 November, available at: http://www.ferghana.ru/article.php?id=4745, accessed 1 May 2009.

Martin, T. (2001) *The Affirmative Action Empire: Nations and Nationalism in the Soviet Union, 1923–1939* (Ithaca, NY, Cornell University Press).

Megoran, N. (2002) The Borders of Eternal Friendship? The Politics and Pain of Nationalism and Identity along the Uzbekistan–Kyrgyzstan Ferghana Valley Boundary, PhD Thesis, Department of Geography, University of Cambridge.

Megoran, N. (2004) 'The Critical Geopolitics of the Uzbekistan–Kyrgyzstan Ferghana Valley Boundary Dispute, 1999–2000', *Political Geography*, 23, 6.

Megoran, N. (2006) 'For Ethnography in Political Geography: Experiencing and Re-imagining the Ferghana Valley Boundary Closures', *Political Geography*, 25, 6.

Megoran, N. (2007) 'On Researching "Ethnic Conflict": Epistemology, Politics, and a Central Asian Boundary Dispute', *Europe-Asia Studies*, 59, 2.

Mirsaidov, N. (2008) 'Porokhovaya bochka. Voennye i SMI sozdayut pochvu dlya tadzhiko-kyrgyzskogo mezhenicheskogo konflikta', *Centrasia.ru*, 9 December, available at: http://www.centrasia.ru/newsA.php?st=1228804260, accessed 1 May 2009.

Mitchell, T. (1988) *Colonizing Egypt* (Cambridge, Cambridge University Press).

Mitchell, T. (1999) 'Society, Economy and the State Effect', in Steinmetz, G. (ed.) (1999) *State/Culture: State Formation after the Cultural Turn* (Ithaca, NY, Cornell University Press).

Mitchell, T. (2002) *Rule of Experts* (Berkeley, University of California Press).

Moore, D. (1998) 'Subaltern Struggles and the Politics of Place: Remapping Resistance in Zimbabwe's Eastern Highlands', *Cultural Anthropology*, 13, 3.

Moore, D. (2005) *Suffering for Territory: Race, Place and Power in Zimbabwe* (Durham, NC, Duke University Press).

Navaro-Yashin, Y. (2002) *Faces of the State: Secularism and Public Life in Turkey* (Princeton, NJ, Princeton University Press).

Navaro-Yashin, Y. (2003) '"Life is Dead Here": Sensing the Political in "No Man's Land"', *Anthropological Theory*, 3, 1.

Nurakun uulu, I. (2008) 'Jilma migratsiyanï toktotuu araketinde', *BBCKyrgyz.com*, 28 February, available at: http://www.bbc.co.uk/kyrgyz/news/story/2008/02/080228_batken_border.shtml, accessed 1 May 2009.

Omuraliev, K. (2008) 'Intsidenty na kyrgyzsko-tadzhikskoi granitse mogut vylit'sya v vooruzhennyi konflikt', *Centrasia.ru*, 5 April, available at: http://www.centrasia.ru/newsA.php?st=1207375260, accessed 2 May 2009.

Passon, D. & Temirkulov, A. (2004) *Analysis of Peace and Conflict Potential in Batken Oblast* (Berlin, German Organization for Technical Cooperation (GTZ)), available at: http://www.policy.hu/temirkulov/index.files/ARC_GTZ-Report-Kyrgyzstan.pdf, accessed 2 May 2009.

Pelkmans, M. (2005) 'On Transition and Revolution in Kyrgyzstan', *Focaal—European Journal of Anthropology*, 45.

Pétric, B. (2005) 'Post-Soviet Kyrgyzstan or the Birth of a Globalized Protectorate', *Central Asian Survey*, 24, 3.

Plenseev, D. (2002) 'Kyrgyz Border Pact with China Stirs Tension in Bishkek', *Eurasianet*, 17 May, available at: http://www.eurasianet.org/departments/culture/articles/eav051702.shtml, accessed 2 May 2009.

Pozharskii, V. (2008) 'Kyrgyzstan—strana bez territorii?', *Delo Nomer*, 5 December.

Rasanayagam, J. (2002) *The Moral Construction of the State in Uzbekistan: Its Construction within Concepts of Community and Interaction at the Local Level*, PhD Dissertation, Department of Social Anthropology, University of Cambridge.

Reeves, M. (2005) 'Locating Danger: *Konfliktologiia* and the Search for Fixity in the Ferghana Valley Borderlands', *Central Asian Survey*, 24, 1.

Reeves, M. (2008) *Border Work: An Ethnography of the State at its Limits in the Ferghana Valley*, PhD Thesis, Department of Social Anthropology, University of Cambridge.

Sahadeo, J. & Zanca, R. (2007) 'Introduction: Central Asia and Everyday Life', in Sahadeo, J. & Zanca, R. (eds) (2007) *Everyday Life in Central Asia: Past and Present* (Bloomington, Indiana University Press).

Satarbaev, A. (2006) *Prichiny i uroky oshskikh i uzgenskikh sobytii 1990 goda (istoricheskii analiz)*, Candidate of Science Dissertation, Department of History, Osh State University.

Scott, J. (1998) *Seeing Like a State. How Certain Schemes to Improve the Human Condition Have Failed* (New Haven, CT, Yale University Press).

Shteinberg, E. (1934) 'Sredneaziatskoe razmezhevanie i protsess natsional'noi konsolidatsii', *Revolyutsiya i natsaional'nosti*, 12.

Skorodumova, E. (2007) 'Trudovaya migratsiya: palka o dvukh kontsakh', *Moya Stolitsa Novosti*, 18 May.

Slim, R. (2002) 'The Ferghana Valley: In the Midst of a Host of Crises', in Mekenkamp, M., van Tongeren, P. & Veen, H.v.d. (eds) (2002) *Searching for Peace in Central and South Asia: An Overview of Conflict Prevention and Peace-Building Activities* (Boulder, CO, Lynne Rienner).

Spencer, J. (2007) *Anthropology, Politics and the State: Democracy and Violence in South Asia* (Cambridge, Cambridge University Press).

Sydykova, Z. (2003) *Khronika Aksyiskoi tragedii* (Bishkek, Kyrgyzskii Komitet po Pravam Cheloveka).

Tabyshalieva, A. (1999) *The Challenge of Regional Cooperation in Central Asia. Preventing Ethnic Conflict in the Ferghana Valley*, Peaceworks 28 (Washington, DC, United States Institute of Peace).

Temir, E. (2008a) 'Kogda polzuchaya migratsiya strashnee cherta', *Vechernii Bishkek*, 3 March.

Temir, E. (2008b) 'Ogni na dal'nykh rubezhakh', *Vechernii Bishkek*, 27 March.

Thurman, J. (1999) *Modes of Organization in Central Asian Irrigation: The Ferghana Valley, 1876 to Present*, PhD Dissertation, Department of Central Eurasian Studies, Indiana University.

UNDP (2001) *Political and Administrative Local Government Programme Preventive Development Component Annual Report 2001* (Bishkek, UNDP).

UNDP (2002) *Second Regional Early Warning Report, Batken Province* (Batken, UNDP).

UNDP (2006) *Coexistence for Northern Tajikistan and Southern Kyrghyzstan* (Dushanbe, UNDP).

Urumbaev, M. (2005) 'Ferganskaya dolina v podveshennom sostoyanii', *Vechernii Bishkek*, 26 October.

Urumbaev, M. (2006) 'Migrant v trekh litsakh', *Vechernii Bishkek*, 4 April.

Urumbaev, M. (2007) 'Batken prorubaet okno v mir', *Vechernii Bishkek*, 29 August.

Urumbaev, M. (2008) 'Moratorii na mezhe', *Vechernii Bishkek*, 2 February.

Verdery, K. (1994) 'The Elasticity of Land: Problems of Property Restitution in Transylvania', *Slavic Review*, 53, 4.

Yeh, E. (2003) 'Tibetan Range Wars: Spatial Politics and Authority on the Grasslands of Amdo', *Development and Change*, 34, 3.

Young, A. (2003) *Ferghana Valley Field Study: Reducing the Potential for Conflict through Community Mobilization* (Portland, OH, Mercy Corps).

Tajikistan's Virtual Politics of Peace

JOHN HEATHERSHAW

SINCE THE FORMAL END OF ITS POST-SOVIET CIVIL war in 1997, Tajikistan has found something proximate to peace and simultaneously been the object of international peacebuilding. Yet peace and peacebuilding are practically related in complex ways. It is problematic to simply assume that the partial achievement of the former is due to the partial completion of the latter. Moreover, the practices and discourses of this peace are far removed from both negative peace (the simple absence of war) and positive peace (the existence of emancipatory structures and cultures of non-violence). It is perhaps better to discuss not the building of peace but the emergence of legitimate order (Heathershaw 2009). Tajikistan has order in that it has established of rules and practices of governance. This order is legitimate in that it is widely resigned to in public discourses and practices which accept its basic validity. It is emergent in that it is not a state but a process and thus incomplete and highly contingent.

This emergence of legitimate order has taken place despite a lack of the very things that both rational choice institutionalists and liberal peace theorists would expect to see. That is, it has taken place amidst the breakdown of the power-sharing mechanisms that were introduced in the 1997 peace agreement (as opposition commanders have gradually been removed from their positions), the absence of formal institutional structures of conflict management (substantial regional autonomy or consociational arrangements for example) and the increasing concentration of power to President Emomali Rahmon, his family and his inner circle from Danghara.[1] Moreover, the inter-regional, ideological and inter-personal conflicts of the 1992–1997 civil war have not simply disappeared, nor have they been channelled into formal institutions, but they have nevertheless been superseded by a 'peace'—a new order of hegemonic governance.

This peace is in part sustained by an informal economic order of exchange founded on corrupt privatisation and land reform (Zürcher 2004), the capture and reappropriation of international aid (Nakaya 2008) and the enormous social impact of seasonal labour migration (Olimova & Bosc 2003). However, what such materialist

---

[1]This is the continuation of a process which Akiner (2001) describes as 'Kulobisation' of Tajikistan's state and society which has increasingly narrowed to indicate the hegemony of a close circle of Rahmon, key family members and associates from the Kulob region of the country. By late 2006 all former opposition commanders who had been awarded senior state positions in the peace accords (such as Mirzo Ziyoev and Mahmudruzi Iskandarov) together with an increasing number of former governmental commanders (such as Ghaffor Mirzoyev) had been removed and in many cases tried and imprisoned (see Heathershaw 2009, esp. pp. 119–24).

accounts fail to explain is the significance of the resources invested by the regime in rewriting history, performing authority and celebrating Tajikistan's emergent sovereignty; and similarly the functions of millions of dollars in international peacebuilding assistance to promote an alternative symbolic and normative order. Symbols provide the interpretative tools by which the new order is made meaningful and according to which other ways of peace appear impossible or unobtainable. According to this emerging symbolic order opposition to the sitting government has become increasingly unpopular and marginalised. Renegade ex-government or ex-opposition commanders who may have tried to launch a rebellion have simply been unable to garner support amongst fellow elite members or their subordinates against a government which is widely considered to be untouchable. Alternatives to the regime have been considered either implausible or undesirable. This is the nature of 'peace' in an emergent order characterised by a growing yet oligarchic economy and pacified discursive environment.

The emergence of this symbolically constituted peace is all the more fascinating given the significant role of international assistance in Tajikistan. From 2000 to 2007, following the formal negotiation, agreement and implementation of the peace accords, a process which ended in 2000, the Security Council-mandated UN Tajikistan Office of Peace Building (UNTOP), the Organization for Security and Cooperation in Europe (OSCE) and many other international development agencies, foreign governments and NGOs strove to bring democracy, security and development to Tajikistan under the maxims of international peacebuilding. Elections were monitored, political parties were supported, border management was reformed, warlords were reintegrated and community conflict resolution projects were undertaken across the length and breadth of the country. However, by the middle of the decade, as Rahmon moved against his rivals, shut down opposition newspapers and parties and gerrymandered referendum, it became evident to many in the international community that peacebuilding was not going according to plan (ICG 2004). Indeed it had achieved a 'virtual' quality, found in other cases of post-conflict intervention such as in Cambodia (Richmond & Franks 2007), where nascent democratisation, development and public sector reform is 'mainly visible to those observing from the outside of the conflict zone in the liberal international community rather than those upon whom this peace is being visited' (Richmond 2005, p. 185). This is seen in the 'success' identified by international monitors and evaluators of aid programmes as well as in the technocratic reduction of peacebuilding to the number of individuals who have experienced training and workshops (Heathershaw 2008).

Given the superficialities of international peacebuilding it is tempting to dismiss it as an irrelevance to the emergence of legitimate order. However, this would be a mistake in at least three respects. First, it is possible that before and during the early 2000s international interventions did, to some extent, achieve the modification of elite behaviour and attitudes in order to achieve modest compromises between Islamists and secularists and between government and the disparate opposition, as earlier policy-oriented research appears to show (Abdullaev & Barnes 2001).[2] Second, the

---

[2]However, it must also be added that recent years have seen the reversal of some of the specific gains in Islamic–Secular dialogue (Seifert & Kraikemayer 2003; Bitter *et al.* 2004) with the introduction of a

indirect effect of international assistance was to provide relatively honest employment and income for a technocratic class of professionals and intellectuals and, more importantly, to provide a basic social safety net for citizens in many regions which the post-conflict state would have been otherwise unable to provide (Heathershaw 2009, pp. 47–50). Third, and most importantly, such a dismissal of international peacebuilding is founded on the illusion that it is merely virtual or symbolic whilst local experiences of peace are real.

This dichotomising of virtual-symbolic and real is a foundational error of materialist analysis which too often dismisses the role of ideas and their representation and simulation in text, images, sound and the built environment as mere afterthoughts to the logic of material exchange. However, it is equally inappropriate to see symbols and discourses as independent variables which directly determine obedience, consent, authority and legitimacy (Wedeen 1999, p. 6). Symbolic exchange is neither entirely decorative nor totally determining. Rather, the theoretical approach adopted here is one where the discursive environment remains significant in a complex and polyvalent fashion. Insofar as these ambiguities are irresolvable they generate a virtual politics characterised by what Jean Baudrillard calls 'hyper-reality' where actors produce, reproduce and respond to signs themselves rather than what they ought to represent.

This essay explores the virtual politics of peace in Tajikistan in terms of its faking, substitution and deterrence effects. Following the pathway carved out by Wilson (2005a) and extending it with the radical theorisation of Baudrillard, the essay discusses virtual politics where international and local discourses, rather than representing politics, both unwittingly misrepresent and unwittingly simulate it. The essay explains the virtual politics of peace as a discursive environment of signs of 'peacebuilding' and 'stability' which are valued in and of themselves despite being detached from the practical and symbolic realities of life in any given context—the world of their ostensible referent objects. In particular, it is shown that international peacebuilding initiatives have helped generate a virtual multi-party system constituted of ambiguous authoritarian–democratic signs. The virtual politics of peace in Tajikistan takes place in attempts to appropriate signs of the democratic peace for conflicting ends and imbue them with contrasting meanings. This is not just a process of faking or misrepresentation (Baudrillard's first order of simulation), but substitution for and deterrence of alternative political realities or non-representation (his third order of simulation). While these orders are irreconcilable it is argued that they are not entirely incommensurable. Both misrepresentation and non-representation are aspects of virtual politics, and an essential dimension of the emergent, fragile and complexly legitimate order which constitutes Tajikistan peace.

This essay draws on examples from the author's recent research monograph to summarise Tajikistan's symbolic and virtual orders of peace and peacebuilding and, more importantly, their mutual interdependence. The data analysed here are largely verbal and taken from extended interviews and observations; some visual and embodied examples of symbolisation are also used. The first part introduces the idea

new school textbook on Islam which is opposed by leading Islamic scholars such as Hoji Akhbar Turajonzoda, and the 2009 religious law which is much more restrictive on the practices and institutions of all religious groups.

of virtual politics as discussed in the context of the post-Soviet space and links it to wider scholarship on virtuality and simulation, particularly that of Jean Baudrillard. The second part turns our attention to Tajikistan and charts the relationship between discourses and practices of 'democracy' and 'authority', demonstrating how international and national actors create simulacra of political representation and thus deter the practice of real politics. The essay concludes with some remarks on how we may rethink the role of international assistance for peacebuilding and democratisation in Central Asia in the context of this understanding of virtual politics.

From symbolic politics to virtual politics

Symbols, as shown elsewhere in this volume, can be 'captured' in the form of specific texts, images, architectural forms and other modes of representation, and instrumentally deployed and manipulated by elites. However, there is a wider meaning of the symbolic developed in the work of Foucault, Bourdieu, Baudrillard and other continental European philosophers that addresses it in terms of discursive environment or field, symbolic orders of exchange and 'the text'. It is through this broad tradition that symbolic politics is understood here. Symbols and symbolic forms (discourses and other forms of representation) are not merely deployed by elites but they themselves do work in generating an environment whereby certain things are unthinkable and others are taken for granted. They are not simply objects of political interactions between individuals and groups but compose a wider inter-subjective context in which things become natural or alien. In that they have functions, symbols have agency—they can be said to do things to other things. In particular, symbols serve to represent: they normalise or legitimate the arbitrary and make meaningful the otherwise barely intelligible. 'Every established order', as Bourdieu remarks, 'achieves the naturalisation of its own arbitrariness' (1977, p. 164).

Therefore a study of symbolic exchange should address not simply individual symbols but the wider discursive order which exists beyond the realm of official discourse and which in various ways challenges or sustains it. This symbolic order includes both public and hidden registers of discourse (Scott 1990). In this wider sense, the work of Lisa Wedeen provides perhaps the best summary of symbolic politics and its logic of representation. It is this distinction of space, between public and hidden registers, which allows Wedeen to perceive 'the difference between what social scientists, following Max Weber, might conceive as a charismatic, loyalty-producing regime and its anxiety-inducing simulacrum' (1999, p. 3). Wedeen's account of the symbolic dimension avoids the Weberian mis-step of a subjectivist treatment of legitimacy and authority. She makes the distinction between obedience and compliance; between genuine reverence and citizens acting as if they revere their leader (1999, p. 6). Yet this politics of the as if—of the subjunctive—is productive and effectual. It creates norms of public behaviour, of acceptable speech and 'clutters the public space with monotonous slogans and empty gestures which tire the minds and bodies of producers and consumers alike' (Wedeen 1999, p. 6). In other words, in Wedeen's work symbols have a political life of their own, becoming 'the very mechanisms of enforcement' which are as, if not more, significant than the military or economic power which they may (or may not) represent. This power of symbols is ironically shown in their very ambiguity—that they 'can be paradoxically both self-defeating and self-serving, both inciting transgression and limiting its content' (Wedeen 1999, p. 31). The importance of Wedeen's account of symbolic exchange is that it provides a non-representational or extra-representational account of the political effects and affects of symbols. Yet insofar as it breaks the linkage between symbol and symbolised, representation and represented, Wedeen's account of symbolic exchange leads us away from the logic of the symbolic. Moreover, it leads us to the realm of virtual politics and the various and contending accounts of this emerging concept.

Wilson's virtuality and reality

In the study of the post-Soviet space, the recent intervention of Andrew Wilson (2005a) has defined the line of inquiry of virtual politics. It constitutes an exceptional attempt to grasp the area between the public and the hidden which remains characteristic of the post-Soviet discursive environment. Wilson's excellent empirical research charts the plots and conspiracies manufactured against the opposition, the faux opposition candidates created to split the anti-regime vote, and various other forms of 'active measures' that have become commonplace in Ukraine, Belarus and particularly Putin's Russia. Furthermore he looks inside the machinery of virtual politics as practised by political technologists and media consultants with names like Nikkolo-M who manufacture fake images and video for public consumption.[3] Politics is thus represented in narrative and theatrical form (understood locally as *dramaturgia*) where opponents are discredited and supporters finally emerge vindicated. Wilson is fully aware of the elements of continuity from the Soviet and even pre-Soviet eras here but argues that it is the post-Soviet era that has seen the birth of virtual politics. 'Unlike traditional authoritarian states', he contends, 'the point is not simply to trap the population in some kind of repressive box, but to trap them in the perception that they are trapped in some kind of box' (2005b).

Despite this triumph of the sign over the substance, Wilson's virtual politics is one which remains in the realm of symbolic politics (the logic of representation) in at least three respects. First, political fakes are controlled by a series of puppet masters operating behind the scenes. Post-soviet virtual politics is a 'radically top-down phenomenon' and is 'created by supply rather than demand' (Wilson 2005a, pp. 48, 42). Second, it is not the only form of politics. In Wilson's rendering, the goals of the virtual 'politics should only exist as a series of designer projects, rather than as a real pattern of representation and accountability' (2005a, p. 39). Yet while this is the ambition it is not one which is ever fully realised. He notes that there are genuine opposition movements, however weak, and that 'other versions of reality creep in at the margins' (2005a, p. 45), whilst 'political technologists are not omnipotent; they

---

[3]Wilson draws a distinction between 'spin doctors' in the Western (particularly British) context who manage the message and 'political technologists' who apply their techniques 'for the construction of politics as a whole'. This includes the management of the media, but also 'the construction of parties, the destruction of others, the framing of general campaign dynamics and the manipulation of results' (2005a, p. 49).

cannot shape the whole world in their own image' (2005a, p. 46). Third, virtuality can be counterposed to reality. Wilson's virtual politics remains a form of symbolic politics in that it remains within the logic of (mis)representation.

> There is so much more (and much less) to post-Communist virtual politics than the triumph of the sign over substance. Politics is 'virtual' or 'theatrical' in the sense that so many aspects of public performance are purely epiphenomenal or instrumental, existing only for effect or to disguise the real substance of 'inner politics'. (Wilson 2005a, p. 47)

Thus, for Wilson, politics is virtual in that skilled elites are able to manipulate the electorate and largely conceal the real objects of political contention.

This partial account of virtual politics is understandable in that it seems to fit the messy empirical 'reality' much better. After all, political technologists are no more omnipotent than any other political actor. However, this individualist version of the virtual—where symbols are deployed and controlled by agents—would be opposed as not nearly radical enough by French late-modern social theorists who have sought to understand the virtual in post-structuralist terms. Whilst Wilson draws on Baudrillard (2005a, pp. 34, 47–48), amongst other exponents of semiotic theory, his concepts are not directly addressed and only partially creep into his analysis and conclusions. Wilson's four 'preconditions' of virtual politics—a cynical elite, a passive populus, a dominated press, and the lack of alternative outlets of information (2005a, p. 41)— suggest a more conventional analysis of authoritarianism. Whilst these four features are not inaccurate they could surely be equally applied to the Soviet state and what Wilson calls 'traditional authoritarian states'. This seems to belie his claim that the virtual politics of authoritarianism is a new, post-Soviet phenomenon. The point here is that the change is less historical, from Soviet to post-Soviet politics, and more interpretative, from an analysis of symbols to an analysis of simulacra and fakes. A better developed concept of virtual politics might help us reinterpret Soviet as well as post-Soviet politics.

Baudrillard's virtuality and hyper-reality

Baudrillard provides an analysis of the complete failure of symbolic politics amidst a world of signs which are detached from their ostensible referent objects and thus have lost all possibility for meaning. The world notoriously described by Baudrillard in *The Gulf War Did Not Take Place* (1995) is one, in Der Derian's words, in which 'origins are forgotten, referents lost, and simulations begin to precede and engender reality' (1994, p. 194). The first Gulf War proves to be an excellent example in that for most of its key protagonists and stakeholders (the citizenry on whose behalf it was being fought) it was neither in the Gulf (but commanded, controlled and observed from afar) nor a war (in that there was very little engagement by allied forces with Iraqi air, naval or land forces who were largely shot whilst in retreat or within their barracks). In both military action and the media representation thereof, the historical context of Iraqi–Western relations were absent and the meaning of war as a strategic contest was substituted for the simulation of war, represented as a surgical operation not directed against the Iraqi people. Whilst clearly a form of organised violence, the war, to

Baudrillard, did not meet the Clausewitzian definition of a 'struggle of wills' brought about by the strategic continuation of policy by other means. This is not to say that the war did not involve a vast amount of violence and human suffering, but that knowledge of these civilian casualties rarely penetrated the discourse of Western decision-makers and publics. The tropes of 'surgical strike' and 'collateral damage' survived despite the physical deaths of perhaps tens of thousands of civilians.

This example of Baudrillard's later work provided a shocking introduction to his thought for many in the academy and beyond. Yet behind this analysis was a long history of post-Marxist scholarship to which it is impossible to do justice here. Since the 1960s Baudrillard has argued that rather than a real or classical political economy, we find ourselves beset by a hyper-real symbolic economy of signs without referents, where simulation triumphs over representation and reality is deterred. He defines simulation simply as 'to feign to have what one hasn't' (1983, p. 5). Yet Baudrillard's understanding of simulation goes beyond the idea of feigning or faking and is radically different from most understandings of simulation or the virtual in political science.[4] Simulation as a strategic exercise in constructing a near-to-reality experience for the purpose of entertainment, training or, even, deception (such as that described by Wilson) is not his focus—although (as will be shown) it can be analysed as part of the wider logic of simulation. It is not just that the Gulf War did not take place but that its simulation disables its real experience and representation. This wider logic—what Baudrillard calls 'precession of the model' (1983, p. 38)—is, he argues, dominant in the entire symbolic economy today where signifiers become objects in themselves. They slip around and become desirous for what they in themselves seem to offer (their hyper-reality) rather than in their objective value as tools, consumables or decorations. As Debrix notes,

> while simulation may be deployed strategically (as a technique to recuperate or reaffirm a certain reality or representation, that of a dominant code or model), it ends up with the fateful disappearance of the real, and the simulated reconstructed reality becomes but a symptom. (2009, p. 59)

It is this triumph of the symptom—also conveyed in other post-Marxist notions such as commodity fetishism—that dominates the sphere of the virtual political. 'Someone who feigns an illness', Baudrillard notes, 'can simply go to bed and make believe he is ill. Someone who simulates an illness produces in himself some of the symptoms' (1983, p. 5).

Wilson is correct to question whether this apparently psychosomatic process is all-encompassing in (post-Soviet) politics where certain representations of objects can remain relatively sedimented and stable over a considerable period of time and thus apparently represent some underlying reality. However, the real value of Baudrillardian conception is less in its reading of the extent of the virtual and more in its reading of its self-referential production and its connotative and conditioning functions. In his first major work, *The System of Objects* (1996), Baudrillard provides a remarkably

---

[4]Some exceptional scholars in International Relations have resourced themselves with Baudrillard's work including Debrix (1999), Der Derian (1994), Luke (1989) and Weber (1995).

prescient analysis of advertising which distinguishes between its imperative and indicative effects. He argues:

> So even though we may be getting better and better at resisting advertising in the *imperative*, we are at the same time becoming ever more susceptible to advertising in the *indicative*—that is to its actual *existence* as a product to be consumed at a secondary level, and as the clear *expression* of a culture. (1996, p. 180, emphasis in original)

Thus, however cynical or sceptical we appear about the authenticity of representations (be they those of Western post-industrial economies or post-Soviet virtual polities), we nevertheless consume and deploy them. Simulacra efface whatever may ostensibly lie beneath signs, divesting them of their symbolic value.

Therefore, 'without believing in the product', Baudrillard argues, 'we believe in the advertising that tries to get us to believe it' (1996, pp. 180–81). In our context this means that whilst post-Soviet subjects may not believe the specific conspiracy theory proffered (in the imperative), they unwittingly accept the premises about politics (in the indicative) as a sphere entirely devoid of ideals and ethics, where the dark arts and conspiracies of elites always prevail. Indeed, cynicism, which is particularly prevalent in post-Soviet societies, furthers virtuality as it erodes all remaining faith in the process of representation—symbolic and political. 'Power can stage its own murder', Baudrillard conjectures, 'to rediscover a glimmer of existence and legitimacy' (1983, p. 37). The point here is not that the virtual becomes omnipotent or omnipresent as Baudrillard's detractors often accuse him of arguing.[5] A better summary of virtuality might be that it is all-encompassing in that it is omnific, or all-creating. It is impossible to communicate politically, to make political objects, without recourse to simulation.

Levels and orders of virtual politics

It should be clear from the above that virtual politics has been interpreted as working on different levels and by different orders. First, we can identify at least two levels: national and international. In the domestic realm, and in a manner similar to that described by Andrew Wilson (2005a), national elites deploy fictive opposition parties and candidates, managed elections and discourses of nation-statehood in order to feign authority and sovereignty. At the international level, in a quite different, but in a certain sense, comparable manner, the international community simulates democratisation and peacebuilding in its absence (Debrix 1999). These international interventions are similarly strategic acts of simulation but not ones which aim to deceive or deter. Rather they constitute a form of simulation which seeks the imitation, emulation and eventual 'internalisation' of democratic practices via 'capacity building' and 'training'. Despite these differences, in process and product international virtual politics may be comparable to those of the national virtual politics insofar as such interventions involve processes of simulation and produce hyper-real effects. In both national and international virtual politics resources are

---

[5]Power and presence are notoriously slippery concepts in semiotic theory. Moreover, Baudrillard criticised Foucault for his understanding of power yet never really developed an alternative approach.

allocated and strategies devised to support processes which do not actually exist in practice but may anyway be 'found' or invented by outside observers. This virtual politics affects the choices and actions of national civil society actors as much as it directs the allocations of international donors. Some recognition of the different levels of the virtual—absent from Wilson's work which is focused on domestic politics—is vital to understand the irresolvable ambiguity of simulacra which are differentially determined by scale as well as by different social groups and political factions. Studying the national alongside the international allows us to see how the manufacture of virtual political parties by regimes is concomitant with the simulation of elections and a multi-party system by the international community. Indeed, foreshadowing the argument which proceeds below, in a virtual multi-party system, internationally sustained parties find themselves existing alongside those manufactured by the regime. The key backers of both types of simulated party are arguably not their supposed popular constituencies but those in either the international community or regime who directly or indirectly provide the political and economic resources to sustain them.

Secondly, virtual politics also works in terms of different orders. The comparisons made above should not lead us to conflate the strategic (misrepresentative) and deterrent (non-representative) functions of simulation. In a manner similar to the distinction he makes between imperative and indicative functions, Baudrillard distinguishes between four orders of simulation. The logic of simulation can be understood first in terms of counterfeiting, second in terms of production, third in terms of simulation in the proper sense of 'masking the absence of a basic reality', and a fourth order 'which bears no relation to any reality whatever' which Baudrillard, heavily influenced by Foucault, charts as emerging in Europe progressively since the Renaissance (1983, p. 83). Wilson's virtual politics is virtual in the imperative sense of Baudrillard's first order, as a form of counterfeiting or a politics of misrepresentation. By contrast Debrix and others in post-structuralist International Relations, following Baudrillard, interpret virtual politics in its most advanced form (the third and fourth orders) where it is no longer possible to determine the more accurate representation of what is real. This is so because simulation supplants or deters reality in its indicative function of creating desire, symptoms and anxieties despite the fact that the simulacra themselves may not be taken at face value. In other words in this advanced form of simulation the referent or represented object is lost and is replaced by slippery and ambiguous signs which are deployed this way and that. In the sense understood by Debrix (1999), peacekeeping is about creating signs of 'peacekeeping' for an audience of the international community rather than actually keeping the peace. Similarly, in Luke's (1989) terms, nuclear deterrence is achieved not by the presence of actual weapons but by signs or discourses of strike and response capability where the credibility of deterrence is maintained not by the actual destructive potential of nuclear war (which is literally unimaginable) but by ideas about usage and the effects thereof. It is the sign which is valued, exchanged and thus significant, not the referent object itself. 'Thus', Debrix, drawing on Baudrillard, notes, 'while simulation may be deployed strategically (as a technique that seeks to affirm a certain reality), it ends up with the fateful disappearance of the real' (2009, p. 57).

How do these different levels and orders of simulation help us understand Central Asian politics? It is the narrow concept of national and misrepresentational virtual politics employed by Wilson (2005a) which is of most obvious utility for the study of Central Asia. Indeed many would argue that the broader non-representational terms employed by Baudrillard are of little use outside of high-technology, post-industrial economies; his Euro-centrism in charting the historical emergence of orders of simulation should certainly lead us to be sceptical of his relevance to Central Asia. These concerns are not unreasonable; as explored below, Tajik society, being without indigenous mass media and a politically engaged civil society, does not require the sophisticated techniques of virtual politics which one might find in Western Europe or Russia. Yet pushing this argument too far implies an Orientalist analysis which essentialises differences between Central Asia and the 'West'. Moreover, it risks conflating the technologies of simulation with its logic—a logic which, according to Baudrillard, 'is the reigning scheme of the current phase [of history]' (1983, p. 83). It is the contention of this essay that the narrow concept is based on a partial theorisation of the virtual which clings to the precepts of objectivity, instrumentality and strategy. Andrew Wilson's work, whilst empirically rich, remains deficient in this respect. Via Baudrillard, we can push Wilson's limited conceptualisation of post-Soviet virtual politics further. This extension of the concept of virtual politics allows us to see the broader functions of international and national strategic acts of simulation in generating a political economy of signs of multi-party politics which are detached from their ostensible referents.

The remainder of this essay argues that there is analytical value in adopting the conceptual resources of the virtual to study the Central Asian context which includes both internationally supported virtual political parties and nationally engineered equivalents, as well as both the strategic or imperative order (the misrepresentative counterfeit or fake) and the indicative order (the non-representative simulacrum as object) of simulation. In as much as consumer durables are the 'must have' objects of post-industrial cultures, perhaps the performance of dialogue, the creation of *faux* political parties and the staging of 'free elections' are the essential signs of post-Soviet politics. In that sense it is in conflicts over these signs (as objects themselves), rather than their ostensible referent objects (a political agenda or value), where politics takes place. Thus, Wilson's conclusion that 'political technology rarely works on its own' (in an imperative sense), without the use of violence and more 'traditional methods' of co-optation (2005b), is a largely accurate account of how short term objectives are reached by post-Soviet elites. However, it risks missing the broader discursive environment of virtual politics which enables the 'success' of these combinations of counterfeiting and coercion to work. Virtual politics makes the primary or foundational site of politics that of the production and contestation of simulacra rather than competition for the real, either through physical violence, material exchange or forms of representation. That is not to say that these things are not a part of inter-elite struggles in Central Asia or elsewhere, but that these struggles remain in a (often hidden) social sphere, are not part of public communication between elites and the populous, and can be regarded as politically unrepresented. This is the corrosive function of virtuality for politics, traditionally conceived, as such politics rests on the logic and practice of representation. It is perhaps a sense of this (hyper)reality which generates the malaise in political culture which Wilson so perceptively describes.

Thus, there are two related but distinct readings of virtual politics. Wilson's reading of virtual politics is that of the imperative or strategic kind in that the virtual can be said to be a counterfeit or misrepresentation of an 'inner politics' equivalent to Baudrillard's first order of simulation. For Baudrillard, however, contemporary political life is virtual in that we lose all ability to judge between different representations as 'simulation envelops the whole edifice of representation as itself a simulacrum' (1983, p. 11). In the Central Asian context, following Baudrillard, we must radically accept that it is impossible to verifiably ascertain whether one public figure is more corrupt than another, what their real agenda is, or who they really represent—themselves, their clan, their patron, their region or their wider economic network. Good political analysis combines these factors rather than declaring one to be the dominant, independent or exclusive origin of political action. However, the situation is much more acute for the subjects of Central Asian societies. They are most often found in confusion, cynicism or, worse, chauvinism in their orientation towards politics. Given this context it is unsurprising that many readers of Baudrillard find his an utterly hopeless and nihilistic account. However, although he failed to provide a systematic account of the possibilities for escape from virtual politics, in the absence of such an account, a starting point for alternative analysis might be in the empirical (or, more accurately, interpretative) study of symbolic fragments of society (invariably spatially localised and temporally momentary) which have not been entirely enveloped by the logic of simulation.[6]

Virtual politics in Tajikistan

In many ways post-conflict Tajikistan makes a less promising case study of virtual politics than Russia or Ukraine. This is not necessarily because physical violence plays a larger role in politics there—as this is not necessarily the case—but because the agents and media of political technology are far less developed. Central Asian politicians often draw on their Soviet experience and that of post-Soviet Russia in their political tactics yet their systems of 'active measures' are both less well resourced and less widespread. Disengagement from politics in Tajikistan is so great that it is perhaps ignorance and disaffection rather than illusion upon which simulacra go unchallenged. Nevertheless, Tajikistan and other Central Asian republics are developing their own fake opposition parties, nominal presidential candidates and manufactured elections. Prior to the February 2005 parliamentary elections, for example, insurrections were orchestrated within the *Sotsialisticheskaya Partiya Tadzhikistana* (Socialist Party of Tajikistan, SPT) and *Demokraticheskaya Partiya Tadzhikistana* (Democratic Party of Tajikistan, DPT) opposition parties in order to unseat their critical leaders. During these elections candidates were fielded often as 'independents' who either suggested that the electorate should vote for the incumbent or who withdrew their candidacy just before election day (in order to reclaim the substantial deposit). In 2006, two

[6]Such an exercise may—but one can only speculate—be compatible with Baudrillard's desire for a renewal of symbolic politics.

'pro-presidential' opposition parties emerged, the *Agrarnaya Partiya Tadzhikistana* (Agrarian Party of Tajikistan, APT) and the *Partiya Ekonomicheskykh Reform Tadzhikistana* (Party of Economic Reforms of Tajikistan, PERT), neither of which had any clear constituency base. Local government officials assisted or actually directed the collection of the 100,000 signatures necessary for the registration of the presidential candidates of these parties and in some cases these same officials themselves established party offices in regional centres. Both these parties and the new officially recognised faction of the SPT nominated relatively unknown candidates to stand against Rahmon in the November 2006 presidential elections.[7]

Systems of signification: making 'sense' of violence and peacebuilding

The discursive milieu within which these moves are made sense of in Tajikistan is complex. We can identify at least three basic discourses of peace(-building), each with public and hidden aspects (Heathershaw 2007, 2009, ch. 3, 4). First, as has been demonstrated globally by Paris (1997, 2004), a narrative of the liberal peace characterises international peacebuilding practice, although it is clear that this discourse can be unpacked into its social justice and conservative order-based graduations (Richmond 2005). This discourse characterises international community policies and programmes in Tajikistan. Secondly, an elite discourse of *mirostroitelstvo* (peacebuilding) emerged from the post-Soviet space and is practised in Tajikistan as the building of authoritative and stable *davlati milli* (national statehood). Finally, a popular discourse, which I denote as one of *tinji* (Tajik: peacefulness or wellness), is a narrative of anti-politics, accommodation and avoidance of conflict, with emphasis placed on the securing of livelihoods. The public aspects of these three discourses are, however, refuted or recast in the hidden spaces of international community, the elite and the poor. Off-duty remarks by peacebuilding practitioners, behind the scenes acknowledgements by government officials, and the stories and complaints of villagers and migrants all bear witness to the limits of the public accounts to properly represent peace and peacebuilding.

It is these hidden spaces where discussion of the violence and abuses of the civil war take place, where a public forgetting of the war is tempered by a communal remembering of violence. Yet those who assume that as a new generation emerges these memories will burst out into the public transcript seem to underestimate the extant salience of the public–private divide in post-Soviet and post-conflict societies. In these hidden transcripts we find very low expectations of what can be expected in terms of peacebuilding, statebuilding or stabilisation in Tajikistan—yet these accounts rarely break through into the public realm. It is this constructed public–private divide which helps explain the absence of anything approaching a meaningful national reconciliation process in Tajikistan involving a truth and reconciliation commission, an international criminal tribunal or another more modest exercise in transitional justice. Thus, in this environment, a straightforward account of symbolic politics is untenable given the hidden transcripts which deny or elide that which is affirmed in public. Both aspects of the discursive environment remain significant.

---

[7]These cases are discussed in Heathershaw (2009, ch. 5).

A symbolic politics, or logic of representation, can thus be found in Tajikistan at least in a negative sense—that of the misrepresentation found in Wilson's virtual politics. The fake political parties and candidates discussed above symbolise not their ostensible referent object but something else. If it is widely acknowledged that these parties and elections are manufactured by the regime—and this is indeed the interpretation found anecdotally in both popular and elite discourses—then these simulacra indicate another meaning: that of the hegemony of the regime. The Agrarian Party represents not real opposition but a real extension of the networks of the regime, not pluralism but uniformity. The frequent failure to speak out against the regime by the most prominent opposition party, the *Hizbi Nahzati Islom* (Islamic Revival Party of Tajikistan, IRP), as well as the co-mingling of the president's party, the *Narodno-Demokraticheskaya Partiya Tadzhikistana* (Peoples Democratic Party of Tajikistan, PDPT), and the *Kommunisticheskaya Partiya Tadzhikistana* (Communist Party of Tajikistan, CPT) in local and national government further indicates the triumph of signs over substance in Tajikistan's multi-party politics.[8] Such evidence suggests a virtual politics which encompasses and extends beyond that described by Wilson. 'Virtual politics' in the strategic or imperative sense of faking are present and functional. Yet, this essay will go on to contend that as a form of symbolic politics they do not merely misrepresent but signify the absence of the very things they ostensibly represent (opposition, dissent and democracy) and indicatively signify the presence of their antonyms (regime hegemony, consent and authoritarianism). More precisely, they indicate or connote the presence of the very kind of orderly 'peace' (established through *mirostroitelstvo* and in *davlati milli*) that regime representatives insist is the only means of conflict resolution. Thus, such virtual political parties both misrepresent and symbolically deter the articulation of meaningful alternatives to these misrepresentations. The second part of this argument (for a Baudrillardian account of virtual politics in Tajikistan) will be further elaborated below.

Virtual politics in the strategic or imperative sense certainly exists in Tajikistan, perhaps as a less sophisticated variety of that described in Russia and Ukraine by Wilson. The existence of virtual politics in the indicative sense is perhaps more difficult to discern. Yet the simulacral or hyper-real political objects have a life of their own beyond that which their producers intended. More precisely, their meanings are multiple, shifting, irreconcilable and beyond the control of both supporters and opponents, be they internal or external. Furthermore, as explored below, internationally supported political parties, NGO programmes and dialogue activities substitute for the lack of democratic politics in Tajikistan and are one factor that deters its practical realisation.

Substitution: signs without referents

Symbolic and virtual politics have played out in Tajikistan over the last decade as a post-conflict stability has emerged in the midst of international intervention for

---

[8]See Heathershaw (2009) for a further discussion of the decline of the IRP as an opposition party (especially pp. 105–06) and the role of 'constructive opposition' adopted by the CP which has even led to its members also being members of the PDP to retain their positions in the state apparatus.

development and peacebuilding. After the first post-conflict parliamentary elections of 2000, international organisations invested in programmes aimed at democratising Tajikistani politics. This has involved countless trainings, seminars and roundtables which brought together officials and representatives of what was cast as civil society—NGOs, the media, business representatives and especially political parties. Based on earlier dialogue activities run by the UN, UNTOP established the Political Discussion Club (PDC), a series of roundtables in towns and cities across the country which ran annually from 2001 to 2006. The OSCE supported a national Islamic–Secular dialogue in cooperation with Swiss and German donor agencies which involved the most prominent figures from government and the former opposition and led to two publications (Kraikemaijer & Zeifert 2003; Bitter *et al.* 2004). At the same time it conducted much lower profile events in regional centres which it called 'Political Plov', where governmental and opposition politicians were brought together to 'chew the fat'. In addition, a number of international NGOs, including the National Democratic Institute (NDI) and the International Foundation for Electoral Systems (IFES), carried out training, funded study tours for party representatives to other 'transition' states, and hosted their own roundtables on particular issues. IFES and the International Research Exchanges board (IREX) also supported voter education drives, particularly aimed at youth and women, around the parliamentary elections of 2005 and the presidential elections of 2006.[9]

Despite these initiatives, by 2007 Tajikistan's nascent democracy was widely perceived to have regressed towards a more authoritarian system in the wake of an increased and overwhelming majority for Rahmon's PDPT in the 2005 elections and the effectively uncontested victory for the president in 2006. More importantly, overall trends in Tajik politics indicated a shrinking space for dissent from the regime. Independent and opposition newspapers such as *Ruzi Nav* were effectively shut down. Political parties were denied registration or, like the SPT and DPT, split into factions due to official interference. In addition, the IRPT Vice-Chair Shamsiddin Shamsiddinov and DPT Chair Mahmadruzi Iskandarov were arrested and convicted on politically motivated charges of, respectively, polygamy and the 'illegal crossing of state borders' (Arman 2004) and terrorism. These events, which intensified after 2003, were by no means a surprise, as admitted in private by international officials, but were publicly greeted with regret and disappointment. Yet, throughout this period, roundtables, dialogues and training courses continued to be funded because they accorded with a normative liberal-democratic vision for Tajik society. Thus, whilst democratisation might appear to have failed or stalled in Tajikistan, it was not widely accepted that the limitations of such international projects led to their failure.

This is evident in the representation of programmes as found in grant applications, programme and project documentation and, most acutely, in the explanations proffered for their limited success in monitoring and evaluation (M&E) exercises during and after the completion of programmes (Heathershaw 2008). In the discourses of international peacebuilding and democratic transition, events such as 'election observation', 'dialogue exercises' and 'study tours' are deemed to create space for

---

[9]For a further discussion of these various initiatives, particularly in the context of the 2005 parliamentary elections, see Heathershaw (2009, ch. 5).

political participation where it would not otherwise exist. Such projects have been lauded by one practitioner as 'substitutes [for] the lack of open political discussion in the parliament'.[10] This substitution function is a useful one to dwell on in terms of virtual politics. It is by no means certain that substitutive or simulated dialogues serve as prototypes of 'real' dialogue; they may indeed have quite different effects. Yet according to the discourse of international peacebuilding, such substitutions are, at worst, neutral in their impact on democratisation. However, time and again local elites have interpreted such events as opportunities to assert the authority of the regime under President Rahmon over political parties and independent groups. What is important here is that international discourses make their purveyors blind to the possibility that these symbolic acts might be self-defeating; that they might function to facilitate authoritarian retrenchment rather than democratic opening.

Even in cases where it is obvious that such initiatives have been met with elite incomprehension or open hostility, and led to a closure of political space, it is assumed that there is a popular demand for political pluralism. The hostility of the government towards 'political' actions by NGOs, according to one programme coordinator, demands that they follow the maxim: 'get government permission in advance, always invite the *hukumat* [local administration]'.[11] When the *hukumat* is unwilling to give permission, even for very small events, it is often necessary to involve the Presidential Administration. Working from day to day in such an environment, the goals of international organisations are diluted in practice. One example from the testimony of the same programme officer noted:

> We organised a workshop with 70 participants and asked the local government to participate in order to work with them—you know the idea was to increase the role of citizens in talking about issues in their area, to have roundtables on priority issues to feed into local government who normally don't listen at all. In actuality the *khukumat* had the say in who is invited and who speaks, but I think you can say that it was a step in the right direction—to get anyone to participate is a positive thing.[12]

A 'step in the right direction' is all that remains of international peacebuilding in this case. However, it is an important superfluous sign; it simulates a process of democratisation despite the absence of any substantive evidence to support that notion.

Amongst Tajikistani political elites these democratisation initiatives are symbolic of something quite different. For example, in Khujond in 2004 the PDC was dominated by governmental elites who used it as an opportunity to demonstrate their loyalty to the state. The meeting was held in a government building. Opposition representatives were for some time shut outside, as the head of UNTOP and senior officials of the OSCE waited inside, before eventually being allowed into the building. A series of governmental speakers praised the regime in front of an audience of hundreds of state servants (*goschinnovniki*) who applauded every speech. When the opposition parties

[10]Author's interview with Jan Malekzade, Dushanbe, Tajikistan, 10 May 2005.
[11]Author's interview with Stephanie Wheeler, IREX, Dushanbe, 23 February 2005.
[12]Author's interview with Stephanie Wheeler, IREX, Dushanbe, 23 February 2005.

were allowed in they had to stand at the sides. After they were eventually given a few minutes to speak they were met with silence.[13] This accords with a vision of civil society propounded by the Mayor of Dushanbe, Mahmadsaid Ubaidulloev, who in a speech to an OSCE dialogue exercise noted,

> I at once want to note that it must not weaken the ability of all branches of government [*vlast*] to command and regulate the situation as it takes shape, and it must not set one group or party against another, and in such a way as to divert it from the fundamental work of supplying rapid economic growth and the reduction of poverty. (2003, p. 62)

This 'fundamental work' reduces 'democracy' to the provision of basic physical wellbeing, and prioritises 'stability' over openness.

On the other hand, elite members have become adept at playing the symbols of the international community when it is strategically beneficial to do so. President Rahmon deemed the elections to be no less important than the international community did and self-consciously adopted the language of international discourses. 'It is in our interests', Rahmon announced on television a week before the 2005 elections, 'to ensure that elections are free and transparent, and that they conform to international standards ... so that this important political event promotes Tajikistan's image in the international arena'.[14] There are a number of different things going on in these examples but two aspects stand out in terms of the interplay of symbolic and virtual. First, at a symbolic level, there are clearly quite different notions of 'democracy' and 'authority' being deployed here—ones that involve the public performance of order and hierarchy. Secondly, in both cases some attempt is being made by the country's elite to play to the virtual political forms of the international community. Even in the Khujond case, the very fact that the PDC was held was seen as a remarkable achievement by the OSCE in the region.[15] In this sense the substitution of signs for referents is symptomatic of processes of simulation found in national and international strategies of 'stabilisation' and 'peacebuilding'. These discourses and positive accounts of international peacebuilding events conceal the absence of a basic reality—a singular symbolic structure through which politics can be interpreted—in Tajikistan's virtual politics of peace. But beyond substitution this virtual politics of the contestations of simulacra has a further effect; that of deterrence.

Deterrence: 'peacebuilding' as peacebuilding

It is perhaps not surprising that, in contrast to its inclusion by the international community, 'opposition' is securitised and symbolically and physically excluded by members of the regime. Such acts could easily be dismissed as instrumental and self-serving moves to misrepresent political rivals. Yet this explanation, in imperative

---

[13]Author's interview with OSCE officer, Khujond, Tajikistan, 18 June 2005; author's interview with political party representative, Khujond, Tajikistan, 21 June 2005.

[14]Author's personal observation, 20 February 2005.

[15]Author's interview with OSCE officer, Khujond, July 2004.

terms, would be incomplete as it ignores the form of political culture which is reproduced in this delegitimation of liberal democracy and legitimation of authority in post-Soviet regimes. Moreover, and more difficult to explain in strategic terms, opposition parties also represent themselves and the party-building activities in which they engage are in terms quite different to international peacebuilding. For example, the Deputy Chair of the *Sotsial-Demokraticheskaya Partiya Tadzhikistana* (Social Democratic Party of Tajikistan, SDPT) in Khujond, described how the party has been increasingly marginalised:

> You know the Political [Discussion] Club, the first time I participated I was glad and was thinking that this was of some use. But after I participated, you know, I noticed that everything stayed the same. There was no response on the part of the *khukumat*. It's as if 'the dog barks but the caravan goes on' [*kak budto sobaka layet, a karavan idiot*].[16] Our opinions don't interest them. They don't consider us. For example, they never invite our party anywhere.[17]

Samadova's account suggests that the ongoing exclusion of political parties by the authorities occurs despite or perhaps because of international initiatives such as the PDC which provide further opportunities for the performance of authority by the regime and the public exclusion of alternatives.

Thus, amongst the small band of activists willing to work on political projects with the international community self-representations are far removed from the portrayal of them found in the international peacebuilding discourse. One such IREX-supported NGO was *Elim* in the Kulob region which administered a small grant to educate women voters through a project entitled 'Vote and Win!'[18] The testimony of the head of *Elim*, Latifahon Rahmonova, is revealing:

> The events that we organised were political events. Moreover, our organisation was non-governmental. That's why we faced many problems. In the first instance this seems to be a very simple thing, but as one gets involved many difficulties come along. For this reason during these four months that I was occupied in this field—firstly because it was my field and secondly because it was a political field—it was a little hard to work with the *Jamoats* [local administration]. The residents of Shahrvand village know that while we were waiting to receive letters from the Ministry of Foreign Affairs and IREX, this created opposition between us and the *Khukumat* [local government]. However, after receiving the letter we came to a consensus and together with the *Khukumat* and the chair of the [official] women's committee of this community could gather all the women and explain to them their voting rights. Until this moment not only the housewives but also women with qualifications did not know the essence of elections. ... I am glad that I came across lots of literature that was made available for us from the American organisations, that we are living in a democratic society, that our community is following this path, and we have to support it.[19]

[16]Literal translation. Figurative sense: 'it's as if everyone carries on regardless'.
[17]Author's interview with Dilbar Samadova, Khujond, 21 June 2005.
[18]Author's interview with Latifahon Rahmonova, Kulob, 2 June 2005.
[19]Author's interview with Latifahon Rahmonova, Kulob, 2 June 2005.

What is interesting here is how tension between local government and an NGO working on 'political events' in a small number of rural villages was overcome by a letter of permission from central government and a subsequent 'consensus' where the *Hukumat* acquires a leading role in implementing this ostensibly non-governmental project. There is an acceptance of patriarchy: Rahmonova went on to comment in the same interview that 'women need to be taught to participate'.[20] Moreover, the voter education material of IREX is presented in conservative and disempowering terms— 'that our community is following this path, and we have to support it'—rather than to empower personal choice and highlight the democratic deficits of Tajikistan. In these interpretations the virtual quality and indicative or deterrence effects of international democratisation initiatives are revealed in two ways. First, they confine opposition to the margins. Samadova, for example, represents international programmes as both failing to meet their ostensible objectives and as having alternative and unacknow- ledged functions of institutionalising the marginality of her party. Secondly, they affirm the domination of the regime. Rahmonova's reading of her voter education project explicitly accepts the nature of 'authority' as purported by the regime. Samadova's reading of governmental 'authority' is critical yet even she accepts the untouchable position of the regime. She opposes the government yet accepts the (hyper-)reality of its authority. It is in this sense that 'substitutes' like Rahmonova's project or the SDPT may in fact deter alternative political 'realities'. They thus become signs without referents which are meaningful amongst the international community for their value as 'first steps' even though they may actually deter the very practices that they ostensibly intend to stimulate.

This becomes clearer when one considers the nature of the SDPT itself. Whilst Samadova's reading of Tajikistani politics may be somehow more authentic than that of the international community, the political party of which she is a leading figure is perhaps the quintessential example of a virtual political party existing in space forged in between national and international politics. The SDPT was registered as a political party in 2002 after its leader, respected jurist Rahmatullo Zoirov, had served as an advisor to the president. However, after Zoriov's falling out of favour with Rahmon, the SDPT found itself in the in-between space of the internationalised 'opposition'. Shokirjon Hakimov, the SDPT's deputy chair, characterises the party as 'intelligent, secular, democratic opposition'.[21] It has gained supporters in this mould, having a few thousand registered members, professionals and NGO administrators, from Dush- anbe, Sughd and Badakhshon. Hakimov notes that because members face 'pressure' from the authorities and may lose their jobs, the party tries to recruit those who 'in economic terms are relatively independent'.[22] Its membership has stayed relatively small and it stays afloat partly because many of its leaders run NGOs which subcontract for international organisations. Zoirov, for example, has often worked as a consultant for the international community including for the UNTOP dialogue project, the PDC (UNTOP/NAPST 2001, p. 16). Hakimov observes, 'as for us all avenues [to government] are closed, we are able to participate in the projects of

[20]Author's interview with Latifahon Rahmonova, Kulob, 2 June 2005, p. 6.
[21]Author's interview with Shokirjon Hakimov, Dushanbe, 4 August 2005.
[22]Author's interview with Shokirjon Hakimov, Dushanbe, 4 August 2005, p. 4.

international community' (2005, p. 6). Here, international programmes serve as the quintessence of hyper-reality in that they provide alternatives to real politics.

One notable exception to this is found in Zoirov's campaign to have the 2003 constitutional changes overturned and the president's victory in the 2006 elections declared illegal and his term of office pronounced as over.[23] In these acts he unsuccessfully sought to reassert the symbolic and representational value of the constitution as a document which actually sets the terms for how governance is practised. However, such public challenges are exceptional and increasingly rare. This bowing to 'authority' and the conscious acceptance by opposition parties of their place on the margins indicates the virtual quality of internationally supported elections, dialogue exercises and political parties. The moderate political opposition is made comfortable and virtual by international programmes, when it might otherwise be spending more time either publicly challenging the regime or being stamped out and serving as a symbol of the lack of democratic governance in Tajikistan. In this sense 'opposition' political parties are tolerated so long as they remain virtual—performing to the symbols of an international audience or to the scripts of their elite producers whilst going largely unheard locally and nationally. They not only substitute for the lack of opposition and dialogue but deter their practical realisation.

Conclusions

Tajikistan's peace is symbolic not just in that it conceals an alternative reality but in that its symbols often indicate the absence of the object which they ostensibly represent—and the presence of its antonym. These signs are constructive of the kind of peace that has emerged in Tajikistan over the last decade and a half. Yet, as this essay has demonstrated interpretively, symbolic politics in Tajikistan is in some respects enveloped by a virtual politics of peace and peacebuilding where such a rendering of presence and absence is illusive. This substitution of an object's fixed meaning by shifting markers which develop a life of their own is an inherent ambiguity found in signs of international peacebuilding and national stabilisation.

What Baudrialllard would call hyper-realities or simulacra are found in Tajikistan's virtual peace(-building) in the form of the 'first steps' of dialogue exercises and the 'substitutes for' democratic politics which elide the categories of presence and absence and situate Tajikistan in some other indefinable place which is neither 'democratic' nor 'authoritarian' nor necessarily somewhere in between. But the processes of substitution for and deterrence of democratic politics constitute the virtual dimension of Tajikistan's peace and are one part of what makes the internationally supported Tajikistani state function. The virtual politics of substitution and deterrence keep international aid flowing and sustain the Tajikistani state as a sovereign and legitimate member of the international community. It effectively limits the ambitions and actions of the more independent and creative members of civil society who often become incorporated into the world of neo-liberal civil society and international and national virtual political parties. Thus, more broadly, civil society becomes virtual in that it is publicly practised according to the technocratic procedures demanded by external

---

[23] *Asia Plus Blitz*, Dushanbe, Tajikistan, email bulletin, 1207, 12 March 2003.

sponsors. This inevitably encourages the continuation of a kind of Soviet-era doublethink by the recipients and participants of peace and peacebuilding where one reality must be attested to in public whilst a quite different reality is assumed behind closed doors. Such an order of virtual politics cannot be considered entirely stable. Thus, Tajikistan's 'symbolic politics' (understood to include symbolic practices of misrepresentation, in Wilson's sense, and properly virtual practices of non-representation in Baudrillard's sense) are together both constructive and deconstructive of the tenuous peace found today in Tajikistan.

The secondary argument of this essay is theoretical. This is that different orders of simulation, both strategic faking and indicative simulation, can be analysed alongside one another in contemporary non-Western cases. However, in such analyses we should be alert to the possibility that the apparent effectuality of strategic faking might be reliant on the triumph of a logic of indicative simulation. Wilson is perhaps correct that virtual politics in the contemporary post-Soviet space is not (yet) all-encompassing. However, it is unclear quite how alternative realities remain distinct from virtual realities. How is such an 'inner politics' sustained, unadulterated by the hyper-realities of the virtual? Once again, we must resist the temptation to uncover a singular hidden reality. Virtual politics in Tajikistan involves strategic attempts to manufacture fake political parties but at the same time these misrepresentations must be seen in the light of non-representation: a larger failure to represent Tajikistani voices, interests and ideas both nationally and internationally. Faking, substitution and deterrence are all processes of virtual politics.

It is hoped that this framing of the virtual is a useful prism through which to view international assistance for development, security and democracy across Central Asia. At a very basic level, the conceptual approach followed here avoids the misstep of assuming international peacebuilding, for all its hyper-real effects, is 'merely symbolic'. Such dismissals equate 'symbolic' with 'tokenistic' and lose all analytical purchase on the nature of international assistance. Elections and political parties for all their 'failures' are far too important to be either ignored as irrelevant by researchers of Central Asia or commodified as a development product by the small army of professional consultants employed by international organisations across the region. This is not least because such failures in practice are discursively reconstructed as 'successes' for an audience of international donors (Heathershaw 2008). The broader approach to post-Soviet virtual politics outlined in this essay demands that we interrogate the hyper-realities of international assistance as well as the space that such projects might allow for moments of symbolic politics—the shattering of simulacra by the public breakout of the hidden transcript. We must also be alert to moves towards alternative modes of politics where opposition parties seek to avoid both national and international virtual politics in favour of representing local social forces, be they progressive or regressive. Interventions, both academic and policy-focused, which reveal the complicity of international actors in virtual authoritarian domination are precisely those which might in a small way revitalise symbolic politics. This essay endeavours to offer one small step in that direction.

University of Exeter

References

Abdullaev, K. & Barnes, C. (eds) (2001) 'Politics of Compromise: The Tajikistan Peace Process', *Conciliation Resources Accord: An International Review of Peace Initiatives*, 10, available at: www.c-r.org/our-work/accord/tajikistan/contents.php (accessed 23 October 2003).

Akiner, S. (2001) *Tajikistan: Disintegration or Reconciliation?* (London, RIIA).

Arman, K. (2004) 'Conviction of Political Leaders Stirs Opposition Ire in Tajikistan', *Eurasianet Human Rights*, 20 April, available at: http://www.eurasianet.org/departments/rights/articles/eav012004_pr.shtml, accessed 23 April 2009.

Baudrillard, J. (1983) *Simulations* (New York, Semiotext[e]).

Baudrillard, J. (1995) *The Gulf War Did Not Take Place* (Bloomington, Indiana University Press).

Baudrillard, J. (1996) *The System of Objects* (London, Verso).

Bitter, J.-N., Huerin, F., Seifert, A.C. & Rahmonova-Schwarz, D. (eds) (2004) *Postroennie doveriya mezhdu Islamistami i sekularistami—Tadzhikski eksperiment* (Dushanbe, Devashtich).

Bourdieu, P. (1977) *Outline of a Theory of Practice* [translated by Richard Nice] (Cambridge & New York, Cambridge University Press).

Debrix, F. (1999) *Re-Envisioning Peacekeeping: The United Nations and the Mobilisation of Ideology* (Minneapolis, University of Minnesota Press).

Debrix, F. (2009) 'Jean Baudrillard', in Edkins, J. & Vaughan-Williams, N. (eds) (2009) *Critical Theorists and International Relations* (London, Routledge).

Der Derian, J. (1994) 'Simulation: The Highest Stage of Capitalism?', in Kellner, D. (ed.) (1994) *Baudrillard: A Critical Reader* (Oxford, Blackwell).

Der Derian, J. (1995) 'The Value of Security: Hobbes, Marx, Nietzsche, and Baudrillard', in Lipschultz, R.D. (ed.) (1995) *On Security* (New York, Columbia University Press).

Der Derian, J. (2001) *Virtuous War: Mapping the Military–Industrial–Media–Entertainment Network* (Boulder, CO, Perseus/Westview Press).

European Commission (EC) (2004) 'EU Programme Management Office for Central Asia Border Management and Drug Control (BOMCA/CADAP) 2004. Joint Border Assessment at the Tajik–Afghan Border', 14–26 August, Bishkek, 11 October, unpublished report.

European Commission (EC) (2005) 'EU Programme Management Office for Central Asia Border Management and Drug Control (BOMCA/CADAP), Response of the International Community to Assist the Government of Tajikistan on the Tajik–Afghan Border', 15–16 February, unpublished meeting minutes.

Heathershaw, J. (2007) 'Peacebuilding as Practice: Discourses from Post-Conflict Tajikistan', *International Peacekeeping*, 14, 2, April.

Heathershaw, J. (2008) 'Seeing Like the International Community: How Peacebuilding Failed (and Survived) in Tajikistan', *Journal of Intervention and Statebuilding*, 2, 3, Autumn.

Heathershaw, J. (2009) *Post-Conflict Tajikistan: The Politics of Peacebuilding and the Emergence of Legitimate Order* (London, Routledge).

International Crisis Group (ICG) (2001a) *Tajikistan: An Uncertain Peace*, Report, 24 December (Osh/Brussels, International Crisis Group).

International Crisis Group (ICG) (2001b) *Central Asia: Drugs and Conflict*, Asia Report 25, 26 November (Osh/Brussels, International Crisis Group).

International Crisis Group (ICG) (2004) *Tajikistan's Politics: Confrontation or Consolidation?* Report, 19 May (Osh/Brussels, International Crisis Group).

Lavrakas, T.A. (ed.) (2004) *Tajikistan: A Guide to the 2005 Parliamentary Elections*, December 2004 (Geneva, CIMERA).

Luke, T. (1989) 'What's Wrong with Deterrence? A Semiotic Interpretation of National Security Policy', in Der Derian, J. & Shapiro, M.J. (eds) (1989) *International/Intertextual Relations: Postmodern Readings of World Politics* (Lexington, MA, Lexington Books).

Nakaya, S. (2008) 'Post-War Exclusion and Violence: Impact of Aid on Transition from War Economies to Oligarchy', Paper presented at the 2008 Annual Convention of the International Studies Association, San Francisco, 28 March.

Olimova, S. & Bosc, I. (2003) *Labour Migration from Tajikistan*, July (Dushanbe, IOM/Sharq Scientific Research Center).

Paris, R. (1997) 'Peacebuilding and the Limits of Liberal Internationalism', *International Security*, 22, 2.

Paris, R. (2004) *At War's End: Building Peace after Civil Conflict* (Cambridge, Cambridge University Press).

Richmond, O. (2005) *The Transformation of Peace* (Basingstoke, Palgrave).

Richmond, O. & Franks, J. (2007) 'Liberal Hubris? Virtual Peace in Cambodia', *Security Dialogue*, 38, 1.

Scott, J.C. (1990) *Domination and the Arts of Resistance: Hidden Transcripts* (New Haven, CT, Yale University Press).

Seifert, A.C. & Kraikemayer, A. (eds) (2003) *O Sovmestimosti politicheskovo Islama i beszopasnosti v prostrantsve OBSE* (Dushanbe, Sharki Ozod).

Ubaidulloyev, M. (2003) 'Ukrepleniye grazhdanskov obshestva v Tadzhikistane', in United Nations Tajikistan Office of Peacebuilding/National Association of Political Scientists of Tajikistan (UNTOP/NAPST) (eds) (2003).

United Nations Tajikistan Office of Peacebuilding/National Association of Political Scientists of Tajikistan (UNTOP/NAPST) (2001) *The Political Discussion Club* (Dushanbe, UNTOP).

Weber, C. (1995) *Simulating Sovereignty: Intervention, the State and Symbolic Exchange* (Cambridge, Cambridge University Press).

Wedeen, L. (1999) *Ambiguities of Domination: Politics, Rhetoric and Symbols in Contemporary Syria* (Chicago, University of Chicago Press).

Wilson, A. (2005a) *Virtual Politics: Faking Democracy in the Post-Soviet World* (London, Yale University Press).

Wilson, A. (2005b) 'Virtual Politics: "Political Technology" and the Corruption of Post-Soviet Democracy', *Johnson's Russia List*, 21 December, available at: http://www.cdi.org/russia/johnson/9324-5.cfm, accessed 6 December 2008.

Zürcher, C. (2004) *Analysis of Peace and Conflict Potential in Rasht Valley, Shuraobad District and GBAO*, Final Report, March (Berlin, Analysis Research Consulting).

Index

Page numbers in *Italics* represent tables.
Page numbers in **Bold** represent figures.

official history 84
Omarov, N. 160
Omuraliev, K. 218
Orange Revolution 44, 62, 63
Organisation for Economic Cooperation
    and Development (OECD) 170
Organisation of Security and
    Cooperation in Europe (OSCE) 33,
    34, 35; chairmanship 22, 42, 45
organised oblivion 84
orthography 126-8, 134-6

passive brands 44
passport nationality 141
paternalism 169
patriarchy 246
patriotism 42; Kazakhstan 177;
    Uzbekistan 177
patronage politics 59, 60
Pauleson, G. 85
peace 229, 230, 241, 248; Tajikistan
    26, 247
peacebuilding 25
perestroika 110, 132
periphery 74, 75, 76; as danger 77
Persian culture 122
personality cults 13, 14, 184-7
Pitkin, H.F. 7
political change 53
political cultures 104
political elite 52, 89, 145, 243; role 83
political exile 29
political legitimacy 58
political manipulation 28, 29, 30
political order: Turkmenistan 90, 91
political parties 241, 242, 245
Political Plov 242
political pluralism 243
political science 1
political symbols 43
political violence 74
politics 3, 197; participation 4, 15, 28
Popkewitz, T. 118
popular protests 27
poverty 244
power 15, 90, 107, 115, 130, 146, 217, 236

power relations 166, 167
Pozharskii, V. 216, 217, 218, 219
preventative development 195
propaganda 16, 23, 24, 35, 70
proxy cults 185, 186
public relations campaigns:
    Kazakhstan 39
public sculpture 84, 85
public space 85, 87, 89, 92, 100
Putin, V. 22, 30

Qodirov, R. 61

Radnitz, S. 26
Rahmon, E. 229
Rahmon, I. 21, 23, 30, 31, 244
Rakimbay uulu, N. 145
rationalism 73
referential symbols 8, 17
reflective symbolism 5
regime change: Uzbekistan 53
regime development 10
regional diversity 175
religion 19, 24, 73
religious extremism 60, 61
religious symbolism 36
religious symbols 24
Renaissance 237
representation 4, 7; constructivist 2;
    intentional 2; reflective 2
repression 164
Richmond, O. 230
riots: Uzbekistan 41
ritual 86, 100, 165
ritual symbols 9, 10
Road to Europe campaign 46
Romm, M. 69, 72, 73, 75, 76, 78, 79
Rose Revolution 41, 62
Ruhnama (Niyazov) 23, 89, 91, 92, 94,
    95, 100, 148
ruling elite 4, 5, 43
Russia 21, 122, 233, 239, 241; symbolic
    power 21, see also Soviet Union;
    Union of Soviet Socialist Republics
Russian Empire 123, 124
Russianisation 136